Peng

Co

Edi

Penguin Modern Economics Readings

General Editor
B. J. McCormick

Advisory Board
K. J. W. Alexander
R. W. Clower
P. Robson
J. Spraos

Cost-Benefit Analysis

Selected Readings

Edited by Richard Layard

Penguin Books

Penguin Books Ltd,
Harmondsworth, Middlesex, England
Penguin Books, 625 Madison Avenue,
New York, New York 10022, U.S.A.
Penguin Books Australia Ltd,
Ringwood, Victoria, Australia
Penguin Books Canada Ltd, 2801 John Street,
Markham, Ontario, Canada L3R 1B4
Penguin Books (N.Z.) Ltd,
182–190 Wairau Road,
Auckland 10, New Zealand

First published 1972
Reprinted with revisions 1974
Reprinted 1976, 1977

Made and printed in Great Britain by
Richard Clay (The Chaucer Press) Ltd
Bungay, Suffolk
Set in Monotype Times

Contents

Part Six
The Case of the Third London Airport 429

Introduction[1]

Should India build a new steel mill or London an urban motorway? Should higher education expand, or water supplies be improved? These are typical of the questions on which cost-benefit analysis has something to say. However, there is no problem, public or personal, to which its broad ideas could not in principle be applied.

The readings in this book concentrate on those issues which are common to all cost-benefit appraisals. However, in making the selection, I searched in vain for any introductory survey that was not only theoretical but also showed how one might tackle a particular problem.[2] I have therefore cast this Introduction in that form, taking an imaginary project and showing how the readings throw light on the analysis. But first a few remarks are needed on the general ideas involved.

The basic notion is very simple. If we have to decide whether to do A or not, the rule is: Do A if the benefits exceed those of the next best alternative course of action, and not otherwise. If we apply this rule to all possible choices, we shall generate the largest possible benefits, given the constraints within which we live. And no-one could complain at that.

Going on a step, it seems quite natural to refer to the 'benefits of the next best alternative to A' as the 'costs of A'. For if A is done those alternative benefits are lost. So the rule becomes: do A if its benefits exceed its costs, and not otherwise.

So far so good. The problems of course arise over the measurement of benefits and costs. This is where many recoil in horror at the idea of measuring everything on one scale. If the objection is on practical grounds, it is fair enough; and many economists

1. I am extremely grateful to P. Dasgupta, C. D. Foster, E. J. Mishan, A. K. Sen and A. A. Walters for detailed comments and suggestions and to E. Baseden and N. J. Krafft for help in preparing the book for publication.

2. The best textbooks are Mishan (1971a) and UNIDO (1972). Good comprehensive survey articles are Prest and Turvey (1965, reading 1), Henderson (1965) reprinted in R. Turvey (1968) and Eckstein (1961) reprinted in R. W. Houghton (1970).

have swallowed hard before making a particular quantification, or have refused to make one. But, if the objection is theoretical, it is fair to ask the objector what he means by saying that A is better than B, unless he has some means of comparing the various dimensions along which A and B differ. Of course, there are some people who believe that one particular attribute of life, such as the silence of the countryside, is of absolute importance. For them cost-benefit analysis is easy: the value of all other benefits and costs is zero. More problematical are those people who believe in the absolute importance of two or more items, for they are doomed to intellectual and spiritual frustration. Whenever A is superior to its alternative on one count and inferior on another, they will feel obliged to do both. Unfortunately, choices between such alternatives have to be made only too often. However, rational choice is not always impossible unless every item has a unique price. Often it will be sufficient to know that the price lies within some finite range; the answer will be unaffected by its exact value. The only basic principle is that we should be willing to assign numerical values to costs and benefits, and arrive at decisions by adding them up and accepting those projects whose benefits exceed their costs.

But how are such values to be arrived at? If we assume that only people matter, the analysis naturally involves two steps. First, we must find out how the decision would affect the welfare of each individual concerned. To judge this effect we must ultimately rely on the individual's own evaluation of his mental state. So the broad principle is that we measure his change in welfare as he would himself value it; that is, we ask what he would be willing to pay to acquire the benefits or to avoid the costs. There is absolutely no need for money to be the numeraire in such valuations. It could equally well be bushels of corn, but money is convenient. Yet the problems of inferring people's values from their behaviour are clearly acute and present the central problem in cost-benefit analysis.

The second step is to deduce the change in social welfare implied by all the changes in individual welfare. Unless there are no losers, this means somehow valuing each man's £1. If income were optimally distributed, £1 more or less would be equally valuable regardless of whose it was, so that each man's £1 has equal weight.

And if income is not optimally distributed, most economists would argue that it should be redistributed by cash transfers rather than through the choice of projects. But what if we think that cash will *not* be redistributed, even if it should be? Then we may need to value the poor man's extra £1 more highly than the rich man's.

However, this raises the kind of question that underlies almost all disputes about cost-benefit analysis, or indeed about moral questions generally: the question of which constraints are to be taken as given. In this case if a government agency knows for certain that cash *will* not be redistributed to produce a desirable pattern of income, even if it *should* be, then the agency should allow for distributional factors when evaluating the project. Equally, it should not allow for these factors, if it can ensure that redistribution is achieved by some more appropriate method. In practice, however, it may not know whether this can be ensured, and until this is settled a rational project appraisal is impossible. Likewise, in the personal sphere it is reasonable to take unalterable features of one's character into account in deciding what is right. But which features are unalterable? In each case the issue is which constraints are exogenous to the decision-maker.

This brings us to the relation between cost-benefit analysis and the rest of public policy. The government's overall aim is presumably to ensure that social welfare is maximized, subject to those constraints over which it has no control, such as tastes, technology and resource endowments. In any economy this objective requires some government activity owing to the failure of free markets to deal with the efficiency problems of externality, economies of scale and inadequate markets for risky outcomes, and also because of the equity problem of the maldistribution of wealth. Three main methods of intervention are open: regulation, taxes and subsidies, and public production. Each of these types of government activity can be subjected to cost-benefit analysis, but it has so far been applied mainly to cases of public production. Here the great strength of cost-benefit analysis is that it permits decentralized decision-making. This is needed because, even if the public sector is small, no one office can hope to handle the vast mass of technical information needed to decide on specific projects. Decentralization deals with that problem, just as the price mechanism does – but it raises the converse one that the right decisions will only result if the prices used by the decision-makers correctly reflect the social values of inputs and outputs at the social optimum, or what are usually called their 'shadow prices'.

In a mixed economy market prices often do not do this, for the reasons mentioned above. So the main problem in cost-benefit analysis is to arrive at adequate and consistent valuations where market prices fail. The government will generally lay down some of the prices (like the discount rate) to be used by public sector enterprises, as well as their decision rule. In a more planned economy the government will lay down more of the prices and could, in principle, by iterative search find a complete set of prices, which, if presented to producers, would lead their production decisions to be consistent with each other and with consumers' preferences.[3] However, in practice no government has tried this, and most rely in part on quantitative targets or quotas, as well as taxes and subsidies, to secure consistency in at any rate some areas of production. If any of the activities of government agencies are non-optimal, this faces the cost-benefit analyst with a second source of difficulty in finding relevant prices, namely whether and how to allow for those divergences between market prices and social values that arise from the action or inaction of government itself.[4]

Broadly the valuations to be made in any cost-benefit analysis fall under four main heads:

1. The relative valuation of different costs and benefits at the time when they occur.
2. The relative valuation of costs and benefits occurring at different points in time: the problem of time preference and the opportunity cost of capital.
3. The valuation of risky outcomes.
4. The valuation of costs and benefits accruing to people with different incomes.

3. This assumes no increasing returns to scale.
4. On the problems discussed in the previous three paragraphs see Sen (1972, reading 4) and Sen (1970b).

Parts Two to Five of the readings in this book deal with these four problems. Part One contains two survey articles, while Part Six contains the only case study, the controversial *Roskill Report* on the Third London Airport.[5] The Introduction follows the same structure. I have also included at the end of the book some practical exercises on which the reader can test his understanding. If anyone unfamiliar with cost-benefit analysis is somewhat dazed by the general notions discussed so far, he can take comfort: we are about to begin at the beginning.

1 The overall approach

Suppose there is a river which at present can only be crossed by ferry. The government considers building a bridge, which, being rather upstream, would take the same time to cross. The ferry is a privately owned monopoly and charges £0.20 per crossing, while its total costs per crossing are £0.15; it is used for 5000 crossings per year. The bridge would cost £30,000 to build but would be open free of charge; 25,000 crossings a year are expected, and the ferry would go out of business. The government send for the cost-benefit analyst to advise them on whether to go ahead with the bridge.

In any cost-benefit exercise it is usually convenient to proceed in two stages: (a) Value the costs and benefits in each year of the project; (b) Obtain an aggregate 'present value' of the project by 'discounting' costs and benefits in future years to make them commensurable with present costs and benefits.

At each stage the appraisal differs from commercial project appraisal because (i) costs and benefits to all members of society are included, and not only the monetary expenditures and receipts of the responsible agency, and (ii) the social discount rate may differ from the private discount rate. The main work goes into step (a), and we shall concentrate on this for the present.

Consumers' surplus and willingness to pay

We need to avoid logical errors in deciding which items are to be included as costs and benefits, and to value those that are included

5. Other applications can be found in other Penguin readings. See, for example, Munby (1968, readings 10, 11 and 12), Blaug (1968, readings 7 and 11) and Rosenberg (1971, reading 9).

correctly. The guiding principle is that we list all parties affected by the project, and then value the effect of the project on their welfare as it would be valued in money terms by them. In this case there are four parties: taxpayers, ferryowners, existing travellers and new travellers (who previously did not cross but now do so at the lower price).

1. The taxpayers lose £30,000 now, assuming the bridge is financed by extra taxes.

2. The ferryowners lose their excess profits of £250 [i.e. 0.05×5000] in each future year for ever (area A on Figure 1).

3. The existing travellers gain £1000 [0.20×5000] in each future year for ever, due to the fall in price (areas A+B).

4. The new travellers. To evaluate their gains is more difficult. We know that the new journey which is most highly valued was nearly made by ferry, and is therefore worth very nearly £0.20; while the journey which is least highly valued is valued only marginally more than its price of £0.00. For the intermediate journeys we have to make some arbitrary assumption and will assume that the value per journey falls at a constant rate from £0.20 to zero. In other words we are assuming that the demand curve is linear. So the average gain to new travellers is £0.10 per crossing and the total gain £2000 [$0.10 \times 20,000$] per year for ever. This figure corresponds to the gain in consumers' surplus on the part of the new travellers, since it represents the sum of the differences between the maximum they would be willing to pay for their journeys and the amount they actually pay, which in this case is zero.[6] Geometrically it is represented by area C – the area under the demand curve and above a horizontal line at the final price (which here is

6. This statement is true if demand is independent of income. In this case the statistic also measures the 'compensating variation' in income, i.e. the amount by which these consumers would have to be taxed after the price fall to make them no better off than before, *and* the 'equivalent variation', i.e. the amount which consumers would need to be given if the price fall did not occur to make them as well off as if it did. Opinions differ on which of these measures is the most relevant indicator of welfare gain. Mishan (1971a, p. 130) favours the compensating variation, assuming, as he does, that the Hicks-Kaldor criterion is used in aggregating the gains of different consumers (see p. 16 below).

zero). In the special case where the demand curve is linear, the value of generated sales will always equal $\frac{1}{2}(p_0-p_1)(q_1-q_0)$, i.e. half the price fall times the quantity increase. This is a formula which is used over and over again in cost-benefit analysis, especially for small changes in prices, when the linearity assumption is a reasonable approximation.

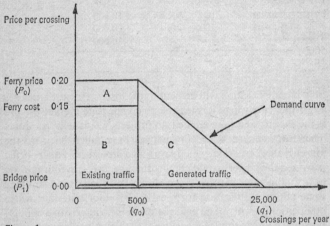

Figure 1

Criteria for a welfare gain

We can now tabulate (Table 1) the overall picture of net benefits (benefits minus costs), discounting all the future permanent flows of net benefits by an arbitrary 10 per cent to obtain their present values.[7]

Can these now be added up? It depends entirely on our approach to the problem of income distribution. If we wish to use the very restrictive Pareto criterion of a welfare improvement, we shall support a project if some people gain and nobody loses. But if some people gain while others lose, the Pareto criterion provides no guidance. If we follow it, we *can* add up the net receipts of all the parties concerned and support the project if they are positive,

7. The reasons for discounting and the choice of discount rate are discussed in Part Three, where we also explain why the present value of a stream of £a per year for ever at a 10 per cent discount rate equals £10a.

Table 1

| | Future net benefits per year for ever | | Present value at 10% discount rate |
	£	Area in Fig 1	
Ferryowners	− 250	−A	− 2500
Existing consumers	+1000	A+B	+10,000
New consumers	+2000	C	+20,000
Taxpayers	—	—	−30,000
Society			?

only if compensation will be paid to the losers. However, there is almost no case where it is feasible to compensate everybody, and if the Pareto rule were applied no projects would ever get done. Therefore many cost-benefit analysts have fallen back on the Hicks-Kaldor criterion, which says that a project can be supported provided the gainers could compensate the losers, even if they do not.[8] In this case net receipts can always be added. However, there is no ethical justification for the Hicks-Kaldor criterion; where compensation will not be paid there seems no alternative to inter-personal comparisons of the value of each man's gains and losses.

This brings us to a second case for unweighted adding up – where interpersonal comparisons are made but it is judged that, in the prevailing income distribution, £1 is equally valuable to all the parties concerned. This may in some cases be quite a reasonable procedure. If not, there are only two alternatives: to use some system of distributional weights (discussed in Part Five) or simply to show the net benefits to each party and let the policy-maker apply his own evaluation. If distributional weights are used they need not of course be unique: it may be that the weights can take a very wide range of alternative values and yet provide an unambiguous verdict on a project. Viewed from this angle the

8. On welfare criteria see Mishan (1971a). For a passionate plea in favour of the Hicks-Kaldor criterion see Harberger (1971). Mishan (1971a) argues that if this criterion is used, as he believes it should be, this is because it corresponds to the 'virtual constitution' of the society. For a fuller discussion of this controversial issue see pp. 57–8.

Pareto criterion is just an extreme case where the distributional weights are allowed to take any value between zero and infinity.

For the time being we shall assume, as many cost-benefit analysts do, that unweighted adding up is permissible. We now learn an important lesson: that the area A disappears from the calculation. The reason is of course that it was a *transfer payment* (monopoly rent) rather than a payment for real goods and services; and if everybody's £1 is equally valuable transfers cannot change social welfare. Consumers used to pay this rent and now they do not, but there is no real saving in resource cost as a result of the non-payment after the bridge is built. The real cost-saving from the demise of the ferry comes from the liberation of resources worth B for production elsewhere in the economy. The only other real future change is the value of the additional consumption (C) – the real value of the first 5000 journeys is neither more nor less than it was before. Thus, if one had wanted to take a short cut to estimating future net benefits (granted all pounds equally valuable) one could have straightaway identified only the 'real' changes, i.e. the cost-saving on the ferry (B) and the consumers' surplus on the generated traffic (C). This is the approach frequently advocated, but it is fraught with danger and the reader is recommended to go the long way round where possible, even if he is ignoring income distribution. He will then see more clearly what he is doing and be able to deal with the problems of valuation that arise.

For example, suppose the shares of the ferry company which were previously worth £2500, fall to zero. Should this also be included as a cost? Clearly not, since when we calculated the capitalized value of the ferry's profits we were in fact approximating the change in welfare of the shareholders, which is measured by changes in the value of their equity. We can use one measure or the other but not both, and it may generally be easier to measure the yield and to ignore changes in asset values.

So let us bravely add up the table. The present value turns out to be negative (– £2500) and the project should be turned down. At this point someone might suggest that the project could be made 'viable' by charging a toll on the bridge. This is nonsense – all that it does is to reduce the number of journeys and hence the gain in the real value of additional consumption, without any corresponding reduction in cost. The reader might like to confirm his understanding of the argument so far by recalculating the table for the case where the government levies a toll of £0.05 per crossing. The moral of this exercise is that the prices charged for the output of a project may profoundly affect its economic desirability.[9] The correct price is generally the marginal social cost per unit of output, which in the case of journeys across an uncongested bridge is zero.

2 Measuring costs and benefits when they occur
Shadow pricing of market items

The matter, however, is not usually as easy as it has been made to appear so far. There are two main problems that arise in valuing net benefits when they occur.

1. For market items, market prices may be either distorted (e.g. by taxes or monopoly) or reflect a market disequilibrium (e.g. unemployment or balance of payments troubles).

2. For non-market items (including public goods and the external effects of market items) we need to devise methods of valuation (e.g. for time, recreational amenities, life and so on).

Both problems are handled by the use of shadow prices, as explained by McKean (1968, reading 3). We can begin with the first. In all economies the price structure is so distorted that it is impossible to estimate with precision the price for each item which would lead to the 'second-best optimum' choice and scale of projects, given the constraints. All that is possible is a partial approach in which the adjustments made to market prices make it more likely that the right decision is made than would be the case using unadjusted prices.

Monopoly. Suppose first that our bridge project uses cement produced by a monopolist and sold at well above its marginal cost. Should we use its market price or its marginal production cost? The answer, as to all questions in shadow pricing, is that it depends on how one expects the rest of the economy to adjust when the project is undertaken. If the national production of cement is

9. See for example Beesley and Foster (1965).

expected to increase by the full amount used by the project, then clearly it should be charged at marginal cost. If, on the other hand, no extra cement will be produced, then the project should value its cement at its alternative use value, which is given by its (market) demand price. If we expect a mixture of the two responses we use a weighted average of price and marginal cost.[10]

Indirect taxes. Similar principles apply where an input is subject to indirect tax. We use the producer's supply price if we expect production to increase by the full amount of the project's demand, and the demand price if we expect no growth in output. For a mixture of the two responses the relevant weighting depends on the elasticities of supply and demand as explained in Harberger (1969, reading 12). Thus if the project consumes $a+b$ units of the input, where b is the number of extra units produced as a result of the project, the relevant price becomes approximately $a/(a+b)$ times the demand price (p^D) plus $b/(a+b)$ times the supply price (p^S) – see Figure 2.

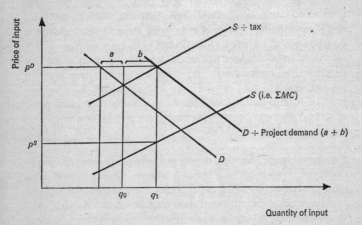

Figure 2

10. This, and what follows, assumes strictly that most goods are competitively produced and untaxed. It also ignores questions of income distribution. In general if other goods are taxed an average rate t marginal factor cost (MC) should be replaced by $MC(1 + t)$.

This whole argument assumes of course that there is no economic rationale for the indirect tax other than the need to raise revenue. Where there is a rationale, such as the correction of external diseconomies (via a fuel tax), the discouragement of 'merit bads' (like smoking) or the redistribution of income, no adjustment may be called for.

Unemployment. Suppose that the bridge is built by workers who would otherwise be unemployed. If there are no macroeconomic costs of employing them (such as more inflation, or reductions in private investment) the cost is not their wage but the value of their lost leisure. This is less than their wage, if they were involuntarily unemployed.

But if the government has already decided on the level of un-employment (i.e. the 'Stabilization Branch' has taken that decision after allowing for its subjective rates of substitution between inflation, growth and employment), then employing people on the project may mean reducing employment and output elsewhere, and the cost of a worker is then measured by his wage. However, in most countries there is a degree of structural unemployment, and the inflationary effects of employing an extra worker depend on who he is and where he lives. In the U.K. extra employment in Northern Ireland might not be inflationary, whereas extra employment in London would. So different costing procedures are needed, relevant to the particular circumstances. In countries worried by sub-optimal investment, the effects on consumption of employing more people must also be allowed for (see Sen, 1972, reading 4 and pp. 49–51 below).

Foreign exchange. Another thorny problem arises over the foreign exchange component of costs and benefits. This is usually considerable, especially when indirect effects are allowed for. On our bridge, for example, the steel used may be imported; or, if produced at home, it may be made by imported equipment or could be exported. Similarly, the extra journeys over the bridge may carry goods to the ports.

Now suppose that the country has an overvalued currency, causing a balance of payments problem which is handled by exchange controls. This means that the demand price for foreign exchange is greater than the official price which the recipients of import licences pay (see Figure 3). How then should we price imports and exports? The standard approach is to use a shadow price of foreign exchange corresponding to the demand price rather than the official price. In this way imports and exports receive prices higher than their nominal prices, so as to measure their social value in terms of the prices of domestic (non-traded) goods. It is easy to see why imports have to be raised in value – their scarcity value is indicated by the demand price for foreign exchange. Exports have to be raised *pari passu*, assuming that £1 worth of extra exports would be allowed to pay for £1 worth of extra imports.

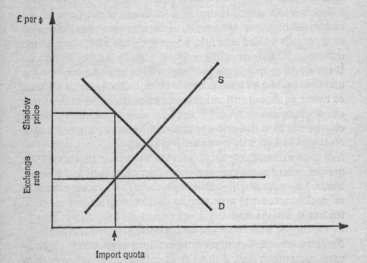

Figure 3

However, Little and Mirrlees (1968, reading 5) have argued that it is far preferable to price exports and imports (and indeed all goods which *in optimal conditions* would be traded internationally) at their unadjusted prices, and to adjust downwards the value of 'non-traded' goods. (Strictly, imports are to be valued at their marginal import cost and exports at their marginal export revenue.) Their proposal has really two elements. The first is to take as numeraire the bundle of goods which a unit of domestic currency will buy on the world market rather than on the domestic market. This is a matter of convenience rather than of principle which Little and Mirrlees justify on the grounds that there are more traded than non-traded goods, which is probably the case for industrial projects with which their *Manual of Industrial Project Analysis* is concerned.

The second element of their proposal is that all goods which are 'tradeable', that is that would be traded in optimal conditions, ought generally to be valued at world prices, even if they are not currently being traded freely because of non-optimal government policies. The purpose here is moralistic, to ensure that countries have the least possible excuse for overlooking the possible gains from trade. As is well known, a price-taking country producing two traded outputs maximizes its welfare by maximizing the value of its output valued at world prices and thus expanding to the maximum (OAB) its consumption possibility set (see Figure 4). If the world price of guns is one ton of butter and a country has an import quota of guns raising their domestic price to 1·1 tons of butter, it should still not produce guns at any cost above one ton of butter unless it is determined to maintain the quota. Doing cost-benefit at world prices is intended to focus planners' minds on the cost of such distorted trading policies.

Not surprisingly, the Little-Mirrlees proposals have aroused a minor hornets' nest. Some critics consider them to have the wrong ideals. For example, Stewart and Streeten (1971) accuse them of an unduly piecemeal approach to development and of ignoring the linkages in the economy which necessitate a strategy of growth in which free trade may not be optimal. Sen (1972, reading 4), though more in favour of the open-economy approach to development, points out that, if this aim is not shared by other government agencies, that constraint should be allowed for in project appraisal. For example, if it would be rational to import a certain input but this is banned by the government, the input should in his view be valued not at its world price but rather at its domestic cost of production.[11]

11. For a reply to criticisms of their approach see Little and Mirrlees (1972 and 1974). On other approaches to the problem see Dasgupta (1972) and Bacha and Taylor (1971).

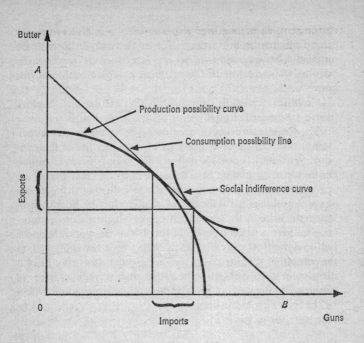

Figure 4

Pricing of non-market items

With non-market goods and services, we do not even have a
market price as a starting point. The marginal value which people
place on a good (A), for which they do not directly pay money,
has therefore to be inferred from the money they would have to
pay for a good (B) which they show themselves to value equally.
In this book we illustrate this approach to only a few examples of
the many items to which it can be applied.

Time. Suppose that our bridge will in fact save travellers time (say
ten minutes) as well as money (the ferry charges). We have a good
deal of evidence on how to value savings of time (Harrison and
Quarmby, 1969, reading 6). Take leisure time first. A crude approach would be based on the theory of labour supply. This
asserts that if a worker has freedom to vary his hours of work, the

marginal value of one hour's leisure can be inferred from his gains from one hour's work, since at the margin he must be indifferent between the two. So one hour's leisure is worth the post-tax wage rate minus the marginal psychic disvalue of one hour's work.

One problem with this approach is that the disvalue of work has to be guessed. Equally problematical, an hour's travelling during one's leisure hours does not deprive one of an hour's leisure; it merely involves using leisure one way rather than another. We want to know the difference in value between an hour's leisure travelling and an hour's leisure in its alternative use.

We have therefore to find cases where individuals can choose to save travelling time at the cost of spending money. Such choices frequently arise in the choice between two methods of transport (say bus versus underground, on the journey to work). Suppose that everybody equally dislikes spending time travelling (T), in the sense that they agree on the money equivalent (say b) of a marginal minute spent at home rather than travelling. Then we can describe the costs (C) of the bus and underground journeys by the following expressions:

$$C_B = a_B + bT_B + M_B,$$
$$C_U = a_U + bT_U + M_U,$$

where a_B and a_U are parameters reflecting the intrinsic pleasures of bus and underground respectively and T and M represent the time and money costs involved. The difference in these costs (ΔC) depends on where a person lives, and turns out to be a good predictor of the probability (P_B) of his travelling by bus rather than underground. One can for example fit a function such as the following:

$$\log\left(\frac{P_B}{1-P_B}\right) = \alpha\Delta C = \alpha(a_U - a_B + b\Delta T + \Delta M).$$

From it we can estimate b and hence the cost of commuting time in terms of its money equivalent. Such studies of 'modal split' (as it is called in the jargon) for commuting in Britain have found costs of commuting time at around 25 per cent of the traveller's gross wage rate. This was the assumption originally used by the Roskill Commission on the Third London Airport, giving an average value of £0.23 per hour. But, after hearing the criticisms of this assumption, they settled for two alternative assumptions of £0.12 and £0.35 (see reading 17).

For working time the problem is simpler since the main cost is the loss of the worker's output, measured roughly by his wage. However, we should also take into account the worker's excess psychic (dis)satisfaction from travelling rather than working. For working time the Roskill Commission finally made two assumptions of £1.46 and £2.58, on either side of the mean business travellers' wage of £2.10.

Recreational facilities. For recreational facilities too attempts have been made to infer valuations from behaviour. Following the method developed by Clawson (1959), Mansfield (1971, reading 7) attempts to estimate the value to the community of the English Lake District National Park countryside viewed as a recreational facility. For this we need to know the excess of the total value which people put upon their visits over the costs they incur in making them. Thus we need to know the demand curve for visits. Since people come to the Lake District from differing distances they incur differential costs in getting there. It seems reasonable to suppose that the number of visits from an area would be proportional to the population of the area, but that this proportion would depend on the costs (and also on car ownership per head of population in the area). Mansfield fits a demand curve using these variables for each area from which visitors come.[12] For visitors from each area the surplus can be readily computed as the area under the demand curve which the equation implies. The total surplus is simply the sum of these surpluses.

There are many problems with the method, in particular its failure to include the price of substitute recreational facilities in the regression analysis. (The reader may like to work out for himself the direction of bias which would result in the estimated surplus, supposing, as seems likely, that the price of substitutes rises as the cost of reaching the Lake District rises.) In addition,

12. His actual demand function is $T = a + bW + cC^{-2}$, where T is trips per head of population, W is cars per head and C is the cost of reaching the Lake District (measured by distance travelled). In similar work C is sometimes approximated by an expression $a' + b'T + M$ like that used above.

as Mansfield points out in the later part of the article quoted, it is very difficult to use evidence on existing facilities to evaluate the creation of new and potentially competitive ones, such as a lake trapped by a barrage across nearby Morecambe Bay. However, the approach is sufficiently interesting to deserve further work. There is also a need for better-designed attitude questions which could be used in social surveys in order to probe the valuation of many non-market items like recreational amenities.

Life. Perhaps the most difficult item of all to value is human life. Yet it is quite clear that countless policy decisions affect the incidence of death, and none of them aim to minimize its incidence regardless of cost. So each decision implies some valuation of human life.

Suppose that each worker on the bridge has a 1 per cent probability of being killed on the job, and there are twenty-five workers. One approach would be to cost the risk of loss of life at 25 per cent times the (average) human capital value per worker. But this immediately raises the question of 'value to whom?' Weisbrod (1961) distinguishes two measures, without committing himself to saying which is relevant to public decisions. The first consists of the present (discounted) value of a man's future lifetime production, measured by his earnings. This measure implies that production is equally valuable, regardless of how many people there are to consume the fruits of it. Alternatively he assumes that all that matters is consumption per living person, in which case the value of someone's life is measured by the effects of his death on the welfare of those who would survive him. This equals the excess of his expected future production over his future consumption, again discounted to the present.

However, neither of these approaches is very satisfactory. The former would, in most countries, support population policies which maximized the birthrate, while the latter would support policies which minimized it.[13] An alternative that has been pro-

13. In Weisbrod's calculations a male has a positive net present value of production minus his own consumption, mainly because he supports his wife. A female presumably has a negative present value. So no conclusions can be drawn for population policy. The remarks in the text are based on the sweeping assumption that the average product of labour declines as labour increases from zero upwards, and that labour is homogenous.

posed is the use of life insurance values, but these could only reflect, if anything, the value of a person's life to his family and not to himself.

Mishan (1971b, reading 8), after reviewing the methods that have been used, concludes that there are three cost consequences of a policy decision which affects the probability of a person's (Jack's) death. First, there is the way in which Jack himself values the extra risk. If he voluntarily assumes the risk, this value is already included in the price he requires for accepting it – this is why bridge-builders get relatively high wages, and there is no need to make any additional allowance for the risk cost to them of their work. If on the other hand the labour was conscript we should have to find a way of valuing the risk. Likewise, we should allow for any risk imposed on people living beneath the bridge who might get killed. The second item is the value which others put on the financial consequences for them of Jack's increased risk of death. This may bear some relation to the measure of his future production less consumption. Where Jack has allowed for this in the terms on which he accepted the risk, it should not of course be double-counted. Finally, there is the psychic value to others of the increased risk of Jack's death, for which again any double-counting must be avoided.

The key feature of this approach is that it does not value death (or life) as such, but only changes in the probability of death. All the valuations are thus *ex ante* and no attempt is made to value the suffering which will actually (*ex post*) be caused if a typical worker dies. Is this right? Suppose, for example, that the suffering which a worker's wife will experience if he dies is equivalent to $-£x$. The expected *ex post* suffering in our example is then $-£0.25x$. What is the *ex ante* valuation of it? If each wife values risky outcomes in terms of her expected utility and knows that the probability of her husband's death is 0·01 and that its utility would be $-£x$, then her *ex ante* valuation of the risk is $-£0.01x$ and the overall *ex ante* valuation (of all twenty-five wives) is $-£0.25x$. The *ex ante* valuation is thus the same as the *ex post* one quoted above. But the wives may instead be ill-informed about the probability of death or may not make a realistic estimate of the suffering they would experience. In this case what does the planner put into his calculation – his own expected *ex post* evaluation or the *ex ante* one expressed by the wives? The answer to this quite general question depends on the degree of paternalism the planner is willing to exercise. If he supports the prohibition of taxation of 'merit bads', like cigarette smoking, on the grounds that the government can foresee the suffering these will cause better than the individual can, then it seems quite logical to adopt the same approach in cost-benefit analysis. The present valuations of the parties affected are then disregarded in favour of their future valuations. How often one would be willing to do this is debatable, but it seems absurd to argue that one should always regard people's present preferences as decisive. Would one on that account have considered the advent of Hitler as the best choice for the Germans in the 1930s?

Reverting to the valuation of life, it remains clear that *ex ante* states of mind are relevant in the sense that, if a wife's life is blighted by the fear of her husband's death, this needs to be taken into account, quite independently of how she would value the actual event of his death. As far as the individual who may die is concerned this fear of death is in fact the only element that enters the calculation, since he will feel nothing once he is dead.

So where does this leave us? How could we calculate the various magnitudes? The answer is that it is very difficult, but, as Mishan points out, it is better to know what it is one should know, even if one cannot know it, than to know something that is irrelevant.

Finally, it is reasonable to ask what light this discussion of death control throws on the apparently parallel question of birth control? It should show that they are not really parallel at all. Death is not the same as non-birth: both death and birth may be costly. In deciding what is right we start from the point where we are, taking into account the probable states of mind of those who may be affected by our decisions. The question of birth control more than any other raises the issue of how the welfare of future generations should be treated in cost-benefit analysis. In much cost-benefit their welfare is ignored, in which case population can be left to find its own level, subject only to the need for financial incentives to counteract any external effects. But if, as I argue later (pp. 39) future generations need to be considered, we have to find some framework for doing this; the one offered there is, unfortunately, the best that is currently available.

Pure public goods and cost-effectiveness analysis. There is, however, a wide range of non-market items which can be valued in one way or another. For example, the cost of noise is discussed in Mishan (1970, reading 18). Nevertheless, there remain other goods for which no meaningful valuation can be made – especially pure public goods, which can jointly benefit many people and where it is difficult to exclude people from the benefits. Owing to the difficulty of exclusion, there is no way of getting people to reveal their valuations of such goods.[14] Whenever cost-benefit analysis becomes impossible, since the benefits cannot be valued, it is still useful to compare the costs of providing the same benefit in different ways. This is called cost-effectiveness analysis and is regularly used in defence, public health and other fields. Apart from not valuing benefits, the procedures are exactly the same as in cost-benefit analysis.

3 The social time preference rate and the social opportunity cost of capital

Suppose we have satisfactorily computed the net benefits of a project in each future year. So we know $B_0 - C_0$, $B_1 - C_1, \ldots$, $B_n - C_n$, where B indicates benefits, C costs and n is the length of time during which the project produces its effects. We still have the problem of aggregating these, to see if in total they are positive. If we have done the job properly, these net benefits represent the changes in consumption brought about by the project, for it is only consumption (rightly defined) that ultimately affects human welfare. So we need to know the value of next year's consumption relative to this year's, and so on for all future years. This relative value is expressed in terms of a time preference rate, or (the same thing) a discount rate. If this rate is 5 per cent, this means that £1 of next year's consumption is worth only about £0.95 of this year's. More generally, if r is the rate, we value each £1 of next year's consumption the same as $£1/(1+r)$ of this year's, r being from this point of view the rate at which we discount next year's benefits. Or, to put the matter the other way round, £1 of this year's consumption is worth $£(1+r)$ of next year's, r being the rate by which present consumption is preferred

14. The Lake District, though it could be classified as a public good, yet involves differential costs of access, so a demand curve can be obtained.

to future consumption. As Feldstein (1964, reading 9) points out, there is no *a priori* reason why the rate at which we discount 1973's pounds to make them equivalent in value to 1972's should equal the rate at which we discount 1983's pounds to make them equivalent to 1982's. But this assumption is almost invariably made. If we make it, the value of a project (valued in terms of today's consumption) becomes

$$PV = B_0 - C_0 + \frac{B_1 - C_1}{1+r} + \frac{B_2 - C_2}{(1+r)^2} + \ldots + \frac{B_n - C_n}{(1+r)^n}$$

and the project should be undertaken if it has a positive value. The project could, of course, be valued in terms of pounds in year n (by multiplying the present value by $(1+r)^n$) or in any other year, but this makes no difference to the decision, since if the value is positive in one year it is positive in all other years and vice versa.

The problem is: How do we choose the discount rate? This is not an academic question. A discount rate of 5 per cent might well lead to twice as much investment as one of 10 per cent, together with an equivalent reduction in consumption. In poor countries in particular, the choice between present and future consumption is truly agonizing. How far in fact is it legitimate to depress present levels of living for the sake of the future? To think about this question it is most useful to begin with a single person economy (Robinson Crusoe) and to apply to his situation the tools of capital theory developed by Irving Fisher.[15]

Suppose that Crusoe's consumption consists only of fish and that he knows he will live for only two years. At present he spends all his time fishing with his existing equipment and catches 100 fish a year. He will do the same next year unless he takes time off to improve his equipment. If he does some investment of this type, he opens up the production possibility curve shown in Figure 5. This schedule consists of a series of projects arrayed from right to left in order of their rate of return – the cost in year 0 is the sacrifice of consumption involved and the return is the gain of consumption in year 1. Only one of these projects is shown separately in the diagram – the most profitable project, costing two fish now and yielding six in the following year.

15. For an excellent exposition of Fisherian capital theory see Hirshleifer (1958) reprinted in B. V. Carsberg and H. C. Edey (1969).

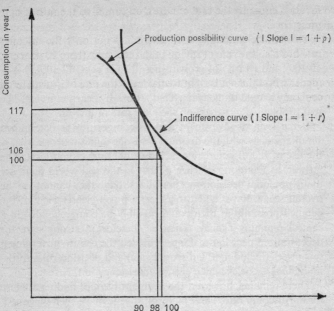

Figure 5

Crusoe chooses from the various production possibilities so as to reach his highest inter-temporal indifference curve. In other words he calculates the amount by which he can increase future consumption by sacrificing a further unit of present consumption and invests until this is equal to the minimum amount of extra future consumption required to induce him to sacrifice a further unit. The first of these amounts is the (absolute) slope of the production possibility curve. Its value corresponds to B_1/C_0 for the marginal project. This can be written as $(B_1 - C_0)/C_0 + 1$, or $\rho + 1$, where ρ is the (marginal) rate of return on investment. The second is the slope of the indifference curve. Its value is MU_0/MU_1, which can be written $(MU_0 - MU_1)/MU_1 + 1$, or $r + 1$, where r is the (marginal) rate of time preference. So the process of choice involves equating the rate of return on capital to the rate of time preference.

This choice simultaneously determines not only the discount rate but also the rate of saving of the economy (here 10 per cent, 10/100) and its rate of growth (here 17 per cent, 17/100).[16] Any reader who thinks it is right to maximize the rate of growth of an economy should think again. That is done by nearly starving. The real problem is to decide on the *right* rate of growth.

If the level of investment and its composition is determined simultaneously with the discount rate, one might well ask what is the use of the discount rate in individual project appraisal. The answer, as mentioned earlier, is that in the real world there are many potential decision-makers who, though they cannot see the overall scene, have, taken together, a much clearer view of the detailed possibilities than could possibly be comprehended in a central planning agency. There is therefore a strong case for decentralized decision-making, provided the central government sets prices (including the discount rate) and decision rules to the individual agencies which ensure consistency in their decisions.

There remains, however, the acute problem of finding a figure for the discount rate. Three main approaches have been suggested.

1. Use post-tax interest rates on long-term risk-free bonds.
2. Make assumptions about the desired growth rate and the intertemporal indifference map.
3. Make assumptions about the desired growth rate and the production possibility curve.

The market rate of interest

In a mixed economy the most obvious indicator of time preference is the market rate of interest. To see how this is determined in a perfectly competitive Walrasian system of general equilibrium we modify the economy of Robinson Crusoe in two ways only: we multiply the human species, and we allow for the possibility of borrowing and lending. The interest rate then adjusts until it equals simultaneously the rate of time preference of all individuals in the society and the rate of return on productive investment (see

16. A savings rate of 10 per cent would not normally produce a growth rate of 17 per cent; this results from the use of the 2-period model.

Stigler, 1966, ch. 17). This is illustrated in Figure 6. The representative borrower, with initial endowment indicated by point D, invests AB and borrows AC; the representative lender, initially endowed at point R, lends PQ. If there are as many borrowers as lenders, PQ must equal AC – the function of the interest rate is to equate the two, and it varies until they are equal.[17] At their equilibrium levels of consumption the borrowers' and lenders' rates of time preference are equated to the interest rate. So does this mean that the interest rate indicates the true rate of *social* time preference?

This is a subject of controversy, but before we embark on the controversy there is one point on which everyone is agreed. If there is inflation the money rate of interest will be adjusted to some extent to allow for the expected rate of change of prices. But we are interested in the subjective rate of substitution between real consumption in one period and another, and so we need to find a 'real' rate of interest which reflects this.[18] If the money interest rate indicates that people are indifferent between £1 now and £$1+i$ next year, it follows that, if I expect prices to rise by a proportion p during the year, I must be indifferent between £1-worth of goods now (at today's prices) and the goods which £$(1+i)/(1+p)$ would buy tomorrow if today's prices still prevailed. This last figure equals approximately £$1+i-p$, so that $i-p$ is the real rate of time preference and the real rate of interest. How price expectations are formed is something we only partially understand. If expectations equalled actual rates of price change, one would have to conclude that the real rate of interest in Britain in 1971 was negative! What can be said quite dogmatically is that money interest rates must be substantially reduced in inflation to obtain a measure of the real rate of interest.

This much is agreed, but there remain many problems with using even an adjusted interest rate as a measure of society's time preference.

17. At this point, assuming no hoarding of money, we also have saving (PQ–BC) equal to investment (AB).

18. In principle, it makes no difference whether we use a money rate of interest and nominal consumption valued at forecast rates of inflation, or a real rate of interest and real consumption at constant prices. However, it is difficult to forecast inflation, so C-B analysis is normally done in constant prices.

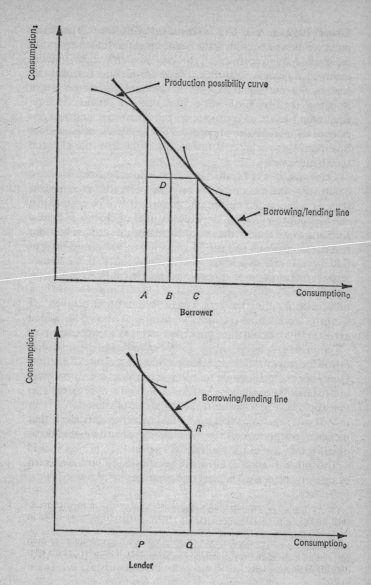

Figure 6

Uncertainty and imperfect capital markets. The future is uncertain and this leads to a multiplicity of interest rates depending on the credit risks involved. Which rate should be used in cost-benefit analysis? It would of course be possible to vary the discount rate according to the riskiness of the net returns of the project, but it is preferable to express all net returns in terms of their certainty-equivalent (see Part Four below). We then need a standard discount rate relevant to certainly-known levels of consumption. This is why the most commonly-used estimate of private (and social) time preference is the rate on long-term government bonds (reduced to allow for expected inflation and income tax payments). These bonds are generally considered free of risk. However, since the future price level is uncertain, there is in fact no truly risk-free rate of interest, nor are there any long-term bonds whose nominal yield is independent of unknown future interest rates, unless they are held to maturity (Arrow, 1969). Nevertheless it remains true that, for the ordinary lender, the adjusted long-term bond rate probably gives as good evidence as we are likely to get on his risk-free time preference.

But whether this is what his time preference would be, given an optimal allocation of resources, is another matter. The fact of uncertainty means that, in the absence of a complete system of futures markets, market prices are of limited welfare significance. For the savings and investment decisions of each individual depend upon his forecast of future incomes and prices, yet these will themselves depend on the decisions made by others. This some believe to be a potent source of under-investment.[19]

Moreover, the imperfections of the capital market mean that the time preferences of borrowers will almost always exceed those of lenders. In principle, the discount rate for each project should be a weighted average of the time preferences of all those affected by the project (Musgrave, 1969, reading 2).[20]

19. For a good discussion of the optimality or otherwise of saving/investment decisions in a market economy see Phelps (1965, ch. 4), reproduced in A. K. Sen (1970b).
20. Strictly the only correct procedure is to evaluate separately for each individual the present value of his net benefit stream, discounted at his own time preference rate.

The influence of money on interest rates. Interest rates have also been criticized on the grounds that they reflect monetary as well as real forces, and therefore should not be used for decisions of real resource allocation. There are, of course, some who maintain that money cannot alter real rates of interest except where there are unanticipated changes in the rate of change of money creation. But most economists would accept that money creation can change real interest rates, through its effect on prices and thus on the public's perception of its real wealth (Metzler, 1951; Mundell, 1963). Given these influences, do interest rates retain any normative significance?

This, as usual, is a question of which constraints are to be taken as given. There must, in principle, be an optimum quantity of money, which could be solved for simultaneously with all the other magnitudes in the economic system, including the implied rate of interest. However, in all probability we do not have the optimum quantity, and project planners, unless they are trying to secure changes in monetary policy, must accept whatever preferences the monetary authorities have helped to create.

Myopia (or 'pure time preference'). A third problem with interest rates is that they reflect each individual's *ex ante* anticipation of the relative value of his future consumption. But individuals may underestimate the pleasure which future consumption will in fact give them, if, as Pigou (1920) alleged, they are victims of 'defective telescopic faculty'. According to Pigou, an individual with the same commitments in both years must, in fact, be as well off if he consumes £100 in Year 0 and £150 in Year 1 or the reverse. That is to say, his indifference map in Figure 5 ought to look the same whichever year's consumption is measured along the horizontal axis. So the indifference curves should be symmetrical about the 45° line from the origin, with the time preference rate being zero when consumption in the two periods is equal. But in fact Pigou surmises that people have 'pure time preference': they value present consumption more highly than future consumption even on the 45° line.

The problem with myopia lies partly in telling whether people have it, though there are certainly stagnant economies with higher interest rates than can be readily explained by risk and capital market imperfections. But even if people do have it and their *ex ante* evaluations fail to equal what the planner knows they will feel *ex post*, there is still the question of how far the planner should impose his own long sight upon the myopic multitude. Marglin (1963a) adopts the view that it is undemocratic for him to do so. But cost-benefit analysis is not in itself a 'democratic' process. It is a thought process which attempts to throw light on what is right, given our knowledge of the consequences of certain actions. If the planners really knew there were myopia they should surely use this knowledge. The main argument against overriding current preferences is that planners may be unlikely to know better than the individuals actually affected, and this argument is a strong one.

External effects in consumption. The problems discussed so far relate to the ability of interest rates to produce an optimum, assuming that all that matters is the welfare of individuals now living and that each individual's welfare is affected only by his own family's consumption stream. But, the reader may say, what about the welfare of future generations? After all, public investments may augment or reduce the consumption of people yet unborn. Surely this should be taken into account?

There are two approaches to this problem. In the first we continue to value only the welfare of those now living, but recognize that this is affected by the consumption available to future generations. Now if my welfare depended only on the consumption available to me and my own heirs, there would be no problem. But most of us do in fact derive pleasure from contemplating the welfare of others and their heirs, and this poses a classic case of externality. For in a free market these external effects are ignored and individuals maximize their own utility, taking the savings decisions of others as exogenous to their own decisions. But if they could bargain or take a collective decision via the political process a better outcome could be obtained.

The original argument about this 'isolation paradox' was propounded by Sen (1961), developed by Marglin (1963a), criticized by Lind (1964) and reformulated in a more general form by Sen (1967, reading 10). His argument is this.

Suppose each individual in society makes the following valuation of one unit of consumption according to who consumes it:

consumed by him now   1
consumed by his heir γ
consumed by others now β
consumed by others' heirs a

Suppose also that one unit of consumption foregone by the present generation leads to k units extra of consumption by the next.

(a) Consider the equilibrium of a competitive market in which each individual makes his own independent saving decision. Assume that, if an individual saves one unit, his heir will benefit by λk and others' heirs by $(1-\lambda)k$, λ depending on the level of taxes, such as death duties. The individual will save till his future return from saving equals his present sacrifice, so that in equilibrium

$$\lambda k \gamma + (1-\lambda) k a = 1.$$

The marginal rate of return on capital $(k-1)$ is thus given by

$$k = \frac{1}{\lambda \gamma + (1-\lambda)a}.$$

(b) Now suppose that whenever one individual saves one unit, every other individual does the same. This could be the case for example if all investment was financed by taxes and all individuals were equally rich. And suppose the decision on whether everyone shall save one more unit is taken by referendum. Then each individual will vote for more saving until the future return (in terms of his own utility) from such saving equals his present sacrifice. If there are N members of the community, each with one heir, each individual's heir can expect to get a $(1/N)$th share of the Nk units of extra future consumption; so in equilibrium

$$k\gamma + (N-1)\,ka = 1 + (N-1)\beta.$$

In this case the marginal rate of return on capital $(k-1)$ is given by

$$k = \frac{1+(N-1)\beta}{\gamma+(N-1)a}.$$

The vital question is whether this equilibrium rate is the same as under competition (i.e. as in (a)). Sen's argument is that it would be pure chance if it was, and in fact he thinks it is lower. It certainly would be if both $\lambda < 1$, as it would if inheritance taxes spread the proceeds of saving, and $1/\beta > \gamma/a$, as it would be if people were more egoistic when comparing their own consumption with their own contemporaries' than when comparing their heirs' consumption with their heirs' contemporaries'. And in this case a free market will produce underinvestment and an excessive interest rate. Whatever one thinks of the values of the various parameters, the approach at least draws attention to the issues raised by external effects in consumption. However, none of those who have argued on these lines has suggested how one would actually get a social discount rate which did allow for these external effects.[21]

The welfare of future generations per se. Nor have we yet considered what allowance should be made for the welfare of future generations *per se*. Is it really right that projects should be judged exclusively in terms of their effects on the welfare of those now living? Most economists would say 'Yes' on the grounds that cost-benefit analysis should be democratic.[22] However, one wonders whether they would apply this reasoning to the evaluation of capital punishment. If one takes the alternative view that cost-benefit analysis aims to throw light on what is right, it is difficult to think of any ethical justification for ignoring future generations.[23] Suppose, for example, that one were to subscribe to the widely-held ethical position that the best course of action is that

21. For Marglin's actual proposal see pp. 43 below.

22. This view is held most strongly by those who would also use the Hicks-Kaldor welfare criterion in project evaluation. It is easy to see why the two approaches are natural bedfellows. The Hicks-Kaldor criterion aims, as far as possible, to separate decisions about production and investment from those about distribution, and acquires whatever plausibility it has from the thought that we could always alter the income distribution by cash transfers. However, distribution between non-overlapping generations in a closed economy can only be altered by decisions about investment. It is therefore convenient if future generations need not be considered.

23. A practical argument is sometimes put forward for ignoring them – that we cannot know their preferences. However, there are many items (like life) where we do not know how they are valued by present generations, and many (like bread) where we can be fairly sure what future generations will feel.

whose consequences one would prefer if one had an equal probability of being each of the people affected by the action.[24] Then clearly future generations must be taken into account in so far as they are affected by the action. But how would one do this by means of a discount rate, when it is essentially a problem of income distribution? The answer is that conceptually the discount rate is an untidy way of proceeding. We should really work out the value of the project to each of the people affected (including the unborn), choosing as the unit for each person £1 of his consumption at some specified point in his life. We should then aggregate across persons using as weights for each individual the relative social value of his consumption at that point in his life. However, supposing that we regard 'me today' as a different person from 'me tomorrow'. Then all inter-temporal problems become distributional. If we can find a satisfactory general solution to the problem of distribution we shall also have solved the inter-temporal problem. This, in a sense, is the approach of 'optimal growth theory' to the discount rate problem.

Making assumptions about the social inter-temporal utility function

The theory of optimal growth, stemming from the seminal work of Ramsey (1928),[25] assumes that there is a cardinal utility-of-consumption function $U(C)$ common to all men, and that total inter-temporal welfare consists of an aggregation of the utilities enjoyed by each man in each period. So, beginning again with Robinson Crusoe, his total inter-temporal welfare is

$$W = U(C_0) + U(C_1).$$

The absolute slope of the indifference curve is

$$\frac{\partial W/\partial C_0}{\partial W/\partial C_1} \quad \text{or} \quad \frac{U'(C_0)}{U'(C_1)}.$$

Now, suppose we assume that the marginal utility of consumption falls steadily, in such a way that for each 1 per cent increase in consumption the marginal utility falls by ε per cent. Then $U'(C)$

24. On possible ethical approaches to the question of fairness see Sen (1971).

25. This is reproduced in A. K. Sen (1970a).

$= C^{-\varepsilon}$. The slope of the indifference curve is now

$$\frac{U'(C_0)}{U'(C_1)} = \frac{C_0^{-\varepsilon}}{C_1^{-\varepsilon}} = \left[\frac{C_1}{C_0}\right]^{\varepsilon} = (1+g)^{\varepsilon} \simeq 1+g\varepsilon,$$

where g is the proportional rate of growth of consumption.[26] So the discount rate equals $g\varepsilon$ – the rate of growth of consumption times the elasticity of the marginal utility of consumption with respect to consumption. If our economy were growing at 2 per cent a year and the elasticity of marginal utility with respect to consumption were, say, $1\cdot5$, the discount rate would be 3 per cent. The faster the rate of growth of the economy the higher the appropriate discount rate, since future income is that much higher than present income and therefore that much less valuable at the margin.

To many people this approach seems to provide the only valid rationale for discounting, rather than investing until the marginal rate of return is zero.[27] Geometrically, it provides an explanation for the convexity of the indifference curves in Figure 5, if one remembers that the rate of growth of the economy is indicated by the slope of a ray through the origin to the point in question on the curve.

So much for Robinson Crusoe. If we turn to an economy of many persons we should presumably calculate social welfare as some aggregation of individual utilities. Supposing, however, that at each point in time income is equally distributed. Then social welfare in a particular period depends on the utility of consumption per head. But is this all or does it also depend on the number

26. The reader will find this approach presented in Eckstein (1957, pp. 75 ff.) and in Eckstein (1961), which is reproduced in R. W. Houghton (1970) where, however, the printing of ε on p. 232 is in some places misplaced. For a more elaborate application of optimal growth theory to the choice of discount rate, see Arrow (1966 and 1969); Arrow however discounts future utilities to allow for some element of pure time preference. See also Arrow and Kurz (1970).

27. For a full discussion of the rationale of discounting, along these lines, see Feldstein (1964, reading 9). Feldstein does not, however, assume a constant ε and therefore provides no actual formula. The reader should note that in optimal growth theory it is necessary for optimality, but not sufficient, that the marginal rate of return equal the proportional rate of decline of marginal utility.

of people enjoying that consumption per head? This is a matter of controversy, which profoundly affects one's approach to the problem of optimal population. However, as far as the discount rate goes, it is enough to note that with a static population the discount rate is the same whichever we assume. With a population growing at rate n the time preference rate is $(g-n)\varepsilon+n$, if welfare depends only on the utility of consumption per head; if it depends on that times the number of people, the rate is $(g-n)\varepsilon$.[28] Whichever assumption we make, the discount rate is lower the faster the rate of population growth, provided ε exceeds unity.

How can we determine the magnitude of ε? It can of course be regarded in two separate lights. One can take the view that there is no place in positive economics for a utility function which says by what proportion a person prefers A to B. And if the same utility function is held to apply to more than one person, this is said to be even more unreasonable, involving as it does inter-personal comparisons of utility. From this point of view therefore the utility-of-consumption function becomes a purely normative device for representing one's ethical position – it is, if you like, a particular form of Bergsonian social welfare function (see Bator, 1957).

Alternatively, it can be argued that we have, from the fact of insurance, some positive evidence that individuals do compare the psychic loss from losing their insurance premium with the psychic loss from losing their houses (Friedman and Savage, 1948). The trouble is that, though the fact of insurance provides evidence of a diminishing marginal utility of income over some range, the fact of gambling suggests that for some people the marginal utility is increasing over some range. We can therefore get no estimate of ε from behaviour towards risk. An alternative approach is one in which the static utility function of the individual is assumed to be additive in two of the items of consumption, such as food and other goods, i.e. the marginal utility of food is independent of the quantity of other goods and vice versa. If this highly questionable assumption is made, the elasticity of the marginal utility of consumption can be calculated from the price and income elasticities of food and from its share in income. The kind of values which

28. For proof of these propositions see the note at the end of the Introduction, p. 64.

are found for ε in this way tend to fall between 1 and 2·5 (Fellner, 1967).[29]

Clearly, the use of any single value of ε is exceedingly arbitrary. Some people's marginal utility of income may indeed rise over some ranges making ε negative; and interpersonal comparisons, though they conform to some of our deepest intuitions about the human situation, are bound to be based on the most intuitive of judgements. Most of those who use the utility-of-consumption function would regard it as having some basis in positive reality, but as being so incapable of empirical investigation that the value assumed for ε is essentially normative: the larger ε the more egalitarian the approach.

And what of the rate of growth of consumption (g)? The problem here is that this is one of the variables which in principle we want to optimize at the same time as the discount rate (see Figure 5). It is of course true that once we have chosen the growth rate we have settled the rate of time preference. But then, assuming our initial decision was correct, we have also settled the marginal rate of return on capital, making it equal to the rate of time preference.

Making assumptions about the production possibility curve

This has led Marglin (1963a) to put forward as an alternative approach the following strategy of decision. First decide on the growth rate you want and then see what investment that would require (see Figure 5). If this is unacceptable, consider different combinations of investment and growth till you have found the one you prefer. This will imply a marginal rate of return on capital, which, since the choice is optimal, must by definition equal the rate of time preference. Use this rate as the discount rate. Critics have argued that this approach is impractical (Prest and Turvey, 1965, reading 1) but it is less likely to produce inconsistent decisions than the approach of pp. 41, where the rate of growth (g) and the discount rate $(g\varepsilon)$ are separately decided, independently of the production possibilities which must in fact link them.

So we are left with two main alternatives. The first allows

29. Harberger (1969) argues that such values are too high to be consistent with the limited amount of insurance purchased by most individuals.

adjusted market interest rates to determine the government's discount rate and hence the rate of investment and the rate of growth of the economy. The other starts by deciding on the rate of growth and infers from it the appropriate discount rate for use in decentralized decision-making. The latter is widely regarded as infeasible, and most cost-benefit analysts to date have followed some procedure where interest rates are taken as starting points for a measure of the social rate of time preference.

The social opportunity cost of capital

However, all the discussion so far has been based on the assumption that the government can bring the economy somehow to the optimal rate of saving and investment, either by inducing the private sector to act or by acting itself. But this may be impossible for various reasons, in which case the cry will be heard, as it is in so many countries: too little growth. We now have a problem in that capital investment, and hence investment displaced by the current project, is socially more valuable than consumption of equivalent monetary value. So if the resources used on the current project would otherwise have been producing investment goods valued at £x in the market, the cost of these resources is greater than £x, since £1 of investment is worth more than £1 of consumption and we choose to measure values in units of consumption.

Let us take a concrete example. Suppose certain products (say shirts) are only produced in the private sector and the government is not permitted to invest funds in the private sector. Suppose too that long-term lending rates (after income tax) accurately reflect private time preference. Nevertheless, owing to Income Tax and Corporation Tax, investors will require from investments in shirts a pre-tax rate of return (ρ) that far exceeds their rate of time preference. The government now considers building our bridge, financing it by borrowing on the capital market, and this borrowing will displace an equal amount of investment in the shirt industry. At what discount rate should the bridge project be evaluated?

The answer is simple – the stream of benefits (consumption generated) and cost (consumption displaced) should (by definition) be discounted at the rate which represents the social value of consumption in different periods, i.e. at the rate of social time preference (r). But what is the consumption stream foregone when £1-worth of resources are diverted from investment in the shirt industry to bridge-building? The investment would have had a rate of return of ρ, so the stream of consumption from an investment of £1 can be approximated by the 'permanent income stream' ρ, ρ, ρ and so on for ever. The present value of this stream when discounted at the time preference rate (r) is ρ/r.[30] So each £1 of cash spent on the bridge should now be costed at £ρ/r (Marglin, 1963b, reading 11). But the social discount rate remains r, and the present value of the project, where C is the initial money cost and B the additional consumption generated per year for ever, is

$$V = -C\frac{\rho}{r} + \frac{B}{r}.$$

The project should be undertaken if this is greater than zero.

The perceptive reader will see at once that this requires that

$$-C + \frac{B}{\rho} > 0.$$

In other words, if the costs are counted in money terms (unadjusted), we get the correct decision if we then compute the present value using ρ as the discount rate. It can, however, be confusing to do so, and is sometimes incorrect; and the reader is recommended to hold on to the notion of discounting by the time preference rate. We shall revert to this point later.

The case we have just quoted, where any government investment displaces an investment of equal monetary cost in the private sector, occurs when there is an absolute savings constraint (i.e. total overall capital rationing). This is sometimes regarded as the standard position in underdeveloped countries, and in such a case the social time preference rate assumed may make little difference to the selection of projects.

30. This extremely useful formula is proved in the note at the end of this Introduction, p. 65. Intuitively, if the rate of interest is r per annum, this means that 1 now has the same value as r per year for ever. Therefore $1/r$ now is equivalent to 1 per year for ever and ρ/r is equivalent to ρ per year for ever.

However, the most general case is where the government is subject to some constraints – it cannot ensure that all projects which ought to be undertaken are, but equally it does have power to alter the overall rate of investment in the economy. Suppose, for example, that it finances the bridge by taxes, and each £1 spent reduces private saving and investment by £θ and consumption by £$(1-\theta)$. Then the cost per pound of bridge-building is $\theta p/r + (1-\theta)$ pounds.

The crucial issue, as usual, concerns which constraints are considered binding. For clarity let us briefly repeat the argument, using the basic Fisher diagram in Figure 7.

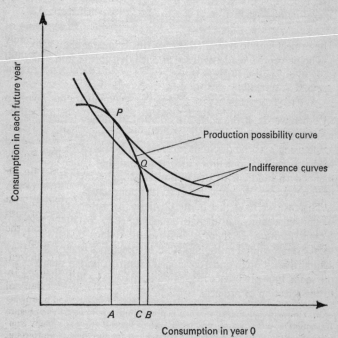

Figure 7

1. If the government can ensure that all projects which ought to be done are done, (i.e. AB is invested) the time preference rate is the (absolute) slope of the indifference curve at P and the opportunity cost of capital is £1 per pound spent.

2. If there is an absolute savings constraint CB, the time preference rate is the slope of the indifference curve at Q; the opportunity cost of capital is the slope of the production possibility curve at Q divided by the time preference rate.

3. If the private sector will undertake no projects less profitable than the marginal project at Q but the public sector can undertake some projects falling within AC, then the time preference rate is the slope of the indifference curve at the final point chosen in consumption space (call it r) and the opportunity cost of capital is $\theta\rho/r+(1-\theta)$, where ρ is the final marginal rate of return on private investment and θ is the rate of displacement.[31]

An even more constrained position is where the volume of private and of public investment are seen as being separately constrained. In this case, the relevant opportunity cost of capital for public sector projects is ρ'/r where ρ' is the marginal rate of return in the public sector.

We have assumed so far that the government cannot invest in private sector projects. If it can, the opportunity cost of capital is always ρ/r. The government can always achieve point P, but the public share in investment will be large. An alternative would be increased investment grants or a cut in those taxes (mainly Corporation and Income Taxes) which discourage private investment. This broad approach is preferred by Musgrave (1969, reading 2). Monetary policy could also be used to reduce interest rates. But the final cost-benefit decision must be consistent with whatever other arrangements are finally decided on, and the calculation of opportunity cost should proceed as indicated.

This approach outlined above has been frequently criticized. Pioneered by Krutilla and Eckstein (1958), and formalized by Marglin (1963b, reading 11), it was sharply attacked by Baumol

31. In an open economy there are possibilities of lending and borrowing abroad which need to be added to the production possibility curve of Figure 7, before we can claim to have society's true consumption possibility frontier. Thus, in principle, we might need to allow for the effect of a project in displacing foreign lending. Equally, if the country is a net borrower, the cost of capital is the present value of the debt service at the margin.

(1968) in a celebrated article which begins by arguing in favour of using the social opportunity cost rate (ρ) as the social discount rate. However, as Arrow (1969, p. 58) points out, he seems here to be dealing with the case of an absolute savings constraint, where, as we have shown, it may in practice be all right to discount by ρ. When, later, he allows for a variable savings rate, he agrees that we have a second-best problem and, given this, the Marglin approach seems correct (Diamond, 1968; James, 1969; Usher, 1969). Mishan (1967) has also argued in favour of using the social opportunity cost rate, provided the government has the power to invest in the private sector. This again seems consistent with the approach outlined above.

There remain three problems. First there is the question of the 'synthetic discount rate'. We saw before that where the cost of capital is ρ/r the correct decisions could sometimes be obtained by valuing all costs and benefits at their nominal value and discounting by ρ. Similarly, if the cost of capital were $\theta\rho/r+(1-\theta)$ we could use a synthetic discount rate $\theta\rho+(1-\theta)r$. This is the approach used by some economists (Diamond, 1968; Usher, 1969) and practised by many governments. However, there are many cases where the approach breaks down, and Feldstein (1973, reading 13) makes out a cogent case against it.

The second problem is of course the assessment of the actual displacement effects of expenditures financed by taxing and borrowing. Harberger (1969, reading 12) outlines a fruitful approach to the problem in the case of borrowing, even though it is couched in terms of the search for a synthetic discount rate. Feldstein (1972, reading 13) argues that it is by no means self-evident that the cost of £1 financed by taxes is less than that of £1 financed by borrowing, once one has allowed for the possible reinvestment of tax-financed interest on the part of those from whom the government borrows.

The third problem is that of reinvestment of the benefits of a project. If savings are suboptimal, reinvested benefits of nominal value £1 are worth more than benefits which are consumed. In underdeveloped countries one of the arguments put forward for public sector rather than private sector production has been that the rate of reinvestment out of profits may be higher. Marglin (1963b, reading 11) shows how the rate of reinvestment can be allowed for by adjusting the cost of capital, but the same result could equally well be achieved by adjusting the benefit stream. Marglin has been criticized by Arrow (1966) for treating the rate of reinvestment as exogenous, rather than as something optimized over time simultaneously with current investment. One should also, in a full treatment, allow for the possibility that ρ and r would change over time and optimally tend to converge (Little and Mirrlees, 1968).

We can now apply the notions we have been developing to our original simple problem of the bridge (p. 13). Suppose the risk-free rate on government bonds is 12 per cent, the rate of inflation in recent years 4 per cent and the marginal tax rate 0·33. Then we might put the rate of time preference at 4 per cent [12(0·66)−4]. (This assumes a fairly perfect market for borrowing and lending.) But the pre-tax nominal rate of return on private investment is, say, 14 per cent, or 10 per cent in real terms. If the bridge is financed by taxation, each £1 spent may reduce private investment by approximately the marginal propensity to save (or rather more) − by say £0·2. Thus the opportunity cost of the bridge is £30,000 times (0·2. 0·10/0·04+0·8) = £39,000. The present value of the perpetual stream of future benefits, assuming none are reinvested, now becomes £2,750/0·04 = £68,750. So the project should be done.

The cost of capital under structural unemployment

Before leaving the question of opportunity cost we must look briefly at a special case which is important in economies suffering from structural unemployment. When we consider the cost of doing something we are normally interested in the value of the activities we shall have to give up, if the general level of economic activity is to be held constant. This corresponds to the procedure, advocated by Musgrave (1959) of making the 'allocation branch' assume that the 'stabilization branch' is doing its job properly. In this case, if resources costing £1 are used in this project, there must be a corresponding reduction of £1's worth in the output of other investment or consumption goods (valued at market prices).[32]

32. As Baumol (1968, p. 792) points out, this need not imply that for a tax-financed project the extra taxes should equal the expenditure on the

But, especially in underdeveloped countries, there may often be resources which are unemployed, even though there are no reasons from a stabilization policy point of view why they need be. In such cases of non-'demand-deficient' unemployment, the spending of £1 which displaces £θ of private investment may displace less than £$(1-\theta)$ of consumption. It may even increase consumption by, say, £φ. In this case we subtract £φ from the cost because it is a positive gain to have this consumption being undertaken. The cost per pound is now £$\theta\rho/r-\varphi$, which may or may not exceed £1.

The most obvious relevance of this is to the shadow wage of previously underemployed rural labourers now employed in urban industry. Suppose their marginal product in agriculture was zero. If no output of investment or consumer goods elsewhere in the economy were displaced by employing them, the cost of employing them would be zero. But the very act of employing them will probably raise their consumption, because they now receive a positive wage. This extra consumption could, of course, be provided by cutting down the consumption of other workers by the same amount (by stiffer taxes, for example); and if this were done the cost of employing them remains zero – there is no change elsewhere in the output of investment or consumption goods. But more likely there will be some increase in the output of consumption at the expense of investment. Suppose in fact that the gain in consumption equalled the full wage (W) and that the project itself produced none of these extra consumption goods. Then each £1 spent in wages would reduce investment by the same amount and the shadow wage would be $W(\rho/r-1)$ (Marglin, 1967, pp. 56–7). This is clearly a special case and a general presentation of the problem can be found in Sen (1972, reading 4).[33]

_____

project. This depends on the propensities to consume of all the parties affected. If the MPC is uniform for all, more taxes need to be raised than expenditure incurred if employment is to be held constant.

33. The reader should note that in Sen's procedure the shadow wage of labour is that cost which in equilibrium should be equated to the *nominal* value of the marginal product of labour. In appraising a project, however, one would normally use a cost for labour which should at the margin be equated to the *social* value of the marginal product of labour. This would mean, for example, rewriting his expression 3.1 for the cost of labour as $w\lambda(s^3-s^2)$ and equating this in equilibrium to $(1+\lambda s^3)q$. In the example

But the basic point is that, when unemployed resources exist in the presence of sub-optimal saving, we have the dual problem that, while the resources can be employed with little loss of output elsewhere, the act of employing them is likely to raise the demand for consumption. Thus, a project may displace other investment, not only through its method of finance, but through the payments which it makes to the hitherto unemployed factors it employs.

Present value versus internal rate of return rules

So far we have assumed that the most convenient way to maximize the present value of consumption is to choose all projects having positive present values or, where there are two or more mutually exclusive projects, to choose the one with the highest present value. However, there is an alternative approach which has often been advocated and even more often used: the rate of return approach. The rate of return is that rate (ρ) which sets the present value of the project at 0. Thus we solve for ρ in

$$0 = B_0 - C_0 + \frac{B_1 - C_1}{1 + \rho} + \ldots + \frac{B_n - C_n}{(1 + \rho)^n}.$$

The rule then is: undertake the project if ρ exceeds the discount rate r.

In very many cases the two approaches give the same answer, and often the rate of return is an interesting and suggestive statistic. However, there are three main arguments against using the rate of return rule for specific decisions. First, it is not the intrinsically correct rule: it is merely a procedure which often gives the same answer.[34] In cases where the discount rate changes from period to period (e.g. falls over time) there is no one value of r with which ρ can be compared, while the present value rule re-

given in the text the former equals $W(\rho/r-1)(1-0)$ and the latter equals $[1+(\rho/r-1)1]q$.

34. Hirshleifer (1958) shows why the present value rule is intrinsically correct for the private investor or for a society which can borrow or lend abroad. In the case of a closed economy the social optimum occurs at a direct tangency between the indifference surface and the production possibility surface. Hirshleifer also sets out the main problems with the IRR approach. For a simplified exposition of some of these points see Baumol (1965, pp. 422–7 and 437–47).

mains well defined. Ignoring this, a second problem arises in the case of mutually exclusive projects, where the internal rate of return may provide the wrong ranking. For example, the table below compares two projects of different size, A and B, in which this is the case. It also compares two projects of different length, A and C, where again the rate of return gives the wrong ranking.

Table 2

Stream		IRR	PV at $r = 0.05$
A	−100, 110	0·10	5
B	− 10, 12	0·20	1·5
C	−100, 6, 6, (for ever)	0·06	20

As Feldstein and Flemming (1964) point out, this problem can, in principle, be overcome by calculating not the separate internal rates of return for each project but the rate of return on the difference between each project being considered (say A) and each of its alternatives. For example, taking A and B above, this is the rate of return on −90, 98 which at nearly 9 per cent is well above the discount rate of 5 per cent. However, the more projects there are the more pairs of projects have to be considered.

Moreover, there remains a third objection. The rate of return calculations may not give a unique answer and in fact may give as many solutions which could have economic meaning as there are sign changes in the stream of net returns. For example, if we take the stream −1, 5, −6 and plot its present value this becomes zero at both 100 per cent and 200 per cent (see Figure 8). At any discount rate on either side its present value is, not surprisingly, negative. Each calculated rate of return tells us that at that discount rate the present value is moving from negative to positive or vice versa, and nothing more. However, if a project can be terminated at will at any point in time, it will have a unique internal rate of return, assuming that for each possible discount rate we choose the optimal life of project (Arrow and Levhari, 1969). But it is not clear how often projects can be usefully regarded as terminable in this way. In real life there may of course be few projects for which the net returns stream changes sign more than once, except in extractive industries where there may be heavy terminal costs (of filling in mines and so on). But the differences in net returns between projects may change signs frequently, and thus for mutually exclusive projects the internal rate of return rule may frequently break down.

Finally, there is the problem of capital rationing, where the correct approach is to select projects in order of their present value per unit of constrained cost until the cost constraint is exhausted.[35] Selection in order of rate of return provides a less general approach.

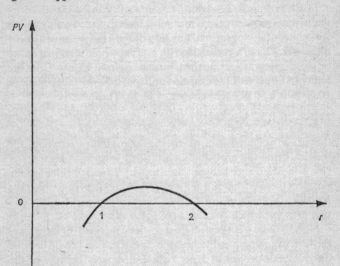

Figure 8

4 The treatment of risk

We have so far studiously avoided the problem of risk. But suppose that we really do not know how much the bridge will cost. It could cost £25,000, but equally well £35,000. How do we

35. At the level of the economy this is the problem of the savings constraint. Here the problem can be handled in the simplified case by costing capital at ρ/r (where ρ is the rate of return on the marginal project within the constraint) and then doing all projects with positive present values. The rule given above in the text is a general rule which should be used also by separate agencies subject to budget constraints.

proceed? If the project were being undertaken by a private firm, which bore all costs and reaped all benefits, and whose discount rate for certainly-known income streams was 5 per cent, it would be likely to cost the bridge at its 'expected' (average) cost of £30,000 and then use a higher discount rate than 5 per cent. The reason is simply that the owners of the firm are averse to risk, and to anyone who is risk-averse a certain prospect of receiving £b is worth more than a 50–50 chance of £0.5b and £1.5b.

Much of human behaviour towards risk can be explained by the hypothesis that people maximize their expected utility, using a cardinal utility-of-income function of the kind we have already discussed. Thus if a person is a risk averter, whose marginal utility of income falls as income rises, we can see from Figure 9 that the utility of £b exceeds the expected utility of a 50 per cent chance of £0.5b plus a 50 per cent chance of £1.5b. The latter is

$$E(U) = 0{\cdot}5U(0{\cdot}5b)+0{\cdot}5U(1{\cdot}5b),$$

that is, a weighted sum of the possible utilities resulting, the weights being the probabilities attaching to each.[36] The cost of risk is the difference between the mean or 'expected value' of the prospect (here $0{\cdot}5 \times 0{\cdot}5b+0{\cdot}5 \times 1{\cdot}5b = b$) and the value which the individual actually places on the uncertain prospect (i.e. the certain prospect which he rates as of equal value, here c).

Now, if there were perfect (and costless) markets for insurance, the firm would not need to bear the cost of risk and could happily discount this project at 5 per cent. But, largely because of the problem of 'moral hazard', such markets generally exist in only a limited form. The securities market makes possible a good deal of pooling of risk among ultimate wealth-owners (Pauly, 1970), but even so private firms generally use discount rates much higher than the rate applying to certainly-known costs and returns, the excess depending largely on the degree of risk of the project.[37]

Should the public sector follow suit? It has been argued that,

36. More generally $E(U) = \Sigma\, p_i\, U(Y_i)$, where p_i is the probability of obtaining income Y_i. Thus in the example we should, strictly, be concerned with the utilities of $y+0{\cdot}5b$ and $y+1{\cdot}5b$, where y is normal income. For a full analysis see Friedman and Savage (1948).

37. This is partly because a manager cannot, like the stockholder, insure against the personal risk associated with a project which he initiates.

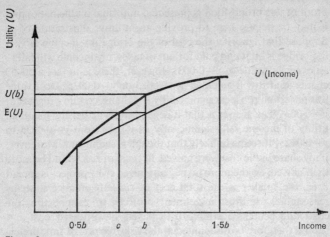

Figure 9

unless it does, it will be led to undertake projects identical in their net returns to those which the private sector would have rejected, and this is sub-optimal. However, Arrow and Lind (1970, reading 14) argue otherwise.

They start with our standard assumption that net returns should be valued as they would be valued by the people to whom they accrue. Thus a risky project undertaken by one man *ought* to be valued at less than its expected value. If insurance is impossible it is absolutely right for a one-man firm with a certainty discount rate of 5 per cent not to undertake a project with only a 5 per cent rate of return, and he ought not to be subsidized to encourage him to do so – the subsidy cannot reduce the social cost of risk.

However, the public sector (or indeed General Motors) is a very large firm with very many shareholders. Our difference between £35,000 and £25,000 when averaged over, say, ten million tax-payers amounts to no more than £1/1000. The question is: is a spread of possible project costs of this order sufficient to make us value the cost of the project to each taxpayer at something higher than its expected value of £3/1000 (assuming each taxpayer pays the same)? Arrow and Lind prove that as the number of taxpayers tends to infinity the cost of the risk tends to zero. The verbal part of their article should be comprehensible to any reader, but the proof of this proposition is presented in formal mathematics and it may be helpful here to provide an intuitive illustration of it. Suppose that ignoring the cost of the bridge my income is y. If the bridge is built and paid for out of taxes, my income will fall to an expected value of $y - 0·003$. However, there is in fact a 50–50 chance that it will be either $y - 0·0025$ or $y - 0·0035$. Do I value this uncertain prospect significantly less than a certain prospect of $y - 0·003$? The answer is that it depends on whether my marginal utility of income falls significantly as y rises from $y - 0·0035$ to $y - 0·0025$. It seems unlikely that the fall is significant. Moreover, if my share in the cost were halved, my cost of risk would be more than halved. So the more taxpayers a given risky project is spread over, the smaller is the total cost of risk. In practice it seems reasonable, for most investment projects, to assume that the costs and benefits accruing to taxpayers have no risk cost and should therefore be discounted at the risk-free rate of time preference.[38]

However, not all the benefits or costs of public projects do accrue to taxpayers as a whole. In the case of our bridge, the cost accrues to the taxpayers but the benefits accrue to the travellers. Whether or not the benefits are sufficiently large and uncertain for any one traveller, for them to be valued at less than their expected value is an empirical question.

For some projects it is unquestionably the case that the projects impose substantial risk cost. Suppose that the bridge was designed to be safe in all normal weathers but would collapse under the influence of a tidal wave of a kind that has happened once in the last 100 years. If one assumed that the probability of disaster in each future year was 1 per cent and one knew the consequences of disaster, one could in principle make an evaluation along the lines we have been discussing – if some utility-of-income function were assumed.

However, sometimes the probabilities attaching to the outcomes of a project may not even be guessable. This provides a case of what Knight called uncertainty and here the only approach is to fall back on game theory. The various possible strategies are discussed in Dorfman (1962, reading 15). No one of them can be said

38. This assumes that the returns to each separate project are independent of national income – that is, that stabilization policy is successful.

to be correct, but they do at any rate provide a way of marshalling one's thoughts.

5 The treatment of income distribution

Finally, we revert to the problem of the distribution of income. Suppose that travellers over the bridge are on average twice as rich as taxpayers but half as rich as ferryowners. Clearly the project will redistribute income. Should this be taken into account in deciding whether to build the bridge? And if so, how?

As we have said, a decision-maker should choose from his available set of actions those which maximize social welfare, subject to all the constraints over which he has no control. Suppose that in his ethical judgement social welfare W depends on the present value Y of the income of each of the n members of society according to the function $W = f(Y_1, ..., Y_n)$. Then a policy which changes the present values by $\Delta Y_1, ..., \Delta Y_n$ should be done, provided

$$\Delta W \simeq \frac{\partial W}{\partial Y_1} \Delta Y_1 + ... + \frac{\partial W}{\partial Y_n} \Delta Y_n \geqslant 0.$$

Only by chance will the weights $\partial W / \partial Y_i$ be equal for different individuals; for any reasonable welfare function they will be higher for the poor than the rich.

But, if the weights could differ in principle, should they be treated as differing in practice? In considering *distributional* policy one must clearly allow for the fact that the weights would differ by an increasing amount as inequality grew. But many economists have argued that, when considering policies for *public production* (like the bridge), distributional considerations should be ignored. Instead the approach should be sequential: first maximize total output (ΣY_i) and then hand it out fairly. In other words, first achieve an 'efficient' allocation of resources and then arrange for an 'equitable' distribution. On this scheme, projects are to be judged by the Hicks-Kaldor criterion and undertaken if and only if the gainers could compensate the losers (i.e. $\Sigma \Delta Y_i > 0$).

But is it possible to adopt this approach? Can the size of the cake be maximized independently of who gets what? The answer would be yes, if transfers between people could be made without affecting their incentives to produce output. But unfortunately all practicable forms of transfer have some incentive effects: an obvious example is the 'excess burden' of the income tax. So the sequential solution is theoretically unsound.

Does this matter in practice? It depends crucially on the number of constraints facing the decision-maker (Sen, 1972, reading 4). Consider first an all-powerful central government, able to enforce the optimal tax-transfer system. In this case, the marginal social value of income $\partial W/\partial Y_i$ will still be somewhat higher for the poor than for the rich, because of the 'excess burden' (fall in total income) involved in effecting a transfer. And since the typical public project, like a bridge, confers its benefits in lump-sum form (even though an excess burden is involved in financing it) inefficient projects (that lower total income) may be socially desirable if they benefit the poor. However, as Musgrave argues forcefully (1969, reading 2), the only projects that get by on this ground are likely to be ones that come quite near to passing the Hicks-Kaldor test.

More serious problems arise if the central government is not all-powerful. There may be political limits to cash redistribution, in which case the marginal social value of income for the poor may greatly exceed that for the rich.[39] Equally seriously, there may be decision-makers outside the central government, for example in local government or specialized agencies, who disagree with the central government's values but have no power to alter the general system of taxes and transfers. Such people are entitled to use their own sets of weights and to pursue inefficient projects (like free transport for old people), which they would not consider if they had control over the distribution of money incomes.

If distributional weights are to be used, how should they be determined? The traditional Benthamite approach argues

39. There are also, as already mentioned, constraints on compensating individual losers. These would raise problems even if general cash redistribution via taxes and transfers were possible. This is because a person's happiness depends not only on income but also on the income he expected. A non-marginal fall in income may cause a greater loss of happiness than an equal rise in income, even if the person whose income falls is richer than the person whose income rises. Governments and electorates are quite rightly sensitive to this point, unlike many economists. Elsewhere we too ignore this point.

that social welfare equals the sum of individual utilities. So $W = \Sigma U(Y_i)$ and $\partial W/\partial Y_i = U'(Y_i)$.

If we use the same utility-of-income function as on pp. 40–41,

$$\partial W/\partial Y_i = Y_i^{-\varepsilon}$$

So the weights attaching to changes in present values are a steadily declining function of individual wealth. However, the traditional utilitarian approach is morally unattractive, since it implies that a given gain in happiness has the same social value whether the person is very miserable or very happy. If we believe that the social value of additional happiness falls the happier someone is, we might assume that $\partial W/\partial Y_i = Y_i^{-\delta}$, where δ is larger than ε, so that the weights decline even faster as incomes rise. If we now assume some value of δ we can recompute the present value of our bridge project. For example, if (for convenience of computation) $\delta = 1$, then the present values to taxpayers, travellers and ferryowners are weighted in the ratios $4:2:1$, and the total present value of the project (in units of ferryowners' present value) becomes $4(-39,000) + 2(75,000) + 1(-6,250)$.[40] It is not quite worth doing.

The problem is of course to determine δ. Eckstein (1961) adopted the Benthamite framework so that $\delta = \varepsilon$, and then argued that the government's estimate of ε should be implicit in the structure of marginal income tax rates. However, as Freeman (1967) has pointed out, if the government sought to maximize the sum of individual utilities, and had a given national income to distribute, it would need to equalize the marginal utility of income of all individuals, i.e. it would aim at complete income equality, by setting taxes equal to $Y_i - \overline{Y}$, where Y_i is individual income and $\overline{Y}$ is average income.[41]

40. The present values to each party are those computed on p. 49.

41. (i) Put another way, the government equalizes the marginal sacrifice (of utility) per dollar of tax. By contrast, the Eckstein approach implies that governments equalize the marginal sacrifice (due to tax) per dollar of *income*; if so, a man with a marginal tax rate of 0·25 could then be assumed to have a marginal utility of income double that of a man with a marginal tax rate of 0·50. However, there is no reason to think that governments do or should pursue this principle – nor the principles of equiproportional sacrifice or equal absolute sacrifice used by Mera (1969) to derive implicit utility-of-income functions.

(ii) P.T.O.

Weisbrod (1968, reading 16) has therefore suggested that the government's weights for different income groups should be inferred from its previous decisions on whether or not to adopt the various projects open to it. This involves the solution of a set of simultaneous equations. There is an obvious logical objection to this approach: either the government's decisions so far have been consistent, in which case why worry about helping it continue to be consistent, or they have been inconsistent, in which case why pretend they were consistent. There is much force in this criticism, especially when it is linked to the difficulties of estimation that arise. However, Weisbrod's article is important in stressing that from now on government decisions should embody some consistent set of distributional weights.

A third, and more limited, approach has been suggested by Marglin (1967). In this, total consumption is maximized subject to some minimum consumption being secured to a given underprivileged group or region. Alternatively, the consumption of the underprivileged may be maximized subject to some minimum total consumption. Any constrained maximization of this kind implies in its solution a relative weight attaching to consumption of the underprivileged as against consumption in general, but this value is determined *ex post*. It is a less general approach to the income distribution problem, but, if no other is available, it is one way of allowing for an important dimension of public policy.[42] The only alternative is that pursued by the Roskill Commission on the Third London Airport (1970), which is to show separately the costs and benefits of different groups in society and let the policy-makers decide their own weights.[43]

(ii) If the government maximizes the sum of individual utilities but tax rates affect production, it should equalize the marginal rates of transformation between pairs of individual incomes to the ratios of marginal utilities of income (Freeman, 1967).

42. For a strong plea to exclude income distribution from formal economic welfare analysis see Harberger (1971).

43. Roskill Commission on the Third London Airport (1970, ch. 29). Separate calculations are not shown in the final report. The Roskill Commission treated foreigners on the same footing as British nationals, whereas some cost-benefit analyses assign them a distributional weight of zero (often without even discussing the issue).

6 The case of the third London airport

The proof of the pudding is in the eating. Perhaps the most ambitious cost-benefit analysis ever undertaken was the Report of the Roskill Commission (1971). The Commission were asked to recommend where a third London airport should be sited, and when it should be built. The second question required them to compare the costs and benefits of extra air travel, but their main calculations related to the first question and consisted essentially of a comparison of costs.[44] But this did not make the task much easier.

The Commission took the view from the start that all costs should, if possible, be computed in monetary units. In other words they rejected the notion that any one of the myriad consequences of choosing a particular site should be regarded as overriding. Instead they decided to laboriously evaluate each consequence and use the total computed cost as a major element in their decision.

As a first step their Research Team provided a draft cost-benefit analysis (volume 7 of the Roskill Commission's papers) which was then subjected to detailed criticism and discussion in the public hearings, as well as to academic comment (Mishan, 1970, reading 18). The procedure was probably more open than any other public inquiry ever held. Finally a revised cost-benefit analysis was presented in the final report. This suggested that Cublington had the smallest present value of net costs of the four short-listed sites; the costs at Foulness were between £156 million and £197 million larger (measured in 1982's pounds).[45]

However, the Commission did not let the sums take the decision for them. They also discussed in detail the 'planning' arguments that spring from the wider external effects of any major decision about land use; but they concluded that the balance of these arguments was unclear one way or the other, and they therefore accepted the ranking given by the cost-benefit analysis. One member of the Commission, Professor Buchanan, dissented in favour

---

44. The benefit side came in in one way: the Foulness site was expected to attract less traffic due to its higher cost. The value of the consumer surplus lost on this traffic was estimated in the usual way as $\frac{1}{2}\Delta p \Delta q$.

45. For map showing the location of the various sites see p. 430.

of Foulness (Buchanan, 1971). The government finally decided against Cublington. The main criticisms of the Report by Buchanan and others that are worth discussing here are as follows.

Cost-benefit analysis is dubious because it adds up a host of items, some of them 'direct costs, which will actually be paid out (e.g. construction costs)' and some of them 'notional costs which will never be paid out (e.g. noise costs)'. This is a most strange objection from those who wish to preserve the quality of life. It reflects the strange awe in which money is held by non-economists: the money costs of constructing an airport are in fact only a tenuous approximation of the value of the production or leisure which the community could have had if the airport were not built. The proper criticism of the Report, if any, is that it included too little rather than too much in its costs and benefits.

'Planning' provides a more useful approach to problems of land use than does cost-benefit analysis. Some extremists indeed hold that cost-benefit analysis is mere 'nonsense on stilts' (Self, 1970) and should be replaced altogether by planning.[46] But this seems to ignore the whole problem of choice. Planning can provide a set of internally consistent scenarios of the future, but we still have to choose that scenario which yields the maximum net benefit. The planners can of course if they like substitute their judgement for any attempt at objective assessment, but it is surely better to aim at developing the latter. The problem with cost-benefit analysis is that the items which can be readily quantified often exclude the wider, and perhaps most quantitatively important, consequences of decisions. On this planners have a great deal to contribute, but their contribution must be set explicitly within a framework of net benefit maximization. On this point Buchanan is unclear. However, in his view the main planning considerations which the Commission failed adequately to allow for were the external effects of a Foulness Airport on employment in its area and the needs of the Midlands for an international airport of their own.

The quiet countryside north-west of London has a value above its value to present local residents. This is the conservationists' case:

46. For a more balanced view see Hall (1971) and Williams (1972).

quiet countryside is an asset which it is virtually impossible to re-create once it has been destroyed. There was therefore a case for putting a high value on the recreational value and housing potential of the area, but the same would presumably apply to the Midlands countryside and to the countryside near Foulness lying north of the Crouch, which is the only land affected by any of the sites that is designated as of Grade A natural beauty. In fact little value was put on such things in the Commission's calculations, though they discussed the issue. Their calculations can of course be interpreted as providing a figure which these differential costs would need to exceed at Cublington if Foulness were to be preferred. Could such costs really be £150 million in terms of present value? It seems unlikely if the relative value of the countryside were to remain at its present level. But, as wealth accumulates, it is possible that this relative value will rise, depending on peoples' taste for country living and country walking as against other things. The Commission would retort to this that at a 10 per cent discount rate the valuations of twenty-first century man are virtually irrelevant. But this leads to a fourth criticism, not often made.

The discount rate of 10 per cent is too high. As we have seen the correct procedure in project evaluation is to discount by the time-preference rate after evaluating costs in terms of their social opportunity costs. The British government by contrast prescribe the use of a standard synthetic discount rate of 10 per cent for all public sector projects – this rate reflecting very heavily the rate of return on displaced private investment. But when one examines the costs of the different Roskill sites the dominant one is travellers' time, and one suspects that this displaces less private investment per £1 of cost than investment in the nationalized industries. If the time preference rate were anything like 10 per cent this would not be worth quibbling about, but, if it is, this means that £1 of consumption in AD 2000 is counted by us now as worth only 6p. Do we really care so little for the future? The conservationists' case depends on the view that the distant future matters more than is suggested by a 10 per cent discount rate. If they were right in believing that the growth rate of income will fall, they would have an additional argument.

Roskill did not envisage a sufficiently active government direction of air traffic. This is a good example of the importance in cost-benefit analysis of which constraints are considered binding. The Roskill Commission assumed that if Foulness was developed, Luton would have to be allowed to develop; this added to the noise and other costs charged to Foulness. But the government, when it decided in favour of Foulness, said it intended to adopt an active carrot-and-stick policy to get the traffic there. If economic theory were heeded, airport charges should be much higher at Heathrow than at Foulness to reflect the differing externalities at the two sites.

Roskill did not use the Pareto criterion. The Commission merely claimed that the gainers could compensate the losers. But the losers fought the Commission and won. There is no reason in principle why losers from airport construction should not be compensated on some crude basis, and cost-benefit analyses are more likely to be accepted in future if they pay more attention to this issue.

The reader must decide on the weight of these various arguments, as against the cogent reasoning of the Commission. If he finds it difficult to reach a decision, this does not mean that the Commission's work was a waste of time. For any reasonable man must admit that their calculations have enormously reduced the area of admissible disagreement on the issues.

No one example can bring out all the pros and cons of a method. There are some problems where cost-benefit analysis can be more helpful than on airport location; these include the selection of industrial projects, fuel policy, and some problems of water management and transport planning. There are other problems which are even less tractable, such as health, or literacy projects. But it is hard to think of any field of public policy where the problem cannot be illuminated, even by some elementary back-of-envelope calculation of critical costs and benefits. And, to revert to our beginning, the notion that all actions have costs and benefits could still do more, if widely accepted, to promote wise behaviour than most of our intellectual formularies.

Note to page 42

If welfare depends on consumption per head, we can write

$$W = \frac{1}{1-\varepsilon}\left[\frac{C_0}{N_0}\right]^{1-\varepsilon} + \frac{1}{1-\varepsilon}\left[\frac{C_1}{N_1}\right]^{1-\varepsilon}$$

$$\frac{\partial W/\partial C_0}{\partial W/\partial C_1} = \frac{(C_0/N_0)^{-\varepsilon}(1/N_0)}{(C_1/N_1)^{-\varepsilon}(1/N_1)}$$

$$\simeq (1+g-n)^\varepsilon(1+n)$$

$$\simeq 1+(g-n)\varepsilon+n.$$

Even if consumption per head is going to be roughly constant, additional consumption will be less useful in period 1 than in period 0 because it is spread over more people. (In this respect Eckstein's approach (1957, p. 75) seems inappropriate. The expression given above is taken from Sen (1968, p. 16, footnote 16) where, however, C should refer to total rather than per capita consumption.)

If welfare depends on population times the utility of consumption per head, we can write

$$W = \frac{N_0}{1-\varepsilon}\left[\frac{C_0}{N_0}\right]^{1-\varepsilon} + \frac{N_1}{1-\varepsilon}\left[\frac{C_1}{N_1}\right]^{1-\varepsilon},$$

$$\frac{\partial W/\partial C_0}{\partial W/\partial C_1} = \frac{(C_0/N_0)^{-\varepsilon}}{(C_1/N_1)^{-\varepsilon}}$$

$$\simeq (1+g-n)^\varepsilon$$

$$\simeq 1+(g-n)\varepsilon.$$

If consumption per head is going to be roughly constant, the effect on welfare per head of a unit gain in consumption per head is equal in the two periods. Additional consumption sufficient to produce a unit gain in consumption per head in period 0 will produce a $1-n$ gain in consumption per head in period 1 and therefore a gain in utility per head $1-n$ as large as the gain in period 0. But this gain is spread over a population $1+n$ as large. So if consumption per head is constant the discount rate is zero.

As to which assumption is reasonable see Meade (1955, ch. 6). The discussion in Feldstein (1964, reading 9) is more general and assumes simply that

$$W = f\left(\frac{C}{N}, N\right).$$

Note to page 45

The present value of a permanent income stream a per year for n years (and paid at the end of each year) is

$$V = a\left[\frac{1}{1+r} + \frac{1}{(1+r)^2} + \dots + \frac{1}{(1+r)^n}\right].$$

Thus

$$V \cdot \frac{1}{1+r} = a\left[\frac{1}{(1+r)^2} + \dots + \frac{1}{(1+r)^n} + \frac{1}{(1+r)^{n+1}}\right].$$

Subtracting the second equation from the first,

$$V\left[1 - \frac{1}{1+r}\right] = a\left[\frac{1}{1+r} - \frac{1}{(1+r)^{n+1}}\right].$$

As n tends to infinity, V tends to

$$V = \frac{a}{r}.$$

References

Arrow, K. J. (1966), 'Discounting and public investment criteria', in A. V. Kneese and S. C. Smith (eds.), *Water Research*, Johns Hopkins Press, pp. 13–32.

Arrow, K. J. (1969), 'The social discount rate', in G. G. Somers and W. D. Wood (eds.), *Cost-Benefit Analysis of Manpower Policies*, Proceedings of a North American Conference, Industrial Relations Centre, Queen's University, Kingston, Ontario, pp. 56–75.

Arrow, K. J., and Kurz, M. (1970), *Public Investment, the Rate of Return, and Optimal Fiscal Policy*, Baltimore.

ARROW, K. J., and LEVHARI, D. (1969), 'Uniqueness of the internal
rate of return with variable life of investment', *Econ. J.*, vol. 79,
pp. 560–66.
ARROW, K. J., and LIND, R. C. (1970), 'Uncertainty and the evaluation
of public investment decisions', *Amer. Econ. Review*, vol. 60, pp.
364–78.
BACHA, E., and TAYLOR, L. (1971), 'Foreign exchange shadow prices:
a critical review of current theories', *Quart. J. Econs.*, vol. 85 no. 2, pp.
197–224.
BATOR, F. M. (1957), 'The simple analytics of welfare maximisation',
Amer. Econ. Review, vol. 47, March, pp. 22–59.
BAUMOL, W. J. (1965), *Economic Theory and Operations Analysis*, 2nd
edn, Prentice-Hall.
BAUMOL, W. J. (1968), 'On the social rate of discount', *Amer. Econ.
Review*, vol. 58, pp. 788–802.
BEESLEY, M. E., and FOSTER, C. D. (1965), 'The Victoria line: social
benefit and finances', *The Journal of the Royal Statistical Society series
A (General)*, vol. 128, pp. 67–88.
BLAUG, M. (ed.) (1968), *Economics of Education 1*, Penguin.
BUCHANAN, C. (1971), 'Note of dissent', *Roskill Commission on the
Third London Airport, Report*, HMSO, pp. 149–60.
CARSBERG, B. V., and EDEY, H. C. (eds) (1969), *Modern Financial
Management*, Penguin.
CHASE, S. B. (ed.) (1968), *Problems in Public Expenditure Analysis*,
Brookings Institution.
CLAWSON, M. (1959), *Methods of Measuring the Demand for and Value
of Outdoor Recreation*, a paper presented at a meeting of the Taylor-
Hibbard Club, University of Wisconsin, 13 January, Resources for the
Future, Inc.
DASGUPTA, P. (1972), 'A comparative analysis of the UNIDO
Guidelines and the OECD Manual', *Bulletin of the Oxford University
Institute of Economics and Statistics*, vol. 34, pp. 33–52.
DIAMOND, P. (1968), 'The opportunity cost of public investment:
comment', *Quart. J. Econs.*, vol. 82, pp. 682–8.
DORFMAN, R. (1962), 'Basic economic and technologic concepts: a
general statement', in A. Maass *et al.*, *Design of Water Resource
Systems*, Macmillan.
ECKSTEIN, O. (1957), 'Investment criteria for economic development
and the theory of intertemporal welfare economics', *Quart. J. Econs.*,
vol. 71, pp. 56–85.
ECKSTEIN, O. (1961), 'A survey of the theory of public expenditure
criteria', in R. W. Houghton (ed.), *Public Finance*, Penguin.
FELDSTEIN, M. S. (1964), 'The social time preference discount rate in
cost benefit analysis', *Econ. J.*, vol. 74, pp. 360–79.
FELDSTEIN, M. S. (forthcoming), 'Financing in the evaluation of
public expenditures', in W. A. Smith (ed.) essays in honour of
Richard A. Musgrave.

FELDSTEIN, M. S., and FLEMMING, J. S. (1964), 'The problem of time stream evaluation: present value versus internal rate of return rules', *Bulletin of Oxford University Institute of Economics and Statistics*, vol. 26, pp. 79–85.

FELLNER, W. J. (1967), 'Operational utility: the theoretical background and a measurement', in W. J. Fellner *et al.*, *Ten Economic Studies in the Tradition of Irving Fisher*, Wiley.

FREEMAN, A. M. (1967), 'Income distribution and planning for public investment', *Amer. Econ. Review*, vol. 57, pp. 495–508.

FRIEDMAN, M., and SAVAGE, L. J. (1948), 'The utility analysis of choices involving risk', *J. polit. Econ.*, vol. 56, pp. 279–304, reprinted in Richard D. Irwin, G. J. Stigler and K. E. Boulding (eds), *Readings in Price Theory*, American Economic Association.

HALL, P. (1971), 'The Roskill argument: an analysis', *New Society*, January, pp. 145–8.

HARBERGER, A. C. (1969), 'Professor Arrow on the social discount rate', in G. G. Somers and W. D. Wood (eds), *Cost-Benefit Analysis of Manpower Policies, Proceedings of a North American Conference*, Industrial Relations Centre, Queen's University, Kingston, Ontario, pp. 76–88.

HARBERGER, A. C. (1971), 'Three basic postulates for applied welfare economics: an interpretative essay', *J. econ. Lit.*, vol. 9, pp. 785–97.

HARRISON, A. J., and QUARMBY, D. A. (1969), 'The value of time in transport planning: a review', in *Theoretical and Practical Research on an Estimation of Time Saving*, European Conference of Ministers of Transports, Economic Research Centre.

HENDERSON, P. D. (1965), 'Notes on public investment criteria in the United Kingdom', in R. Turvey (ed.), *Public Enterprise*, Penguin.

HIRSHLEIFER, J. (1958), 'On the theory of the optimal investment decision', *J. polit. Econ.*, vol. 66.

HOUGHTON, R. W. (ed.) (1970), *Public Finance*, Penguin.

JAMES, E. (1969), 'On the social rate of discount: comment', *Amer. Econ. Review*, vol. 59, pp. 912–16.

KRUTILLA, J. V., and ECKSTEIN, O. (1958), *Multiple Purpose River Development*, Studies in Applied Economic Analysis, Johns Hopkins Press.

LIND, R. C. (1964), 'The social rate of discount and the optimal rate of investment: further comment', *Quart. J. Econs.*, vol. 78, pp. 336–45.

LITTLE, I. M. D., and MIRRLEES, J. A. (1968), *Manual of Industrial Project Analysis in Developing Countries, vol. II, Social Cost Benefit Analysis*, Development Centre of the Organization for Economic Cooperation and Development.

LITTLE, I. M. D., and MIRRLEES, J. A. (1972), A reply to some criticisms of the OECD manual *Bulletin of the Oxford University Institute of Economics and Statistics*, vol. 34, pp. 153–68.

LITTLE, I. M. D., and MIRRLEES, J. A. (1974), *Project Appraisal and*

Planning for Developing Countries, Heinemann Educational Books. (A successor volume to Little and Mirrlees 1968.)

MAASS, A., *et al.* (1962), *Design of Water Resource Systems*, Macmillan.

MCKEAN, R. N. (1968), 'The use of shadow prices', in S. B. Chase (ed.), *Problems in Public Expenditure Analysis*, Brookings Institution, pp. 33–65.

MALINVAUD, E. (1969), 'Risk-taking and resource allocation', in J. Margolis and H. Guitton (eds), *Public Economics*, Macmillan.

MANSFIELD, N. W. (1971), 'The estimation of benefits from recreation sites and the provision of a new recreation facility', *Regional Studies*, vol. 5, no. 2, pp. 55–69.

MARGLIN, S. A. (1963a), 'The social rate of discount and the optimal rate of investment', *Quart. J. Econs*, vol. 77, pp. 95–111.

MARGLIN, S. A. (1963b), 'The opportunity costs of public investment', *Quart. J. Econs.*, vol. 77, pp. 274–89.

MARGLIN, S. A. (1967), *Public Investment Criteria*, Allen & Unwin.

MEADE, J. E. (1955), *Trade and Welfare*, Oxford University Press.

MERA, K. (1969), 'Experimental determination of relative marginal utilities', *Quart. J. Econs*, vol. 83, pp. 464–77.

METZLER, L. A. (1951), 'Wealth, savings, and the rate of interest', *J. polit. Econ.*, vol. 59, pp. 93–116.

MISHAN, E. J. (1967), 'Criteria for public investment: some simplifying suggestions', *J. polit. Econ.*, vol. 75, pp. 139–46.

MISHAN, E. J. (1970), 'What is wrong with Roskill?', *Journal of Transport Economics and Policy*, vol. 4, no. 4, pp. 221–34.

MISHAN, E. J. (1971a), *Cost-Benefit Analysis*, Unwin University Books.

MISHAN, E. J. (1971b), 'Evaluation of life and limb: a theoretical approach', *J. polit. Econ.*, vol. 79, pp. 687–705.

MUNBY, D. (ed.) (1968), *Transport*, Penguin.

MUNDELL, R. (1963), 'Inflation and real interest', *J. polit. Econ.*, vol. 71, pp. 280–83.

MUSGRAVE, R. A. (1959), *The Theory of Public Finance*, McGraw-Hill.

MUSGRAVE, R. A. (1969), 'Cost-benefit analysis and the theory of public finance', *J. econ. Lit.*, vol. 7, pp. 797–806.

PAULY, M. V. (1970), 'Risk and the social rate of discount', *Amer. econ. Review*, vol. 60, pp. 195–8.

PETERS, G. H. (1968), *Cost Benefit Analysis and Public Expenditure*, Eaton paper 8, 2nd edn, The Institute of Economic Affairs.

PHELPS, E. S. (1965), *Fiscal Neutrality Toward Economic Growth*, McGraw-Hill.

PIGOU, A. C. (1920), *The Economics of Welfare*, 4th edn, Macmillan.

PREST, A. R., and TURVEY, R. (1965), 'Cost-benefit analysis: a survey', *Econ. J.*, vol. 75, pp. 683–735.

RAMSEY, F. P. (1928), 'A mathematical theory of saving', *Econ. J.*, vol. 38, pp. 543–59.

ROSENBERG, N. (ed.) (1971), *The Economics of Technological Change*, Penguin.

(ROSKILL) COMMISSION ON THE THIRD LONDON AIRPORT (1970), *Papers and Proceedings*, vol. 7, HMSO.

(ROSKILL) COMMISSION ON THE THIRD LONDON AIRPORT (1971), *Report*, HMSO.

SELF, P. (1970), 'Nonsense on stilts: the futility of Roskill', *New Society*, July, pp. 8–11.

SEN, A. K. (1961), 'On optimizing the rate of saving', *Econ. J.*, vol. 71, pp. 479–96.

SEN, A. K. (1967), 'Isolation, assurance and the social rate of discount', *Quart. J. Econ.*, vol. 81, pp. 112–24.

SEN, A. K. (1968), *Choice of Techniques*, 3rd edn, Basil Blackwell.

SEN, A. K. (1970a), *Growth Economics*, Penguin.

SEN, A. K. (1970b), 'Interrelations between project, sectoral and aggregate planning', United Nations' *Economic Bulletin for Asia and the Far East*, vol. 21, pp. 66–75.

SEN, A. K. (1971), *Collective Choice and Social Welfare*, Oliver & Boyd.

SEN, A. K. (1972), 'Control areas and accounting prices: an approach to economic evaluation', *Econ. J.*, vol. 82, no. 325 S, pp. 486–501.

STEWART, F., and STREETEN, P. (1971), 'Little-Mirrlees Methods and Project Appraisal,' *Bulletin of the Oxford University Institute of Economics and Statistics*, vol. 34, pp. 75–92.

STIGLER, G. J. (1966), *The Theory of Price*, 3rd edn, Macmillan.

TURVEY, R. (ed.) (1968), *Public Enterprise*, Penguin.

UNIDO (United Nations Industrial Development Organisation) (1972), *Guidelines for Project Evaluation*, United Nations, Authors: P. Dasgupta, S. A. Marglin, and A. K. Sen.

USHER, D. (1969), 'On the social rate of discount: comment', *Amer. econ. Review*, vol. 59, pp. 925–9.

WALSH, H. G. and WILLIAMS, A. (1969), *Current Issues in Cost-Benefit Analysis*, CAS occasional paper no. 11, HMSO.

WEISBROD, B. A. (1961), 'The valuation of human capital', *J. polit. Econ.*, vol. 69, pp. 425–36.

WEISBROD, B. A. (1968), 'Income redistribution effects and benefit-cost analysis', in S. B. Chase (ed.), *Problems in Public Expenditure Analysis*, Brookings Institution, pp. 177–209.

WILLIAMS, A. (1972), 'Cost-benefit analysis, bastard science? and/or insidious poison in the body politick', *J. of Public Econs*, vol. 1, no. 2, July.

Part One
General Surveys

Prest and Turvey's is the classic survey article on cost-benefit analysis and deals with all the main issues that arise. In a more recent paper Musgrave concentrates on the social discount rate and the treatment of income distribution, as well as setting cost-benefit analysis in the wider context of the general theory of public finance.

1 A. R. Prest and R. Turvey

The Main Questions

Excerpt from A. R. Prest and R. Turvey, 'Cost-benefit analysis:
a survey', *Economic Journal*, vol. 75, 1965, pp. 685–705.

Preliminary considerations
Statement of the problem

Cost-benefit analysis is a way of setting out the factors which
need to be taken into account in making certain economic
choices. Most of the choices to which it has been applied involve
investment projects and decisions – whether or not a particular
project is worthwhile, which is the best of several alternative
projects, or when to undertake a particular project. We can,
however, apply the term 'project' more generally than this.
Cost-benefit analysis can also be applied to proposed changes in
laws or regulations, to new pricing schemes and the like. An
example is furnished by proposals for regulating the traffic on
urban roads. Such schemes involve making economic choices
along the same lines as investment schemes. As choice involves
maximization, we have to discuss what it is that decision-makers
want to maximize. The formulation which, as a description, best
covers most cost-benefit analyses examined in the literature we are
surveying is as follows: the aim is to maximize the present value
of all benefits less that of all costs, subject to specified constraints.

This formulation is very general, but it does at least enable us
to set out a series of questions, the answers to which constitute the
general principles of cost-benefit analysis:

1. Which costs and which benefits are to be included?

2. How are they to be valued?
3. At what interest rate are they to be discounted?
4. What are the relevant constraints?

Needless to say, there is bound to be a certain degree of arbitrariness in classifying questions under these four headings, but that cannot be helped.

A general issue

Before we can take these questions seriatim it is convenient to discuss an issue which involves more than one of these questions. It arises because the conditions for a welfare maximum are not likely to be fulfilled throughout the economy. If they were, and so resource allocation were optimal, the marginal social rate of time preference and the (risk-adjusted) marginal social rate of return from investment would coincide. A single rate of interest would then serve both to compare benefits and costs of different dates and to measure the opportunity cost of that private investment which is displaced by the need to provide resources for the projects in question. As things are, however, no single rate of interest will fulfil both functions simultaneously; in a non-optimal world there are two things to be measured and not one.

The problem has been discussed by a number of authors, including Eckstein (1958; 1961), Steiner (1959), Marglin (in Maass *et al.*, 1962) and Feldstein (1964a, b and c). They suggest that the costs and benefits of a project are the time streams of consumption foregone and provided by that project. The nature of this approach emerges clearly from Feldstein's remarks on the social opportunity cost of funds transferred from the private sector to the public sector:

Part of the money taken from the private sector decreases consumption immediately, while the rest decreases investment and therefore future consumption. A pound transferred from consumption in a particular year has, by definition, a social value in that year of £1. But a pound transferred from private investment is worth the discounted value of the future consumption that would have occurred if the investment had been made. The original investment generates an income stream to investors and workers. Some of this income is spent on consumption and the remainder is invested. Each of these subsequent investments generates a new income stream and thus consumption and further investment. The final result is an aggregate consumption time-stream generated by the original investment. It is the current value of this aggregate that is the social opportunity cost of a one pound decrease in private investment (Feldstein, 1964c).

The application of this approach to both costs and benefits produces a complicated expression for the present worth of a project's benefits less its costs. Nobody has as yet succeeded in quantifying such expressions, however,[1] so at present the approach can only serve as a reference-standard for judging simpler but more practicable ways of tackling the problem. Meanwhile, we note that the problem arises to the extent: (i) that a project's benefits are reinvested or create new investment opportunities, or (ii) that some of the funds used for the project would otherwise have been invested or that the project renders impossible some other and mutually exclusive investment project. If neither of these conditions is fulfilled; if, in other words, benefits and costs both consist exclusively of consumption (directly provided and, respectively, precluded by the project), then these complications do not arise, and the problem is reduced to one of choosing an appropriate social time preference rate of discount.

The main questions
Enumeration of costs and benefits

Definition of a project. In most cases the scope and nature of the projects which are to be submitted to cost-benefit analysis will be clear. For the sake of completeness, however, we must make the point that if one authority is responsible for producing A goods and B goods, then in judging between A goods investment projects of different sizes it must take into account the effect of producing more A goods on its output of B goods. There are all sorts of complications here: relationships between A and B goods may be on the supply or demand side, they may be direct (in the sense of A influencing B) or indirect (in the sense of A influencing C, which influences B) and so on. One illustration is the operations of an authority responsible for a long stretch of river; if it puts a dam at a point upstream this will affect the water level, and hence the operations of existing or potential dams downstream.

1. 'Estimating many of the variables and parameters needed to calculate net social benefit may indeed be difficult' (Feldstein, 1964a, p. 126).

Construction of a fast motorway, which in itself speeds up traffic and reduces accidents, may lead to more congestion or more accidents on feeder roads if they are left unimproved. All that this amounts to saying is that where there are strong relationships on either the supply or the demand side, allowances must be made for these in cost-benefit calculations. We shall return to this point later (see p. 97 *infra*), when discussing investment criteria.

Externalities. We now come to the wide class of costs and benefits which accrue to bodies other than the one sponsoring a project, and the equally wide issue of how far the sponsoring body should take them into account. We shall discuss the general principles at stake and then apply them to particular cases.

McKean (1958, ch. 8) discusses the distinction between technological and pecuniary *spillovers* at length. The essential points are that progenitors of public investment projects *should* take into account the external effects of their actions in so far as they alter the physical production possibilities of other producers or the satisfactions that consumers can get from given resources; they *should not* take side-effects into account if the sole effect is via prices of products or factors. One example of the first type is when the construction of a reservoir by the upstream authority of a river basin necessitates more dredging by the downstream authority. An example of the second type is when the improvement of a road leads to greater profitability of the garages and restaurants on that road, employment of more labour by them, higher rent payments to the relevant landlords, etc. In general, this will *not* be an additional benefit to be credited to the road investment, even if the extra profitability, etc., of the garages on one road is not offset by lower profitability of garages on the other, which are now less used as a result of the traffic diversion. Any net difference in profitability and any net rise in rents and land values is simply a reflection of the benefits of more journeys being undertaken, etc., than before, and it would be double counting if these were included too. In other words, we have to eliminate the purely transfer or distributional items from a cost-benefit evaluation: we are concerned with the value of the increment of output arising from a given investment and not with the increment in value of existing assets. In still other words, we measure costs and benefits on the assumption of a given set of prices, and the incidental and consequential price changes of goods and factors should be ignored.[2]

No one can pretend that this distinction is a simple one to maintain in practice; there may well be results from investment which are partially technological and partially pecuniary. Nor is the task of unravelling made easier by the fact that some of the transfers occasioned by investment projects may affect the distribution of income significantly, and hence the pattern of demand. But as a general guiding principle the distinction is most valuable.

We now consider the application of this principle. First of all, an investing agency must try to take account of obvious technological spillovers, such as the effects of flood control measures or storage dams on the productivity of land at other points in the vicinity. In some cases no explicit action may be needed, e.g. these effects may be internal to different branches of the same agency, or some system of compensation may be prescribed by law. But in others there should at least be an attempt to correct for the most obvious and important repercussions. Although in principle corrections are needed whatever the relationship between the interacting organizations, it must be expected that in practice the compulsion to take side-effects into account will be much greater if similar organizations are involved, e.g. one local authority is more likely to take account of the costs it imposes on other bodies if those mainly affected are one or two other local authorities than if they are a large multitude of individuals.

Secondary benefits. The notion that some pecuniary spillovers are properly included in benefits has appeared in a particular guise in arguments about secondary benefits. The American discussion of this matter has centred on the benefit estimation procedures used by the Bureau of Reclamation in respect of irrigation projects. In their analyses of the problem, McKean (1958), Eckstein (1958) and Margolis (1957) all start by describing these procedures. The essential principle can be made clear by taking the case of irrigation which results in an increase in grain production, where the

2. Apart from allowances necessary to get a measure of the change of surplus (see p. 80 *infra*).

direct or primary benefits are measured as the value of the increase in grain output less the associated increase in farmers' costs.

The increased grain output will involve increased activity by grain merchants, transport concerns, millers, bakers and so on, and hence, it is asserted, will involve an increase in their profits. If the ratio of total profits in all these activities to the value of grain at the farm is 48 per cent then secondary benefits of 48 per cent of the value of the increase in grain output are credited to the irrigation project. These are called 'stemming' secondary benefits. 'Induced' secondary benefits, on the other hand, are the extra profits made from activities which sell to farmers. The profit rate here has been computed as averaging 18 per cent of farmers' purchases.

All the three authors mentioned are highly critical of these notions, as they were set out by the Bureau of Reclamation in 1952. We shall not give a blow-by-blow account of the arguments of each author, but instead attempt to provide our own synthesis.

Where the output of a project has a market value this value plus any consumers' surplus can be taken as the measure of the gross benefit arising from the project. But where the output either is not sold or is sold at a price fixed solely with reference to cost-sharing considerations, it is necessary to impute a value to the output. Thus, in the case of irrigation water, a value is obtained by working out what the water is worth to farmers as the excess of the value of the increased output which it makes possible over the cost of the necessary increase in all the farmers' other inputs. The question now arises whether we should not impute a value to the increased farm output just as we have imputed one to the water instead of taking the market value of that output. Thus, supposing (to simplify the argument) that wheat is the only farm output, that all the wheat is used to make flour and that all the flour is used to make bread, why should we not value the water by taking the value of the increased output of bread and deducting the increase in farmers', millers' and bakers' costs? Consumption is, after all, the end of all economic activity, so is not what matters the value of the increase in consumption of bread made possible by the irrigation project less the sacrifice of alternative consumption involved – as measured by increased farming, milling and baking costs?

The answer must be that a properly functioning price mechanism performs the function of imputing values for us. It does so not only as regards the increase in farmers' costs (as the argument implicitly assumes) but also as regards the increase in their output (as it seems to deny). The market demand for wheat is a derived demand, and so reflects the value of extra bread and the marginal costs of milling, baking, etc. Imputation of values by the analyst is thus necessary only where there is no market for a product, i.e. only for the water itself.

We conclude, therefore, that if the conditions for optimal resource allocation are fulfilled in the rest of the economy the estimate of benefits obtained by using the price of wheat and the price of farming inputs constitutes an adequate measure. Putting the matter the other way round, we need worry about secondary benefits (or, for that matter, costs) only to the extent that market prices fail to reflect marginal social costs and benefits. The real problem concerning secondary benefits (and costs) is thus a matter of second-best allocation problems.

Project life. Estimation of length of life is clearly a highly subjective process depending on assessments of the physical length of life, technological changes, shifts in demand, emergence of competing products and so on. The effect of any error will depend on the rate of discount adopted; the higher this is, the less do errors of estimation matter. Some investigations seem to show that different assumptions about lengths of life do not affect the viability of schemes to an enormous extent (Foster and Beesley, 1963). We have here, incidentally, one example of the scope for sensitivity analysis, where the calculations are repeated many times for different values of variables. This is an extremely important tool when estimates of costs and benefits are uncertain.

Valuation of costs and benefits

The relevant prices. When we are dealing with costs and benefits which can be expressed in terms of money it is generally agreed that adjustments need to be made to the expected prices of future inputs and outputs to allow for anticipated changes in relative prices of the items involved (including expected changes in interest rates over time), but not for expected changes in the *general* price level. The essential principle is that all prices must be reckoned on the same basis, and for convenience this will usually be the price-level prevailing in the initial year.[3] Future developments in output levels have also to be taken into account, e.g. it is customary in cost-benefit studies of highway improvements to allow for the long-term trend of traffic growth.

Non-marginal changes. With the exceptions discussed below, market prices are used to value the costs and benefits of a project. Difficulties arise when investment projects are large enough to affect these prices. In the case of final products, the benefits accruing from investment cannot be measured by multiplying the additional quantum of output either by the old or the new price. The former would give an over-estimate and the latter an under-estimate. What is needed, as has long been recognized (Dupuit, 1952), is a measure of the addition to the area under the demand curve, which, on the assumption that the marginal utility of money remains unchanged, is an appropriate measure of the money value of the benefits provided, in the sense of assessing what the recipients would pay rather than go without them. When the demand curve is linear an unweighted average of before and after prices will suffice; but more complicated techniques are necessary for other forms of demand function – when they are known. In the case of intermediate products, the demand curve is a derived one, and so it can only be a perfect reflector of social benefit if the optimum welfare conditions are met all along the line. If this condition is satisfied the gross benefit arising from a project concerned with intermediate products is measured by the market value of sales plus any increase in consumers' and producers' surplus in respect of any final products based on the intermediate ones.

On the costs side there is a double problem, clearly distinguished in Lerner's treatment of indivisibilities (1944). First, it is necessary to adjust prices of factors so as to eliminate any rental elements, which will be measured by excesses over transfer earnings in their next best alternative use. Second, one has an exactly analogous

3. Hirshleifer *et al.* (1960, p. 143) argue that, since the 'true' interest rate lies below the 'monetary' one when prices are expected to rise, a downward adjustment should be made to market rates to allow for this.

problem to the demand side, in that as more and more of a factor is absorbed in any one line of output the price of the alternative product which it might have been making rises further and further. Therefore we are faced with the choice between valuation of factors at the original price (i.e. that ruling prior to the expansion of output of the commodity in question), the ultimate price, or some intermediate level. On the assumption of linearity, a price half-way between the original and ultimate levels will meet the bill, as on the demand side. Obviously, either or both of these two types of adjustments may be necessary at any particular time, and so to this extent the adjustments for indivisibilities on the costs side are likely to be more complex than those on the benefit side.

Market imperfections. Departures from Pareto-optimum situations arise when monopolistic elements or other imperfections in goods or factor markets are such as to twist relative outputs away from those which would prevail under competitive conditions. In cases of this kind investment decisions based on valuations of costs and benefits at market prices may not be appropriate; failure to correct for these distortions is likely to lead to misallocations of investment projects between different industries.

The relevance of this point for public decisions concerning investment is several-fold. First, if a public authority in a monopolistic position behaves like a private monopolist in its pricing and output policy its investment decisions will not comply with the principles of efficient allocation of resources unless the degree of monopoly is uniform throughout the economy. Secondly, complications may arise when there is monopolistic behaviour at a later stage in the production process. This can be illustrated by the example of an irrigation project which enables more sugar-beet to be grown, and hence more sugar to be refined. If the refiners enjoy a monopolistic position the sugar-beet farmers' demand for irrigation water will not be a sufficient indication of the merits of the irrigation project. If the refiners were producing at the (higher) competitive level they would absorb more beet, and this would in turn react back on the demand for irrigation water.

A third illustration is in respect of factor supplies. If the wages which have to be paid to the labour engaged on an investment project include some rental element and are greater than their marginal opportunity costs, then a deduction must be made to arrive at an appropriate figure: conversely, if wages are squeezed below marginal opportunity costs by monopsony practices.

Fourthly, there may be an excess of average over marginal costs. This raises the well-known difficulty that if prices are equated to short-run marginal costs, as they must be to ensure short-period efficiency, the enterprise will run at a loss. Various ways (see, e.g., Hicks, 1962) of getting over the problem have been suggested, but there are snags in all of them. Charges can be made, e.g. by means of a two-part tariff, but this is likely to deter some consumers whose marginal valuation of the output exceeds its marginal cost. Various systems of discriminatory charges can be devised, but these may imply inquisitorial powers on the part of the authorities. Voluntary subscriptions can be asked for, but this runs into the Wicksell objection in respect of collective goods.[4] If none of these solutions are acceptable one must be prepared to countenance losses. So this is still another case where investment decisions have to be divorced from accounting computations of profits. Instead, they must be based on notions of what people would be willing to pay or what the project 'ought to be' worth to customers, as Hicks (1962) puts it. It must be emphasized that this is not a case where prices of goods or factors are imperfect measures of benefits and costs *per se*, but where the present value of net receipts no longer measures benefits.

These are all examples of what is fundamentally the same problem: the inapplicability of investment decision rules derived from a perfectly competitive state of affairs to a world where such a competitive situation no longer holds. It should be noted that there are two possible ways of making the necessary accounting adjustments: either a correction can be made to the actual level of costs (benefits), or the costs (benefits) arising from the market can be taken as they stand but a corresponding correction has to be made to the estimation of benefits (costs). Normally, the first of these two methods would be less complicated and less liable to cause confusion.

Taxes and controls. Imperfect competition constitutes only one case of divergence between market price and social cost or benefit.

4. See *infra*, p. 87.

Another is that of taxes on expenditure. Most economists prefer to measure taxed inputs at their factor cost rather than at their market value, though the latter would be appropriate when the total supply of the input in question has a zero elasticity of supply, e.g. an imported item subject to a strict quota. A possible extension of this particular example relates to the cost of imported items in an economy with a fairly high level of tariff protection where it could be argued that price including duty is the best measure of social cost, because in the absence of protection the country's equilibrium exchange rate would be lower. Perhaps the most important example of a tax which it has been decided to exclude from costs occurs in the estimation of fuel savings resulting from road improvements (Coburn *et al.*, 1960).

Public decisions may properly differ from private ones in the investment field in respect of direct tax payments too. While private profit-making decisions should allow for income and profits tax payments, this is not apposite in the public sector. What one is primarily concerned with here is a measurement of cost which corresponds to the use of real resources[5] but excludes transfer payments. Hence profits or income taxes on the income derived by a public authority from its project are irrelevant.

As an example of government controls, we may take agricultural price supports and production controls. There seem to have been cases in the past in the United States (e.g. the Missouri Basin project) where estimates of the benefits from sugar-beet production were made without taking any notice of existing sugar-beet quotas or considering whether sugar-beet production would actually be allowed to increase! Hard as it is to cope with refinements of this sort, obviously some attempt must be made to take cognizance of the more blatant discrepancies.

Unemployment. A divergence of social cost from private cost which is sometimes of major importance arises when there is

5. Additional government expenditures necessitated by a public authority project should be included as part of its costs. But whether these expenditures are, or are not, financed by taxes on that authority is irrelevant.

When public projects are being compared with private ones there must obviously be a common standard of comparison in respect of transfers to and by government, the simplest being to ignore them.

unemployment. When there is an excess supply at the current market price of any input that price overstates the social cost of using that input. Furthermore, when there is general unemployment, expenditure upon a project, by creating a multiplier effect, will create additional real incomes in the rest of the economy. Hence the use of market values to ascertain direct costs and benefits of a project overstates its social costs and underestimates its total benefits (by the amount of 'induced benefits'). Under these conditions almost any project is better for the country than no project, so that, to achieve sub-optimization, autonomous public agencies should bring these considerations into their benefit and cost calculations, while agencies subject to central government control over their expenditure should either choose the same or be told to do so. This simple picture only holds, however, when there is but one issue to decide: shall a particular project be initiated or not? But such a choice never exists in this solitary state. The Government can choose between public works and other methods of curing unemployment. The agencies responsible for the public works can choose between a number of possible projects, some of them mutually exclusive (e.g. the choice between building a four- or six-lane motorway along a particular alignment). And it is not at all obvious that unemployment-adjusted estimates of costs and benefits constitute the right tool for making these choices.

The arguments against correcting costs for an excess of the market price of factors over the price which would clear the market for them and against including multiplier effects in benefits are largely [6] practical (cf. McKean, 1958):

(a) It is easier to allow for the overpricing of labour which is to be used in constructing or operating a project than to allow for the overpricing of equipment, fuel, materials, etc., which are overpriced because they, too, include in their costs some overpriced labour. Yet if correction is made for project labour costs only, the

6. But not entirely: it is possible to conceive of an unemployment situation in which shadow cost pricing would make a very large number of investment projects pass a cost-benefit test – in fact, a larger number than would be needed to reach full employment. The problem is to fix the shadow prices so that one can select the best projects but not so many of them that one has more than full employment.

relative social costs of project labour and of other inputs may be more poorly estimated than if no correction at all is made.

(b) Correcting future costs requires estimates of future unemployment. Government agencies are not usually equipped to make such forecasts, and governments may be reluctant to provide them on a realistic basis in view of the difficulty of keeping them out of public notice.

(c) The effect of a project upon unemployment depends not only upon the expenditure which it involves but also upon the way it is financed, and this may not be known to the people doing the cost-benefit analysis (e.g. in the case of an agency financed by government grants).

These arguments suggest that in most cases it is best for unemployment policy to be left to the central government and for the agencies responsible for public works to confine their corrections of market prices on account of under-employment (i.e. over-pricing) to divergences which are local or which relate to some specialized factor of production. National unemployment, to take an example, should be no concern of the National Coal Board, but the alleged lack of alternative employment opportunities for miners in certain coalfields should.

Collective goods. Market prices clearly cannot be used to value benefits which are not capable of being marketed. Thus we meet the collective goods issue (Samuelson, 1954; 1955; 1958; Musgrave, 1959; Head, 1962). The essential point is that some goods and services supplied by Government are of a collective nature in the sense that the quantity supplied to any one member of the relevant group cannot be independently varied. For example, all members of the population benefit from defence expenditure, all the inhabitants of any given district benefit from an anti-malaria programme, and all ships in the vicinity benefit from a lighthouse. The difference between separately marketable goods and such collective goods can be shown as in Figures 1 and 2, following Bowen (1948).

Whereas aggregation of individual demand curves is obtained by *horizontal* summation in the Figure 1 case, it is obtained by *vertical* summation in the Figure 2 case. This reflects the fact that

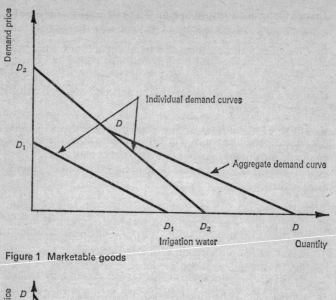

Figure 1 Marketable goods

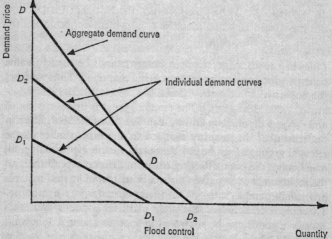

Figure 2 Collective goods

though individuals may differ in their marginal valuation of a given quantity of a commodity, they all consume the same amount, in that each unit is consumed by all of them. For example, flood control afforded to different individuals is a joint product.

Ever since Wicksell, it has been recognized that any attempt to get consumers to reveal their preferences regarding collective goods founders on the rock that the rational thing for any individual consumer to do is understate his demand, in the expectation that he would thereby be relieved of part or all of his share of the cost without affecting the quantity obtained. Although a number of people (notably Lindahl) have attempted to find ways out of this impasse, it seems safe to say that no one has succeeded. In fact, the difficulties have multiplied rather than diminished, as Samuelson (1954; 1955; 1958) and Musgrave (1959) have demonstrated that even if the non-revelation of preferences problem is ignored, there is still another major snag, in that there is no single best solution but rather a multiplicity of alternative optimum solutions.

The relevance of this discussion for our purposes is that where commodities are supplied at zero prices or at non-market clearing prices which bear no relationship to consumer preferences, there is no basis for arriving at investment decisions by computing the present values of sales. Of course, the problem does not apply to collective goods alone; a whole range of other goods and services may be supplied free (or at nominal prices) by Government for a whole variety of reasons.

Intangibles. Some costs and benefits (such as the scenic effect of building electricity transmission lines) cannot be quantified, and others, although they can be quantified, cannot be valued in any market sense (e.g. a reduction in lives lost). Such costs and benefits have been called intangible costs and benefits. They are obviously important in many cases and, equally obviously, have to be presented to the decision-maker in the prose which accompanies the cost-benefit arithmetic, since they cannot be incorporated in the arithmetic itself. It may be possible to gain some idea of their importance on the basis of consumer questionnaires, but one has to be careful of the well-known difficulties inherent in such efforts (Yates, 1960).

There is one possible exception in the case of quantifiable items. Consistency requires that the net marginal cost of, say, saving an average citizen's life be the same whether it be achieved by hiring more traffic police or by having more ambulances. If there were consistency and if the marginal cost were known, then it would measure how much decision-makers were ready to pay to save a life, and hence it could be used for valuing lives saved. So the importance attached to particular 'intangibles' may sometimes be inferred from private or public behaviour. Thus, one might suggest that British public standards of visual amenity are higher than the private standards manifest in most back gardens!

Choice of interest rate

The social time preference rate. The literature on the choice of appropriate interest rates for public investment projects is voluminous, and we cannot hope to survey it in detail. But starting from the constellation of rates that one finds in the private sector, various questions have to be raised. Even if one can select a single or average risk-free long-term rate, it is not clear what significance can be attached to it. Straightaway we come up against all the old arguments about whether market rates of interest do bear any close relationship to the marginal productivity of investment and time preference or whether the relationship is so blurred as to be imperceptible. This is partly a matter of different interest theories (neo-Classical, Keynesian, Robertsonian, etc.) and partly a matter of how particular economies tick at particular times – do governments intervene in capital markets with any effectiveness, how well organized and unified is the capital market in a country, etc.? Both pure theory and imperfections in the capital market are thus involved.

Another issue is whether any market-determined interest rate would suffice for community decisions even if neo-classical theory is accepted and a perfectly functioning capital market assumed. Some writers believe that social time preference attaches more weight to the future than private time preference and that it is the former which is relevant for determining the allocation of society's current resources between investment and consumption. A number of arguments in favour of such a proposition have been produced over the years. Pigou (1932), for instance, suggested that individuals were short-sighted about the future ('defective tele-scopic faculty') and that government intervention might be needed to give adequate weight to the welfare of unborn genera-tions (*op. cit.*, pp. 24–30). More recently, other arguments, which seek to avoid the objection that the Pigou position is a funda-mentally authoritarian one, have been put forward (Eckstein, 1961; Marglin, 1963a). One point made really relates to a special kind of externality. It is that any one individual's preference for current consumption, relatively to future consumption by himself or his successors, will be less if there is some sort of government-organized programme for imposing sacrifices on everybody – or at least on a large section of the population – than if the solution is left to the market. More generally, one might follow the lines indicated by Feldstein (1964b) and distinguish between: (1) mar-ket preferences; (2) preferences expressed through the ballot box; (3) what the Government in its wisdom thinks is good for this generation; and (4) what the Government thinks is good for this generation and future generations taken together.

Whatever the ultimate pros and cons of these arguments, there are two difficulties, if one tries to give effect to them. The first is actually to determine the social rate of discount. Marglin accepts that this does pose serious difficulties, but goes on to suggest that one can set about it by choosing the growth rate for an economy and thence (on the basis of the marginal capital/output ratio) determine the rate of investment; the social rate of discount must then be equated with the marginal productivity of investment. The practicability of such a procedure does not commend itself to us; but we must leave this to others to judge.

Another difficulty of operating with a social rate of discount is that we have the very awkward problem that different rates of interest would be used in the public and private sectors. There is then likely to be considerable inefficiency in the allocation of funds inside the investment sector – in the sense that if the Govern-ment is, say, responsible for electricity and the private sector for oil, inferior projects of the former kind will supplant superior projects of the latter kind.[7] This particular difficulty leads us right back to the point discussed on pp. 74–5, i.e. that one rate of

7. Defining 'infer ior' and 'superior' in terms of present values of net benefits.

interest cannot perform two functions in a non-optimal situation. One way out of this is to recommend making the situation an optimal one. For instance, Hirshleifer *et al.* (1960) have suggested that the Government should take action to push down market rates of interest to the social rate, so that all investment decisions, whether in the public or private sectors, should be taken on the same basis. While applauding this idea in principle, other writers quite reasonably feel that in practice economists will still have to deal with sub-optimization problems.

The social opportunity cost rate. The government borrowing rate is a popular and easily applicable measure of costs, both because it is a financial cost in the case of government financed investment and, more academically, because it can be regarded as 'the' risk-free rate of interest.[8] Yet despite the recent empirically founded recrudescence of belief in the interest elasticity of private investment, no one has demonstrated that the latter's marginal efficiency does actually equal the interest rate. A direct attempt to measure marginal rates of return on private investment is therefore required. Even if such a measure were made, however, it would be relevant only in so far as the costs being evaluated consisted exclusively of displaced private investment.

Recognizing this problem, Krutilla and Eckstein (1958) assumed that the alternative to public investment would be a tax cut, considered the ways in which a likely tax cut would affect income groups, and then asked how the notional recipients would utilize their hypothetical receipts, thus finally arriving at a weighted average rate of return. An alternative postulate was that the additional public investment would be offset by tighter monetary policy; it was then asked which individuals would suffer and what sort of weighted interest rate could thence be derived. The general result from both assumptions was that Federal capital in the United States in the late 1950s had an opportunity cost of 5–6 per cent. Quite apart from the logical and statistical problems associated with the techniques of assigning tax cuts to the different income groups, etc., as Eckstein himself has noted (1961), this approach deals with only two out of many relevant alternatives (e.g. more public investment might be met instead by less public

8. Abstracting from uncertainty about the price level.

consumption). It has also been severely criticized by Hirshleifer *et al.* (1960) on the grounds that the composite interest rate finally derived has an unknown allowance for a risk premium in it. Feldstein has also commented on this approach (1964c).

Adjustment for uncertainty. The various ways in which uncertainty impinges upon cost-benefit analysis are discussed by Dorfmann (in Maass *et al.*, 1962, ch. 3), McKean (1958, ch. 4), Eckstein (1961, section 5), Hirshleifer *et al.* (1960, pp, 139–41) in their admirable surveys, and we need only add two remarks here. The first point is that there is no reason to argue that public invest-ment projects are free of uncertainty (see, especially, Hirshleifer *et al.*, 1960). The second is that allowances for uncertainty can be made: (1) in the assessments of annual levels of benefits and costs; (2) in the assumptions about length of life; and (3) in the discount rate. The first is most appropriate if the risk of disper-sion of outcomes (or inputs) is irregularly, rather than regularly, distributed with time. If the main risk is that there may be a sud-den day of reckoning when benefits disappear or costs soar, the second type of adjustment is needed. The third correction, a premium on the discount rate, is appropriate where uncertainty is a strictly compounding function of time.

The need for an interest rate. When the problem of choice involves no opportunity cost of capital – as happens when all of a fixed budget is to be spent – there is obviously no need for an oppor-tunity-cost rate of interest. It has been argued by some authors, e.g. McKean (1958), that in this case there is no need for a social discount rate of interest either. This can be generally true, how-ever, only if the maximand is not the present worth of benefits less costs, for if it is, some rate of discount is obviously required. We shall not elaborate this point here, since one of us has already published a purely expository note on the subject in this Journal (Turvey, 1963).

Principles vs. *practice.* Discussions about social rates of time preference, social opportunity cost, etc., do not cut very much ice in most empirical work, and we have not been able to discover any cases where there was any convincingly complete application of such notions.[9] Nor do ideas about allowing for future changes in interest rates seem to receive much attention. In practice, the most usual kind of procedure is to select an interest rate or rates, on the basis of observed rates ruling at the time, for calculating present values, etc. For example, Weisbrod (1960) takes a rate of 10 per cent to represent the opportunity cost of capital in the private sector (on the basis that the observed yield of 5 per cent for corporate stocks should be grossed up to approximately double that figure to allow for the corporate profits tax)[10] and one of 4 per cent to represent the cost of Federal Government borrowing. He then makes his present value calculations on both bases. It can obviously be said that this may give ambiguous results, e.g. that project A is preferable to project B on one basis, but project B is preferable on the other. This is indisputable; but there are also examples to show that the choice of varying discount rates does not, within the 4–8 per cent band, make much difference to assessments of a project (Foster and Beesley, 1963), though the same conclusions do not necessarily hold for a rather wider band. The truth of the matter is that, whatever one does, one is trying to unscramble an omelette, and no one has yet invented a uniquely superior way of doing this.

Relevant constraints

Introduction. Eckstein (1961) has provided a most helpful classification of constraints. First, there are physical constraints. The most general of these is the production function which relates the physical inputs and outputs of a project, but this enters directly into the calculation of costs and benefits. Where choice is involved between different projects or regarding the size or timing of a particular project, external physical constraints may also be relevant. Thus, one particular input may be in totally inelastic supply, or two projects may be mutually exclusive on purely technological grounds.

Next there are legal constraints. What is done must be within

9. Eckstein (1961) concluded after several pages of discussion 'thus the choice of interest rates must remain a value judgment' (p. 460).

10. It might be argued that a further correction should also be made to bridge any gap between earnings yield and dividend yield. This would make for a wider spread of the rate band.

the framework of the law, which may affect matters in a multiplicity of ways, e.g. rights of access, time needed for public inquiries, regulated pricing, limits to the activities of public agencies and so on. Third, there may be administrative constraints, related to limits to what can be handled administratively. Fourth, uncertainty can be introduced by constraints, for example, by the introduction of some minimum regret requirement. Finally, there are distributional and budgetary constraints; these need more extended discussion.

Distributional constraints. The notion that the choice between projects can be made solely on the grounds of 'economic efficiency', because any unfavourable effects on income distribution can be overcome by making some of the gainers compensate some of the losers, is rarely applicable in practice.

It is perfectly possible to compensate property-owners not only for property which is expropriated but also for property which is reduced in value. Similarly, it is possible to levy a charge in respect of property which has been enhanced in value. These payments of compensation and charges, being lump sums, are not likely to have any direct effects upon resource allocation. Another way in which extra money can be raised from the beneficiaries of a project without affecting resource allocation arises where some of the project outputs are sold and intra-marginal units of these outputs can be priced at more than marginal units. (Thus electricity consumers may be charged on a two-part tariff.)

In general, however, attempts to get beneficiaries to pay more than the marginal social cost of the project outputs they consume will affect the allocation of resources. Such attempts may be made either because of a desire not to raise the real income of the beneficiaries to an extent regarded as unfair or because of a desire to raise funds to compensate a group who are made worse off by the project or simply because of a general belief that projects ought to break even. Whatever the reason, the pricing policy adopted will affect project outputs, and hence project costs. Tolls on a motorway, for instance, will affect the volume of traffic, and this may affect the appropriate width at which it should be constructed. Thus, benefits and costs are not independent of pricing policy.

This can affect cost-benefit analysis in either of two ways. The first is relevant when pricing rules have been laid down in advance in the light of political or social notions about income distribution. Here the task is to maximize the present value of benefits less costs subject to certain specified financial requirements, i.e. subject to one or more constraints. The second way in which income distribution requirements may affect cost-benefit analysis occurs when the authorities have not laid down any specific financial rules but do clearly care about income distribution. In this case it is up to the analyst to invent and present as alternatives a number of variants of a project which differ both as regards the particular people who pay (or are paid) and the prices charged and, in consequence, as regards outputs and inputs. For each alternative, the analyst will have to set out not only total costs and benefits but also the costs and benefits for those particular groups whose economic welfare is of interest to the decision-maker.

In cases like this the choice can be formalized – if the decision-taker allows it – by expressing it in terms of maximizing the excess of total benefits over total costs subject to constraints on the benefits less costs of particular groups. Alternatively, it can be expressed in terms of maximizing the net gain (or minimizing the net loss) to a particular group subject to a constraint relating to total benefits and costs. Whether or not this is helpful in practice is not known, but at least it may explain why income distribution considerations have been brought into this survey under the heading of constraints.

It should be noted that these considerations may relate to many different kinds of groups. In one context notions of 'fairness' to workers may predominate, while in another it may be notions of 'equity' between different geographical areas which are important. If one is taking a regional, rather than a national, viewpoint the assessment and measurement of costs and benefits may be quite markedly different. For instance, it has been argued that one of the benefits of the Morecambe Bay barrage scheme would be the attraction of more industry to the Barrow area. This would no doubt benefit Barrow; but it is perfectly conceivable that there would be equivalent or even greater losses to South Lancashire, or for that matter other regions of the United Kingdom. Therefore one gets an entirely different picture of benefits and costs, if one looks at them from the viewpoint of the Barrow area, from that prevailing for the whole of the North-west or the whole of the United Kingdom.

Budgetary constraints. Discussions of this topic combine (and sometimes confuse) three issues: first, ought such constraints to exist; second, what form do they take; and third, how can they be incorporated into investment criteria? We shall deal with the third issue shortly when we reach the general subject of investment criteria. We do not propose to discuss the first point, but might note that Hirshleifer *et al.* (1960) have argued that if the budgeting authorities are worth their salt the amount allocated to the sub-budgets will take account of the productivity of the projects available to them and the costs of obtaining the necessary funds. If this is not done, it is argued, the answer is to recast the system of budget allocation rather than to go into python-like contortions at the sub-budget level. This argument, however, is rather unrealistic. For the present, at any rate, many decisions are in fact taken within the framework of a budget restraint, and the economist might as well help people to sub-optimize within this framework, even if, as a long-run proposition, he thinks in his private capacity that it should be changed.

On the second issue there is not much to be said in general terms. There may be a constraint upon total capital expenditure over one or more years, as, for instance, when the projects undertaken by a public agency have to fit within a budget framework determined in advance. The sums involved may be either maxima which do not have to be reached or amounts which are to be spent entirely.[11] In the first case, but not the second, the expenditure in question has an opportunity cost, since once the decision is made to use funds, they are effectively a bygone. There can be other kinds of constraint applying to capital expenditure, such as a prescribed percentage of self-financing, and constraints can also apply to current expenditure and/or to revenue, for example, a financial target for gross or net accounting profits.

11. 'Maximum' or 'specific' rationing to use the convenient terminology of Hirshleifer *et al.* (1960).

Final considerations
Investment criteria

We believe that the most common maximand where projects involve only costs and benefits expressed in terms of money is the present value of benefits less costs. Other maximands are possible, however, such as capital stock at a final date. We shall not attempt to argue the relative merits of different maximands, but, continuing to accept present value, now introduce the subject of investment criteria or, as they are sometimes called, decision algorithms.

Where no projects are interdependent or mutually exclusive, where starting dates are given and where no constraints are operative, the choice of projects which maximizes the present value of total benefits less total costs can be expressed in any of the following four equivalent ways:[12]

1. select all projects where the present value of benefits exceeds the present value of costs;

2. select all projects where the ratio of the present value of benefits to the present value of costs exceeds unity;

3. select all projects where the constant annuity with the same

12. Symbolically, these criteria can be summarized as follows.

Let $c_1, c_2, \ldots, c_n$ = series of prospective costs in years $1, 2, \ldots, n$;
$\quad c$ = constant annuity with same present value as $c_1, c_2, \ldots, c_n$;
$b_1, b_2, \ldots, b_n$ = series of prospective benefits in years $1, 2, \ldots, n$;
$\quad b$ = constant annuity with same present value as $b_1, b_2, \ldots, b_n$;
$\quad s$ = scrap value;
$\quad i$ = appropriate rate of discount for annual compounding;
$\quad r$ = internal rate of return.

Then we may write the rules as follows: select projects where

$$\frac{b_1}{(1+i)}+\frac{b_2}{(1+i)^2}+\ldots+\frac{b_n+s}{(1+i)^n} > \frac{c_1}{(1+i)}+\frac{c_2}{(1+i)^2}+\ldots+\frac{c_n}{(1+i)^n} \qquad 1$$

$$\frac{b_1/(1+i)+b_2/(1+i)^2+\ldots+(b_n+s)/(1+i)^n}{c_1/(1+i)+c_2/(1+i)^2+\ldots+c_n/(1+i)^n} > 1 \qquad 2$$

$$b > c. \qquad 3$$

Finally, select projects where $r > i$, where r is given by

$$\frac{b_1-c_1}{(1+r)}+\frac{b_2-c_2}{(1+r)^2}+\ldots+\frac{b_n-c_n}{(1+r)^n} = 0.$$

present value as benefits exceeds the constant annuity (of the same duration) with the same present value as costs;

4. select all projects where the internal rate of return exceeds the chosen rate of discount.

Once the various complications just assumed away are introduced, more complicated rules are required. We shall explain the impact of these complications in terms of the present-value approach without claiming that it is always the most convenient one. Which approach is most convenient will vary with the facts of the case. Where a rule which is not algebraically equivalent to the present value approach is used, the issue is not one of convenience, but involves either error[13] or a different maximand.

Where the costs and/or benefits of two schemes A and B are interdependent in the sense that the execution of one affects the costs or benefits of the other (see pp. 75–6 *supra*), they must be treated as constituting three mutually exclusive schemes, namely A and B together, A alone and B alone. Thus, if one wants to improve communications between two towns one has the choice between a road improvement, a rail improvement and a combination of road and rail improvements.

Mutual exclusivity can also arise for technological reasons. Thus, a road intersection can be built as a cross-roads, a roundabout or a flyover. Similarly, a large or a small dam, but not both, may be put in one place. Whatever the reason for mutual exclusivity, its presence must be allowed for in formulating investment rules.

Where there is a choice of starting date it must be chosen so as to maximize the present value of benefits less costs at the reference date.

Constraints cause the biggest complications, particularly when there is more than one of them and when mutual exclusivity and optimal timing are also involved. Indivisibilities also complicate matters when constraints are involved.

We shall not venture into the algebraic jungle of constructing

---

13. A naïve error in early writings was the use of benefit–cost ratios to choose between two mutually exclusive projects. One project may have the lower benefit–cost ratio, yet will be preferable if the *extra* benefits exceed the *extra* costs. This is clearly brought out by McKean (1958, pp. 108 ff.).

decision algorithms. Anyone who seeks examples can turn to Dorfmann in Marglin's discussion of income distribution and budgetary constraints in his exemplary synthesis of much of cost-benefit analysis (Maass *et al.*, 1962) or to his monograph on dynamic investment planning (Marglin, 1963b). A most useful discussion is also to be found in an article on capital budgeting by Dryden (1964).

Second-best matters

Since cost-benefit analysis is essentially a practical tool for decision-making, it is not worth our while pursuing the second-best problem into the higher reaches of welfare economics. The non-fulfilment of the conditions for a welfare maximum elsewhere in the economy is relevant to cost-benefit analysis only in so far as it makes the market values of outputs and inputs obviously biased measures of benefits and costs. Small and remote divergences from the optimum will cause biases in these measures which fall within their margin of error, while large divergences of an unknown sort create unknowable biases which are necessarily irrelevant to action. Only those divergences which are immediate, palpable and considerable thus deserve our attention. We have discussed some of these already, and will bring in further examples in our survey of particular applications of cost-benefit analysis.

Ideally, all such divergences should be taken into account, for otherwise a sub-optimum will not be achieved. Yet it does not follow that public agencies ought always to take account of them; the ideal involves administrative costs. It has to be recognized that public agencies have defined spheres of competence and that the responsibility for wide issues lying outside these spheres rests not with them but with the Government which created them and their tasks. It is not the business of, say, the Scottish Development Department to decide whether or not the currency is overvalued, for instance, and it is not within its competence to put a shadow price upon the foreign-exchange content of proposed expenditure. Either it must value imports at their import price or it must be told to adopt a shadow rate for planning purposes by the central government, whose function it is to consider such matters. The division of labour in administration which is necessary if the public sector is to avoid monolithic sluggishness requires each part of the machine to act as if the rest were doing its job properly. After all, to continue with this example, it may be better if all government agencies value foreign exchange at a uniform but incorrect exchange rate than if they each have their own different shadow rates.

References

BOWEN, H. R. (1948), *Toward Social Economy*, Holt Rinehart & Winston.

COBURN, T. M., BEESLEY, M. E., and REYNOLDS, D. J. (1960), *The London–Birmingham Motorway: Traffic and Economics*, Road Research Laboratory Technical Paper no. 46, DSIR, HMSO.

DRYDEN, M. M. (1964), 'Capital budgeting: treatment of uncertainty and investment criteria', *Scottish J. polit. Econ.*, vol. 9.

DUPUIT, J. (1952), 'On the measurement of utility of public works', *International Econ. Papers*, vol. 2 (translated from the French), pp. 83–110.

ECKSTEIN, O. (1958), *Water Resource Development*, Harvard University Press.

ECKSTEIN, O. (1961), 'A survey of the theory of public expenditure criteria', in J. M. Buchanan (ed.), *Public Finances: Needs, Sources and Utilization*, Princeton University Press.

FELDSTEIN, M. S. (1964a), 'Net social benefit calculation and the public investment decision', *Oxford Econ. Papers*, vol. 16, pp. 114–31.

FELDSTEIN, M. S. (1964b), 'The social time preference discount rate in cost-benefit analysis', *Econ. J.*, vol. 74, no. 2, pp. 360–79.

FELDSTEIN, M. S. (1964c), 'Opportunity cost calculations in cost-benefit analysis', *Public Finance*, vol. 19, no. 2.

FOSTER, C. D., and BEESLEY, M. E. (1963), 'Estimating the social benefit of constructing an underground railway in London', *J. Royal stat. Soc.*, vol. 126, part 1.

HEAD, J. G. (1962), 'Public goods and public policy', *Public Finance*, vol. 17.

HICKS, J. R. (1962), 'Economic theory and the evaluation of consumers' wants', *J. Business*, vol. 35.

HIRSHLEIFER, J., DE HAVEN, J. C., and MILLIMAN, J. W. (1960), *Water Supply: Economics, Technology and Policy*, University of Chicago Press.

KRUTILLA, J. V., and ECKSTEIN, O. (1958), *Multiple Purpose River Development*, Johns Hopkins Press.

LERNER, A. P. (1944), *The Economics of Control*, Macmillan.

MAASS, A. (1962), *Design of Water Resource Systems: New Techniques for Relating Economic Objectives, Engineering Analysis and Governmental Planning*, Macmillan.

MCKEAN, R. N. (1958), *Efficiency in Government through Systems Analysis*, Wiley.

MARGLIN, S. A. (1963a), 'The social rate of discount and the optimal rate of investment', *Quart. J. Econ*, vol. 77.

MARGLIN, S. A. (1963b), *Approaches to Dynamic Investment Planning*, North-Holland.

MARGOLIS, J. (1957), 'Secondary benefits, external economies, and the justification of public investment', *Review of Econ. and Stat.*, vol. 39.

MUSGRAVE, R. A. (1959), *The Theory of Public Finance: A Study in Public Economy*, McGraw-Hill.

PIGOU, A. C. (1932), *The Economics of Welfare*, 4th edn, Macmillan.

SAMUELSON, P. A. (1954), 'The pure theory of public expenditure', *Review Econs. and Stats.*, vol. 36, pp. 387–9.

SAMUELSON, P. A. (1955), 'Diagrammatic exposition of a theory of public expenditure', *Review Econs. and Stats.*, vol. 37.

SAMUELSON, P. A. (1958), 'Aspects of public expenditure theories', *Review Econs. and Stats.*, vol. 40.

STEINER, P. O. (1959), 'Choosing among alternative public investments in the water resource field', *Amer. Econ. Review*, vol. 49, pp. 893–916.

TURVEY, R. (1963), 'Present value versus internal rate of return – an essay in the theory of the third best', *Econ. J.*, vol. 73.

WEISBROD, B. A. (1960), *Economics of Public Health: Measuring the Economic Impact of Diseases*, University of Pennsylvania Press.

YATES, F. (1960), *Sampling Methods for Censuses and Surveys*, Griffin.

2 R. A. Musgrave

Cost-Benefit Analysis and the Theory of Public Finance

R. A. Musgrave, 'Cost-benefit analysis and the theory of public finance',
Journal of Economic Literature, vol. 7, no. 3, 1969, pp. 797–806.

A theory of public finance remains unsatisfactory unless it comprises both the revenue and expenditure sides of the fiscal process. The classical (Ricardo-Mills-Edgeworth-Pigou) tradition of a 'taxation-only' view neglected this axiom. Holding expenditures unproductive, or disregarding them altogether, the task was to arrange taxes so as to impose equal (or least total) sacrifice. As a theory of taxation, this approach collapsed with the old welfare economics; and as a theory of public finance, its exclusive concern with taxation bypassed the central problem of how to allocate resources for the provision of social goods. Subsequently, various attempts were made to combine the revenue and expenditure sides in a more satisfactory system. We shall note these briefly, and then consider how cost-benefit analysis fits into the picture.

Past approaches

The first attempt also came from A. C. Pigou. Although the early editions of his *Public Finance* stayed largely in the classical mold, subject only to added concern with announcement effects, it does contain an aside on public-sector theory (1928, part I, ch. 7), drawn in the image of his prior *Economics of Welfare* (1924). The composition of public expenditures should be selected so as to equate their marginal social benefits; the composition of taxes should be chosen so as to minimize total social cost; and the size of the budget should be carried to the point where marginal benefits and costs are equal. There is nothing wrong with this view, but it says little beyond demanding in general terms that the public sector should be efficient. The real question is how costs and benefits are to be determined, and how they are related to each other.

Tax-costs in terms of taxpayer sacrifice cannot be determined unless cardinal utility schedules are comparable and known. This was denied (perhaps too vehemently so) by the new welfare economics. But, apart from this, the Pigovian model remains inadequate because it offers no mechanism by which benefits are to be measured. 'If a community were literally a unitary being, with the government as its brain,' as Pigou says, 'expenditures (paraphrasing) and taxes could be pushed up to the point where marginal benefits and costs are equal' (1928, p. 50). This formulation allows for both sides of the problem, but it still bypasses the main issue: the community is not a unitary being, and benefits must be valued (in the absence of specific reasons to the contrary) in terms of the preferences of consumers. While Pigou's welfare model is compatible with this requirement, it fails to show us how the requirement can be met.

Such was the state of affairs when I first studied the problem. Then came the Keynesian revolution, which elevated the fiscal mechanism to a strategic position in macroeconomic theory and policy. As distinct from the earlier emphasis on allocation and distribution, primary concern was now with fiscal effects on total demand. In the initial stages at least, exclusive emphasis was with the level of deficit and the expenditure side of the budget. When 'functional finance' reintroduced taxation as a policy tool (Lerner, 1944, ch. 24), it was as an agent of deflation only, with the balanced-budget theorem the symbol of the both-sides approach. The traditional issues of efficient resource use and distribution were swamped by the newly discovered multiplier, or at best reduced to the 'ditch-digging' case against careless selection of public works.

A concerted return to the basic issues of allocation and distribution occurred in the fifties, when English-language literature first viewed the theory of public finance as one of social goods. The nature of social goods was defined in terms of goods the consumption of which is non-rival; and the conditions for efficient resource use in the provision of social goods were stated in terms of the 'new' welfare economics. In some respects, this was but a catching up with Knut Wicksell, who had written along these lines half a century before, and with Erik Lindahl's development thereof.[1] But the job was now to be done more thoroughly. Paul Samuelson's (1954; 1969) statement of Paretian efficiency for a world with both private and social goods was the basic step. While Samuelson referred to his formulation as a 'theory of public expenditures', this was too narrow a term. The formulation does not constitute an 'expenditure-only' approach, analogous to the classical taxation-only version. The opportunity cost of social goods use is made an integral part of the analysis, and the entire picture is included.

If taxation in the usual sense does not enter, neither do public expenditures. The generality of the formulation soars above such institutional trivia. An omniscient planner to whom available resources and techniques are given and all individual preferences are known, determines the choice of efficient outputs (including the division between public and private goods, and the assignment of the latter among consumers) for all possible states of welfare distribution, and then chooses the optimum optimorum by application of a social welfare function.

The special case of social goods was thus firmly incorporated into the general theory of welfare economics, but the new formulation left little or no footing from which to build a bridge towards an operational theory of public finance. Choosing this more parochial objective, I have preferred therefore to stay with the Wicksell-Lindahl tradition of separation between allocation and distribution issues. This separation can be reconciled with Samuelson's general formulation;[2] and while I admit that nothing

1. See excerpts of Wicksell's and Lindahl's writing in Peacock and Musgrave (1958).

2. To spell out this point, assume a world with private goods only, and no externalities or other causes for market failure. Competitive pricing then offers an efficient pricing rule. Given such a rule, there exists a desired state of welfare distribution which may be translated into a corresponding distribution of money income. We may then argue that public policy should be directed at (A) market-structure policies which will enable this pricing rule to function, and (B) distribution policies which are directed at obtaining the

is gained thereby in the omniscient-planner context, the separation of issues becomes essential if one is to link the normative model with the real-world problem of budget determination.

In that setting, an initial state of distribution exists, making it necessary to assign the opportunity cost of public resource use to individuals. Also preferences are unknown, so that a mechanism is needed to induce their revelation. These needs are met via a voting process which joins the tax and expenditure decisions, and the policy task is to design this process to implement an efficient pricing rule. Distribution objectives may then be met by redistributing money income, having in mind the pricing rule by which social goods are allocated and their cost charged. Allocation objectives may be met by approximating efficient project choice within the context of this pricing rule.

This much for past doctrine, as I see it. More recently, a new approach has emerged and become of major interest to the younger generation of fiscal economists. This is the application of cost-benefit analysis to the determination of expenditure policy. While this approach has proved of great practical value in applying efficiency considerations to expenditure decisions, our concern here is not with its pragmatic use. Rather, I wish to examine how cost-benefit analysis relates to the central theory of social goods. Seen in this context, is it a step forward, or a throwback to a one-sided view of the budget, compensating, as it were, by lagged Hegelian logic for the taxation-only sins of the twenties?

'proper' (given this pricing rule) distribution of money income. This may be contrasted with an approach which argues that in the absence of proper distribution there is no presumption in favor of Pareto optimality; and that policy should always be ready to condone departures from Pareto-efficient pricing since such departures may be validated in a broader efficiency sense by resulting gains in distribution. The latter may be held as the best available solution if efficient decisions are precluded by political or other factors, but it does not seem suitable for a normative model.

Precisely the same problem arises in the case of social goods, except that the choice of pricing rule (now through the political process) is less obvious. Nevertheless, some political mechanisms or voting systems are more efficient than others, and the task is to develop the system which offers the best approximation to an efficient solution. For further discussion see my article 'Provision for social goods' (1969).

While this is a tempting interpretation of doctrinal development, it may also be too harsh a view. Whereas the classical theory of taxation only dealt with minimizing the costs of taxation without allowing for expenditure benefits, cost-benefit analysis by its very nature includes both the cost and benefit sides. An objective function is to be maximized, with both costs and benefits as arguments in that function. But this is not enough to make a theory of the public sector. The question is how costs enter the picture, and how they are related to the benefit side.

Measuring benefits

Consider first the question of what benefits should be included, and how such benefits should be measured. Unless distributional considerations are to be inserted into the objective function, cost-benefit analysts agree that purely pecuniary benefits should not be allowed for, but that all others (internal or external, direct or indirect, tangible or intangible) should ideally be included (Prest and Turvey, 1965). However, they cannot all be measured. Evaluation is easy where the goods provided are in the nature of private goods, and provision is through public sale, so that benefits can be measured by market price. In this case, the planner merely performs functions usually assumed by the private firm, and the economics of that firm apply. The theory of public enterprise, selling private goods and producing without externalities, does not belong in the theory of public finance.

The more germane situations arise where there are inherent reasons for market failure. Among these, our concern is mainly with the provision of social goods, i.e. goods which are non-rival in consumption. Since their use by any one consumer does not interfere with that by another, it would be inefficient to make consumption contingent on a price payment, even where exclusion could be readily applied. Tolls are inappropriate for an uncrowded bridge.[3] The fact that exclusion frequently cannot be applied, or at great cost only, further strengthens the conclusion that the auction system of the market is not available to evaluate

3. Such is the case, at least, for an existing bridge. If a series of new investment is considered, the inefficiencies of charging tolls (while there is still traffic slack) may have to be weighed against those of decision by political process.

the benefits.[4] A political process is needed, and this involves tax and expenditure determination through the voting system.

Such at least is the case for social goods of the final or consumer good type. Uncrowded highways for pleasure driving, the delights of public parks, or the TV spectacle of a moon-landing, are cases in point. Here the benefit side of cost-benefit analysis collapses: while costs can be measured, benefits have to be stipulated if an optimization procedure is to be applied. Such stipulation is not provided by cost-benefit analysis. In some cases, the cost of complementary private goods (travel costs to reach a park) may give some guidance to valuing the social good (enjoyment of the park itself) (Mack and Myers, 1965), but at best this sets only a lower limit to the benefit. Generally speaking, cost-benefit analysis provides no substitute for the basic problem of evaluation in the case of final social goods. All it can do is to expedite efficient decision-making after the basic problem of evaluation is solved. At the same time, cost-benefit analysis, even if based on arbitrary evaluations of final benefits, may be helpful: viewing the benefit as the dependent variable, the analysis may provide a test for how high evaluation must be to justify the outlay.

The situation is more manageable, however, where benefits are reflected in price change, or are made calculable with reference to price. Thus, the benefits from irrigation may be measured in terms of increased agricultural output; flood control results in cost-saving since measurable damage to capital assets or resources is avoided; better roads reduce automotive costs and save trucking time, which can be valued; public health measures reduce remedial care cost; investment in education raises earning power, and so forth.

The common characteristic of these cases is (1) that the social good is not a final but an intermediate good, i.e. a good which enters into the production of further output; and (2) that this further output is in the nature of a private good which may be valued efficiently at the market. While external effects on produc-

4. Only where exclusion is inapplicable in the case of goods with rival consumption, does the inapplicability of exclusion become a primary and distinct cause for market failure. Improvement in exclusion technology then becomes the preferred solution.

tion cost have been dealt with in the general theory of externalities, the specific case of social goods *qua* intermediate goods has been neglected in the development of social good theory, nearly all of which has dealt with final goods.[5]

The intermediate social good has the same characteristic of non-rival use, as has the final good; but this non-rival use is now by producers rather than consumers. Since it enters into a final private good, the benefit of such a social good *can* be measured in terms of the market price of this final (private) good. This measure of benefit can be inserted into the objective function, and the maximizing procedure can be applied. It is thus in the case of the intermediate social good that cost-benefit analysis can perform most effectively. Notwithstanding past preoccupation of social goods theory with final goods, a large part of the social goods basket is clearly of this intermediate type, and this may explain why provision for social goods is in reality not as intractable as the theory suggests.

Investment decisions

Until recently, at least, the primary application of cost-benefit analysis has been to public investment, rather than to the provision of short-lived goods. This may be due to concern with investment planning in developing countries, as well as the economist's fascination with the niceties of time discount analysis. Also, the very choice of the discount rate involves an externality problem, in that the social rate is usually held to fall short of the private rate. For our purposes, two aspects of the investment problem are of particular interest, i.e. (1) the relation between investment mix and total investment, and (2) the way in which the means of finance enter the profitability calculation.

Total investment v. investment mix

This problem may be seen most clearly if we suppose that the capital market is perfect, so that all rates of return, subject to risk

5. I am indebted to John Head for pointing out to me that the intermediate goods case was dealt with in a brief note by Keimei Kaizuka (1965). Kaizuka shows that the efficiency condition (analogous to the consumer good case) now requires the sum of the marginal rates of substitution to be equal to the marginal rate of transformation. I also wish to thank Elisha Pazner for helpful discussion of this case.

differentials, are equalized. In this setting, we can speak of *the* internal rate of return on private investment, which in turn will equal *the* private rate of discount, r_p. If we assume that the social rate of discount r_s equals r_p, a public investment will be undertaken if present value equals cost when using the discount rate r_p, or (which comes to the same) if its internal rate matches r_p. No conflict arises.

Now let $r_s < r_p$, which happens if investment involves social-goods type benefits which are not accounted for by the private market (Eckstein, 1959; Marglin, 1965 and 1963b; Feldstein, 1964b). In this case, the level of investment generated by the private sector will be too low from the social point of view. This may be compensated for either by raising private investment through monetary policy or other incentives, such as an investment subsidy; or it may be compensated for by adding public investment. If the former option is open, there is no prima facie case for public investment to be selected as a corrective for deficient total investment. The best solution, clearly, is to achieve both the proper level of total investment *and* the proper mix between public and private. This involves first a monetary or subsidy policy which equates the market rate of return with r_s, then a mix of public and private investment so as to equate returns at the margin, discounting by r_s in both cases.

But cost-benefit analysts tend to proceed without this two-step sequence. The prevailing discrepancy between r_s and r_p is taken as given and analysis then proceeds by the second best rule, that public investment should be made if it does not displace a 'better' private investment (Marglin, 1963a, p. 276). To compare the value of alternative investments, the same social discount rate r_s is to be applied. A public investment is undertaken if the present value of the consumption stream which it generates exceeds its opportunity cost; and the latter is measured as the present value of the consumption stream foregone because the private investment is not made. But though no superior private investments are displaced, public investment as a policy instrument can neither raise the level of private investment to include projects which would be profitable if r_p were reduced to r_s, nor can it lengthen the structure of private investment to that which would hold at r_s.

These defects are avoided if the two policy objectives (adjustment in total investment, and its distribution between public and private) are distinguished and two instruments (equalization of the private rate of return with r_s, and public investment) are used instead of public investment only. Cost-benefit analysts are aware of this but the trouble, they argue, is that the official who decides on public investment does not control fiscal or monetary policy. He must take the world with its given constraints, and if a pro-public investment bias results, this second best solution is still the best which the circumstances permit him. True enough, provided that the pragmatic nature of the approach is recognized and the need to loosen the constraints is not forgotten in the process.

Sources of finance

Given the assumption of *perfect capital markets* and provided the government uses the private rate of discount r_p, the investment decision is independent of the source of finance. If resources are withdrawn from private investment, the least profitable invest-ments (yielding r_p at the margin) will be surrendered. The present value of the consumption stream foregone, discounted at r_p, will be one dollar per dollar of investment that is withdrawn. If resources are withdrawn from consumption, the opportunity cost per dollar of present consumption foregone is again valued at one dollar. Since the capital market is in equilibrium, the opportunity cost will be the same in both cases and the source of finance does not matter.

If the government uses a social discount rate r_s where $r_s < r_p$, the source of finance matters, even in the case of perfect capital markets (Feldstein, 1964a). If the resource withdrawal is from investment, the foregone consumption stream is discounted at r_s and the opportunity cost per one dollar of private investment lost exceeds one dollar. But in the case of withdrawal from consump-tion, the opportunity cost will still be one dollar. The opportunity cost will thus be greater where withdrawal is from investment. Accordingly, public investment is more likely to 'qualify' if tax financed, where withdrawal is more largely from consumption than if loan financed, where withdrawal is more largely from investment. Matters are complicated further if reinvestment rates are to be considered. Since these differ among private investments, the result further depends on which particular investment is withdrawn. The outcome for loan finance thus depends upon the type of debt instrument which is issued.

Turning now to *imperfect capital markets*, we begin with a situation where a given rate r_s is applied. If the resource withdrawal is from private investment the opportunity cost now varies not only with the reinvestment rate, but also depends on the profitability of the particular investment which is displaced. The consumption stream foregone will differ, and so will its present value as discounted by r_s. If the resource withdrawal is from consumption, opportunity cost presumably is again valued on a one for one basis. Since tax finance, as previously noted, tends to fall on consumption while loan finance falls more largely on investment, the finance choice now matters even more in determining the opportunity cost.

Next, consider a situation where planners do not work with a given level of r_s but wish to apply the private rate of discount r_p. If the resource withdrawal is from private investment, the consumption stream foregone again differs with the particular investment which is replaced. But there is now the additional difficulty of having to determine the level of r_p by which to discount both the private consumption stream which is foregone and the public stream which is to be gained. For lack of a single rate, some average of market rates has to be chosen. The government's borrowing rate, adjusted to include tax revenue foregone, may be a rough indicator (Harberger, 1968).

A new twist enters if the resource withdrawal is from consumption. The particular rate, or combination of rates, available to the person whose consumption is reduced, is now selected as the appropriate rate by which to discount the income stream generated by the public investment.[6] Since rates available to various consumers differ, the result depends on just what taxes are used and

6. See Krutilla and Eckstein (1958, ch. 4). While this procedure is ingenious, its meaning in a setting of imperfect capital markets is puzzling. If the rate of substitution of future for present consumption differs among consumers, and different rates of transformation apply in private investment, it is difficult to see why the rates applicable to the particular taxpayer should be controlling. To be sure, it is *his* consumption that is reduced, and this is relevant if distributional weights are to be attached. But I see little merit in applying the market rates available to him as a normative guide.

on how they are shifted. Since low income consumers borrow at higher rates, public investment will be less profitable and of shorter maturity with regressive than with progressive taxes. Since the bulk of public investment is financed by taxes, and since taxes fall largely on consumption, differentials in the interest rates confronting the consumer (rather than in the yields of displaced investments) are thus moved to the center of the stage.

In summary, the sources of finance do not matter for the case of perfect capital markets with the use of r_p, but they are vitally important once r_s is used and especially if capital markets are imperfect. Since the choice of revenue policy determines whether displacement is in private investment or consumption, the revenue side affects the public investment decision. But revenue policy is taken as given, and is not linked (except via opportunity cost and the discount rate) to the basic task of evaluating the benefit stream. The linkage thus differs altogether from that demanded by a theory of social goods, where both sides of the budget are determined simultaneously, and neither side can be separated from the other.

Allowing for distributional objectives

The addition of distributional considerations provides another instance where multiple targets are arrived at by use of a single instrument.[7] Distributional considerations may be included in the objective function by setting constraints regarding distributional effects, or by aiming at a 'grand efficiency' (Weisbrod, 1968) which assigns value weights to particular distributional results.

It has been suggested that such weights may be derived from past policy, by assuming that past Congressional action, be it in setting income tax rates[8] or in choosing investment projects,[9] did

7. Among those favoring inclusion of distributional objectives are Eckstein (1959, p. 447), Marglin (1962; 1965), Weisbrod (1968) and others.

8. See Mera (1969). To begin with, I have no intuition as to the type of equal sacrifice (absolute, proportional, marginal) which Congress intended to implement. Nor do I know whether one should use actual liabilities (with loopholes) or statutory liabilities (without them). These difficulties arise, quite apart from the basic assumption that the legislative record could be taken to reflect a social welfare function.

9. See Weisbrod (1968, p. 199). If past investment decisions may be assumed to have been correct, why is cost-benefit analysis needed to validate future decisions?

in fact reflect the true social welfare function. These techniques do not seem convincing to me, and I would prefer an explicit assignment of weights, based on deviation of income from the norm set by the poverty line, or some such concept. Let the Administration, through the Bureau of the Budget, announce its scale of weights, and require all Departments to use that scale. This, however, is not my main concern. Rather, it is with the very inclusion of such weights into the objective function for the particular investment, as against considering a policy package which combined various instruments to secure various targets.

Consider these two situations: in case I the choice is between building a park in location A or B, where A is a mountain top and B is a swamp, but the potential customers in A will be rich while those in B will be poor; and in case II the choice is between building a shipyard in D or E, where D is Norfolk and E (to give an extreme illustration) is West Virginia. The cost will be lower in D but the income of potentially employed workers is lower in E. The objective function without redistributional weights calls for A and D; but with such weights B and E may win.

As I see it, the efficient choice is A and D, supplemented by the necessary distributional adjustment through a tax-transfer mechanism from A or D to B or E. This is simply another aspect of what I consider to be the pragmatic case for the separation of allocation and distribution objectives. However, certain qualifications are in order.

1. The political situation may be such that, for reasons of political strategy, the distributional objective can be 'put over' via investment in B and E, but not via a tax-transfer mechanism. In this case, the *political* economist may favor B and E; though the solution is second best in the absence of political constraints, he may consider it the best available measure to implement his views.[10]

2. The community may prefer to redistribute by providing income in kind (the case for B) or by giving employment (the case

10. The political case for including distributional objectives because policy constraints prohibit direct distributional adjustments need be distinguished from the quite different analytical proposition that in Samuelson's model allocation and distribution issues are inherently inseparable.

for E) as against cash support. The employment choice in particular may make good sense; but the social advantage of such decisions should then be specified and measured against its opportunity cost, be it the inferior park in case B or the higher cost in E.

3. In addition, and as a more technical objection, it has been suggested by Marglin that the excess burden involved in the redistribution process must be allowed for if equivalent policy packages (investment in B and E, or investment in A and D plus redistribution to B and E) are to be compared. This is a valid point, since by definition, distributional adjustments cannot be made through lump sum taxes and lump sum transfers. They must, by their very nature, be related to income, thus posing an excess burden problem. But it goes too far to conclude that, therefore, inclusion of distributional objectives becomes a 'matter of judgement' (Marglin, 1965, p. 21). The question is how heavy the excess burden will be.

If the investment is made in D, let the cost be C_D, and if it is made in E, let it be $C_E = (1+a)C_D$. If e is the excess burden as per cent of the tax dollar, the total cost in D equals $(1+e)C_D$ and the total cost in E equals $(1+e)(1+a)C_D$. But investment in D requires additional transfer payments in E, equal to $(1+a)C_D$, and corresponding taxation in D. Both these involve an excess burden, so that the total cost $\hat{C}$ for investment in D becomes

$$\hat{C}_D = (1+e)C_D + 2e(1+a)C_D,$$

while that in E equals

$$\hat{C}_E = (1+e)(1+a)C_D.$$

There is thus a case for construction in E if $\hat{C}_E < \hat{C}_D$, that is if $a < 2e/(1-e)$. If we set e equal to, say, 2 per cent,[11] we obtain $a < 0.041$ as the condition for investment in E. It would seem that the excess burden factor can offset relatively minor cost differentials only. Even if extreme cases, such as our shipyard example, were discarded, a will typically be substantially larger, so that a strong case remains for a multiple instrument approach.

11. Arnold C. Harberger's estimate for the excess burden of capital taxes is about 3 per cent of yield (Harberger, 1966) while for the income tax the estimate is about 2 per cent (Harberger, 1964).

Finally, if distributional effects of expenditures are included in the objective function, this would seem to call for a similar inclusion of the distributional effects of the financing mechanism (Freeman, 1967). This may be bypassed by ranking alternative public investments, while holding the source of finance constant, so that the distributional effects on the revenue side are the same. But they should be included in the function in the more general case where there is no budget constraint, and the scope of the public investment is to be determined.

In this case, revenue policy enters cost-benefit analysis not only via its bearing on opportunity cost and the rate of discount, but also through the distributional changes to which it gives rise. Moreover, revenue choice may be made a policy variable. Thereby, the approach becomes somewhat similar to the Pigovian welfare model, except that policy weights are substituted for direct utility comparisons of disposable income. However, the basic weakness of the Pigovian model is also retained. The tax and expenditure sides of the budget continue to be determined independently, and unrelated to the basic problem of benefit evaluation. The essential question of how to value final social goods – the essence of my 'allocation branch' problem – remains outside the system. Although the distribution function is included, it is permitted to enter into the allocation choice, rather than (as I think it should be) handled through a separate adjustment.

In concluding, let me note again that I do not wish to deprecate the practical value of cost-benefit analysis. Much is gained if a comprehensive assessment of project costs is made, accepting the existing policy constraints, and if benefits are measured for inter-mediate goods where this is possible. Having spent much of my time on tax analysis, which is equally partial, it would ill behoove me to deny the same treatment to the expenditure side. At the same time, it is well to note that cost-benefit analysis, even if com-bined with traditional tax analysis, does not provide a substitute theory of public finance. Though opportunity cost is allowed for and the revenue structure enters in peculiar ways, there is no basic linkage between the revenue and expenditure side, and hence no way to solve the valuation of final social goods. More-over, by taking policy constraints for granted, and thus saddling the single instrument of public investment with multiple objectives (mix of public and private investment, correcting the level of total investment, correcting income distribution), the second-best nature of the approach is accepted perhaps too readily, thereby reducing its normative value where the use of multiple instruments (which can also be framed in cost-benefit terms) could give better results.

References

ECKSTEIN, O. (1959), 'A survey of the theory of public expenditure criteria', *Conference on Public Finances: Needs, Sources and Utilization.* National Bureau of Economic Research, New York.

FELDSTEIN, M. S. (1964a), 'Net social benefit calculation and the public investment decision', *Oxford econ. Pap.* (NS), vol. 16, pp. 114–31.

FELDSTEIN, M. S. (1964b), 'The social time preference discount rate in cost-benefit analysis', *Econ. J.*, vol. 74, no. 2, pp. 360–79.

FREEMAN, A. (1967), 'Income distribution and planning for public investment', *Amer. econ. Review*, vol. 57, pp. 495–508.

HARBERGER, A. C. (1964), 'Taxation, resource allocation and welfare', *The Role of Direct and Indirect Taxes in the Federal Revenue System*, conference report of the National Bureau of Economic Research and the Brookings Institution, Princeton University Press.

HARBERGER, A. C. (1966), 'Efficiency effects of taxes on income and capital', in M. Krzyzaniak (ed.), *Effects of Corporation Income Tax*, Wayne State University Press.

HARBERGER, A. C. (1968), 'On the opportunity cost of public borrowing', *Economic Analysis of Public Investment Decisions: Interest Rate Policy and Discounting Analysis*, Hearings Before the Joint Economic Committee, 90th Congress, 2nd Session, USGOP, Washington.

KAIZUKA, K. (1965), 'Public goods and decentralization of production', *Rev. econ. Statis.*, vol. 47, pp. 118–20.

KRUTILLA, J. V., and ECKSTEIN, O. (1958), *Multiple Purpose River Development*, Johns Hopkins Press.

LERNER, A. P. (1944), *The Economics of Control*, Macmillan.

MACK, R. P., and MYERS, S. (1965), 'Outdoor recreation', in R. F. Dorfman (ed.), *Measuring Benefits of Government Investments*, Brookings Institution.

MARGLIN, S. A. (1962), 'Objectives of water-resource development: a general statement', in A. Maass *et al.*, *Design of Water Resource Systems*, Harvard University Press.

MARGLIN, S. A. (1963a), 'The opportunity costs of public investment', *Quart. J. Econ.*, vol. 77, pp. 274–89.

MARGLIN, S. A. (1963b), 'The social rate of discount and the optimal rate of investment', *Quart. J. Econ.*, vol. 77, pp. 95–111.

MARGLIN, S. A. (1965), *Public Investment Criteria*, MIT Press.

MERA, K. (1969), 'Experimental determination of relative marginal utilities', *Quart. J. Econs*, vol. 83, pp. 464–77.

MUSGRAVE, R. A. (1969), 'Provision for social goods', in J. Margolis and M. V. Posner (eds), *Analysis of the Public Economy*.

PEACOCK, A., and MUSGRAVE, R. A. (eds) (1958), *Classics in the Theory of Public Finance*, Macmillan.

PIGOU, A. C. (1924), *The Economics of Welfare*, Macmillan.

PIGOU, A. C. (1928), *A Study in Public Finance*, Macmillan.

PREST, A. R., and TURVEY, R. (1965), 'Cost-benefit analysis: a survey', *Econ. J.*, vol. 75, pp. 683–735.

SAMUELSON, P. A. (1954), 'The pure theory of public expenditure', *Rev. Econ. Statist.*, vol. 36, pp. 387–9.

SAMUELSON, P. A. (1969), 'Pure theory of public expenditures and taxation', in J. Margolis and M. V. Posner (eds), *Analysis of the Public Economy*.

WEISBROD, B. A. (1968), 'Income redistribution effects and benefit-cost analysis', in S. B. Chase, Jr (ed.), *Problems in Public Expenditure Analysis*, Brookings Institution.

Part Two
Measuring Costs and Benefits
When They Occur

The first hurdle in cost-benefit analysis involves finding a set of
prices by which to compare costs and benefits at the time
when they occur. McKean, a pioneer in cost-benefit analysis,
discusses the main problems in finding appropriate 'shadow'
prices and is rather pessimistic about the possibility of
achieving great precision. Sen, reviewing some recent
controversies in shadow pricing, concludes that the issue is
almost always about which constraints the decision-maker
should take as given. Thus, where Little and Mirrlees in their
famous *Manual of Industrial Project Analysis* advocate the use
of world prices in project appraisal, Sen argues that, even if
free trade is the optimal policy, projects should not be planned
as if tariffs and quotas did not exist, unless the government is
going to abolish them. Likewise, where savings are constrained
at a sub-optimal level, Sen shows how this affects the shadow
wage of labour.

There follow three papers on the shadow pricing of
particular items. Harrison and Quarmby survey the work that
has been done on the valuation of travel time – a good
example of how consumers' values of non-market items can
be inferred from their behaviour. Mansfield uses the 'Clawson
method' to measure the consumers' surplus benefit obtained
from the recreational use of the English Lake District National
Park. Finally, Mishan tackles the highly controversial topic of
the value of life.

3 R. N. McKean

The Use of Shadow Prices

Excerpt from R. N. McKean, 'The use of shadow prices', in S. B. Chase (ed.), *Problems in Public Expenditure Analysis*, The Brookings Institution, 1968, pp. 33–52.

In any industry it is possible to substitute some of one input for amounts of others in order to produce particular outputs. H_2, S, and O_4 go together in fixed proportions to produce sulphuric acid, yet sulphur can be substituted for oxygen in limited amounts if a firm reallocates its effort, being less careful in caring for inventories of sulphur and more careful in preventing 'waste' of oxygen. Also it is possible for consumers to substitute one product for others in attaining a given level of satisfaction. Even Robinson Crusoe had to reckon, either explicitly or implicitly, with such substitutions. The marginal exchange ratios or rates of substitution among items – inputs to either production or consumption – can be regarded as ratios of prices.

When prices are explicitly used to exchange items freely, they are called market prices. If gasoline is thirty cents per gallon and kerosene is ten cents per gallon, these prices tell one that a gallon of gasoline can be obtained by sacrificing three gallons of kerosene. When the prices are *implicit* in exchanges that should be made to maximize a particular objective function (or to minimize a cost function), they are called 'shadow prices'.[1] Such exchange relationships emerge from the shadows if one minimizes the cost

1. An excellent standard treatment of the concept is in Dorfman, Samuelson and Solow (1958), various pages. For a clear elementary presentation of the idea (although the term 'shadow price' is not used), see Alchian and Allen (1967, pp. 165–74).

of providing a specified number of nutrients in a daily diet. A sequence or family of shadow prices emerges if one traces out a combined production-possibility schedule (maximum Y for each amount of X to be produced) from individual production-possibility sets. Such a sequence also emerges when one derives a production-possibility schedule in terms of values rather than physical commodities – *if* one adopts a particular value structure or preference function (for example, if he accepts the particular value structure that results from a voluntary exchange process).

Such exchange ratios lurk in the shadows under communism just as much as under capitalism. Like death and taxes, they are always with us. Note that the appropriate shadow prices depend upon the function one wishes to maximize. Remember, too, that there is no preference function that is inherently correct in decisions affecting several persons. One person can have a utility function that is unambiguously correct *for him*. Three persons may conceivably agree upon every choice, or they can agree to abide by the results of majority rule or of free markets in a specified framework or of delegation of all authority to one of the three persons. If one dissents, however, he may suffer in silence, attempt to persuade the others, or fight – but there is no 'right' choice or ultimately correct group preference function to be maximized.

This can be seen clearly if one visualizes himself and two others choosing a movie to be seen by all three together (or deciding anything else that affects all three). If there is disagreement, what should be the criterion: maximize the utility of one individual? Maximize the utility of one subject to constraints on the other utilities? Abide by majority rule? Avoid violence? Maximize aggregate utility (if individual utilities could be measured)? Or accept the results of voluntary exchange (which enables each person to maximize his utility as long as he does not reduce anyone else's utility)? Logic does not compel one to prefer any of these outcomes – there is no test of the fundamentally correct course of action. And, accordingly, there is no unique set of shadow prices that is the correct one.

Government expenditures are group decisions – that is, choices that affect many persons. This is not to say there is such an entity as a group that makes decisions. Choices are made by individuals

– in government, by individual senators, congressmen, officials, employees, organization members, voters, and so on. But each person, in taking his stand, takes into account the wishes expressed or sensed, the rewards offered, and the penalties threatened by others. Thus individuals make decisions, yet those choices are by no means independent of other persons' views. Similarly, in a bowl of marbles, individual marbles rather than groups take action, but the action taken by each depends upon the positions and actions of the others.

Choices about government expenditures, then, are 'group choices' for which (as noted above) there is no ultimately correct preference function – choices whose preferredness cannot be subjected to any *ultimate* test. A corollary of the proposition that group choices cannot be subjected to any ultimate test is that there is no uniquely correct set of prices or tradeoff ratios. If I am dictator, one set of tradeoffs is appropriate. If you are dictator, a different set is correct. If we agree to abide by the results of majority rule, whatever preference function (or family of functions) this implies – if it could be identified – would call for another set of exchange ratios. If we agree to accept the results of voluntary exchange starting with a given wealth distribution, still another set of shadow prices becomes correct. Actually, any government is guided by a complex mixture of rules, constraints, and discretionary authority. There is always an inherent uncertainty about the preferences implied by a collective decision-making process, about the preferences of any subaudience to which an analysis might be directed, about the constraints that should be taken as given and those that should be regarded as negotiable, about the technological facts and substitution-possibilities, and so on. In the face of such uncertainties, one has an even murkier perception of the values that should be attached to alternative outcomes and of the tradeoffs that are appropriate.

Whatever preference surfaces and shadow prices are used, it should be kept in mind that prices play a pervasive role in economic analyses of federal expenditure programmes. Their general function, as mentioned earlier, is to provide appropriate substitution ratios enabling an economy to achieve efficiency, but prices perform this function at all stages of analysis – not merely in whatever final exhibits are presented to higher officials. When benefit-cost analyses are made available to Congress, for example, they usually contain estimates of costs and gains for one design of the Hungry Horse project, one design of a cross-Florida canal, one or perhaps two proposals for research and development (R & D) on oil shale, one or at most a few alternative missile forces. The estimates resulting from the prices embedded in these analyses are supposed to help one decide whether or not to go further in substituting missiles for aircraft, R & D on oil shale for R & D on coal, irrigation projects for canal facilities.

In earlier stages of the analyses, however, alternative designs for each proposal are considered. In these earlier stages, prices are supposed to reveal appropriate substitution ratios among cement and gravel, labor and earthmoving equipment, alternative processes for extracting fuel from oil shale, manpower and check-out equipment in missile systems, warhead size and guidance mechanisms, and so on. The substitution possibilities at these early stages are extremely important, for efficient choices are not reached by comparing well-designed canal proposals with stupidly designed irrigation proposals or well-designed missile forces with stupidly designed aircraft systems. In short, the role of prices is to serve as appropriate substitution ratios among inputs, intermediate outputs, and end-items in the whole sequence of choices – designing alternative systems, redesigning the alternatives, and comparing the alternatives in the narrower menu of proposals that is finally presented to higher authorities.

Pareto optimality and limitations of market prices

Let us assume initially that by unanimous agreement government is to seek 'Pareto optimality' or, as it is often referred to, 'economic efficiency' – that is, the results that would obtain if each person were made as well off as possible, as *he* perceives *his* well-being, without making anyone else worse off, as *he* sees *his* well-being.[2] There is, of course, a whole family of Pareto-optimal points, one for each initial distribution of wealth. Let us assume

2. See Koopmans (1957, pp. 41–66) or Dorfman, Samuelson and Solow (1958, pp. 390–416). To achieve Pareto optimality, many conditions have to be fulfilled, but the following statement may clarify the general notion: a voluntary exchange between two persons which affects no other person leads the economy 'closer to' Pareto optimality, for it makes one or both

that the government seeks the particular subset of efficient points implied by the distribution of wealth as it will be affected by the going tax structure and the expenditure choices. (This is still somewhat ambiguous, for even different ways of building a dam will lead to slightly different wealth distributions and therefore efficient points. Moreover, the implications of uncertainty are being neglected. But it will be helpful to look at this vastly over-simplified case.)

It should be repeated that there is nothing sacrosanct about Pareto optimality. There is nothing illogical about my not wanting individual X to maximize his utility as *he* sees it. Indeed, if we are candid, economic efficiency in this sense is no one's first choice, for each of us would prefer to distribute wealth, encourage the use of some products, and discourage the consumption of others, according to his own fancy.

But, having made the assumption that the government seeks Pareto optimality, one can make some observations about ideal price ratios. In effect it will be assumed *initially* that the government is a huge industry catering to consumers, accepting consumers' valuations, and trying to attain economic efficiency in the usual sense.[3] (Naturally, if government is conceived of as a separate economy like that of another planet, everything changes.)

First, a few words about market prices. There are enough things wrong with observed prices to make one's hair stand on end. Most of the time they are defective representations of the appropriate substitution ratios. The only good thing one can say about market prices is that they are usually better than the alternatives – prices that are derived rather than observed. The reason is that markets provide an enormous amount of information at a relatively low cost, even though the information is still short of being

---

of the individuals better off, in terms of their individual preferences, without making anyone worse off.

3. The difficulties associated with public goods – those for which it is costly to exclude nonpayers so as to get information about consumers' subjective values – will be considered in connection with externalities and goods for which there are no markets. As will be seen later, the choice of prices to be used in such cases depends upon making judgements about, and weighing, the gains from having better information against the costs of acquiring it.

perfect.[4] This information has some relevance as long as one's preference function gives some weight to the desirability of having voluntary exchange. Markets put millions of persons into the business of providing information about substitution possibilities. Markets induce millions of people to adjust their purchases and sales to prices, so that those prices reflect (approximately) what an extra unit would be worth to all users. Because of market imperfections, there are no doubt more appropriate exchange ratios in principle, but in most cases it would be extremely expensive to acquire the improved information. Therefore, as the shortcomings of market prices and the possibilities of deriving shadow prices are discussed, one thing should be kept in mind: the existence of defects in market prices does not mean that some derived price or alternative procedure would automatically be better. This point will come up again later on. For the moment, let us simply stress that one should not disregard the costs of seeking improved substitution ratios.

Imperfect markets

Market prices may fail to reflect appropriate substitution ratios for several reasons that are discussed in the literature on the theory of second-best.[5] Sometimes it is especially difficult to perceive what is second-best – the best one can do, given various constraints. For example, it is obvious that market imperfections alone cause prices to deviate from marginal cost. Suppose the price of A is higher than marginal cost, where marginal cost means the market value of resources used to produce A.[6] To reflect appropriate substitution ratios, should the price of B to consumers also be higher? The answer is yes, if one could control those prices (and there were no other commodities and no other distortions and the controls had no side effects).

But should a benefit-cost analyst, who cannot control market prices, use a higher-than-marginal-cost price for B or a lower-than-observed price for A, in the analysis of policies producing

4. See later discussion based on the work of Harold Demsetz. In fact, my indebtedness to Demsetz is too pervasive for me to insert acknowledgements at many of the places where they would be appropriate.

5. This topic was prompted by Lipsey and Lancaster (1956–7).

6. Rather than the utility foregone by giving up a unit of A.

or employing A and B? It depends. If the government project would produce or consume marginal units of A without affecting the monopolist's output of A, the marginal units would be provided to or taken from consumers of A. The marginal value produced, and the marginal cost in the sense of the value sacrificed by pulling a unit of A from consumers, would be measured by the observed price of A. The same statements would be true for extra units of B produced or employed by a government project. If, however, the project's production of A simply reduced the monopolist's output, he would release resources, and the project's output would really be the alternative value that these resources could produce, that is, the marginal cost in the sense of the market prices of the resources released. Or, if the project's purchase of A simply increased the monopolist's output, he would hire resources, and the sacrifice to the economy would be their alternative products, that is, the marginal cost of the inputs. In these circumstances, to use the observed prices of A and B would distort the true substitution ratios.

In fact, a project's production of A would in part increase the amount of A consumed and in part release resources to other uses; and a project's consumption of A would deprive consumers of some units but to some extent induce the monopolist to expand his output. Thus to accept the observed prices for a benefit-cost analysis (prepared with economic efficiency as a criterion) would not be completely correct. If one considers other situations, there are similar difficulties in choosing correct substitution ratios. If the government project would yield or employ inputs to the production of A and B, or an input used by numerous monopolists with diverse ratios of output-prices to marginal costs, the observed prices of those inputs would certainly not be fully appropriate in benefit-cost analyses.

Other constraints on resource use

If unions restrict entry so that the price of electricians' services is above its value in competitive equilibrium – if entry into the field of medicine is hampered so that the value of doctors' services is higher than it would be with free entry – should lower prices for these services be employed in benefit-cost analyses? (Some government programmes might involve producing medical services as outputs, and others might involve using them as inputs. In either instance, the matter of prices or substitution ratios would come up.) The answer is no – if the government's action would make more of these services or less of these services available to consumers. If that were true, the marginal evaluations of consumers should be used. It does not matter whether it is God or man that imposes the restriction on supplies. What matters is whether or not the restriction is expected to be binding. Needless to say, if the restriction is about to be ended, then consumers' marginal evaluations – marginal cost in the sense of value sacrificed by using another unit – will go down, affecting the substitution ratios that will be appropriate thereafter.

The same argument applies to restrictions on imports, as in the case of petroleum products, lead or zinc. What is sacrificed by employing units of these ingredients in a project and what is gained by producing extra units in some program? If import quotas are to continue unchanged, the incremental values under discussion are the users' marginal evaluations in the going circumstances. Whether or not the quotas stem from acceptable reasons – for example, values consciously attached to self-sufficiency – is irrelevant. The relevant issue is whether the restrictions are to persist. Of course, if a change in the quota situation is expected, or if the project itself would somehow bring about a change, then the relevant prices would be something else. (If the discussants of a proposed project wished to call attention to quotas they disapproved, they might want to use adjusted prices for tactical reasons. But that is a use of benefit-cost analysis that is off-limits in this paper.)

Price-support programs

Where subsidies exist for the production of certain items, similar arguments apply – as long as the output is offered for sale, and consumers are free to adjust at the margins. Again, whether God or man's mistaken calculations expand supplies, the value of the marginal unit (as long as we seek Pareto optimality) is what consumers are willing to pay for it. The subsidies may exist because a group of persons who receive side-benefits join forces and contract to subsidize an industry. The subsidies may exist because a majority of voters believe there are spillover benefits and therefore condone government subsidies. Or the subsidies may exist because producers' pleas are such a nuisance that voters would rather subsidize than resist. The underlying reason is immaterial – what matters is whether the subsidies are expected to persist.

Price-support programmes, however, introduce a more complicated issue, for the subsidy may take the form of purchasing the output at a stated price and then (in effect) throwing part of it away. In this circumstance, what is the sacrifice entailed by consuming a unit in building a project or the value obtained by producing a unit as the output of a project?

Suppose consumption of extra units to build a project caused increased production, depriving consumers of alternative products. The cost of the extra units would be the cost of the resources used. If, however, the extra units to build a project came from storage units that would otherwise be destroyed, they would cost nothing. The cost of units that would partly have been destroyed would entail a cost somewhere between the market price and zero.

What about a project that produced instead of consumed units of this product? The value of its extra units produced would be zero if they were simply going into storage to decay, somewhere between zero and the market price if they were entering storage to deteriorate partially. I suppose one could argue that here, too, voters condone the price-support program because they like to handle these products in this fashion – just as a consumer might buy rock-and-roll records because he enjoyed smashing them – and that the observed price is therefore still the appropriate one to enter into substitution ratios.[7] But in this instance my personal judgement is that an adjusted price could measure the marginal value better than the observed price.

Anticipated changes in supply and demand conditions

Perhaps it should go without saying that observed prices are inappropriate if a benefit-cost analysis pertains to the coming decade and price-ratios are expected to change in a predictable manner next month. To get the most from resources (with a given

7. If people are attaching a value to another type of 'product' – wealth distribution *through this particular mechanism* – one could also regard these substitution ratios as being appropriate.

value system) one should use the substitution ratios that are appropriate at the time the substitutions are to be made. One should not make choices today in accordance with circumstances in 1850 any more than he should make choices in the United States on the basis of substitution ratios on Mars. This, too, turns out to depend on the costs of information and therefore to call for heroic judgements. Markets generate a great deal of information about current substitution ratios and, through future markets, some probabilistic information about a few substitution ratios several months hence. But the cost-per-unit of high quality information about substitution ratios five years from now is usually like the per-unit cost of Holy Grails: it is very high. Supply-and-demand conditions for many items – such as water, the rare earths, recreational facilities, particular skills and automation equipment – are likely to change drastically in the years ahead. But how far to go in adjusting current prices for purposes of evaluating federal programs will depend on judgements about the costs and gains from seeking the improved information.

A special case is the situation in which the government's program is itself expected to alter prices. A program might, for example, use such a lump of fissionable material, or produce such a lump of power, or yield such a large technological advance that it significantly affected the prices of the items involved. In deciding whether to substitute the programme for other activities, one should include as benefits whatever people are willing to pay for those lumps, whether large or small. (In the examples mentioned, the benefits would include the area under the relevant portion of the demand curve for power, and the costs would include the area under the relevant part of the marginal-cost curve for fissionable material.) In deciding whether to make subsequent substitutions among fissionable materials, power and other items, the new prices would indicate their new marginal evaluations. Again, of course, information costs are the key to decisions about the prices to be put into benefit-cost analyses.

Unemployed resources

Observed prices are also misleading when at the going price part of a resource is involuntarily unemployed. There is no need to go into the theory of unemployment here; inputs are sometimes idle yet would be employed if aggregate demand ceased falling or rose. In such circumstances the sacrifice entailed by using those inputs is not reflected by observed prices and may be virtually zero in the case of manpower. Should the benefit-cost analyst insert an adjusted or shadow price wherever a government project would employ such inputs?

The answer depends on the real-world situation *at the time the input would be used*. Unemployment today does not necessarily imply unemployment two years from now when the project would be completed. It does not strike me as reasonable, particularly in this latter half of the twentieth century, to assume that mass unemployment will persist year after year.[8] If a depression exists and a project would begin shortly, it might be appropriate to charge a zero price for manpower during the first year of the project, though as a general rule comparisons of alternative proposals are likely to be more accurate if ordinary levels of employment are assumed. In the evaluation of some projects, such as training programs for new or underprivileged immigrants, it may be appropriate even during prosperity to assume a low level of employment. Again, unfortunately, the answer will be different for different analyses; these principles provide general guidelines but not specific guidance.

External effects

Another phenomenon that casts doubt on the use of observed market prices is the existence of external effects. If an action uses up valuable resources but the owner's voluntary consent is purchased, the sacrifice is 'internalized'.[9] If an action uses valuable resources, but no one's consent is purchased, the sacrifices caused by the action will not be fully recognized; there is an external cost. Similarly, if a benefit is produced but no price is charged for it, the benefit will not be fully recognized; there is an external gain.

8. 'Moderate' amounts of unemployment, although it may sound callous to say so, are often more valuable than alternative uses of the resources. The 'idle' are often seeking information that has more value, both to them and in terms of Pareto optimality, than would the jobs at hand. And the fact of unemployment sometimes produces information of value – that a location or occupation should have fewer resources devoted to it.

9. Not only contracts and markets, but also the possibility of lawsuits for damages, can internalize what would otherwise be externalities.

Why should such things happen? Sometimes they happen because of the legal framework – for example, ocean fishing rights are not assigned to anyone in particular. Sometimes they happen because the contracting costs would be too high in relation to the gains [10] – for example, purchasing the consent of householders who do not like throwaway papers or handbills thrown on their lawns. [11] In many instances externalities persist because the effects have 'public-good' (or 'public-bad') characteristics. That is, it is expensive to exclude nonpayers from reaping benefits so that a price of admission could be charged – or, in the case of the public 'bad', expensive to exclude those whose consent to suffer costs is not purchased. If someone eats an apple, others are automatically (that is, costlessly) excluded from eating the apple. If someone listens to a concert, however, others can be excluded so as to charge a price of admission only if special barriers are erected. If a glue factory emits noxious odours, persons whose air-space is being used without purchasing their consent cannot be excluded except at enormous cost. Sometimes it turns out to be economical to erect the barriers and charge admission, but often the costs of excluding those who do not enter the agreement and of policing it are too high. In most instances, mixtures of exclusion cost and contracting cost keep effects from being internalized.

Now, to achieve Pareto optimality, external effects should be taken into account – whenever the gains from doing so exceed the costs. When markets are economical – such as the sale of garbage to pig-farmers – the transactions provide information [12] about what consumers are willing to pay for the item and what the costs or alternative gains are – and simultaneously the markets eliminate the externality. When markets are uneconomical, questions are left up in the air because the worth of external benefits and the size of external costs are usually uncertain, precise determination of these magnitudes being infinitely expensive (that is, impossible) and improvements in the quality of estimates being of uncertain

10. See Demsetz (1964).

11. There is no public-good characteristic, or cost of exclusion, involved here. Only contracting costs would be entailed.

12. For many of the ideas here I am especially indebted to Armen A. Alchian and Harold Demsetz for discussions of the costs of acquiring information. The fundamental issues are discussed by Demsetz in 'Some aspects of property rights' (1966).

value. Government may or may not decide that intervention would be worthwhile.

But our problem here is not whether to intervene because of externalities; it is whether, in choosing among alternative projects or actions, to modify observed prices of inputs and outputs so as to allow for externalities. In this situation officials are not setting up markets; they are not concerned with the costs of exclusion and contracting. They are simply concerned with whether to use one set of prices or another set of prices in preparing or interpreting a benefit-cost analysis – that is, in evaluating alternative actions. Real-life government officials will decide on the basis of their own preference functions and the gains and costs they feel. The result will rarely be an all-out effort to achieve Pareto optimality.

But in terms of Pareto optimality what should be done? What are the costs of taking externalities into account in choosing among irrigation projects or training programs? The costs seem to be the opportunities foregone in preparing and refining estimates. And the gains, it should be stressed, should allow for uncertainty about the estimates. They may be of such low quality as to have a negative value. (Misleading estimates are not hard to imagine; we do not know whether certain prison or training or recreational facilities increase or reduce juvenile delinquency.)

Suppose vaccinations were one of the outputs of a government project. The observed price would hardly reflect the full incremental value, since it would not include the value of each vaccination to all other citizens. (As noted before, it would be too costly for private markets to exclude those who would not pay for the external benefit and too expensive also to contract for the sale of benefits that would be tiny per transaction from millions of vaccinated persons to millions of beneficiaries.) Should the benefit-cost analyst adjust the free-market valuation to allow for external impacts? It depends upon what it would cost to get information of various qualities and therefore information having various values. If a government official judges that an estimate worth more than the cost can be prepared, he should undertake to allow for the external effects. In the case of vaccinations, many of us judge that it would be economical to allow for the external benefit and estimate a shadow price. (A government agency should presumably regard spillover costs as negative gains, for from that agency's standpoint they would not be resources foregone but negative outputs.) But note that cases must be considered on an ad hoc basis, for the decision rests on judgements about the worth of unknown bits of information and the costs of a sequence of probes for information. Note, too, that since subjective judgements must be made, legitimate disagreement may ensue.

To repeat, the choice regarding derived or adjusted prices seems to hinge on the costs and value of extra information about external effects. Officials must decide how far to go in estimating what people would pay for incremental smog-control or noise-abatement, and what the derived value of smog- or noise-creating products should therefore be. Such decisions depend upon the costs and worth of alternative degrees of refinement in preparing the estimates. (I see no way to compare these costs and worths except on the basis of a personal judgement followed by a sequence of information searches and more personal judgements. Yet these are judgements that we cannot sidestep.) This is not a very helpful conclusion. It gives no operational guidance. Yet in my view it is better to offer a correct but general statement about the way to look at the choices than to offer specific guidance that is incorrect.

It may appear that there is another category of products for which we need shadow prices – products produced by government that are not sold through markets. Clearly government programs can produce many items of value – such as defense capabilities, the saving of lives, improvements in race relations, better maintenance of law and order, a greater degree of equity, noise-abatement and court decisions – for which there are no markets. These items are of value, for many people are willing to pay for increments in output. There are no markets, for it is evidently uneconomic to define rights to the products, police the rights set-up, exclude nonpayers (in some instances), transfer these rights, and so on. Moreover, government programs can produce many items of negative value – such as loss of life, impairments of race relations, deterioration of law and order, inequities, noise, and bad court procedures and decisions – for which there are no markets. Throughout the process of producing these positive and negative values, substitution possibilities are pervasive. Since there are no markets, what about shadow prices?

Actually, the matter has already been discussed. These impacts are in reality our earlier acquaintance: externalities. If the Los Angeles government bought permission from householders to use their sound-space by banging trash cans together early in the morning, it would be like their purchase of the oil company's permission to use the fuel in the vehicles. There would be no externality. Or, if householders paid extra to have the trash collected very quietly, there would be a different distribution of wealth but again no externality. But a market for this noise-abatement is too expensive to be worth operating, and the noise is inflicted without anyone having the option of agreeing to a fee.

Similarly, if government could economically exclude non-payers and sell the spillover benefits from vaccination, they would no longer be spillovers, for the result would be like selling any other product. People would adjust to their best positions in the light of all costs and gains. No benefits would be created that people did not voluntarily buy. Again such marketing arrangements would be too costly, and the economy is left with externalities. Hence, 'goods' or 'bads' for which there are no markets turn out to be externalities. As noted earlier, whether or not to impute shadow prices, and how far to go in refining estimates of such prices, depends upon heroic judgements about the value and cost of acquiring such information. In my view, the analyst and government should at least take the almost costless step of describing the principal external effects. In some instances it is worthwhile to make specific estimates and in effect to introduce shadow prices showing the tradeoffs between, say, vaccinations and noise abatement. In other instances, the cost of producing estimates and shadow prices may exceed their value (in view of their quality).

Many persons may feel that this discussion grossly exaggerates the cost of information, for they visualize correctly that a hundred thousand dollars would buy a lot of numbers. But cost depends on the quality of the output that is being considered. Even for an output like Minuteman squadrons, it would cost little to provide some sort of shadow prices, yet it might be infinitely costly to prepare appropriate ones. Similarly it would not cost much for me to build 'a' chair or to write 'a' short story; yet it would cost a great deal for me to build a good chair, and the cost of my writing a Somerset Maugham story would probably be infinite.

As stressed repeatedly, what to do depends upon one's judgements about the cost and worth of the alternative results.

Market prices and nonmarket values

In reality, as mentioned earlier, government officials attach values to many items that are customarily omitted from the individual's list of products. For example, officials may attach greater value to additional economic growth than is implied by individual choices. They may attach high values to self-sufficiency, cohesiveness or discipline, or certain redistributions of wealth. Such values may be sanctioned by a majority of the voters. In addition, even with democratic procedures, officials end up with some discretionary authority, and they are likely to introduce additional aims that may or may not be condoned by controlling coalitions of voters. For instance, through the actions of numerous officials, a value may be attached to having relatives on the payroll, carrying out pet schemes, subsidizing particular religions, developing Alaska, controlling certain prices, or having more personal convenience.

There is nothing wrong or right about these values from the economist's point of view, any more than there is anything wrong or right about a taste for oranges or castor oil. In some instances one may regard these various preferences as introducing constraints that prevent the attainment of the usual production-possibility boundary (or alter the particular point that is attained). Or one can view them as constraints that depart from consumers' evaluations and alter the boundary. In that case one has to redraw the boundary to allow for these constraints. The more general way of thinking about the matter is this: these values may simply introduce other items that can be produced by sacrificing alternative outputs, items that are not usually considered when discussing the Pareto-optimal boundary, but items that need be no more foolish than any other element in individuals' utility functions.

There are complications, of course. For one thing, such valuations are thrust upon large blocs of persons without the fine discrimination and voluntarism that markets permit. If the majority or a dictatorial clique sets a high value on economic growth, it is different from allowing each individual to buy $5, or $1000 or $0 worth of economic growth. Since compulsion for some individuals is involved, it is a far cry from Pareto optimality in the usual sense. But the revised set of values and constraints does imply some sort of production-possibility boundary.

For another complication, the process may result in inconsistent valuations. One part of the government may make choices implying that positive values are attached to agricultural products, while another may make choices implying that zero or negative prices are attached to them. Also, the introduction of these values at different levels and in different portions of government may sometimes imply 'nontransitivity' – for example, a preference for A over B, and for B over C, yet for C over A.

The most fundamental complication is the absence of markets for the items concerned. There are no explicit bids to buy and offers to sell units of economic growth, national self-sufficiency, placements of relatives on the payroll, the development of Alaska, and so on. Government cannot simply raise its bids for such items and find that market prices adjust so as to reflect these valuations. Since there are no markets for these items, the observed prices for various inputs do not necessarily reflect the values attached to these final items. In principle, therefore, many observed prices would be incorrect in analyses intended to help decision makers maximize whatever modified preference function is implied. If governing officials in a nation, underdeveloped or otherwise, attach a high value to economic growth, their judgement presumably implies that the price of steel facilities, one type of investment, should rise relative to the price of bowling alleys, another type of investment. Similarly the appropriate exchange ratios among investments shift about in a consumer-oriented economy if the demand for airline service increases relative to the demand for railway service. But in the mixed economy under discussion here, and the kind we live in, observed market prices do not necessarily indicate the appropriate substitution ratios.

Ways of deriving shadow prices

The use of programming techniques to solve maximization problems highlights appropriate trade-offs or substitutions, and for this reason the concept of shadow prices has been developed mainly in connection with linear programming. However, the imputed prices derived through programming techniques are no more appropriate than the assumed preference functions and technological interrelationships that underlie them. Such calculations have turned out to be relatively successful in connection with blending problems for which the objective function and the interrelationships could be specified with confidence and completeness. For entire economies or sectors of economies, however, it is almost impossible to conceive of complete and appropriate preference and production functions. As one might expect, therefore, programming and econometric models do not so far have a good record when used to make predictions.[13] By the same token, the shadow prices generated by such models can hardly be regarded as promising substitution ratios to use in evaluating alternative government actions. Shadow prices from a pretend-economy have a good chance of being no more relevant than shadow prices from the economy on Mars.

Another method of imputing prices is to take over price relationships observed in markets for similar items or in markets for the same items in other countries. For example, in trying to value a public beach or recreational facility, one often resorts to using the prices that people pay for similar beaches or facilities that are operated commercially. A major difficulty in using this approach is determining how similar these items are. A slight difference in location, sand, water currents, popularity with others, adjacent services, and so on, can make a great difference in what individuals are willing to sacrifice for the use of a particular facility. Some products, restaurants and recreational ventures succeed, while others fail because of slight and hard-to-discern differences. The appropriate prices of even close substitutes like butter and oleo may vary considerably. Similarly, for well-known reasons, the correct prices of the same item in different countries may be far apart. For the purpose of exploring a technique, it may be useful to insert a few US prices in computations for an underdeveloped economy, but for evaluating alternative policies seriously, the adoption of prices generated in another economy has severe disadvantages that should be weighed

13. See Carl Christ (1951) (based in part on earlier work of Andrew W. Marshall) and Harold J. Barnett (1954).

against the gains. The hazards of producing misleading evaluations are great indeed.

A third method of deriving what I am calling shadow prices is to determine the prices implied by other governmental choices. In procuring equipment that saves lives, military officials and congressmen are expressing a willingness to spend so much but not more to save a life. Similarly, health policies, safety regulations, and features of highway construction imply a willingness to incur some cost to save a life. Tradeoffs of a less serious nature are implied by most government decisions. The number and type of elevators installed, the number of typists hired, the duplicating services available, the percentage of tax returns checked – all reflect decisions about possible substitutions between one input and other inputs or between one service and other services. When one concludes that government is spending too much on A (buildings) and too little on B (salaries), he is pointing to an implied substitution ratio and is suggesting that the government has failed to stop at the correct ratio. People often object to rules-of-thumb in government agencies (and in universities and other organizations) that prevent appropriate substitutions.

Even these few statements should indicate, however, that these implied price ratios are not necessarily the appropriate ones for the maximization of a particular preference function. First, decisions by different officials imply the assignment of a variety of values to the same item. In the absence of markets, there is no reason to expect the marginal evaluations of one set of decision makers to coincide with the marginal evaluations of others. Individual agencies adjust their rates of purchase of many items, such as the saving-of-lives, to their own marginal valuations.[14] Similarly, if several individuals buy oranges at different prices in separate markets, instead of adjusting their rates of purchase to a single market price, the marginal utility of oranges (to use old-fashioned terminology) will not be the same for these different individuals. Second, even if only one implied value exists within government,

14. If agencies could and would get together and adjust their life-saving policies until the marginal cost of saving lives was the same in all programs, it would be possible to save more lives for the same budget. But the issue in this paper is whether one can regard an implied evaluation by one agency as an appropriate shadow price.

there is no assurance that it is the correct one to use in maximizing some (unspecified) preference function. As noted above, other officials and observers often criticize the tradeoffs embedded in a decision. There is disagreement; and one does not know what preference function should be used, how to specify it, or how appropriate the implied price relationships are.

A final catch-all means of deriving shadow prices is the adjustment of market prices to allow for considerations that are not reflected in those market prices. That is, taking observed prices as the point of departure, one might make adjustments to allow for the estimated effects of externalities, anticipated changes in import restrictions, anticipated changes in domestic restrictions, monopoly elements, anticipated changes in subsidy programs, the effects of price-support activities, and expected changes in supply-and-demand conditions in general. Again, however, the information costs are formidable. The imputed values of externalities are not subject to market tests, changes in supply-and-demand conditions are inherently uncertain, and the impacts of removing restrictions are hard to gauge.

The purpose of this section is not to damn the use of imputed or shadow prices. It is merely to emphasize that using them, like adopting almost any other action, does not amount to enjoying a free lunch. There are costs associated with whatever direction one takes in seeking correct substitution ratios. (A corollary that was mentioned before and treated elsewhere by Demsetz bears repetition: a system of markets is a fantastic information-generating device. It yields information of tremendous value, provided one accepts something like the preference function implied by a voluntaristic society – information that would be extremely expensive to obtain in other ways.)

References

ALCHIAN, A. A., and ALLEN, W. R. (1967), *University Economics*, 2nd edn., Wadsworth Publishing.

BARNETT, H. J. (1954), 'Specific industry output projections', *Long-Range Economic Projection*, Princeton University Press for National Bureau of Economic Research.

CHRIST, C. (1951), 'A test of an econometric model for the United States, 1921–1947', *Conference on Business Cycles*, National Bureau of Economic Research.

DEMSETZ, H. (1964), 'The exchange and enforcement of property rights', *Journal of Law and Economics*, October, pp. 11–26.

DEMSETZ, H. (1966), 'Some aspects of property rights', *Journal of Law and Economics*, October, pp. 61–70.

DORFMAN, R., SAMUELSON, P. A., and SOLOW, R. M. (1958), *Linear Programming and Economic Analysis*, McGraw-Hill.

KOOPMANS, T. C. (1957), *Three Essays on the State of Economic Science*, McGraw-Hill

LIPSEY, R. G., and LANCASTER, K. (1956–7), 'The general theory of second best', *Review of Economic Studies*, vol. 24, pp. 11–32.

4 A. K. Sen

Feasibility Constraints: Foreign Exchange and Shadow Wages

A. K. Sen, 'Control areas and accounting prices: an approach to economic evaluation',[1] *Economic Journal*, vol. 82, 1972, pp. 486–501.

A prerequisite of a theory of planning is an identification of the nature of the State and of the Government. The planner, to whom much of planning theory is addressed, is part of a political machinery and is constrained by a complex structure within which he has to operate. Successful planning requires an understanding of the constraints that in fact hold and clarity about precise areas on which the planners in question can exercise effective control. The limits of a planner's effective control depend on his position *vis-à-vis* the rest of the Government as well as on the nature of the political, social and economic forces operating in the economy. This paper is concerned with an analysis of some aspects of these interrelationships in the specific context of project appraisal and benefit-cost evaluation.

In section I, the problem is posed. In section II, the OECD *Manual of Industrial Project Analysis*, prepared by Professors Little and Mirrlees (1968), is critically examined in the light of the approach outlined in section I. In section III, the approach is illustrated in the specific context of fixing a shadow price of labour in benefit-cost analysis.

1. This is based on a seminar given at Nuffield College, Oxford, in the summer term of 1969–70. For useful discussions I am grateful to Partha Dasgupta, A. Harberger, Ian Little, Stephen Marglin, James Mirrlees and Maurice Scott.

I Spheres of influence and control variables

For any planning agent the act of planning may be viewed as an exercise in maximizing an objective function subject to certain constraints. In the absence of non-convexities it is relatively easy to translate the problem into a framework of shadow prices. Corresponding to the maximizing 'primal' problem one could define a 'dual' problem involving the minimization of a function where there will be one shadow price (acting as a value-weight) corresponding to each constraint in the original problem. All this is straightforward and mechanical and there is not really very much to argue about. The interesting questions arise with the *selection* of the objective function and the constraints.

If $W(x)$ is the objective to be maximized through the selection of choice variables in the form of a vector x subject to a set of m constraints, $F_i(x) \leqslant R_i$, for $i = 1, \ldots, m$, then the dual related to any particular constraint F_i will correspond to the additional amount of maximized W that would be generated by relaxing the constraint by one unit, i.e. by raising R_i by a unit. Thus, the dual p_i corresponding to F_i can be viewed as the marginal impact of R_i on W, the objective, and if R_i is the amount of a given resource then p_i is the marginal contribution of R_i to W (not necessarily corresponding to the marginal product in terms of market evaluation). It may be convenient to view p_i as the shadow price of resource i. Since the value of p_i is essentially dependent on the objective function $W(x)$ and on the other constraints, the shadow price of any resource clearly depends on the values of the planner reflected in the objective function W and on his reading of the economic and other constraints that bind his planning decisions.

Consider now a project evaluator. What does he assume about other agents involved in the operation of the economy, e.g. the private sector (if any), the households and the other government agencies? Presumably, in so far as he can influence the private sector and households directly or indirectly he builds that fact into his description of the exercise, but except for this the operation of the private sector and households will constrain his exercise. He may express this either in the form of specific constraints or in the form of implicit relations embodied in other constraints or even in the objective function. The actual form may not be very important but the inclusion of these elements is, of course, a crucial aspect of realistic planning. In principle, the position outlined above may be fairly widely accepted, though I would argue later that the implications of this position are frequently overlooked.

What about the relation between the project evaluator and other planning agents and how does his role fit in with the rest of the government apparatus? This question has several facets, one of which is the problem of co-ordination, teamwork, decentralization and related issues. This basket of problems has been discussed quite a bit in the literature and will not be pursued here.[2] Another facet is the problem of conflict between the interests of the different government agencies. This is particularly important for a federal country since the relation between the State Governments and the centre may be extremely complex. But even between different agencies of the Central Government there could be considerable conflict of interests, e.g. between the road authorities and the nationalized railways, to take a narrow example, or between the department of revenue and the public enterprises, to take a broader one. Whenever such conflicts are present a question arises about the appropriate assumption regarding other agencies of the Government in the formulation of the planning exercise by any particular agency.

A third facet is the question of the impact not of government policy on the private business sector but of the private business sector on government policy. The control variables are affected by such influences but they are often not affected in a uniform way. For example, a public sector project evaluator may think that certain taxes cannot be imposed because of political opposition, but somewhat similar results could be achieved through variations in the pricing and production policy of the public sector.

In a very broad sense taxes, tariffs, quotas, licences, prices and outputs of the public sector are all control variables for the Government as a whole. But they are each constrained within certain ranges by administrative, political and social considerations. For a project evaluator, therefore, it is important to know

2. I have tried to discuss the relation of this range of issues to the exercise of project evaluation (Sen, 1970).

which variables are within his control and to what extent, and in this respect a feeling of oneness with the totality of the Government may not be very useful. This aspect of the problem has been frequently lost sight of because of the concentration in the planning models on a mythical hero called 'the Planner', and unitarianism is indeed a dominant faith in the theory of economic planning.

II The use of world prices

A distinguishing feature of the Little-Mirrlees *Manual* (henceforth, LMM) is its advocacy of the use of world prices in the evaluation of commodities. For 'traded' goods produced in the economy the evaluation is at the import price (c.i.f.) or the export price (f.o.b.) depending on whether it would potentially replace imports or be available for exports; and a traded good used up is valued at the import price if its source (direct or indirect) is imports and at the export price if it comes from cutting out potential exports. When opportunities of trade are present these values reflect the opportunity costs and benefits. The nontraded goods are also related to trade indirectly since they may be domestically produced by traded goods, and the nontradables involved in their production can be traced further back to tradables. 'Following the chain of production around one must end at commodities that are exported or substituted for imports.'[3]

This is not the place to discuss or evaluate the nuances of the LMM. Problems such as imperfections of international markets are taken into account by replacing import and export prices by corresponding marginal cost and marginal revenue considerations. Externalities are somewhat soft-pedalled partly on the ground that there is 'little chance, anyway, of measuring many of these supposed external economies',[4] and also because a discussion of the main types of externalities generally emphasized makes the authors 'feel that differences in those external effects, which are not in any case allowed for in our type of cost-benefit analysis, will seldom make a significant difference'.[5] These and other considerations may be important in practical decisions but

3. Little and Mirrlees (1968, p. 93).
4. *ibid*, p. 37.
5. *ibid*, p. 219.

I do not want to discuss them here. These problems are essentially factual in nature and can only be resolved by detailed empirical work.

The crucial question lies in deciding on what is to be regarded as a 'traded' good. The LMM proposes two criteria, *viz.* '(a) goods which are actually imported or exported (or very close substitutes are actually imported or exported),' and '(b) goods which would be exported or imported if the country had followed policies which resulted in an optimum industrial development.'[6] It is the second category that relates closely to the question we raised in section I of this paper.

Suppose it appears that project *A* would be a worthwhile investment if a certain raw material *R* needed for it were to be imported but not if *R* were to be manufactured domestically (assuming that *R* is not economically produced in the economy). 'Optimal industrial development' requires that *R* be not manufactured in the economy but be imported. Suppose the project evaluator examining project *A* finds that the country's trade policies are not 'sensible', and *R* would in fact be manufactured, no matter what he does. It does not seem right, in these circumstances, to recommend that project *A* be undertaken on the ground that 'if the countries had followed policies which resulted in an optimal industrial development' then *R* would not in fact have been domestically produced; the question is whether or not *R* will be domestically produced *in fact*.

The question at issue here is the theory of government underlying the planning model of the LMM. Little and Mirrlees explain their approach thus:

Sometimes, our guess about whether a commodity will be imported or not may be almost a value judgement: we think that a sensible government would plan to import some, so we assume that it will do so. Of course, if one of our assumptions required government action in order to be fulfilled, this should be drawn to the attention of the appropriate authorities.[7]

The judgement would readily become a fact if the appropriate authorities would do the 'sensible' thing whenever their attention

6. *ibid*, p. 92.
7. *ibid*, p. 106.

is drawn to such action. There is no logical problem in this approach; the only question is: *Is this a good theory of government action?*

One could doubt that this is a good theory on one of many grounds.[8] Some people may doubt whether governments typically do think sensibly. Often enough, evidences of sensible thinking, if present, would appear to be very well concealed. But more importantly, something more than 'sensible thinking' is involved in all this, and it is necessary to examine the pressures that operate on the government. There would certainly be some interest groups involved, e.g. those who would like to produce good R under the protection of a quota, or an enhanced tariff, or some other restriction. By choosing project A and thus creating a domestic demand for R (or by augmenting the demand that existed earlier) one is opening up this whole range of issues involving protection and domestic production. If the project evaluator thinks that the pressures for domestic production of good R will be successfully crushed by the government agencies responsible for policies on tariff, quota, etc., it will certainly be fair to choose project A. But what if the project evaluator thinks that it is very likely that if project A is chosen then there will be irresistible pressure for domestic production of good R inside the economy? Similarly, what should the project evaluator do if he finds that there already exists a quota restriction on the import of good R so that the additional demand for R will be met by domestic production unless the trade policies are changed, and he does not believe that they will change because of political pressures in favour of the continuation of these policies? It is not a question of *knowing* what is the 'sensible' policy in related fields but of being able to *ensure* that these policies will in fact be chosen. This would depend on one's reading of the nature of the State and of the Government and on one's analysis of the influences that affect government action. And on this should depend the appropriate set of accounting prices for cost-benefit analysis.

It is possible to argue that if one uniform assumption has to be made about the actions to be undertaken by other government agencies, then the LMM assumption is as good as any. It may

8. See also Sen (1969) and Dasgupta (1970). Further, Dasgupta and Stiglitz (1971).

well be better to assume that the actions taken by the other agencies will be all 'sensible' in the sense defined rather than be 'distorted' in a uniform way in all spheres of decision taking. But there is, in fact, no very compelling reason for confining oneself artificially to assumptions of such heroic uniformity. The correct assumption may vary from country to country and from case to case, and may also alter over time, since the projects sometimes have a long life and the political and social influences on the tax and trade policies may change during the lifetime of the project. What the L M M approach seems to me to do is to assume implicitly that either the project evaluator is very *powerful* so that he can ensure that the rest of the government machinery will accept his decisions in other fields as well (and the political acceptance of 'sensible' tax, tariff and quota policies is ensured), or that he is very *stupid* so that he cannot be trusted to make a realistic appraisal of the likely policies and should be better advised to assume a rule of uniform simplicity.

III Cost of labour in project analysis

This section will be concerned with the valuation of labour cost and will be divided into six subsections. In (*a*) a general expression for the social cost of labour will be suggested, and in (*b*) some of the other formulae will be compared and contrasted with the one proposed here. In the subsequent subsections the problem of evaluation of specific value weights will be discussed in the line of the general questions raised earlier in the paper.

(a) Social cost of labour: an expression

Let w be the wage rate of the kind of labour with which we are concerned and let these labourers be drawn from a peasant economy. The reduction of output in the peasant economy as a consequence of someone being withdrawn from there is m, and the value of income which the person thus drawn away would have received had he stayed on in the rural area may be y. If there is surplus labour, we have $m = 0$, but y is, of course, positive. Even when m is positive and there is no surplus labour, it will often be the case that $y > m$ since the marginal product of a labourer may be considerably less than the average income per person. When the peasant in question moves away as a labourer in the urban area, his income goes up from y to w, and those remaining behind experience an increase in income equal to $(y-m)$. However, as a consequence of the departure of one member of the family those remaining behind may also work harder, and the value of more sweat is a relevant constituent of the social cost of labour. Let z^1 and z^2 be the increase in work effort respectively for the peasant family and for the person who moves to the project in question.[9]

A part of the respective increases in income may be saved, and we may assume that the proportions saved out of the marginal earnings of the peasant family and of the migrant worker are respectively s^1 and s^2. The proportion of project profits that are saved[10] may be denoted s^3. The marginal impact on project profits of the employment of one more man is given by $(q-w)$, where q is the relevant marginal product. Thus the total impact on the different groups can be summarized as follows:

Category	1 Increase in income	2 Increase in savings	3 Increase in efforts
1 Peasant family	$y-m$	$(y-m)s^1$	z^1
2 Labourer migrating	$w-y$	$(w-y)s^2$	z^2
3 Project	$q-w$	$(q-w)s^3$	

Taking v^{ij} to be the relevant marginal weight for the jth item in the ith row in the social welfare function W, we obtain the following expression for the change in social welfare as a consequence of the employment of one more man in the project:

$$U = v^{11}(y-m)+v^{12}(y-m)s^1+v^{13}z^1+v^{21}(w-y)+v^{22}(w-y)s^2$$
$$+v^{23}z^2+v^{31}(q-w)+v^{32}(q-w)s^3. \qquad 1$$

If there is no other restriction on the use of labour, the optimal policy would be to expand the labour force as long as U is positive, and making the usual divisibility assumptions the optimal position will be characterized by $U = 0$.

9. If project work is more or less backbreaking than peasant farming an adjustment for this may be included in z^2.
10. It is conventional to assume that $s^3 = 1$ if it is a public project. But there are problems of group consumption for project employees and they may be tied to project profits.

U is in one sense the social cost of labour, and indeed the shadow price of labour in this sense must be zero since there is no binding constraint on labour in addition to the relations that have already been fed into the expression of social welfare. However, the shadow price is frequently used in the sense of *that* value of labour which, if equated to the marginal product of labour, will give the optimal allocation of labour.[11] In this sense the shadow price of labour (w^*) is the value of q for $U = 0$. This is readily obtained from **1**:

$$w^* = [w\{(v^{31}-v^{21})+(v^{32}s^3-v^{22}s^2)\}-y\{(v^{11}-v^{21})+(v^{12}s^1-v^{22}s^2)\} + m(v^{11}+v^{12}s^1)-(v^{13}z^1+v^{23}z^2)]/(v^{31}+v^{32}s^3). \qquad 2$$

(b) Some other expressions

In the basic model in my *Choice of Techniques* (Sen, 1968), henceforth COT, I made the following assumptions which are here translated into the terminology used in subsection (a) above:

(i) all current consumption is equally valuable, i.e. $v^{11} = v^{21} = v^{31}$;

(ii) all saving is equally valuable and marginally more valuable than consumption, i.e. $v^{12} = v^{22} = v^{32} = \lambda > 0$;[12]

(iii) marginal disutility of efforts are negligible, i.e. $v^{13} = v^{23} = 0$;

(iv) the peasant economy has surplus labour, i.e. $m = 0$;

(v) the savings propensity of the workers and peasants are equal at the margin, and less than that out of project profits, i.e. $s^1 = s^2 < s^3$.

Taking consumption as the numeraire, i.e. putting $v^{11} = 1$, we can obtain from **2**:

$$w^* = \frac{w\lambda(s^3-s^2)}{1+\lambda s^3}. \qquad 3.1$$

Certain distinguished cases may be commented on. First, in the Polak-Buchanan-Kahn-Tinbergen criterion the shadow price of labour is taken to be zero in a surplus labour economy. This follows from taking consumption and savings to be equally valuable at the margin, i.e. $\lambda = 0$.

$$w^* = 0. \qquad 3.2$$

11. See Sen (1968), Little and Mirrlees (1968) and Stern (1972).
12. λ is a 'premium' since savings get a weight anyway as part of income.

The case associated with the names of Dobb (1960) and Galenson and Leibenstein (1955) corresponds to the assumption that the growth rate should be maximized, which amounts to maximizing the savings rate with no weight on consumption, i.e. taking λ to be infinitely large, and this leads to

$$w^* = \frac{w(s^3 - s^2)}{s^3}.$$ 3.3

With the further assumption of no savings out of wages, i.e. $s^2 = 0$, we get

$$w^* = w.$$ 3.3*

The case of using taxes in a manner such that the savings propensities of the different classes are equated, as put forward by Bator (1957), will lead to 3.2, as is readily checked by putting $s^3 = s^2$ in 3.1.

The LMM takes a set of assumptions that are equivalent to (i)–(iii) and (v) above, but omits the assumption (iv) of surplus labour, and in addition assumes:

(vi) $s^1 = s^2 = 0$;
(vii) $s^3 = 1$.

This yields from 3 the following expression [13]

$$w^* = \frac{w\lambda + m}{1 + \lambda}.$$ 3.4

The following aspects of the problem will now be discussed:

(a) the premium on investment, i.e. λ being positive;
(b) the question of distributional weights, reflected in v^{11}, v^{21}, v^{31}, etc.;
(c) the valuation of efforts, i.e. the choice of v^{13} and v^{23}; and
(d) the question of the relation between the intake of labour into the project and the outflow of labour out of the peasant economy.

These are not the only problems that deserve comment, but they do seem to be related closely to the general issues raised in the earlier sections of the paper.

13. See Little and Mirrlees (1968, p. 167). Their formula is the same as 3.4 but for notational differences.

(c) Premium on investment

The question of whether λ should be positive depends on whether at the margin investment is regarded as more important than consumption. It is assumed to be so in the COT as well as in the LMM. The underlying assumption is one of sub-optimality of savings. The question is why should such an assumption be made?

The tendency for market savings to be below optimal has been argued from various points of view. One reason is the presence of an externality in the form of members of the present generation having some concern for the well-being of the future generations which is, therefore, like a public good in the Samuelsonian sense. Another reason is the presence of a tax system which makes the private after-tax rate of return lower than the social rate of return to investment. In the underdeveloped countries with surplus labour it can also be argued that the private rate of return falls short of the social since wages are a cost for the individual investor whereas the social opportunity cost of labour may be much lower so that the market under-estimates the rate of return. There are other possible arguments and Phelps (1970) has provided a critical survey of the literature.

All these, however, amount merely to demonstrating that the level of market-determined savings may be sub-optimal. But this is not a good enough reason for taking λ to be positive, because that would require us to assume that savings are sub-optimal *even after* any possible government policy that could be used to change the rate of saving. If the savings as given by the market are too low, why not raise their level through taxation, subsidies, deficit spending, etc., to make it optimal and then proceed to do the project selection exercise without having to bother about raising the rate of savings through project evaluation itself? This is precisely where the argument relates to the main question with which this paper is concerned. We have to look at the relevant constraints that restrict the planners.

The project evaluator may find the savings rate to be sub-optimal for one of two different reasons. First, his judgements about the relative importance of present consumption *vis-à-vis* future consumption may be different from that of the planners in charge of taxes and other policies that influence the national rate of savings. He may wish to attach a higher weight on savings than that which is reflected in the government policy concerned with macro-economic planning. Second, the planners in charge of taxes, etc., may themselves regard the savings level to be suboptimal but be unable to set it right through taxes, etc., because of political constraints on taxation and other instruments.

In putting an extra weight on savings in the determination of the shadow price of labour one is essentially exploring the possibility of raising the savings rate through project selection and the choice of capital-intensity of investment.[14] It raises the question as to whether such a means of savings generation can be utilized when there are constraints that prevent the savings rate from being raised through more taxes. In one case savings are raised by income being taxed away and in the other savings are raised by choosing a lower level of employment in the project design thereby reducing disposable wage income and cutting down consumption. I have tried to discuss elsewhere the mechanism as well as the plausibility of using choice of techniques as a means of raising savings (Sen, 1968, ch. 5), so that I shall not go into the problem further here. I would only point out that the question rests on two propositions, viz. (i) the project evaluator finds the savings rate to be sub-optimal which implies more than finding that the *market-determined* savings rate is sub-optimal since the possibility of government action (through taxes, etc.) is present, and (ii) the project evaluator believes that the political or other constraints that rule out raising savings through taxes would not rule out raising savings indirectly through an employment policy. The whole problem turns on the precise reading of the area of control for the project evaluator.

(d) Income distributional considerations

Should there be differences in the weights attached to different kinds of income on grounds of distribution? In expressions **1** and

14. The problem of optimal development in an economy with constraints on taxation and savings and with a wage-gap (i.e. in a dual economy) is, of course, a complex one, and the precise determination of q must be posed as a variational problem involving inter-temporal optimality. On this question see Marglin (1966), Dixit (1968), Lefeber (1968), Stern (1972) and Newbury (1972).

2 this will take the form of v^{11}, v^{21} and v^{31} being not necessarily equal, and similarly v^{12}, v^{22} and v^{32} being different. The simplicity of expressions 3.1–3.4 arose partly from neglecting these differences. What could be said in defence of such a procedure?

The most common argument is that income distributional changes are best brought about by taxes and subsidies and other general policy measures and not by affecting project designs. If lump-sum transfers were permitted then the force of this argument is obvious, but in an important paper it has been demonstrated by Diamond and Mirrlees (1971) that even in the absence of the possibility of lump-sum transfers social welfare maximization requires that production efficiency be preserved, given some assumptions, including constant returns to scale. If the incomes of two factors of production are valued differently in making production decisions it could conceivably violate production efficiency. The rate of substitution between the factors in the production process to be decided on may then be different from that in the rest of the economy, and this will amount to production inefficiency.

Once again the question turns on the possibilities of taxation. While Diamond and Mirrlees (1971) do not necessarily assume the availability of any taxes other than commodity taxes, they do assume that there are no constraints on the quantum of such taxes, e.g. there will be no political difficulty in having a tax rate of, say, 1000 per cent on some commodity if the optimization exercise requires this. This may or may not be a good assumption, but what is our concern here is to note that the question relates once again to the identification of political and other influences on the operation of the government machinery; and also that the result depends on the ability to tax *all* commodities if necessary. There is a clear link here with the problem discussed in the last section. If wages could be taxed and the rise in income of the peasant family could also be taxed, then the question of using employment policy as a vehicle of savings adjustment will diminish in importance; COT, LMM and other frameworks do imply a certain inability to tax all commodities (including labour). It may in fact turn out that this is not a limiting constraint for the problem of income distribution, but the question will have to be posed in the context of commodity taxes *with* some constraints even in that sphere and not in terms of a model where any tax rate on any commodity is possible.

In addition to this aspect of the problem viewed from the angle of the totality of the planning set-up, there is, of course, also the problem of the project evaluator being constrained by the operation of the tax system on which he may not have more than a small amount of control. *Given* the tax system he might feel the necessity to violate efficiency by introducing income distributional considerations even though he might have preferred to do the adjustment through changing the tax system rather than affecting the project selection. The question relates again to the identification of areas of control.

This problem may also arise in the context of locational planning. In many developing countries an important constituent of planning is the regional allocation of investment. To take an illustration from India, in spite of the higher rate of return (in the absence of distributional considerations) from investment in fertilizers to be used in wet land *vis-à-vis* that from investment in irrigation in the dry areas, the appropriateness of the policy of emphasizing fertilizers and ignoring irrigation is open to question on distributional grounds. The problem would disappear if inter-regional transfers could be arranged so that more income might be generated through an appropriate production policy and the distribution to be looked after through transfers. But the question of inter-state transfers in a federal country like India has important political limits and the choice of agricultural policy must, therefore, depend on a reading of the areas of control.

Another set of illustrations from India relates directly to the question of social cost of labour for projects. Given the limitations of regional transfers there are considerable social pressures on the location of big industrial projects, and this seems to have been an important consideration in a number of locational decisions. The inoptimality of it has been well discussed by Manne (1967) and others. The question does, however, depend on the constraints that bind. By attaching a higher weight on the income of workers from the backward regions it is possible to alter substantially the benefit-cost balance sheet. But there remains the question of the control that the project evaluator can, in fact, exercise on the actual choice of manpower for projects. It is not uncommon for a project evaluator to decide to locate a project in a backward region on grounds of income distribution, and then for project managers to recruit labour from outside. When project selection is guided by one set of shadow prices and the performance of the project manager judged by profits in the commercial sense at market prices, this can easily happen. In some of the major industrial projects in India local labour has not really been much absorbed; project managers have seen considerable advantage from the point of view of 'performance' in using labour from areas with earlier industrial experience. However, from the point of view of the project evaluator the ranking may be in descending order: (1) project A in the backward region with the use of local labour, (2) project A in a non-backward region closer to the traditional sources of supply of industrial labour, and (3) project A in the backward region with importation of labour from traditional sources. If the area of control of the project evaluator extends to the location of the project but not to the exact recruitment policy, the use of shadow prices with distributional weights may conceivably make the situation worse from every point of view than ignoring distribution altogether. This complex range of issues is involved in the choice of appropriate weights and much depends on a clear perception of the exact sphere of the project evaluator's influence.

(e) Valuation of sweat

Neither the COT model nor the LMM model attaches any value to greater effort on the part of the peasant family in cultivation after the departure of the labourer for the project. In the COT model it is assumed that the disutility of labour up to a point is zero, and this feature produces surplus labour in that model.

A similar assumption about no disutility of labour may have been implicitly made by Little and Mirrlees (1968) since the 'plausible simplified utility function' for the labouring community as presented in the *Appendix for Professional Economists* takes individual utility to be a function only of individual income without any account of efforts. But if this is really so then there clearly must be surplus labour in the peasant economy, since the marginal rate of substitution between income and leisure will be constant at zero; and constancy (at zero or not) is known to be the necessary and sufficient condition for the existence of surplus labour (Sen, 1966). However, surplus labour is not assumed in the LMM model, and unlike in the COT model the value of m (alternative marginal product of a labourer) is not assumed to be zero.

It would, thus, appear that in the LMM model the peasants do dislike more work in the relevant region but this dislike is not to be reflected in the social objective function. That is, the peasant's attitude to work is accepted in the LMM model as a constraint that binds the planner but not as an element that directly enters the objective function.

If, on the other hand, it is assumed that if the peasants dislike more sweat then it must be reflected in the social objective function, then the problem will require reformulation. The positivity of m will imply that v^{13} must be positive. It should also be added that even if m is zero, i.e. even if there is surplus labour, it does not follow that v^{13} should not be positive. Surplus labour will exist whenever the marginal rate of substitution between income and leisure is constant in the relevant region and this rate need not necessarily be zero. Thus the existence of surplus labour may still require a positive shadow price of labour even in the absence of a premium on investment, i.e. even if $\lambda = 0$. The movement of labour from the peasant economy may not reduce the output there since those who remain behind may work harder, but then the enhanced effort of the remaining members requires some valuation in the planning exercise. In this view the peasants' attitude to work will be treated not merely as a constraint but also as a constituent of the social welfare measure.

(f) Control of migration

The point has been raised that when there is a wage differential between a protected urban labour market and the average earning in the rural sector from which the labourers come, there will be a tendency for more people to move than the number of jobs created.[15] Migration from the rural to the urban sector may equate the expected value of earnings in the urban area with that in the rural area, and if w is the urban wage rate, p the probability of employment in the urban area and m the level of rural marginal

15. See Todaro (1969) and Todaro and Harris (1970).

product, then the migration will be up to the point that would guarantee

$$pw = m. \qquad\qquad 4$$

Further, if the probability of employment p equals the proportion of urban labour force that is employed, then the migration equilibrium will exactly equate the wage rate of the employed people to the alternative marginal product sacrificed in the rural sector as a consequence of the movement of labour. For every employed man with w wage rate there will be $1/p$ men in the urban labour pool (including the employed and the unemployed), and m/p will be the amount of output sacrificed in the rural sector. And thanks to **4**, w must equal m/p.

Thus in the absence of considerations of savings premium, income distribution and effort variation, the market wage rate will be the appropriate shadow wage rate for project evaluation in spite of the existence of dualism and the wage-gap, i.e. in spite of $w > m$. There is much force in this argument. Professor A. C. Harberger, who is responsible for this form of the argument, has also extended it to the case where the migrant labourers may not maximize the expected value of earnings.[16] Suppose they are risk averse and pw exceeds m at equilibrium; it could still be argued that they regard the probability p of w income to be equivalent to the certainty of m, so that for project choice w is still the right measure of labour cost if social welfare must be based on the individual's measure of expected utility. There is scope for dispute in this, since it is arguable that social welfare should be based not on the *expected* utility of the labour force (all of whom had probability p of getting a job) but on the *realized ex post* utility of all of them (making a distinction between those who got the job and those who did not). And when pw is not equated to m by expected utility calculus it will make a difference whether *ex ante* expected utility (Neumann-Morgenstern type) or *ex post* realized utility (certainty type) is taken.

There is also the question as to whether the migrant regards m or y as the value of income that he is sacrificing by moving. His income while in the peasant economy was y and his marginal

16. Presented in a seminar in Nuffield College, Oxford, in May 1970.

product m, which might or might not have been zero depending on whether surplus labour existed or not. If he acts from the point of maximizing *family welfare* then m is the cost that he should consider, but if he wants to maximize his personal welfare then the relevant cost is y. The equilibrium condition will then be

$$pw = y. \qquad\qquad 5$$

In explaining the gap between the urban wage rate and the marginal product of labour in the rural sector, it has often been suggested that the migrant views his loss in terms of his income rather than in terms of the income of the previously joint family, and it is even possible to take a model[17] where $w = y > m$. This type of personal motivation will, of course, reduce the incidence of urban unemployment as a device of marginal equilibrium, and in the case where $w = y$, the problem will disappear altogether. Also, the correctness of the thesis that the market wage rate is the right wage rate even in the presence of a gap between w and m depends on these considerations.

IV Concluding remarks

One of the most complex aspects of the exercise of project appraisal is the precise identification of the project evaluator's areas of control. This will affect the nature of the exercise that he has to solve and the shadow prices that will be relevant for his evaluation. Much of the paper was concerned with demonstrating how variations in the assumptions about areas of control will radically alter the nature of the appropriate shadow prices.

The important approach to project evaluation developed by Professors Little and Mirrlees was studied in this context. The procedure of using world prices for project evaluation was critically examined and it was argued that that procedure required a rather extraordinary assumption about the project evaluator's areas of control.

The relation between the project evaluator's control areas and the appropriate shadow prices was illustrated in terms of the question of labour cost. The relevance of a premium on savings over consumption, weights based on income distributional considerations, valuation of efforts by the peasant family and the

17. See Lewis (1954). See also Jorgenson (1961).

labourers, and the impact of employment creation on migration, were analysed in this context. The determination of the appropriate shadow price of labour is impossible without a clear understanding of the extent of influence that the planner exercises over the relevant variables in each category. There was an attempt in the paper to relate differences among schools of thought on the accounting price of labour to differences in assumptions (often implicit) about the areas of control and the motivation of the relevant economic agents.

References

BATOR, F. (1957), 'On capital productivity, input allocation and growth', *Quart. J. Econ.*, vol. 71.

DASGUPTA, P. (1970), 'Two approaches to project evaluation', *Industrialization and Productivity*.

DASGUPTA, P., and STIGLITZ, J. (1971), 'Benefit-cost analysis and trade policies', mimeo; forthcoming in the *J. polit. Econ.*

DIAMOND, P., and MIRRLEES, J. (1971), 'Optimal taxation and public production: I and II', *Amer. Econ. Review*, vol. 60.

DIXIT, A. K. (1968), 'Optimal development in the labour-surplus economy', *Review of Economic Studies*, vol. 35.

DOBB, M. H. (1960), *An Essay in Economic Growth and Planning*, Routledge.

GALENSON, W., and LEIBENSTEIN, H. (1955), 'Investment criteria, productivity and economic development', *Quart. J. Econ.*, vol. 69.

JORGENSON, D. W. (1961), 'The development of a dual economy', *Econ. J.*, vol. 71.

LEFEBER, L. (1968), 'Planning in a surplus labor economy', *Amer. Econ. Review*, vol. 58.

LEWIS, W. A. (1954), 'Economic development with unlimited supplies of labour', *Manchester School*, vol. 22.

LITTLE, I. M. D., and MIRRLEES, J. A. (1968), *Manual of Industrial Project Analysis in Developing Countries*, vol. 2, OECD.

MANNE, A. S. (1967), *Investment for Capacity Expansion: Size, Location and Time-Phasing*, Allen & Unwin.

MARGLIN, S. A. (1966), 'Industrial development in the labor-surplus economy', mimeo.

NEWBURY, D. M. G. (1972), 'Public policy in the dual economy', *Econ. J.*, vol. 82.

PHELPS, E. S. (1970), *Fiscal Neutrality Toward Economic Growth*, ch. 4; reproduced in A. K. Sen (ed.), *Growth Economics*, Penguin.

SEN, A. K. (1966), 'Peasants and dualism with or without surplus labour', *J. polit. Econ.*, vol. 74.

SEN, A. K. (1968), *Choice of Techniques*, 3rd edn, Blackwell.

SEN, A. K. (1969), 'The role of policy-makers in project formulation and evaluation', *Industrialization and Productivity*, bulletin 13.

SEN, A K. (1970), 'Interrelations Between Project, Sectoral and aggregate planning', *United Nations Econ. Bulletin for Asia and the Far East*, vol. 21, pp. 66–75.

STERN, N. H. (1972), 'Optimum development in a dual economy', *Review econ. Studies*, no. 118, pp. 171–85.

TODARO, M. P. (1969), 'A model of labor migration and urban employment in less developed countries', *Amer. Econ. Review*, vol. 59. no. 118, pp. 171–85.

TODARO, M. P., and HARRIS, J. R. (1970), 'Migration, unemployment and development: a two-sector analysis', *Amer. Econ. Review*, vol. 60.

UNIDO (1972), *Guidelines for Project Evaluation*, United Nations.

5 I. M. D. Little and J. A. Mirrlees

The Use of World Prices

Excerpt from I. M. D. Little and J. A. Mirrlees, *Manual of Industrial Project Analysis in Developing Countries, vol. II, Social Cost-Benefit Analysis*, Development Centre of the Organization for Economic Cooperation and Development, 1969, pp. 105–14.

Accounting prices for traded goods

In this section, and the succeeding ones, we shall discuss the principles that should govern the estimation of the various accounting prices. Accounting prices, like ordinary market prices, may vary from year to year: and we are always looking ahead, and estimating what they will be in future years.

If some of the demand for a commodity will be satisfied from imports, or some of the supply exported, we call it a *traded good*. Other goods and services are referred to as *nontraded*. Whether or not a particular commodity will be a traded good or a nontraded good, an import or an export, in some future period, depends on how the economy is going to develop between now and then. Sometimes, our guess about whether a commodity will be imported or not may be almost a value judgement: we think that a sensible government would plan to import some, so we assume that it will do so. Of course, if one of our assumptions required government action in order to be fulfilled, this should be drawn to the attention of the appropriate authorities.

In theory, all we need to do to get a good method of project selection is to estimate *relative* accounting prices: so that, for example, we know the ratio of the price of electricity to that for steel. But it is convenient to measure prices in terms of something. We shall try to measure everything in terms of its 'foreign exchange equivalent' – that is, the amount of foreign exchange that is just as valuable to the economy as having an extra unit of the commodity. (We shall sometimes express the unit of foreign exchange in terms of the local currency; this makes no difference provided we always convert, say dollars into rupees, at the same exchange rate. We can speak indifferently of 'an accounting rupee' or 'one rupee's worth of foreign exchange'.)

Imported goods

Suppose that raw cotton can be purchased from the world market at a definite price, which is virtually independent of the amount bought. If the project is going to use some raw cotton, we shall charge it the amount of foreign exchange that has to be spent to buy the raw cotton. If a bale of cotton costs $x and the official exchange rate is 7 rupees to the dollar, we shall take the accounting price to be $7x$ rupees. A charge must also be made for the cost of transporting the goods from boat to factory, including insurance and trading costs; the details of this will be discussed later.

What is the justification for the above rule? The answer is that it ensures that the use of, say, 1000 accounting rupees in buying any one imported commodity costs the economy the same as its use in buying any other imported commodity. For instance, if instead of using raw cotton that costs 1000 rupees of foreign exchange (say $143 worth), raw jute costing 1000 rupees is used (bought from another country that happens to use rupees as currency), that in itself makes absolutely no difference to the economy. These two inputs cost the economy exactly the same. Thus purchase taxes and import duties are excluded from accounting prices; for the project should not be encouraged to use inputs that happen to have low tariffs or taxes on them, since that might lead the country to spend more foreign exchange to no advantage.

The rule that one should ignore duties and purchase taxes would not be a good one if the government was using these duties deliberately as a means of discouraging one import as compared to another, for reasons that demanded respect in project evaluation. Indeed, governments should, when considering changes in the tariff structure, keep very much in mind the possible effects of tariffs on production decisions. But, in reality, one cannot pretend that the structure of tariffs, as we find it in any country, is designed to provide just the influence on imports and hence internal production decisions, that the government would now deliberately choose to exert.

The structure of tariffs in most countries is far more the result of a series of historical accidents than of a deliberate attempt to influence production decisions so as to get more of this used and less of that. The import duty might be higher on one commodity compared to others, because it is an important import and therefore a useful source of revenue; or because of past programmes to encourage domestic production of the commodity; or because negotiated tariff reductions had involved the second commodity but not the first. Usually, the reasons for tariffs are irrelevant to the decision whether to use one input or another in production.

There is, however, one exception. The rule that the accounting price should be the foreign exchange cost of a unit of the commodity is correct only if the price the country pays for the commodity is independent of the amount it wants to buy. If this is not true, there is a case, at any rate in terms of narrow national interest, for discouraging use of that commodity. The reason is that an increase in demand will increase the foreign exchange cost of what is already being bought; so that the actual foreign exchange cost is more than the price of the extra amount demanded. In this case, one might well want to have a tariff on imports, and this is a tariff one would want to include in the accounting price. This might happen either because the country's demand for the commodity was a very important part of total world demand, or because any expansion in demand would force the country to resort to more expensive suppliers. The first reason for having an accounting price above the world price is applicable only rarely to the case of a developing economy. The second reason arises more frequently.

The general rule is that the accounting price for an imported commodity is the total foreign exchange cost, including any increase in the cost of existing purchases, of increasing imports by one unit. The technical term for this quantity is the *marginal import cost*. It will seldom be easy to tell just how much higher the marginal cost is than the world price. Probably there are few cases where the difference would matter very much. But a similar point arises in connection with exports; and there it is liable to be much more important.

It may be as well to emphasize that the world price of the imported commodity is the one to use whether the commodity is being used as an input or being produced as an output. The same accounting price should be used for a commodity whatever its role in the economy. After all, it is just as useful to the rest of the economy for a project to make 10,000 rupees worth of steel, as it is for it to save 10,000 rupees worth of steel; we want to encourage both to exactly the same extent, and therefore assign the same price to each. It should also be emphasized that a good is normally considered as an imported good even if it is actually purchased for the project from a domestic supplier, provided that some of the total supply would in any case be imported. The justification is that someone else will have to import instead of buying from this domestic supplier. In some particular year, a commodity that would normally be imported, may in fact be available from a domestic producer with excess capacity. This is hard to predict far ahead, but might be known to apply to a piece of capital equipment to be bought early in the life of the project. The accounting price can then be less than the price of imports as was explained in chapter 8 [not included here]. It becomes, effectively, a nontraded good (see pp. 170–72 below).

Exported goods

We can now compare a commodity that is exported with a commodity that is imported. If the exported commodity can be sold at a fixed price (in terms of foreign exchange – i.e. neglecting taxes and subsidies, special exchange rates, etc.), that price is the accounting price for the commodity. It is as valuable to obtain 1000 rupees by exporting cotton piece goods as to save 1000 rupees by reducing the import demand for tin. Similarly, when comparing two commodities that are both exported, it is obvious that what the projects provide the economy with, is the foreign exchange earned; in comparing the two commodities, one should look only at the prices they will fetch in world markets.

Thus, if the project produces a commodity that is being exported, it must be credited with the foreign exchange equivalent (less the appropriate transport and distribution costs). This is correct even if the output of the project will not itself be exported, but used in some other domestic industry. For, given the demands of this domestic industry, the output of the project still has the effect of increasing exports, as compared to what they would otherwise have been. Some indirect effects are here neglected, which might occasionally be important. This point will be taken up later.

Unfortunately, the above description of an exported commodity sounds rather unrealistic. Countries seldom feel that they can export as much as they choose of any specified commodity, without significantly affecting the price they can hope to receive. Perhaps the developing countries are apt to exaggerate the difficulties of selling goods abroad; often the problem is not so much that of finding markets as of maintaining adequate quality on a sufficient volume of production. But sometimes countries face, or feel seriously threatened by, the prospect of impenetrable trade barriers erected by the more industrialized countries.

If, on reflection, project planners decide that the limit on the export of bicycles is the rate at which good quality production can be expanded, then no special problems arise in evaluating particular production proposals (once they are reckoned to be genuinely feasible). If, however, increased production will have to be sold in less and less favourable markets, it may be necessary to reduce prices to all purchasers if exports are to be expanded. This is certainly the position in many of the markets for primary commodities; if cocoa producers try to increase production too rapidly, the price is forced down. In that case the extra foreign exchange, which will be earned by producing more, is less than the actual foreign exchange receipts from the new sales, since the price reduces the earnings of existing production.

In such a case, it is a good idea to discourage production by crediting the project with rather less than the ruling price for the commodity; this is the reason for the export taxes discussed earlier [not included here]. This lower price, which is the increase in foreign exchange earnings per unit of extra exports, is called the *marginal export revenue*. It is analogous to the marginal import cost discussed in the previous section. The general rule for determining the accounting price of a commodity that is being exported is that the accounting price is equal to the marginal export revenue.

In fact, most commodities are produced by a number of countries, and one country acting on its own cannot usually get a significantly better price for its production by restricting its own output. For this reason there are sometimes agreements among the producers of primary commodities to reduce overall production, in order to keep prices from falling too far. In such cases – the International Coffee Agreement is an example – the various producing countries are given quotas which limit the amount of the commodity that they should export. The accounting price for a commodity which is exported under a quota of this kind should not be very different from the world price (for quota exports), provided domestic demand for the commodity is small. But if the country's own demand for the commodity in question is large, and the level of exports is given, the commodity should be regarded for the purposes of project analysis as a nontraded good. The accounting price must, of course, be less than the world price (otherwise it would not be worth exporting at all).

It may be thought that we have still not covered all possibilities. It often seems that the exports of some particular commodity are given in *both* quantity *and* price. What is the project planner supposed to do then? In fact, the planner may be too quick to suppose that both quantity and price are fixed. He is, after all, planning for the future, and not for today. There is time to try to expand markets by offering lower prices, mounting selling campaigns, and so on. Very occasionally, export contracts – e.g. for bilateral trade – may be fixed well in advance, specifying both quantities and prices, and productive capacity is established precisely for this purpose. In such a case it is obvious what the foreign exchange earnings of the outputs are! But we suspect that, in general, it is merely a matter of statistical convenience to suppose that future export demand is a given quantity, which cannot be expanded except with the most expensive difficulty; and not an accurate statement of export possibilities.

On the other hand, in the new export lines that are the particular concern of the industrial planner, export sales require the gradual development of markets, as selling agencies are built up, designs developed, reputations established, the characteristics of different markets learned, and so on. It may then be sensible to act as though exports could be expanded easily up to a certain point, without prices being much affected. This point will be changing through time, and may well not be where the planners think it is going to be. But, while planning production within these limits, the expected prices may be used as the accounting prices in evaluating projects, at any rate when uncertainty about probable markets is not too great. It would be better if one knew how much one could expand sales by spending still more on selling efforts, so that rational decisions could be taken about export promotion. But no one seems to be very well informed about this.

Particular problems and exceptions should not blind us to the essential point of the argument. If the commodity in question is going to be exported or imported in the year under discussion, planners have to decide the accounting price by looking at the foreign markets from which the country buys or to which it sells. Often, it will be enough to forecast the price at the port. Sometimes an 'ideal' import or export tax may be allowed for in the accounting price, so as to discourage an export or import that would have a harmful effect on the world price. But one would not look to domestic market prices at all.

Accounting prices for nontraded goods

We do not discuss labour for the moment, since it is desirable to treat it in a rather special way. We shall first discuss goods and services that will not be traded at all; and then certain special cases of commodities which, though to some extent imported or exported, have to be treated as nontraded goods.

Commodities that do not enter into foreign trade

Some nontraded goods like construction work, electricity and banking services, are almost always produced in the country because it is very awkward and very expensive to produce them elsewhere and then import them. In this case, it is obvious that the goods or services will not be traded. In other cases it is not obvious, and one has to predict rather carefully whether the commodity is likely to be traded or not. Sometimes, the question whether or not the commodity will be traded is to be settled by the decision on the investment project. In none of these cases can one estimate the accounting price simply by forecasting the state of the world market.

Let us first agree that the same accounting price should be used for the commodity in all its uses (apart from the differences that must arise because of transport or transmission costs). If the project uses a hundred thousand kilowatts of electricity, the purpose for which it is used does not alter the sacrifice which society must make in allowing the project to use electricity at that rate. Similarly, the value of an extra unit of electricity to the nation is the same whatever means are used to produce the electricity, or even if the extra electricity is made available by using less electricity in other projects.

The general long-run principle is that the accounting price should equal the social cost of providing a little more of a non-traded good. (In economic jargon this is the *marginal social cost* – MSC.) If this cost varies with output, the level of demand will need to be predicted. If mistakes are made about this, a case may arise for making the accounting price for users temporarily higher or lower than the long-run MSC. For instance, if capacity is insufficient to meet the demand, and cannot be quickly expanded, there is a case for postponing projects which are heavy users of this nontraded good. This can be done by using a higher accounting price than the MSC for a few years – until such time as output can be expanded to satisfy the demand. Similarly, though this is less common, excess capacity may arise – in which case, an accounting price rather below the long-run MSC will be appropriate for a few years.

We have seen that the future level of demand may need to be predicted. This depends not merely on accounting prices, but also on the actual prices charged to different users. In the case of a public utility, these have to be set, for different types of customer, in accordance with government policy. We cannot go at length in this manual into the problem of optimum tariff-making. But, unless excess capacity arises, actual prices charged should not be lower than the accounting price: they may be higher either if there is a temporary shortage of capacity, or if the nontraded good enters into private consumption and is a suitable medium for taxation.

To help understand the operation of these principles, let us suppose that the planners have set an accounting price of 1 rupee for peak-period electricity from now until 1975. How do we know if they are right? On what grounds might we, for instance, say in 1975 that it has proved to be too high? A higher rather than lower accounting price will have reduced the amount demanded (more accurately, the amount demanded will be less for each actual price charged). This is because (1) public sector projects that use a lot of electricity will have been discouraged, and (2) anticipating too high a social cost, the government may have disallowed extensions of supply such as, say, some schemes for rural electrification. At the same time, the sanctioning of generating stations will have been encouraged. Thus, the accounting price will have proved too high if, in 1975, there is either more capacity than required to meet the demand, or if, to prevent this, actual charges have to be lower than the long-run MSC (or lower than desirable, if some revenue should have been raised but now cannot be). In this situation, the accounting price must be lowered, since too much producing-capacity has been encouraged, and too little using-capacity.

For similar reasons, if the accounting price has been set too low, the demand will exceed the supply unless the actual price (net of any desirable tax element) is raised above the MSC, or unless some form of rationing is applied. In either event, some users will have less electricity than they would have been willing to buy, paying as much as it costs the economy to supply: and the accounting price should then be raised, since more capacity is justified.

We now turn to the problem of estimating the MSC. This is relatively easy if costs do not vary significantly with the amount of capacity constructed – for, in this case, one need not worry about the level of demand. To show this, let us consider the case of electricity a little further.

Except for hydroelectricity, most of the inputs (oil or coal, and equipment) are traded goods, and will, therefore, be valued at c.i.f. or f.o.b. prices. Let us suppose that the shadow wage rate has also been determined, so that the accounting prices for all inputs are known. Further, suppose that supplying any amount of electricity is simply a matter of building more or fewer coal-burning generating stations of the same type (of course, we are simplifying!). Now there will be a minimum accounting price for electricity which will make it socially profitable to build any power station – so that, if the accounting price were less than this, the project selection procedures would not permit the production of any electricity. But if the accounting price were significantly higher than the minimum, there would be good reason to build a limitless number of power stations. So, in this case, there is an unambiguous accounting price, which is equal to the MSC, and which is quite independent of the amount of electricity demanded and supplied. There is thus no need, in estimating the accounting price, to worry about the prices that householders ought to pay, nor about such things as the licensing arrangements which should govern private producers of electricity nor anything else that affects the demands made upon the public supply. Needless to say, the electricity authorities must still worry; for they have to estimate actual future levels of demand (as affected by the accounting price, together with any regulations or rationing the government may impose), in order to decide how many power stations to build.

There are, however, many ways of making electricity. The accounting price of electricity might be too low to allow production by one means, but still higher than is required to allow production by other means. The correct accounting price is the one that is so low that the best of all the available methods of production is just worth using. Then the price reflects the total use of foreign exchange involved in producing the electricity; and, at the same time, it makes sure that no more foreign exchange is used in making electricity than is strictly necessary. For instance, the accounting price might be such as to permit coal-fired stations but disallow oil-fired ones – or *vice versa*.

As already indicated, the problem is theoretically more complicated if, say, the marginal social cost of electricity would be lower if the extension of planned supply was greater rather than smaller. Then one needs to estimate the demand at various accounting prices, and choose that accounting price which will result in a level of demand such that the marginal social cost of supplying that level of demand is also equal to the accounting price. This is obviously much more difficult for it requires knowledge both of how social costs decline with increased output, and of how demand reacts to changes in price. Fortunately, the use of electricity in most industrial projects is a sufficiently small part of costs to make such sophisticated attempts at precision unnecessary.

The discussion has so far been couched in terms of a single nontraded commodity. We have assumed that only one accounting price remained to be determined, all the others being known already. For instance, in discussing inputs into electricity, the nontraded input of construction was left out. Is that not cheating? In fact it is not, for we are providing ourselves with an equation corresponding to each nontraded commodity – the equality of supply and demand. Some of these equations will depend on several of the accounting prices we want to calculate. But there will be as many equations as prices. We can confidently assert that these equations do have a solution. It is theoretically possible that they might have more than one solution: but it will be clear, when we come to discuss the estimation of the accounting prices, that this particular problem is much less troubling in practice than in theory.

We have at this stage done no more than establish the principles governing the accounting prices of nontraded goods. The problem remains of how to estimate them in detail. Discussion of this is reserved for chapter 12 [not included here]: here we need say only that, in our view, serviceable methods are available.

Ambiguous cases

The investment rules used by project planners should fit in with the government's tax policies, rationing arrangements, licensing procedures, and so on. If the government deliberately, as a matter of long term policy, makes arrangements that lead to a certain rationed demand for automobiles, accounting prices should be such that just this demand is supplied. (Sometimes governments like to use queues as a means of restricting demand, so that supply is apparently less than demand – but not less than the demand the government wants to be supplied. We do not think this is a good method of restricting demand; but if it is done, project selection should not fight against it.)

Sometimes this requirement, that project selection should take account of the ways in which the government influences demand, may force us to regard a commodity that is being imported (or exported) as a nontraded good for the purpose of estimating its accounting price. A straightforward and obvious case is when the country is receiving foreign aid in the form of a fixed amount of some commodity – say wheat – but the government has no intention of importing any more of the commodity than is provided by way of aid. In such a case, any increased use of the commodity in question must be provided by domestic production; and, if there is no possibility of export, increased production must be absorbed by domestic users; in no case will the quantity of imports or exports be affected, and the world price of the commodity is therefore of little help in estimating the accounting price.

A slightly less obvious case of the same situation is when the government imposes a fixed quota on imports of the commodity. The quota might be so ungenerous that many potential users would be willing to use the commodity even if its accounting price was substantially higher than the price of imports. If the quota will really not be influenced by decisions on projects that produce or use the commodity, it may be necessary to use a price above – or possibly below – the foreign exchange cost of importing; after all, one has to make sure that the demand is not in excess of the supply. In such a case as this, the government is obviously unwise to operate a fixed quota. It is absurd to produce a commodity domestically at a foreign exchange cost greater than the cost of importing the commodity. Project planners can point this out. Indeed, planning for the long run as they are, they may be tempted to take production decisions – or rather decisions not to produce – that will force the government to relax the import quota when the time comes.

Another case where a good which may normally be traded becomes temporarily a nontraded good may arise when there is excess capacity. Extra demand may then have no effect on imports of the good itself, and its accounting price becomes the accounting cost of the current inputs of the labour, fuel and materials required to make it. Such excess capacity cannot normally be anticipated except sometimes in the case of equipment to be installed at the beginning of the life of a project.

Finally, it will be realized that the distinction between traded goods and nontraded goods is not always as sharp in practice as in theory. One may want to regard textile piece-goods as traded goods, because exports are quite an important part of total production. But the particular kinds of textile goods that are exported will usually be rather different from the kinds that are produced for the domestic market. It is obvious in this case that the whole output can be regarded as traded goods for the purpose of accounting price estimation, at any rate when the different goods are of fairly similar quality. We shall discuss the details later. But there may be awkward cases, where, say, small work-shops produce goods of inferior quality for the domestic market; one would not necessarily want to assume in this case that the accounting price and market price were identical, just because market prices and accounting prices are identical in the case of the products of large modern firms.

How far one should go in worrying about the proper classification of a commodity depends, as does the amount of work that should be devoted to estimating the accounting price, on the importance of the commodity for the project in question. In project analysis, troubles tend to come singly. Most of the inputs and outputs will be quite easy to deal with.

6 A. J. Harrison and D. A. Quarmby

The Value of Time

Excerpts from A. J. Harrison and D. A. Quarmby, 'The value of time in transport planning: a review', in *Theoretical and Practical Research on an Estimation of Time-Saving*, European Conference of Ministers of Transports, Report of the Sixth Round Table, Paris, 1969.

Brief outline of paper

Part 1 deals with the theory of valuation. The basis in economic theory of deriving values for time is considered and the nature of the assumptions underlying the derivation of values from the analysis of choice behaviour is described and the validity of these assumptions assessed. A final section deals with some general theoretical problems. Part 2 is concerned with the empirical realization of the theoretical approaches discussed in part 1. The methods used by recent workers in the field are described and the conditions under which valid empirical results can be obtained are defined, and the possible contribution of each methodology assessed.

Before beginning, an explanation of some of the terms used in the paper may be helpful. The expression 'the value of time' is commonly used as a shorthand for the value to be attached to saving time. But even this expression can be misleading, since this in turn is compressed and potentially ambiguous. There are two basic reasons why time savings are valued: first, the obvious reasons, above all for working time, that time savings allow further activities to be engaged in. In the case of working time this is the predominant reason; if working time is saved then in general more economic value can be produced with the labour released. In the case of leisure time similar reasoning applies: if time is saved, other existing activities can be conducted at a more leisurely and pleasant pace, or alternatively, other new activities can be engaged in.

The second reason is particularly important for leisure time. For most occasions, travel can be assumed to have positive disutility, different conditions of travel will result in different degrees of disutility to the traveller and hence different values of time. Thus a typical commuting journey, involving walking, waiting, travel and interchange time, is best treated in terms of the different components, since each of these stages will, to a given traveller, convey different amounts of disutility because of the basic conditions under which the time is spent. In these circumstances a change in the composition of overall journey time may be accounted valuable even where total journey time remains unaltered. Thus 'time saving' is a composite entity taking on different attributes in different situations – freedom from irritation at delays, freedom from physical effort, from overcrowding. Reductions in the lengths of time that have to be devoted to enduring these various conditions may be accounted valuable in themselves, even though no explicit consideration is given to expanding a traveller's range of activities, and hence 'saving time' may be valued, even though the savings are not seen in any way as productive. This point will be seen to be important below where certain types of time saving are considered which do not obviously allow further activities to be undertaken.

One important consequence of there being different degrees of disutility attached to time experienced in different ways is that it is desirable wherever possible to refer to these conditions explicitly: hence a distinction will be made frequently in the paper between walking time, waiting time and in-vehicle or overall travel time. In principle, a much finer categorization of time would be desirable reflecting the wide range of conditions surrounding travel, but these are all it is practicable to make at the present time.

In the whole of the paper a basic distinction will be made between working and non-working or leisure time. Working time includes all journeys made in the course of work, i.e. during time which is paid for by the employer; non-working time includes all other journeys, i.e. during time which is not paid for, including in particular journeys to work as well as journeys on personal business, holidays, etc. As we will see below, there may be a case for further subdividing this category.

While the distinction between the two categories is obvious enough, there are some categories of trip maker which fall uneasily between the two, e.g. the self-employed or certain categories of employee whose salaries are invariant with the length of time actually spent working. Such people may take time savings in the form of leisure or extra work. This problem is, however, essentially a practical one and in principle could be overcome by applying some of the methods of analysis described below. Once these have established the division in practice, then it is a matter of convenience into which category they are placed. Apart from a brief discussion in part 1, this group will be ignored.

1 Theory of valuation
Working time

A number of approaches have been suggested for the evaluation of working time.[1] The most usual has been to estimate value by reference to wage rates, often known as the cost savings approach: the obvious theoretical backing for this approach is the marginal productivity theory of factor rewards. Employers hire labour until it is no longer worth their while to do so. As it is normally assumed that all workers of a given type are paid the same, then the average wage equals the marginal value product; hence the wage rate is a satisfactory measure of the value of production gained or lost by changes in the labour force, as long as the changes under consideration are small relative to the markets in which the prices are set, and as long as there are no subsequent changes in wage levels.

A first qualification is that the wage rate must be taken to mean the total cost to the employer of employing the class of labour under consideration. Thus for purposes of practical calculation such costs as social insurance, employment taxes and costs such as the provision of uniforms, etc., which are borne by the employer are included as wages. The following paragraphs review a number of objections to the cost savings method.

Objection 1: imperfections in the labour market may mean that

1. For a listing, see National Co-operative Highway Research Programme Report 33.

the value in other uses of labour using road transport is not adequately represented by the wage rate.

Comment: there are many reasons why the wage paid to a class of labour may inadequately reflect its opportunity cost: union restrictions, customary relativities sometimes based on convention, notions of equity, etc., or the special conditions pertaining in the profession, e.g. the armed forces or other jobs subject to discipline or special dangers. There may, too, be groups who are paid less than their opportunity cost – possibly nurses or other workers giving personal service (cf. Evans, 1969). None of these factors are likely to be of major importance for those occupational groups who make up the bulk of the travellers in working time – professional drivers, salesmen, service engineers, etc. These are all groups where there is a high degree of mobility in and out of the profession, strong unionism in some cases, but not in the restrictive sense relevant here and not subject to notions of 'service' or status. Obviously as nearly all occupations travel in working time, though by no means to an equal extent, a proportion of this category of time saving must accrue to those whose time is 'wrongly' valued, but for practical purposes this effect may in our view be discounted.

Objection 2: the release of resources assumed in theory may not take place, because of labour restrictions.

Comment: in some cases, however, labour restrictions are in force which do have implications for the economic value of working time saved. In the United Kingdom some agreements among specialist haulage firms provide for a fixed average speed of working which is invariant to the specific conditions obtaining on a given route and which are only gradually responsive to overall changes in travel time, while in the United States, hauliers are licensed on, and restricted to, individual routes. In this situation gains in working time are converted into leisure time and should be valued as such (although one may doubt whether the value of free time during nominal working hours is equivalent to leisure time under genuinely free conditions). However, the situation becomes more complex if one considers the normal context in which time values are adopted for the purpose of evaluation, i.e. an ongoing continuing investment process, not typically an isolated scheme. Over time, restrictions are relaxed, productivity agreements negotiated and the time savings realized at their face value. There may therefore be a case for making some assumption about the date at which savings are fully realized – though tests run on the present values of schemes have shown that the effect is not large, especially when one allows for the fact that the savings have value at least as leisure time and that most users of roads in working time are flexible and hence responsive to change. In certain circumstances, however, one may doubt if there is any justification for assuming deferment. If, because of previous investment or other changes such as improvements in vehicle performance, there is already scope for adjustment of schedules as such, then the effect of a further lump of investment may be to 'tip the balance', and consequently lead to a greater than expected saving. Thus, unless it is the case that the negotiation of schedules is on a regular 'n' year basis and one makes the further restrictive assumption that one is only considering investment over a period which does not include negotiation, the use of the average values at their face value may be justifiable even where labour restrictions are obtained. It has, however, to be conceded that the counter-arguments rest on a number of assumptions (e.g. on the distribution of the probabilities of realizing time savings) which may not be empirically valid.

Objection 3: the same problem may arise because of inability of road-using enterprises to convert time savings into resource savings.

Comment: the same type of argument may be applied to the next problem. Firms may be unable to convert time saved into economic value for many reasons, including managerial incompetence, but the major problem raised in this context is that of indivisibilities. Thus, typically, even fairly large investments yield savings that are both absolutely and proportionately small in relation to the effective unit of work – the trip or the working shift. In this situation, it is frequently alleged that the savings have no or little value. As this problem is common to all types of time savings, it will be discussed in a separate section below on general theoretical problems.

Objection 4: the assumption that resources have other alternative uses may not always hold.

Comment: time savings accruing to commercially used vehicles represent an increase in the potential capacity of the road trans-port industry, but there is, at the same time, no necessary increase in demand to take up the extra capacity for work. Hence, if all other things were equal resources would be released for other purposes. In practice, however, the general growth in demand for road transport common to all countries is such as to prevent this happening in most cases and hence the issue does not arise. In certain cases where there is persistent structural or localized un-employment and demand is growing slowly, if at all, the oppor-tunity cost of driving time may be less than the wage rate by a considerable amount, and it may be appropriate to use a shadow price adjusted to allow for the less than unit probability of the displaced driver being employed elsewhere (it would, of course, be appropriate in this circumstance to use a similar shadow price for local labour when estimating the cost of the construction of the road concerned for purposes of investment appraisal. The implicit assumption of this argument is, of course, that wages are, for institutional reasons, sticky downwards). [...]

Objection 5: it values working time purely from the point of view of the employer and does not consider the value the em-ployee might place on the savings in journey time and hence the way his work time is spent.

Comment: the degree of disutility which the employee attaches to his work varies with a wide range of factors; one relevant factor is the actual task he is involved in: for those who spend only part of their working day driving, e.g. delivery or salesmen, a reduction in the driving task means an increase in the amount of time spent on other tasks. In principle, therefore, an allowance should be made for their perception of this difference. In the long term, the difference should show in the wage paid, i.e. if more driving were welcomed, then wages would fall or rise less fast, and the benefit could be estimated this way. In practice, this solu-tion appears non-feasible, but so also is direct attribution of changes in the disutility of work, since it is not clear which way the adjustment should go.

Objection 6: it treats time purely as a disutility: in some cases travel time may be used productively.

Comment: in some cases journey time may be used produc-tively, e.g. where the mode of transport allows work to be carried out in the course of a journey, e.g. time spent on a train may be used for reading. This case is likely to be unimportant for road transport since (except for bus travel which is little used in working time) there is little opportunity for such activities. Passengers may at times use their time productively, e.g. if chauffeur driven, but this is relatively rare.

Objection 7: for some classes of worker, no distinction can be drawn between working and non-working time.

Comment: the problem is posed by those whose hours of work are not fixed, or who are paid according to work done, or who are self-employed. If such people save time during a work journey (if indeed it is possible to determine into which category the journey falls!), they may choose to work more, or they may prefer to have more leisure, or, probably, a combination of the two. In this situation the theory outlined here is inappropriate and the derivation of values must rest with the empirical methods discussed below. The objection must be allowed in principle: on what information is available in the United Kingdom, this group is unlikely to form more than a small proportion of total travellers in working time.

Most investment appraisal involves a prediction of future levels of benefits, hence a method of predicting future values of time is required. This problem is relatively straightforward with working time; given the theoretical framework outlined above, the value of working time is determined by its productivity and hence all that is required for predicting future values is a view as to the future rate of growth of labour productivity in real terms (per man hour). This rate can then be applied to the total wage cost. The normal method of deriving a rate of growth of productivity produces an average value of time; if this figure is used for predicting marginal value, there is an implicit assumption that marginal and average values will grow at the same rate. While it is difficult to justify this assumption, it is more difficult to find a better one. [...]

Non-working time

(*a*) *Classical theory.* The traditional economist's starting point for the consideration of the value of leisure time has been the labour market: it would appear obvious that in a free market for labour the marginal value of leisure to the consumer is equal to what he foregoes by way of extra earnings. This theory has come in for some criticism (cf. Moses and Williamson, 1963) on the ground that the length of the working week is given as far as most individuals are concerned: hence all that can be said from the observations that people do in fact work is that the total utility gained from earnings outweighs the total loss of leisure; nothing can be said about marginal values (and there can be no presumption that marginal and average values are equal).

Recent theoretical development has, however, shown that the simple formulation is wrong for a further reason in that it ignores the disutility attached by the consumer to the work situation *per se*: the fact that different categories of work gave rise to different degrees of disutility has been recognized in economic theory since the last century at least, but has not, until recently, been embodied in the theory of the allocation of time. When this is allowed for the equilibrium situation is defined by an equation of the form[2]

$$\frac{U_l}{U_y} = P + \frac{U_w}{U_y},$$

where the marginal rate of substitution between income and leisure, U_l/U_y, is defined as the sum of two terms, the first, as in traditional theory, the money wage P, and the second the marginal rate of substitution between income and time spent at work U_w/U_y. Thus the marginal utility of leisure time is equal to the wage rate less the marginal disutility of work. Accordingly the value of leisure time should be some amount below the average wage rate, even in a free market, but the extent of this divergence is determined by the value of the second term, in which *a priori* considerations shed no light. The value of travel time will again differ from this measure to the extent that the disutility attached to travel is different from that attached to work. Where disutility of travel is negative (i.e. the journey is valued for itself) then a time saving can have zero or even negative value.

2. An equation of this form has been developed independently by a number of authors. See Johnson (1966), Oort (1969), Evans (1969) and also Philips (1969). See Evans for a general development of the theory of consumer behaviour, and Philips for a consideration of the implications of the Johnson-Evans-Oort approach for empirical studies.

Further considerations supply further reasons why the traditional marginal equivalence should not hold. These can be seen from considering the consumer also as a producer in the sense that he may (a) buy certain commodities not for their utility but because of their ability to create it as intermediate goods, and (b) choose to supply services directly to himself or buy them in (e.g. household repairs). The longer a consumer works, the more he is likely to have to buy convenience goods, labour-saving devices, obtain domestic help and not do it himself. Thus his effective net wage at the margin is much less than what he actually earns. It may in fact be negative if he prefers work to housework – not an implausible situation for the married, childless wife.

Thus, to sum up, the classical theory even when adapted and extended does not yield a method for deriving a value for leisure time, still less of travel time specifically. Other methods must therefore be adopted.

(b) *Behavioural approaches.* While some have accepted traditional theory, most of the empirical workers in the field have ignored it, on the presumption that the value of personal time is best measured by observing how people in practice trade off travel time savings against cost. The traditional theory does not, of course, imply a particular value. The problems of this approach as a *method* will be discussed below: here all that is relevant is an appreciation of it as a principle of valuation. Before it is acceptable as an applied principle certain empirical conditions should be satisfied: for example, that the choice makers were aware of their choice and had had time to adjust to the alternative facing them. It would probably be considered unacceptable, for example, to infer values from behaviour where people had little notion of what they were 'purchasing' or where emotions were strongly involved, as would arise in connection with safety or health. In this case, it might be thought that an 'administrative' judgement was preferable, partly because one would not expect much stability in the values obtained from such circumstances and partly because it was held that in the circumstances the consumer was not the best judge of the value of what he was consuming and, while resources may be allocated in the private sector according to the whim of the consumer, it is frequently an aim of public policy to reduce the extent to which it occurs (e.g. by legislation on trade descriptions, advertising, etc.).

Second, as the section on definitions indicated, the value of time savings depends not on the use to which such time saved would be put, but on the disutility attached to the travelling time saved. Walking time and waiting time are examples of types of time which may well have different disutilities to the traveller, and different again from actual travelling time in a vehicle. Hence, as a second requirement, any method for deriving values of time using empirical analysis of travellers' choices in trade-off situations should be able to disentangle the effects of the different time types in the whole journey; otherwise the value of time measured is a specific average of the values of the different time types occurring in the situation being analysed and is not, unless the 'mix' is constant, a meaningful number. Early studies using the revealed trade-off technique did not make this distinction between types, and their results contain significant biases (see p. 191 ff.).

Not only are different time types a source of different values of time; any empirical situation will contain a population of choice-makers who in general will collectively exhibit a distribution of values of time. Much of the variability can be attributed to real differences in personal or household circumstances – for instance, income – and some indeed may derive from differences in psychological attributes which lead to fundamentally different attitudes to the trade-off situation. In so far as any or all of such *ex hypothesi* sources of variability may exist in the empirical situation under view, a further requirement in the approach to the trade-off method of valuation is to establish by whatever means possible the effects of such factors, if any, on the overall average value of time. This can sometimes place considerable demands on the skill and ingenuity of the researcher; more than one of the earlier studies lacks generality because no check was made at the time of the effect of a factor which even without the benefit of hindsight one might have suspected to have affected the derived time values.

A third requirement is that the individual's judgement as to the value of his time can be accepted as valid in a social calculation. In many fields of public expenditure, e.g. health and education, government policy is designed to correct, as much as cope for, certain trends in consumer behaviour. In the field of transport there appears to be no reason why such principles apply; it is not obviously an aim of public policy that travel time should be reduced except in so far as people wish it to be. This would not be true if it could be shown that productivity, health, etc., or other facts not taken into account by the individual were important, but there appears to be no reason to think that they are. [...]

(c) *Prediction of values.* Finally, the 'measurement' approach may also be applied to the problem of predicting future values, where it is possible to associate values with independent variables which can themselves be predicted. One obvious candidate is income since it is apparent from the theoretical considerations outlined above that future income levels will be a prime determinant (and this is confirmed by empirical studies). However, it is also necessary to consider the other terms in the equation given above. If they remain constant, then the value of non-working time will grow at the same absolute rate as working time, i.e. proportionately faster. However, it is perfectly possible that the disutility of work and the disutility of travel will alter, partly for reasons of change of taste and income and partly because of changes in objective conditions, such as work environment, average congestion levels, etc. As between modes a further relevant factor is the extent to which other activities may be engaged on in travelling. If it is possible to read or otherwise use time productively then there will be a damping effect on growth in values, and vice versa. This has obvious implications for the values of time as between transport modes.

General theoretical problems

This section discusses a number of aspects of time valuation common to both working and non-working time.

(a) *Size of time saving.* This problem is put in two basic forms: first, is one saving of ten minutes worth ten savings of one minute; and second, do savings under some given amount have any value at all. Before these questions can be tackled, some theory must be developed as to the way in which time savings are of value to people. In the introduction it was pointed out that time might be valued for two reasons: first, because of the opportunities it presents for other activities to be undertaken, and second, because of its relative disutility. The full theory obviously comprises both these reasons in one utility maximizing model.

If we consider the first reason, it is apparent that it would be naïve to suppose that time savings of all sizes could be, on all occasions, recognized as economically valuable at the same rate. This would be to suppose an unreal degree of flexibility among transport users. An obvious development is some sort of probabilistic model on the following lines: if we assume that there exist indivisibilities and constraints which prevent users adjusting perfectly to the traffic situation facing them, then we may also assume that some margin of slack or idle-time exists within their current arrangements. We may further assume a continuous and uniform distribution between perfect adjustment and some maximum level of maladjustment. Thus if we consider a ten-minute time saving in relation to ten one-minute savings, it is obvious that the probability of the large saving allowing readjustment to take place is greater than any of the individual one-minute savings. However, on the assumptions given, there is no reason to suppose that the former probability is greater than the sum of the probabilities over all the one-minute savings, since even a small saving would be sufficient to allow those just below the margin of maximum maladjustment to make some rearrangement and realize time savings much larger than the single minute saving. In fact a model of this sort is equivalent to assuming a continuous demand curve, on which there are always marginal users ready to respond to small changes in the conditions facing them. It is not difficult to construct simple arithmetic examples which show the equivalence of the numerous small savings with the single large saving, but it is apparent that any argument for equivalence must depend heavily on the validity of the probability distribution assumed. A number of plausible alternative distributions would not produce the required equivalence, and there is little or no empirical evidence one way or another. We are concerned here mainly with pointing to the existence of a theoretical justification of some plausibility for disregarding size of time saving.

It is obvious that this line of argument can be deployed to

justify attaching value to small time savings even where these are much smaller than the unit of output (say the journey). A further and important line of argument may also be addressed to this problem. The normal context in which time values are used is that of a continuing expenditure programme or a total traffic plan. Such programmes typically consist of large numbers of individual items which may be analysed separately. Let us take the example of a traffic management scheme for an urban area: each component may be small and present very small gains: similarly some of the measures brought in to increase pedestrian safety (e.g. crossings) may impose very small delays. In these circumstances it would obviously be fallacious to ignore small time savings on the grounds that they were too small to be noticed; if this were done, there would be pedestrian crossings everywhere and no vehicular traffic. Thus to deny value to small time savings is to start on a very slippery slope since it is by no means obvious by reference to what criteria time savings would become worthwhile.

Consideration of the second basis for valuing time savings suggests a further reason for not ignoring small savings. In the case of pedestrian crossings, roundabouts, etc., the main effect (at moderate levels of flows) is to interrupt free flow and lead to an irregular and more tiring driving experience even where total journey time is not affected (as these may not be in certain conditions). Thus as far as leisure time is concerned, the main source of benefit from this kind of saving may lie with factors correlated with time saving rather than time saving *per se*. This implies one of two courses: (a) to attempt to disaggregate time savings into components such as 'reductions in discomfort', reduced tension, etc., or (b) to develop a series of specific values of time, the appropriate ones to be selected according to the situation concerned.

Finally, a different kind of consideration. In both public and private sectors, resources are devoted to saving consumers small amounts of time: for example, telephone switchboard capacity is determined by reference to acceptable very small delays in obtaining service. Similarly, a large number of convenience goods or labour-saving devices are purchased which produce similar orders of saving.

A. J. Harrison and D. A. Quarmby 185

(*b*) *Variance in journey times*. One effect of replacing a congested road by a road on which free flow speeds are attainable is to increase the probability that a journey can be achieved within a given time limit. Congested conditions can, of course, be anticipated, but the effect of random events – breakdowns, accidents, etc. – is much greater when roads are near or in excess of the capacity than when there is plenty of capacity spare. It is not difficult to show that a reduction in journey length variance is equivalent to a time saving of similar (though normally rather less) extent. Thus if we assume extreme conditions when a deadline or schedule must be adhered to and the probability of not achieving it reduced effectively to zero by the traveller, then the time allowed for the journey must be the maximum expected time, however infrequent that is. If the variance is reduced even without any corresponding reduction in mean journey time, users will experience a benefit – in this extreme case equivalent to the whole of the reduction. Normally, of course, mean times will be reduced simultaneously, but this effect remains an independent source of benefit, which has been, as far as we are aware, neglected. Again, alternative distributions will produce different answers.

(*c*) *Marginal and average values*. The question is often raised, though rarely answered: are marginal and average values of time identical? Sometimes this is a version of the first problem discussed above, but the treatment suggested has effectively evaded the issue since it suggested that a small time saving may lead to a large one being realized and a large one may lead to only a small effective saving. Hence no inference with regard to marginal and average values may be drawn.

An alternative interpretation of this question concerns the validity of using the same unit values for isolated schemes as for large investment programmes: a small scheme may have only a small effect on any individual, but large schemes, e.g. the creation of an intercity motorway network, may be felt to represent more than marginal changes. One may on empirical grounds question the force of the distinction. Long journeys are infrequent in leisure time, and hence even a large programme has only a small effect on the majority of individuals, even though it may have a large effect per unit of long distance trip making. And with regard to journeys in working time even a large motorway network will carry less than 5–10 per cent of total trips and no remarkable change in the labour force required in the road haulage industry and hence in the wage rate to be paid is to be anticipated. At a theoretical level, however, it has to be allowed that the valuation determined at the existing margin may not adequately reflect the importance of all changes in aggregate, since there can be no general reason to suppose the equality of marginal and average values. In the case of working time, it is, of course, normal to draw rising labour supply curve to an industry, not a horizontal one (at least in developed countries); while with regard to non-working time, the classical theory as reformulated suggests a similar conclusion. In our view, however, the effect of even a large investment programme is insufficiently large for there to be large divergences in practice between marginal and average values.

A final problem is put in the form of the question: is it always marginal time which is saved? There are obvious cases where intra-marginal time is involved – for example, where hold-ups are unexpected and where as a consequence time may be valued very much in excess of its values where time tables were adhered to. But it is not customary (perhaps wrongly) to assume any variation in the unexpected; what can be said of the expected? One model of behaviour suggests that firms (with regard to working time) and individuals (with regard to non-working time) will adjust their behaviour so that the marginal value of time is equal at the margin of each activity.[3] Thus the firm will adjust its labour force and its schedules while the individual will adjust his pattern of behaviour.

Where constraints exist – for example, because of fixed hours of work and fixed hours of a participation in certain leisure activities such as theatre going – it is probable that adjustment will not be perfect and time will possess different values at different times of day, and hence it could be argued that on some occasions intra-marginal time will be saved. This only presents difficulty if (as is in fact the case at present) valuations can only be obtained for 'constrained' time of day. If a wide enough range of trips is observed, then this difficulty disappears.

3. See Evans (1969) for a more precise formulation.

2 Measurement

Working time

If the marginal wage theory is accepted, then problems of measurement are relatively simple; what problems exist as far as wage and related elements are peculiar to the statistical deficiencies of each country; nothing of general interest arises. We do not wish to imply that the practical problems may not be severe. They can be, but it is not appropriate to discuss them here, since little of a general nature can be said.

An exception to this is the estimation of the proportion of overhead cost – the marginal wage increment as defined above, for which no readily available statistics are available from standard series. Overhead wage–cost ratios are often quoted for production workers or higher executives, but these are of little interest, since they are normally obtained by dividing some total cost figure by the number of employed in the relevant class, and hence bear little relation to the required measure, which refers solely to those costs which vary with the level of employment, but not with the level of production.

Some pilot work on this problem has been done in the United Kingdom for the Ministry of Transport (see Harrison, 1969): basically there are three approaches: interviewing accompanied by case studies of firm's actual costs; development of a production function from historical or cross-section data; estimation of a production function from engineering cost accounting data.

All of these are difficult to apply as general techniques although they may be successful in some cases. In MOT's own investigations, the first and third approaches were tried, the second failing for lack of relevant data. The first yielded meagre results; most firms found it difficult to recognize the concept being investigated – and certainly had not measured it themselves. But some were able to provide information on particular cost items, associated closely with the employment of staff – personal equipment such as tools and uniforms, rest rooms, etc. Severe difficulties arose, however, when attempting to estimate savings of long-run costs and no firm estimates have been possible.

The third method has so far been employed on a limited basis, by considering the cost structures of firms using road transport and attempting to estimate by a prior reasoning and informed judgement exactly which cost components might be expected to vary with the output–employee ratio. This method seems practical for commercial vehicles, since cost structures are relatively homogeneous; it is less easy for users of car transport, since such users come from a wide range of industries and carry out, when off the road, very different functions. Little progress has been made with this type of road user.

Very little work has been done on the problems listed above in the discussion of principles. Some work has been done in America by Fleischer and Haning and McFarland (1963), and in the United Kingdom by one of the present authors (Harrison, 1967), on the question of the utilization of time savings, but this is, for various reasons, limited in its scope. The work by Fleischer is a detailed case study of a particular long distance trucking operation, tracing its development over time, as successive improvements occurred to the highway on the route it involved. The study brought out the fact that because of the constraints under which trucking operations take place – limited driving periods in particular – time saving on the road could not always be utilized immediately but had to wait until further improvements took place and an entire rescheduling of the operation took place.

The obvious point to make about this finding is that the case study is of a scarcely typical type of road transport operation, especially in the smaller countries of Western Europe, and it is typical in another sense, the degree of regulation to which it is exposed. Most road using operations are more flexible, being over shorter distances, where the impact of hours, regulations, etc., is slight. And, of course, for commercial road users of cars there is no restriction whatsoever. These, in United Kingdom conditions, and including only time savings to persons, are more important than all heavy goods vehicle operations.

It is difficult to assess the work reported by Haning and McFarland – or at least that part concerning the utilization of time savings. Using 'scaling measurement and subjective judgement', they suggest that (in the short run) common carriers (route restricted to the United States) enjoyed only 40–60 per cent of potential value, private carriers from 80–100 per cent, with specialized carriers in between 60–80 per cent. They point out, however, that all time savings are of value – they may be used for additional maintenance, better service, etc., but it is difficult to assess how valuable. It remains unclear how long the short-run is, how valuable these other activities are and, finally, how the scaling measurements turn out in practice to compare with actual experience.

The work done by one of the present authors (Harrison, 1967) on the London–Birmingham motorway was much less thorough than the Fleischer study and laid no claim to statistical rigour; it was rather a pilot survey to assess the problems involved. From it only an impressionistic judgement could be reached.

In some way the Fleischer findings were confirmed; about 150 operators provided information, but among these one-third said that although they used the motorway it was a minor influence and its effect had not been noticeable. There was some evidence that it was the hauliers for whom the motorway represented the largest relative savings (i.e. those with a London or Birmingham base) who were most likely to be able to turn time savings into resource savings. Nearly one-third of the respondents mentioned labour relations as an obstacle to the utilization of time savings. This was especially true of the trunk haul operators. In only a very small number of cases was precise information forthcoming.

The empirical methods so far employed in assessing the value of working time illustrate some of the problems of working in this field: the large number of firms involved, the range and variety of their operations, their general lack of cost consciousness as well as the ever-present problem of *ceteris non paribus*. The problem is made even more difficult if the theoretical model outlined in the above of the utilization of time savings is accepted, particularly if the proportion of firms actually utilizing any given saving is a small proportion of the total. For if this were so, the sample required to obtain statistically satisfactory solutions would have to be very large. One may doubt whether, in the face of the difficulties which empirical work is faced with, if such a sample could be obtained and analysed satisfactorily.

One obvious method, of which more will be written below, is to observe the reaction of commercial vehicle users and those using cars in business time in those circumstances where a time trade-off is present. No systematic analysis of these seems, however, to have taken place in recent years with one exception of dubious worth (Gronau, 1970). *Pace* the difficulties facing studies of this type, which will be gone into in detail below, it would seem worthwhile to attempt to verify the current values by this means.[4] The appropriate statistical methods are discussed in the next section.

Non-working time

In part 1, it was established from classical theory that the value of non-working time was likely to be less than the average wage rate, but it was not possible to say by how much. The principle was put forward that given certain conditions the value of non-working time was best estimated by discovering empirically what value people themselves placed on their travelling time outside working hours.

In this section we discuss at some length various empirical methods for determining values of time from analysing the revealed behaviour of travellers. This has over the past few years proved itself to be a fruitful area of work, and a considerable number (over a dozen) of empirical studies have been carried out. First of all, we discuss some general characteristics of the methods of analysing revealed behaviour, with a note on the empirical conditions which, as a distillation of the various studies done, appear to be necessary for deriving 'good' values. Next, specific methodology is reviewed in each of the main areas where empirical work has been done, and various studies are assessed for their methodology. Finally, there is a discussion of some general issues on the use of input data and on the interpretation of outputs. [...] In principle, all these methods could be used for deriving a value of working time – i.e. by analysing the behaviour of those travelling in working time. But, as made clear in part 1, there are good reasons for choosing as a value the opportunity cost of time to the employer.

There are a number of different methods that have been used in recent years, but they nearly all have one fundamental approach – to derive a value of time by analysis of situations where people can make choices between different 'packages' of time,

4. This may be attempted in studies being commissioned by the Ministry of Transport.

cost and other travel characteristics. For instance, workers who choose trains rather than buses to travel to work are buying a particular travel, for which they are prepared to pay to save time, compared with travelling by bus. There are a few quite distinct kinds of travel decisions, and each one is potentially susceptible to this sort of analysis. This list is of areas of choice where work has been attempted:

(a) Choice of destination to travel to, or frequency of trip-making to a particular destination.
(b) Choice of mode of travel.
(c) Choice of route.
(d) Choice of speed at which to drive.
(e) Choice of relative locations of home and work.

We shall examine each of these choice areas in turn subsequently; firstly, we discuss some general characteristics of methods of analysing choices.

When travellers make choices in any one of the choice areas mentioned above, they may well not be making a conscious trade-off between time and money; indeed there are usually very many other factors that both consciously and unconsciously affect their choices. For the researcher intent upon estimating a value of travel time, there is a danger in principle in trying too hard to find a value of time in situations where time or cost may not be important variables at all. All of this points to the need to approach the analysis of a choice situation with the primary object of trying to explain the choice, rather than trying to derive a value of time. If in fact a value of time emerges from the explanation of choice – then the effort is rewarded; if it does not, then nothing can be gained by twisting the explanatory relationships so as to yield a time value. This is an obvious point of research methodology and does not need labouring, but it is worth noting that the point could be made of more than one of the empirical studies mentioned here.

Basically the method is to formulate some models for topography which purports to explain rationally either the collective or, on a probabilistic basis, the individual behaviour of travellers, and to assign relative weights to different factors. Because such a model may well not appear to explain behaviour in specific individual cases, we must deal statistically with large numbers of people, and we then use statistical techniques to derive quantitative values for the model or hypothesis. Immediately, this imposes certain conditions which both the model and the data must meet if the method is to yield valid results. In order to demonstrate these conditions, and to illustrate the sorts of behavioural model and statistical techniques that are being referred to, a particular model in a particular choice area will now be described.

This is a relatively successful model that has been used in recent years to explain choice of travel mode, in nearly every case for commuters travelling to and from work. It is based on a linear function of the relative characteristics of one mode with respect to the other – which some researchers (including the present authors) like to think of as a 'relative disutility of one mode with respect to the other' – and a relationship for the probability of choice of one mode with respect to the other as a logistic function of this relative disutility:

$$L(X) = a_0 + \sum a_i x_i$$

and $$P_1(X) = \frac{e^{L(X)}}{1 + e^{L(X)}},$$

where X is a vector of values of relative characteristics of the two modes (time, cost, etc.), a_i is a vector of parameters whose values are to be determined by analysis, and $P_1(X)$ is the probability of

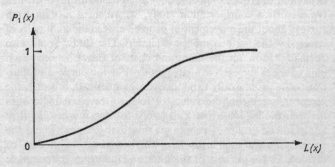

Figure 1

a traveller (or proportion of a group of travellers) characterized by the vector X choosing mode 1 for this journey. This general approach has been used, with variations in the statistical methodology, by Warner (1962), Quarmby (1967a), Lisco (1968), Thomas (1967) [this was for route, not mode, choice], Research Projects Ltd (1969), Local Government O.R. Unit (1968), Lave (1969) and Mercadal (1968).

This model has been used by most researchers in the first instance to explain modal choice rather than to derive a value of time; the emphasis has therefore been largely on obtaining as good an explanation of choice behaviour as possible, with whatever variables have been available in the data and have been shown to be significant. The model itself is something whose form can be derived *ex hypothesi*, either from economic concepts of disutility (see Philips, 1969, and Quarmby, 1967b) or from statistically based analogies in the physical sciences (see Wilson, 1968). The statistical methods to establish a set of significant x's and a set of a's to go with them are various; discriminant analysis, multiple linear regression, and probit methods have all been used. The value of time is, then, the ratio of the appropriate coefficients a_i/a_j, where i is the time variable and j is the financial cost variable.

The model has generally been used by researchers to analyse individual choices, that is, using as data the actual choice made by each individual together with the values of travel characteristics facing that individual. It can also be used to analyse the behaviour of groups of people on a zonal basis: for instance, in a typical urban transportation study, where there is data from surveys about the movement of people between different pairs of zones, by the various modes available. The study would also normally throw up the times and costs of travel between each pair of zones for each available mode. For the purpose of illustration we assume only two modes are available. In this case, the vector x_i represents the values of relative travel characteristics between modes for a particular zone-to-zone journey, as they apply to the group of people making that journey (where the zones represent unit areas into which a conurbation may be divided, for the purpose of analysing and modelling the complete travel patterns of the conurbation). And $P_1(X)$ is the proportion of travellers choosing mode 1, so that multiple regression can be performed by transforming as follows:

from $\quad P_1(X) = \dfrac{e^{L(X)}}{1 + e^{L(X)}},$

$$L(X) = \log_e \dfrac{P_1(X)}{1 - P_1(X)}.$$

Thus with observed data about $P_1(X)$, since

$$L(X) = a_0 + \sum a_i x_i,$$

regress $\quad \log_e \dfrac{P_1(X)}{1 - P_1(X)}$

on $\quad a_0 + \sum a_i x_i.$

We now examine at some length the five choice areas mentioned above, and discuss both the general methodological approach in each area, and the ways in which various researchers have attempted to derive time values. No attempt is made at this stage to review studies for their actual empirical results – we are only concerned with reviewing studies for their methodology.

(a) Choice of destination to travel to, or frequency of trip making to a particular destination

The alternatives in the title exist because of different hypotheses about the substitutability of trips to A for trips to B, and because of real differences in substitutability between different trip purposes. The basic approach is the same, however – to relate the amount of trip making to a particular place to the time and distance costs (and any other components of 'cost') associated with getting there, using as data either trip making to many different places from one origin, or trip making to one place from many different origins. One of the many alternative forms of the 'gravity distribution model' will provide an *a priori* model to establish an explanation of the observed data, in cases where some substitutability of trips can be assumed. One such form is[5]

$$T_{ij} = \frac{O_i A_j f(C_{ij})}{\sum\limits_k A_k f(C_{ik})},$$

where T_{ij} is the number of trips in unit time made from area or zone i to area or zone j; O_i is the *total* number of trips generated by zone i; and A_j is a measure of the attractiveness of zone j. $f(C_{ij})$ is a decaying function of the overall cost or disutility of travel C_{ij} between zone i and zone j. The bottom line serves to 'balance' the model, i.e. to constrain that

$$\sum_j T_{ij} = O_i.$$

In the case where the data refer to trip making to several destinations from one origin, then $O_i / \sum\limits_k A_k f(C_{ik})$ is constant for all observations, and the model reduces to

$$T_{ij} = k A_j f(C_{ij}).$$

The most common algebraic forms of $f(C_{ij})$ are $e^{-\lambda C_{ij}}$ and C_{ij}^{-n}, and sometimes the two in combination. Then the model reduces to

$$\frac{T_{ij}}{A_j} = k e^{-\lambda C_{ij}} C_{ij}^{-n}.$$

Whence $\log \dfrac{T_{ij}}{A_j} = k' - \lambda C_{ij} - n \log C_{ij}.$

We suppose the travel 'cost' from i to j can be represented as a linear function of in-vehicular time, distance, other types of time (e.g. walking), parking charges, etc., describing the journey from i to j. It is the relative weights (a_h) of the different components (x_h) that we want to find

$$C_{ij} = a_1 x_1 + \ldots + a_h x_h + \ldots + a_n x_n,$$

since the ratio of a for travelling time to a for cost gives us the

5. Gravity-type distribution models, as used in a transport context, can take a number of forms, depending on the precise conditions and constraints which the model-builder wishes to impose. The model described here is reckoned by the authors as suitable for modelling travel movements in either urban or inter-urban areas for journeys other than to or from places of work. For a discussion of alternative forms, see Wilson (1968).

value of time. With several observations of T_{ij}, A_j and the associated x's, then multiple regression can be performed iteratively with the following, where, substituting for C_{ij},

$$\log \frac{T_{ij}}{A_j} = k' - \lambda(a_1 x_1 + \ldots + a_n x_n) - n \log (a_1 x_1 + \ldots + a_n x_n).$$

There must exist variations in speed between routes to different places, otherwise the time and cost variables in the C_{ij} will be so highly correlated that no meaningful regression co-efficients, and hence no implied time/cost trade-offs, can be derived. There are no published studies of attempts to establish values of time from this method applied to data on trip making from one origin to several destinations. The alternative approach, using data on trip making to one destination from several origins, has recently been attempted by Mansfield (1969a) on recreational trips to the Lake District. In terms of the gravity distribution model above, much less is now constant over the data: since the $O_i / \sum_k A_k f(C_{ik})$ is different for each origin, only the A_j is constant over the data. However, if insignificant substitutability between the Lake District and other destinations can be assumed, then the model effectively reduces to something of the form

$$T_{iL} = kO_i f(C_{iL}),$$

where T_{iL} is the number of trips from zone i to zone L, the Lake District, etc. Proxies for O_i, in the form of population and car ownership levels, can be used to facilitate data gathering about many different origin zones. C_{iL} can be decomposed into its time, cost and other parts, and regressions performed.

For a more detailed methodological discussion of trip distribution models and the value of time, see Mansfield (1969b). Generally this is an interesting method which with care could throw light on certain values of time not readily obtainable by the more 'classical' methods as applied to modal choice – for instance, on social and recreational trips, and on long distance trips.

So far it has hardly been tried at all by researchers – probably because data is not easily available or easily obtainable, and probably because the task of meeting the empirical and statistical conditions could be formidable. However, the objective of this method could be described as trying to formulate a 'generalized cost' function – i.e. to set up a good, reliably quantified linear function for C_{ij}.

(b) Choice of mode of travel

As has already been indicated, this has been one of the most successful areas for value of time work. Although Warner (1962) was the first to develop an individual-based model to explain the binary choices of commuters, the structure of his variables did not yield a value of travel time, as he used the logarithm of ratios of costs and of times as a measure of the relativeness of one mode against another. In other words, where the model is of the form discussed above, i.e.

$$L(X) = a_0 + \sum a_i x_i$$

and $\quad P_1(X) = \dfrac{e^{L(X)}}{1+e^{L(X)}},$

x_1 would be

$$\log \frac{\text{time by mode 1}}{\text{time by mode 2}}$$

and x_2 would be

$$\log \frac{\text{cost by mode 1}}{\text{cost by mode 2}}.$$

The interesting implication of this form of variable structure is that time is valued solely in proportion to the total journey time, and cost is valued in proportion to the total journey cost. So it would be possible to say that for a journey of so many minutes and so many pence there is a trade-off between time and money of so much. But that trade-off is only defined for that particular journey cost and time. Now it may be that the value of time saved does vary with the total journey time but unfortunately Warner tested no other variable structures to see if they gave better explanations of behaviour.

Beesley was the first to attempt to derive a trade-off value for time and cost from modal choice data, only he did not explicitly use a model of the above form: his method can, however, be shown (Quarmby, 1967b) to be formally equivalent to the discriminant analysis method of determining the parameter a_i in the

$L(X)$ equation above, where x_i are the *differences* between time, cost, etc. However, it actually operates much more simply and more crudely. Using information about the times and costs for preferred and alternative modes of travel for each member of a group of travellers (for their journeys to work) then rational choices made would fall into one of three categories:

(i) those choosing cheaper and faster modes;
(ii) those choosing cheaper but slower modes;
(iii) those choosing more expensive but faster modes.

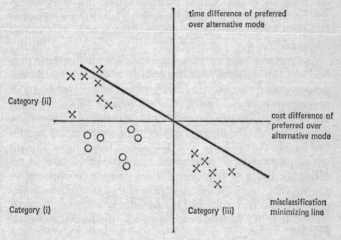

Figure 2

The method depends on being able to find a straight line through the origin of the graph shown, so as to minimize the proportion of observations on the 'wrong' side of the line. The basis of the method is that if the line is to represent the rate at which people will trade-off time savings against money savings, then none of those (or at least a minimum) actually choosing – say – a cheaper but slower mode (i.e. in quadrant ii) should be in a position of incurring more extra time than they are willing to incur for the money they are saving. So none of those in quadrant ii should be on the north-east side of the line (they should be in

A. J. Harrison and D. A. Quarmby 199

quadrant ii using the other mode then), and none of those in quadrant iii should be on the north-east side of the line. The first results on British data showing a value of time between 30 per cent and 50 per cent of gross personal income of the commuters were obtained using this method, but were found in the light of subsequent modal choice studies to over-estimate the value of travelling time itself. Apart from the fact that Beesley was using very small samples (less than 40 observations), the travelling time which he valued actually contains some walking and waiting time. Subsequent studies have shown walking and waiting to have rather higher values of time than in-vehicle; this may help to explain why Beesley's value of time is higher than the values of in-vehicle time obtained by other researchers in the United Kingdom.

As a method, there are three main criticisms: firstly, it can only deal with two variables, since it operates graphically in two dimensions. Secondly, it offers no formal tests of significance or goodness of explanation. Thirdly, it cannot reliably obtain a straight line other than through the origin; although this can in theory be done by transposing the quadrant iii points over into quadrant ii and finding the minimum misclassification line without fixing it through the origin, in practice there is too much 'noise' in the data to permit it to be found with any degree of confidence. In consequence, it must always be assumed that at zero time difference and zero cost difference the traveller is indifferent between modes. It is like forcing a_0 to be zero in the formal analytical method.

However, the method can give a very good intuitive idea of what the trade-off technique is all about, and since it can be done quickly without a computer it can be useful for looking at data prior to computer analysis. The Beesley method was used by Barnett and Saalmans in a (1967) GLC study of travel to and from work at County Hall; they obtained slightly lower values of time than Beesley did, but the same basic criticisms apply.

(c) Choice of route

This is concerned with drivers' choice of route over a road network. The most easily identifiable binary trade-off situations are between fast motorway and slower all-purpose road, and between paying tolls to cross estuaries by bridges or ferries and driving more mileage round the end of the estuary. Generally the same methodology as for modal choice is applicable here – the linear estimating equation and logistic probability transformation – and the only successful derivation of a value of travelling time from route choice did in fact use this (Thomas, 1967).

The principal empirical difficulties, which Thomas was mostly aware of and went to great length to try and overcome, are that the time and cost variables are usually even more highly correlated than in modal choice; secondly, there is often too little variation within the variables to allow a reliable estimating equation to be derived – this usually happens at tolled estuary crossings where nearly everyone is faced with the same time and cost differences; thirdly, the cost differences are largely made up of differences in car running costs (e.g. between crossing an estuary or going 'round the end') which are difficult to estimate as perceived by the driver, and it is found that values of time are even more sensitive to the mileage cost rate used than in modal choice analysis; fourthly, most of the route-choice situations in the United Kingdom that could lend themselves to this sort of analysis have a high proportion of non-regular journeys such as holidaymakers who cannot be presumed to have particularly accurate information about the alternatives facing them. Mention has already been made of the Claffey Study, in which the analytical model was inconsistent with the behavioural hypothesis; however, even when re-analysed in a consistent model (Quarmby, 1967c), no reliable values of time were obtained, principally because of very high multi-collinearity between travel time differences and cost differences, for the different pairs of tolled motorways and free all-purpose roads examined. The Road Research Laboratory study (Dawson and Smith, 1959) has already been mentioned too – this did not disguise between different kinds of time, and with a somewhat unsatisfactory analytical method obtained a very high value of time. However, even when re-analysed using discriminant analysis, no reliable value of time was obtained (Quarmby, 1967c), as the overall level of explanation was too low – probably because many of the travellers did not have sufficient information in which to make rational choices. [...]

(d) Choice of speed at which to drive

On the face of it this is a legitimate area of choice in which drivers trade-off increased operating costs with higher speeds and therefore lower travel times. However, it presumes that drivers are sufficiently well aware of the relationship between speed and operating cost so as to choose an 'optimum' speed. But there is no evidence that drivers have a sensitive enough awareness. It could be argued that there are many other factors that influence free-flow speed – such as safety. There is no evidence that cars with more passengers travel faster than those with fewer. Mohring (1965) attempted to derive a value of time on this basis; while it turns out to be not a ludicrous value, it can hardly be accorded much weight because of the method.

(e) Choice of relative locations of home and work

For core-orientated cities, it is possible to establish an economic model to indicate trade-off between commuting costs (including time costs) and location rent of housing. The main difficulty about using such a model empirically is firstly that the location rent is difficult to extract from all the other factors that influence the rent or value of a housing parkage – such as amenity, quality of building, and so on. Secondly, accessibility to a single area of work is not the only accessibility that the location rent is likely to be dependent on – even in very heavily core-orientated cities like London accessibility to non-central work places is important except for very high income commuters, and accessibility to other facilities can be important as well. However, Mohring (1960) did carry out analysis with this basic model, and obtained values of time which are not out of line in percentage terms with British values but rather less than other American values. Mohring himself recognizes important shortcomings both in the data and in the use of this model. A study by Pendleton (1963) obtains a value by the same general method as part of an attempt to explain real estate values. While there is no definite conclusion on time values, there is a useful discussion of the problems of using this method, e.g. treatment of vehicle operating costs, the appropriate discount rate, the level of trip-making of accessibility with other variables, e.g. age and density of the housing stock. Generally this is not likely to be a fruitful area until much more comprehensive general urban models exist, out of which sub-models for time-cost trade-off analysis might be carved.

(f) Some general issues on input data and interpretation

This section is concerned with some general problems that are common to a number of different studies, and methods already discussed, and which are not intrinsic to the methodology but substantially affect the resulting values of time. The first problem area is concerned with perceived values as against objectively assessed values; the second with interpretation of values of time for individuals or vehicles, earners or all adults, and so on.

Most of the early studies – whether on route or modal choice – used 'objective' estimates of car operating cost, and it was never actively considered by any of the researchers that drivers might not in fact be aware or want to be aware of the actual costs of running their cars; except that Dawson, in the RRL study of 1959, did discover that he had to reduce the car costs to petrol costs alone, otherwise nearly all the drivers who opted to drive round the Forth estuary would have found it quicker *and* cheaper to cross by the ferry. The question of car mileage costs matters for two reasons – firstly, because there is a big discrepancy between the 'real' marginal costs of car mileage and the costs which, by a variety of direct and indirect methods, researchers have found that motorists 'perceive' or at least base their behaviour on. Including fuel, oil, maintenance, tyres and mileage-dependent depreciation, most private cars show a marginal cost of between 4d and 7d a mile. Various empirical methods indicate 'perceived' costs between 2d and 4d a mile (in the period 1966–9). These methods range from direct interviews – asking people the cost of particular journeys (see Harrison, 1969) and Local Government O.R. Unit (1968) – to finding those mileage costs which best explain their travel behaviour (see Quarmby, 1967b). The second reason all this matters is that in both route choice and in modal choice (involving a car alternative), the value of time derived is extremely sensitive to the car mileage rate used to derive a travel cost by car. In the Leeds modal choice study (Quarmby, 1967b) it was found that the derived value of time was over twice as large when 4d a mile was used compared with when

2d a mile was used, although there was relatively little movement in the value of time between 1½d and 3d a mile. Three different analytical methods were used to find the mileage rate which most appropriately explained commuters' decisions, and a value of 2½d a mile was finally arrived at (this was from a survey in Spring 1966, when petrol cost 4s 6d to 5s a gallon; compared with mid-1969 petrol prices of 6s to 6s 8d a gallon).

In any trade-off situation where use of a car is involved (except in the carefully chosen case like Thomas', where mileages were the same by either route), it is clearly absolutely essential to use a mileage cost rate which is known or believed to reflect the drivers' perceptions of cost, or to reflect the revealed behaviour of drivers.

In the absence of an on-the-spot method of determining perceived or 'behaviour' mileage cost in a particular empirical study, the researcher should at least explore the sensitivity of his derived value of time to a range of mileage cost rate inputs. In any case, the researcher should not use an objective marginal cost as his best estimate, if there is no local empirical evidence as to perceived costs, unless the situation is so far removed from circumstances where there is empirical evidence (like a different country where the pattern of costs of fuel, maintenance, tyres, etc., is very different). In arriving at a good initial estimate for another European country it would seem from the direct interview studies that the best way to interpret the United Kingdom perceived mileage cost of 3d a mile or so is as the cost of petrol plus ½d or so for other dimly perceived mileage-dependent costs such as oil, etc.

Most of the American studies have yielded values of time rather higher – as a percentage of income – than the British studies. Part of this difference may be explained by the use of a higher mileage cost in these studies than the above discussion would warrant (except in the case of Thomas' study). Although Lisco, in his modal split study of Chicago commuters, found that the value of time did not vary much with two different levels of car operating costs, his lower figure was still as high as 6 cents per mile (higher 9 cents) which with gasoline at 30–35 cents a (United States) gallon is still very much more than gasoline costs. It would have been interesting to know how the value of time varied with mileage costs lower than 6 cents a mile. Although

Lisco is one of only a few American researchers to allow some uncertainty in what the mileage costs should be, he does not go very deeply into the actual problem of estimating what their perceived value is.

The difference between reality and how people perceive it – and indeed the difference between how people perceive it consciously and how their perception of it actually influences their behaviour – is at the heart of the above problem on mileage costs, but it also potentially affects every item of input data into a behaviour-explaining model. In modal and route choice studies of individual behaviour (as opposed to behaviour of groups), the researcher can use either the individuals' reported travel time and costs, or some objectively measured times and costs.

The problem is: which is more likely to give a reliable explanation of the individual's behaviour? We have already discussed the problem of the car mileage rate, but this alone can be reduced to a single unit quantity for which evidence can be sifted. No such treatment can be given to estimates of time – travelling, walking, waiting – and we are at the present time reduced to *a priori* arguments. There are arguments on both sides:

1. Objectively measured times can only be averages, and there may be real differences in the experience of individuals, for which their reported times are better approximations in each case.

2. If there are real discrepancies between reported and the directly equivalent objective time, it may be that people rationalize their choices (of mode or route) by under-estimating their preferred alternative, and over-estimating their rejected alternative.

3. Travellers may really not have reliable information about their rejected alternative; but it could be said that this is the information they base their decisions on, reliable or not.

4. Behaviour may not be best explainable in terms of either the consciously perceived characteristics or the objective measurements, but it is likely to be nearer the former than the latter.

Until research is done on this particular topic, the issue cannot be fully resolved; the authors generally prefer to use reported characteristics, in spite of the important argument about rationalization (2 above). It can be important: in Thomas' study, the value of time using perceived differences in travel time was over twice that using measured differences. In the case of a route choice study, where results are highly geared to smallish differences in driving times, there is a case for using perceived or reported times, if only to express the real variations (even in United States) in driving speeds and time experiences by drivers.

The other major question in this section refers to the interpretation of a value of time, and the specific issue of how a value of time derived for a vehicle and for an earner (and particularly a value derived from commuting studies) can be generalized to a value for people in general, for whom a planning agency might wish to estimate the value of time savings. The route choice studies in general derive a value of time for a vehicle, and the question is whether this wholly represents the value of time for the driver, or for all the occupants equally; the modal choice studies in general derive a value of time for a commuter who earns – while this value can be attributed to him, what can we deduce about the value of time for other members of his household, and in so far as the value of time is empirically found to relate to income, should it be linked to personal income of the earner, or to the household income? 'And what can we say about non-commuting journeys? These are important issues where there may be, between studies and between countries, differences in car occupancy, in earners per household, in household size, etc., and where we wish to generalize between studies, and particularly where our most reliable values derive from commuting studies. All these questions relate in principle to the social psychology of the household and of its members, and while it is possible to argue on *a priori* grounds whether husbands treat their wives like themselves or not, in terms of spending money on saving time, it is also possible to carry out psychologically based research studies to find out.

6. Lee and Dalvi (1969; 1971) discuss this briefly: they argue that a household-based quantity is probably more appropriate for describing behaviour, but that a personal-based quantity is more accurately obtainable as data in surveys. The authors tend to agree.

References

BEESLEY, M. E. (1965), 'The value of time spent travelling: some new evidence', *Economics*, vol. 32, May.

CLAFFEY, P. J. (1961), 'Characteristics of passenger car travel on toll roads and comparable free roads', St. Clare's College and N. Weider, *Highway Research Bulletin*, no. 306.

DAWSON, R. F. F., and SMITH, N. D. S. (1959), 'Evaluating the time of private motorists by studying their behaviour', Report on a pilot experiment, Road Research Laboratory, Research Note 3474.

EVANS, A. (1969), 'A general theory of the allocation of time', unpublished paper, University of Glasgow.

FLEISCHER, G. A. (1962), *The Economic Utilization of Commercial Vehicle Time Saved as the Result of Highway Improvements*, Stanford University.

GRONAU, R. (1970), 'The effect of travelling time on the demand for passenger transportation', *J. Polit. Econ.*, March/April.

HANING, C. R., and MCFARLAND, W. F. (1963), 'Value of time saved to commercial motor vehicles through use of improved highways', *Bulletin no. 23*, Texas Transportation Institute.

HARRISON, A. J. (1967), 'Road transport and the motorway', *Bulletin of Oxford Inst.*, vol. 25, no. 3.

HARRISON, A. J. (1969), *Estimation of the Marginal Wage Increment*, Time Research note 8, Highway Economics Unit, Ministry of Transport.

JOHNSON, M. E. (1966), 'Travel time and the price of leisure', *Western econ. J.*, Spring.

LAVE, C. A. (1969), 'Model choice in urban transportation: a behavioral approach', unpublished Ph.D. thesis, University of California.

LEE, N., and DALVI, M. Q. (1969), 'Variations in the value of travel time', *Manchester School*, September.

LEE, N., and DALVI, M. Q. (1971), 'Variations in the value of travel time: further analysis', *Manchester School*, September.

LISCO, T. (1968), 'The value of commuters' travel time: a study in urban transportation', dissertation submitted to the Social Sciences Faculty, University of Chicago.

LOCAL GOVERNMENT OPERATIONAL RESEARCH UNIT (1968), *Modal Split: Factors Determining the Choice of Transport for the Journey to Work*, report no. C32.

MANSFIELD, N. W. (1969a), 'Recreational trip generation', *J. Transport Econs. and Policy*.

MANSFIELD, N. W. (1969b), *Trip Generation Functions and Research into the Value of Time*, Time Research note 1, Highway Economics Unit, Ministry of Transport.

MERCADAL, M. (1968), 'Choice of mode of transport', paper resented to ECMT 3rd Round Table on Economic Research.

MOHRING, H. (1960), 'Highway benefits: an analytical framework', Transportation Centre, Northwestern University.

MOHRING, H. (1965), 'Urban highway investments', in R. Dorfman (ed.), *Measuring the Benefits of Government Investments*, The Brookings Institution.

MOSES, L., and WILLIAMSON, H. (1963), 'Value of time, choice of mode, and the subsidy issue in urban transportation', *J. Polit. Econ.*, vol. 71.

OORT, C. J. (1969), 'Evaluation of travelling time', *J. Transport Econs and Policy*, May.

PENDLETON, W. B. (1963), *Relation of Highway Accessibility to Urban Real Estate Values*, Highway Research Record no. 16.

PHILIPS, J. (1969), 'Valuing travel time: some implications of recent theories', report submitted by Economic Consultants Ltd to Ministry of Transport.

QUARMBY, D. A. (1967a), 'Choice of travel mode for the journey to work', *J. Transport Econs. and Policy*, vol. 1, no. 3.

QUARMBY, D. A. (1967b), 'Factors affecting commuter travel behaviour', Ph.D. thesis, University of Leeds.

QUARMBY, D. A. (1967c), 'Values of non-working time: a re-analysis of two studies', M.A.U. Note 76, Mathematical Advisory Unit, Ministry of Transport.

RESEARCH PROJECTS LIMITED (1969), 'Modal choice – a study of use and non-use of public transport in the Greater London Area', RPL.

THOMAS, T. C. (1967), *The Value of Time for Passenger Cars: An Experimental Study of Commuters' Values*, Stanford Research Institute.

WARNER, S. L. (1962), 'Stochastic choice of mode in urban travel: a study in binary choice', Transportation Centre, Northwestern University.

WILSON, A. G. (1968), 'A statistical theory of spatial distribution models', *Transportation*, vol. 1, no. 3.

7 N. W. Mansfield

The Value of Recreational Facilities

Excerpt from N. W. Mansfield, 'The estimation of benefits from recreation sites and the provision of a new recreation facility', *Regional Studies*, vol. 5, 1971, pp. 56–9.[1]

Marshall (1920) defines consumers' surplus as

... the price which a person pays for a thing can never exceed, and seldom comes up to that which he would be willing to pay rather than go without it: so that the satisfaction which he gets from its purchase generally exceeds that which he gives up in paying away its price; and he thus derives from the purchase a surplus of satisfaction. The excess of the price which he would be willing to pay rather than go without the thing, over that which he actually does pay, is the economic measure of this surplus satisfaction. It may be called *consumers' surplus*.

In mathematical terms, where there is a relationship between price and quantity demanded of the sort: $p = f(q)$ then consumers' surplus can be measured by the integral

$$\int_0^q f(q)\, dq - p \cdot q,$$

that is, total utility less actual revenue paid for the good in question.

[1]*Editor's note:* This reading is part of a wider study designed to evaluate the benefits of providing a new recreational facility at Morecambe Bay in North-West England. In order to illustrate the method Mansfield begins (in the excerpt reprinted here) by calculating the existing benefits of the nearby Lake District National Park.

In practice it is rarely possible to derive the basic relationship $p = f(q)$, especially in the sphere of recreation where most activities are available free, or at a nominal charge. However, it was pointed out by Clawson (1969) that the user of a recreation facility invariably has to spend both time and money in transporting himself to the site, and both Clawson and later writers have found an inverse relationship between this 'travel cost' and the number of people in a given population who made use of the facility. Generally, the travel cost–recreation demand relationship bears a striking resemblance to the formal 'gravity model' of transport planning, which, as Harrison and Quarmby (1970) state, can for a single destination be expressed as

$$T_{iL} = k \cdot O_i f(C_{iL}),$$

where T_{iL} are trips from zone i to zone L, the single-destination recreation area; O_i (normally in transport models the total number of trips from an origin zone) can be approximated by use of car ownership and population proxy variables. In this case the consumers' surplus calculation becomes

$$\sum_i \int_{C_i}^{C_0} T_{iL} \, dC_{iL},$$

where C_0 is the cost for each zone at which zero trips would take place. (In economic terms, the travel cost procedure and the gravity model both follow the Walrasian formulation of the quantity–price relationship, rather than the Marshallian form most usually considered in welfare economics.) Use of this integral is a short-cut procedure to the estimation of benefit, since it is implicit in a Clawson-type demand curve. The latter was not explicitly derived for this study, as it was less concerned with overall demand at different 'prices' than with the total benefit from a recreation area.

Some writers (notably Smith and Kavanagh (1969) and Burton and Wibberley (1965)) include as part of the benefits derived from a recreation site the money payment (if any) made for the use of the facility, i.e. the cost of an angling or sailing licence. This is largely on the grounds that recreation can be provided at zero cost, so that any charge represents either an economic rent or producers' surplus, as well as a measure of utility. It might be argued that this item should be included as a site-specific benefit in the present case, where such charges are levied.

It can be accepted that benefits are obtained by the recreationalist at least equal to the money price or travel cost he has to bear. However, the usual rule of consumer equilibrium theory that the marginal utilities from each good are in constant proportion to the price of that good means that should use of the site suddenly be denied to the recreationalist, he will be able to rearrange his expenditure to achieve the same amount of utility (excluding surplus elements) as he got from it before. (If he could get more afterwards, this implies disequilibrium at the margin, and that the recreationalist would have been better off to have arranged his previous expenditure away from the site under consideration, despite its continued existence.)

Hence, although the revenue obtainable from charging for the use of a site will be of interest to an entrepreneur, as well as consumers' surplus items, if his policy is to maximize utility over a given set of independent projects, neither revenue nor travel cost should properly enter a *social* benefit calculation. Nationally, expenditure on a single recreation site is purely marginal, and is unlikely to have noticeable Hicksian income effects. The net benefit to the nation from its existence is therefore only the surplus foregone were the site to suddenly disappear, the 'real resources' being released in such an eventuality being capable of redeployment to yield as much value as in its former use, and so having no welfare connotations. In the Morecambe Bay study it was assumed that no producers' surplus element was concealed in either charges or the 'travel cost' proxy price, and these were ignored in estimating total surplus.

Surplus from the Lake District

The amount of consumers' surplus derived from two of the three basic recreation activities in the Lake District during 1966 (namely full-day trips and half-day trips) was estimated from trip distribution equations of the following general form

$$T_{iL} = K + bW_i + cC_{iL}^{-n} + e,$$

where T_{iL} = day trips or half-day trips on an average peak day per 1000 population from each origin zone i, W_i = cars owned per 100 households in each origin zone i, C_{iL} = cost (expressed in terms of 'distance units') of travel to the Lake District from each original zone i, e = an error term, and n an exponent set arbitrarily at 2.

The data employed was based on an earlier study on recreational trip generation by Mansfield (1969), which investigated the distribution of trips to the Lake District during several peak weekends in 1966. For each zone considered, consumers' surplus was calculated from the definite integral

$$\sum_i \int_{C_i}^{C_0} T_{iL} \, dC_{iL} = \sum_i [(k+bW_i)C_{iL} - cC_{iL}^{-1}]_i^0,$$

giving a value of surplus in terms of distance units.

Although it is a reasonable proposition that journey costs vary proportionately with distance, and that therefore the value of each 'distance unit' is constant whatever the total number of 'distance units' in the value of surplus, finite cost values are needed to convert the latter into £p. It has been stated that travel cost on the journey to a recreation site includes the expenditure of both time and money. The fundamental question is what value ought to be placed (if any) on each element.

It can be argued that travellers positively enjoy the time they spend travelling while on recreation trips, or are at least indifferent at the margin to time spent in such a way. If this were so, it would be wrong to include any 'value' for the cost of travel time in the surplus value, since motorists would not be willing to pay to have it reduced (or might even pay *not* to have it reduced). Knetsch (1963) has claimed that the use of a distance–decay function as the form of the travel costs–trips relationship implicitly assumes time and money are not substitutable. However, in a situation like the Lake District where journey times and road distances are almost totally correlated, the functional form used in this study is compatible with some underlying 'generalized cost' relationship, incorporating a finite value of time as well as operating costs. (See Mansfield (1970) for a more detailed discussion of the theoretical assumptions in trip distribution functions.) As Knetsch rightly points out, to ignore the time element in travel completely would lead to the Clawson procedure over-estimating consumers' surplus.

Such evidence as there is on the subject, relating to the Lake District (Mansfield, 1969) and the Forest of Dean (Colenutt, 1969) suggests that motorists *are* responsive to variations in the journey time to a recreation area, even though they may not be while driving for pleasure within (say) a National Park. In arriving at the final surplus value it was accordingly assumed that motor-ists travelling to the Lake District valued their time at between 8s 6d and 9s 3d (42·5p and 46p) per car party, consistent with the results reported by Mansfield. At an average journey speed of 48 kph (30 mph), these values imply a 'time-cost' element of 6·8d to 7·4d (2·8p to 3·1p) per 'distance unit'.[1]

Again, there is room for debate on the value attributable to vehicle operating costs. At one extreme, there is the full cost of motoring, including all depreciation and maintenance costs, at up to 1s 6d (7½p) per mile. To a motorist who owned his car solely to go on recreation trips, this may be the effective marginal opera-ting cost. At the other extreme, there is the basic petrol cost of 1½d (½p) per mile for a car-user who has a business car main-tained at the expense of his employer. Basically, however, one is measuring 'utility' in consumers' surplus calculations, and there-fore should be valuing costs at what motorists think they are paying, and not what they actually pay. Vehicle operating costs have therefore been assumed to be 3d (1·25p) per mile, following Quarmby's findings regarding the perceptions of travel cost by motorists in Leeds (Quarmby, 1967). This value is also supported by some unreported findings by Smith (1969) in his study of trout fishing at Grafham Water, and follows current practice with regard to the treatment of perceived costs at the Department of the Environment. Adding together the time and cost elements, a value is obtained for each 'distance unit' in 1966 of 12·8d (5·3p) on full-day trips, and 13·4d (5·6p) on half-day trips.

Two problems had to be overcome in using the basic distribu-tion equations as a foundation for calculating consumers' surplus, since they were not suitable in their general form for the purpose.

1. It should be realized that these values are implicit in the model, which is based on Mansfield's data, and not an exogenous addition to total travel cost.

This was because the functions approach the trips and cost axes asymptotically, and the model can only take zero values where one or other of the variables reaches infinity, or through the influence of other factors, such as car ownership levels.[2] In the particular case considered, the nature of the data was such that, except for three zones in the day-trip model, there was a finite point along the cost axis at which predicted trips equalled zero. This value for each zone was used as the upper limit of the surplus integral since it reflected zone specific influences on demand. For the three zones where the curve stretched to infinity, a cost of 120 distance units (miles) was used for the cost level at which zero trips would be forthcoming. This represented a weighted average of the 'observed' cost levels at which zero trips were predicted in the remaining zones. Actual values in these other zones varied from 100 – for Tyneside (the area with fewest cars) – to 190.

The second problem was more difficult to overcome. Except for one or two zones, predictions based on the single equation of the model varied somewhat from actual observed trip numbers, due to factors not subsumed in the variables considered. For example, the actual road distance from one zone was seventy-two miles, but even after allowing for its low car-ownership level, the zone only generated the number of trips to be expected at a distance of eighty miles. (The model could not be reformulated to eliminate these errors.) The procedure used in calculating consumers' surplus involved integration of the trip distribution functions from a lower limit which could be either the actual observed cost of travel in terms of distance units, or the cost implied by a solution of the model to obtain the actual observed trip numbers. In practice, however, there was little difference between the two methods of integration, and that using observed cost levels as a lower limit was adopted in subsequent calculations.[3] The results are given in Table 1.

A slightly different procedure was adopted in the calculation of

2. Examination of the equations used, with their negative constant terms and positive relationship with car ownership levels, showed that any variation in the point where predicted trips equalled zero was largely a function of the different car ownership levels in each zone.

3. To consider a hypothetical example, take Figure 1 relating trip levels to travel costs.

the consumers' surplus accruing from holiday trips to the Lake District. The thirty-two geographical zones into which the original data was divided were revised to form nine broad distance bands, concentric to the Lake District, of between ten and fifty miles in width. This was done in an attempt to make the zones sufficiently homogeneous with respect to factors not taken into account directly into the model, so that a better explanation of trip distribution would be achieved. As can be seen from Table 2 below, an exponential fall-off of trips with distance was thus pro-

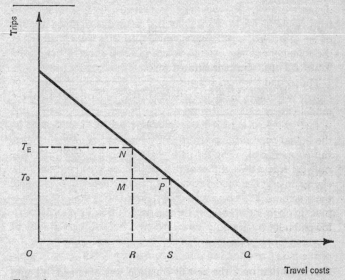

Figure 1

Let actual observed trips be OT_0, but the expected trip level be OT_E. To measure consumers' surplus one has the alternative of integrating under the demand curve between the points R and Q, or S and Q; in the latter case, the travel cost actually incurred is not $OSPT_0$, but $ORMT_0$, and the value represented by $MPRS$ is somehow 'lost' because of the inexactness of the model. Conversely, if the integration took place between R and Q, the area MNP is added incorrectly to the calculation of surplus, since it relates to trips which did not take place. $MPRS$ is included correctly, however, as a surplus item. It is clear that the true level of surplus must lie somewhere between these two values, and depending on the elasticity of demand, nearer to that calculated using observed costs rather than trips.

Table 1 Estimated surplus from day and half-day trips –
average day, Lake District National Park 1966

Zone	Full-day visitors £	Half-day visitors £
Within 25 miles of National Park	1231	757
Lancashire	1705	342
North-East England	300	20
Yorkshire	391	21
Rest of England	109	—
Total consumers' surplus per average day	3736	1140

Table 2 Trips from concentrated zones

Zone (miles)	Journey cost in weighted distance units	Holiday trips per 1000 population	Population (000s)
30–39	32	0·9222	417·5
40–49	42	0·6997	290·2
50–69	64	0·4644	2598·7
70–89	73	0·3125	7779·2
90–119	103	0·2008	3102·4
120–149	138	0·1697	3144·4
150–199	163	0·1188	5174·6
200–249	226	0·0987	13,163·7
250 plus	301	0·0826	9843·4

duced, so that once the best-fit equation was obtained, it could
be treated in the same way as described previously to obtain an
estimate of total surplus.

The best explanation of holiday trip distribution was obtained
from $T_{IL} = kO_I f(C_{IL})^\beta$ fitted to the data above as a logarithmic–
linear equation by least squares regression. In order that the
fitted demand curve should intersect both axes, an arbitrary addition of 1 was made to all observations of recorded trips per 1000
population. (This follows a procedure adopted previously by
Knetsch (1964), and Smith and Kavanagh, to derive demand
curves with a finite limit of zero trips.) The value 1 (rather than

0·80 as used by Knetsch) has the advantage of being mathematically neutral, since $\log_e 1 =$ zero, while constraining the logarithm values to be positive for all observations.

The equation finally obtained to explain variations in weekly holiday trips was (translated back from logarithmic values into real numbers):

Holiday Trips per 1000 population =
$$-1·00$$
$$+4·33 \text{ (Distance Units to the power of minus } 0·259).$$

The percentage level of explanation was 90·07 per cent. This equation predicted that zero trips occur at a cost level of 288 Distance Units (or thirteen below the maximum recorded). Since trips from both the furthermost band and the penultimate one were underpredicted by the model, for purposes of estimating consumers' surplus they were treated as one, with a mean journey cost of 226 Distance Units. A value of 12d (5p) was used[4] for each distance

Table 3 Estimated surplus from holiday
trips – average week, Lake District 1966

Zone (miles)	Total trips per average week	Estimated surplus per average week (£)
30–39	385	1136·58
40–49	203	689·08
50–69	1207	4613·81
70–89	2431	12,283·27
90–119	623	3245·11
120–149	534	1932·33
150–199	615	2046·43
200–249	1294	1012·81
250 plus	810	740·82
Totals	8102	27,700·24

4. As there was no direct evidence from the data used in the study concerning the value of time on holiday journeys, use was made of the values quoted in Harrison *et al.* (1969). An occupancy rate of 2·2 adults and 0·8 children per car was assumed, giving an overall value of 7s 6d (37·5p) per car hour.

unit in calculating consumers' surplus using the integral

$$\sum_i \int_{C_i}^{C_0} T_{iL} \, dC_{iL} = \sum_i \left[\frac{4.33}{0.74} C_{iL}^{0.74} - C_{iL} \right]_{C_i}^{C_0}$$

with $C_0 = 288$ and C_{iL} the number of Distance Units from the centroid of band i to the Lake District. The results are presented in Table 3.

References

BURTON, T. L., and WIBBERLEY, G. P. (1965), *Outdoor Recreation in the British Countryside*, Wye College, University of London.

CLAWSON, M. (1959), 'Methods of measuring the demand for and value of outdoor recreation', *Resources for the Future*, reprint no. 10, Washington D.C.

COLENUTT, R. J. (1969), 'An investigation into the factors affecting the pattern of trip generation and route choice of day visitors to the countryside', Ph.D. thesis, University of Bristol.

HARRISON, A. J., *et al.* (1969), 'The value of time savings in transport investment appraisal', Directorate of Economics Technical Note no. 3, Ministry of Transport.

HARRISON, A. J., and QUARMBY, D. A. (1970), 'The value of time in transport planning', ECMT Occasional Paper, Paris.

KNETSCH, J. L. (1963), 'Outdoor recreation demands and benefits', *Land Econ.*, vol. 39, pp. 387–96.

KNETSCH, J. L. (1964), 'The economics of including recreation as a purpose of eastern water projects', *J. Farm Econ.*, vol. 46.

MANSFIELD, N. W. (1969), 'Recreational trip generation – a cross section analysis of weekend pleasure trips to the Lake District National Park', *J. Trans. Econ. Policy*, vol. 3, no. 2.

MANSFIELD, N. W. (1970), 'Trip distribution functions and the value of time', a review in N. W. Mansfield (ed.), *Papers and Proceedings of a Conference on Research into the Value of Time*, Department of the Environment.

MARSHALL, A. (1920), *Principles of Economics*, ch. 6, 8th edn, Macmillan.

QUARMBY, D. A. (1967), 'Choice of travel mode for the journey to work', *J. Trans. Econ. Policy*, vol. 1, no. 3.

SMITH, R. J., and KAVANAGH, N. J. (1969), 'The measurements of the benefits of trout fishing', *J. Leisure Res.*, vol. 1, no. 4.

8 E. J. Mishan

The Value of Life

E. J. Mishan, 'Evaluation of life and limb: a theoretical approach',
The Journal of Political Economy, vol. 79, no. 4, 1971, pp. 687–705.

As cost-benefit studies grow in popularity, it is increasingly important to make proper allowance for losses or gains arising from changes in the incidence of death, disablement, or disease caused by the operation of new projects or developments. What is at issue is not the reliability of the current estimates of economic gains or losses arising from the saving or losing of life or health but the appropriateness of the ideal or conceptual measures about which, so far, there is no consensus among economists. I propose, therefore, first to argue that the more familiar concepts employed in evaluating the loss or saving of life are all unsatisfactory and, second, by referring to the basic rationale of economic calculation, to determine how such losses and gains should, in principle, be evaluated.

Since the analysis of saving life is symmetrical with that of losing it, it will simplify the exposition if, initially, we confine ourselves to the analysis of loss of life and limb – or, more briefly, to loss of life alone – indicating the necessary extensions in the latter part of the paper.

1. Despite repeated expressions of dissatisfaction with the method, the most common way of calculating the economic worth of a person's life and, therefore, the loss to the economy consequent upon his decease is that of discounting to the present the person's expected future earnings. A precise expression for the loss to the

economy calculated on this method would be L_1, where

$$L_1 = \sum_{t=\tau}^{\infty} Y_t P_\tau^t (1+r)^{-(t-\tau)}.$$

The Y_t is the expected gross earnings of (or, alternatively, value added by) the person during the tth year, exclusive of any yields from his ownership of nonhuman capital.[1] The P_τ^t is the probability in the current, or τth, year of the person being alive during the tth year, and r is the social rate of discount expected to rule during the tth year. This kind of calculation is occasionally supplemented by a suggestion that auxiliary calculations be made in order to take account of the suffering of the victim, the loss of his utility due to his demise, and/or of the bereavement of his family.[2] More recently, and as an example of the economist's finesse, it has been proposed that such calculations be supplemented by the cost of 'premature burial'[3] – the idea being that the present discounted value of the funeral expenses is higher if they are incurred sooner owing to an untimely death.

2. A second method, which might be thought of as more refined than the first, is that of calculating the present discounted value of the losses over time accruing to *others only* as a result of the

1. For the returns on his (nonhuman) assets continue after his death, or during his disablement.

2. For example, see Kneese (1966, p. 77) and Ridker (1967, p. 34). The suggestions, needless to remark, have not been taken up. Presumably they are made in response to an uneasy conscience about the methods actually being employed.

3. The expression occurs in Ridker's book (1967) on the costs of pollution. For those prone to morbid curiosity, the formula used is on page 39, and takes the form

$$C_a = C_o \left[1 - \sum_{n=a}^{\infty} \frac{P_a^n}{(1+r)^{n-a}} \right],$$

where C_a is the present value of the net expected gain from delaying burial at age a; C_o is the cost of burial; P_a^n is the probability that an individual age a will die at age n; and r is the discount rate. It is not impossible that these calculations were made with tongue in cheek and, if so, it is perhaps an oversight on his part that he omitted a countervailing consideration; namely, that if the unfortunate person died at a very early age, some useful savings might be effected from the lower cost of a smaller coffin.

death of the person at age τ. A precise expression for the loss to the economy based on this method would be L_2, where

$$L_2 = \sum_{t=\tau}^{\infty} P_\tau^t (Y_t - C_t)(1+r)^{-(t-\tau)},$$

where C_t is the personal expenditure of the individual during the tth period that is expected at time τ. This kind of measure (sometimes referred to as being based on the 'net output' approach in order to distinguish it from the 'gross output' approach associated with the L_1 measure), although occasionally mentioned in the literature – for instance, by Devons (1961, p. 107) and Ridker (1967, p. 36) – has not been employed apparently because of the assumed policy implications.

3. A third possible method would repudiate any direct calculation of the loss of potential earnings or spending. Instead, it would approach the problem from a 'social' point of view. Since society, through its political processes, does in fact take decisions on investment expenditures that occasionally increase or reduce the number of deaths, an implicit value of human life can be calculated. This approach receives occasional mention – for instance, by Fromm (1965, p. 193) and by Schelling (1968, p. 147) – and, indeed, the appeal to the political, or democratic, process is sometimes invoked to provide guidance on broader issues.[4]

4. Indeed, Rothenberg (1961, pp. 309–36) ends his examination of social welfare criteria by proposing that the democratic process itself be regarded as such a criterion. More recently, Nath (1969, pp. 216–17) proposes that the task of the economist be limited to that of revealing the locus of 'efficient' economic production possibilities available to society, leaving it to democracy to select the collection of goods it wishes. If one favors a majority decision rule or some other democratic decision rule for top level choices, the question must arise: on what grounds is this decision rule withheld (in favor of the potential Pareto criterion) at lower levels of *optima* – for instance, in generating a locus of 'efficient' collection of goods? A movement from a nonefficient point *inside* the boundary to an efficient point *on* the boundary of production possibilities can claim no more than can a movement from a top-level nonoptimal boundary point to a top-level optimal boundary point. Both of such movements have distributional implications, both meet the 'Scitovsky' criterion and both may be negated by the Kaldor-Hicks criterion.

4. The insurance principle is a departure from any of the afore-mentioned methods. Predicated on the premium a man is willing to pay, and the probability of his being killed as a result of engaging in some specific activity, it is thought possible to calculate the value a man sets on his life. An example is given by Fromm (1965, p. 194).

Each of these four possible methods of measuring the loss of life is now briefly appraised.

Method 1, turning on the loss of potential future earnings, can be rationalized only if the criterion adopted in any economic reorganization turns on the value of its contribution to GNP, or, more accurately, to net national product. But although financial journalists manage to convey the contrary impression, maximizing GNP is not an acceptable goal of economic policy. Notwithstanding its usage, most writers have mental reservations about its validity and tend to regard it as only part of the total measurement. For instance, Schelling (1968) makes a distinction between the value of likelihood, which is the L_1 measure, and the value of life, which poses a perplexing and possibly unsolvable problem.

The so-called net output method (2) might seem, at first glance, more acceptable than the gross output method. For, taking a cold-blooded attitude, what matters to the rest of society is simply the resulting loss, or gain, to society following the death of one or more of its members. This *ex post* approach, however, appears to strike some writers as either absurd or dangerous.[5] If accepted, it certainly follows that the death of any person whose L_2 measure is negative confers a net benefit on society. And this category of persons would certainly include all retired people irrespective of their ownership of property. Yet, from this undeniable inference, no dread policy implications follow. If the method were satisfactory on economic grounds, the inference would not, of itself, provide any reason for rejecting it. But the method is not satisfactory for the simple reason that it has no regard for the feelings of the potential decedents. It restricts itself to the interest only of

5. For example, Devons (1961, p. 108) concludes ironically: 'Indeed if we could only kill off enough old people we could show a net gain on accidents as a whole!' As for Ridker (1967, p. 36), the net output method 'suggests that society should not interfere with the death of a person whose net value is negative.'

the surviving members of society: it ignores society *ex ante* and concentrates wholly on society *ex post*.

As for the method (3) which would build on implicit values placed on human life by the political process, the justification appears somewhat circular even when we ignore the political realities of Western democracies. Assuming that democratic voting alone determines whether or not a particular investment project or part of a project is to be adopted, the idea of deriving quantitative values from the political process is clearly contrary to the idea of deriving them from an independent economic criterion. Where the outcome of the political debate calls upon the economist to provide a quantitative evaluation of the project under consideration, the economist fails to meet his brief insofar as he abandons the attempt to calculate any aspect of the project by reference to an economic criterion and, instead, attempts to extricate figures from previous political decisions.[6] By recourse to a method that refers a question, or part of a question, received from the political process back again to the political process, the economist appears to be concealing some deficiency in the relevant data or some weakness in the logic of his criteria.

Finally, there is method (4) based on the insurance principle. This has about it a superficial plausibility, enough, at any rate, to attract some attention. An early attempt, for instance, was made by Fromm (1965, pp. 193–6) to attribute a value for loss of life raised on the implied assumption of a straight-line relationship between the probability of a person being killed and the sum that he would pay to cover the risk. If, therefore, the premium y corresponding to the additional risk p is known, the value he places on his life is to be reckoned as y/p. Thus, if a man would pay \$100 to reduce his chance of being killed by 1 per cent – say, from an existing chance of one-twentieth to two-fiftieths the value he places on his life is to be estimated as \$10,000. (Or, to use Fromm's own calculation, if the probability of being killed in air travel were to be reduced from the existing figure of 0·0000017

6. Which is not to deny that the economist's criterion or criteria – although independent of the outcome of any particular political process that is sanctioned by the constitution – must be vindicated ultimately by reference to value judgements widely held within the community. The reader interested in this aspect is referred to Mishan (1969, pp. 13–23).

per trip of 500 miles to zero, a person who values his life at $400,000 should be willing to pay sixty-eight cents to reduce the existing risk to zero.)

The implied assumption of linearity, which has it that a man who accepts $100,000 for an assignment offering him a four-to-one chance of survival will agree to go to certain death for $500,000, is implausible, to say the least. And, indeed, this linearity assumption was later criticized by Fromm himself (1968, p. 174) when it was incidentally posited by Schelling (1968). But even if it were both plausible and proved, the insurance principle does not yield us the required valuation. For the insurance policy makes provision, in the event of a man's death, only for compensation to *others*. Thus, the amount of insurance a man takes out may be interpreted as a reflection, *inter alia*, of his concern for his family and dependents but hardly as an index of the value he sets on his own life.[7] A bachelor with no dependents could have no reason to take out flight insurance, notwithstanding the fact that he could be as reluctant as the next man to depart this fugacious life at short notice.

The crucial objection to each of these four methods, however, is that not one of them is consistent with the basic rationale of the economic calculus used in cost-benefit analysis. If we are concerned, as we are in all allocative problems, with increasing society's satisfaction in some sense, and if, in addition, we eschew interpersonal comparisons of satisfactions, we can always be guided in the ranking of alternative economic arrangements by the notion of a Pareto improvement – an improvement such that at least one person is made better off and nobody is made worse

7. An ingenious paper by Eisner and Strotz (1961), after some theorizing on the basis of the Neumann-Morgenstern axioms about the optimal amount of insurance a person should buy, addresses itself to the question of why people continue to buy air-accident insurance when ordinary life insurance is cheaper. They suggest, among other things, that flight insurance could be a gamble (related formally to the increasing marginal-utility segment of the income-utility curve), and they point also to the existence of imperfect knowledge, imperfect markets, and inertia. However, the paper does not, and is presumably not intended to, throw any light on this question of the valuation of human life. The observation that a man does not insure his life against some specific contingency cannot be taken as evidence that he is indifferent as between being alive and being dead.

off. A *potential* Pareto improvement,[8] one in which the net gains *can* so be distributed that at least one person is made better off, with none being made worse off, provides an alternative criterion, or definition, of social gain. This alternative, as it happens, provides the rationale of all familiar allocative propositions in economics and, therefore, the rationale of all cost-benefit calculations.[9]

When the full range of its economic effects is brought into the calculus, the introduction of a specific investment project will make some of the community of n members better off on balance, some worse off on balance, the remainder being indifferent to it If the jth person is made better off, a compensating variation (CV) measures the full extent of his improvement, this CV being a maximum sum V_j he will pay rather than forego the project, the sum being prefixed by a positive sign. *Per contra*, if the jth person is made worse off by the introduction of the project, his CV measures the full decline of his welfare as a minimal sum V_j he will accept to put up with the project, this sum being prefixed by a negative sign.[10] If, then, in response to the introduction of this specific project, the aggregate sum

$$\sum_{j}^{n} V_j > 0$$

8. A 'potential Pareto improvement' is an alternative and simpler nomenclature than 'hypothetical compensation test'. The problems associated with the concept are important, but need not concern us here if we accept the fact that cost-benefit analyses take place within a partial context, one in which changes in the prices of all the nonproject goods can be ignored. If this much is granted, the relevant individuals' compensating variations, which is what we are after, will be uniquely determined.

9. For the arguments that tend to this conclusion, see Mishan (1969, pp. 66–73).

10. These sums may be calculated as annual transfers or as capital sums according to the method being used in the cost-benefit study. Since the flow of costs and benefits is to be valued at a point of time, consistency would require that the CVs also be reckoned as a capital sum at that point of time. If there are no external effects of saving for future generations, as posited by Marglin (1963), the existence of imperfect capital markets will result in different rates of time preference among the persons concerned. In that case, capitalizing their CVs reckoned as annual sums at some single rate of discount will result in corresponding capitalized CVs which would differ from those chosen directly by these same persons, which latter sums should, of course, prevail.

(where j runs from 1 to n) – if, that is, the algebraic sum of all n individual CVs is positive – there is a potential Pareto improvement, its positive value being interpreted as the excess of benefits over costs arising from the introduction of the project.[11]

Consistency with the criterion of a potential Pareto improvement and, therefore, consistency with the principle of evaluation in cost-benefit analyses would require that the loss of a person's life be valued by reference to his CV; by reference, that is, to the minimum sum he is prepared to accept in exchange for its surrender. For unless a project that is held to be responsible for, say, an additional 1000 deaths annually can show an excess of benefits over costs *after* meeting the compensatory sums necessary to restore the welfare of these 1000 victims, it is not possible to make all members of the community better off by a redistribution of the net gains. A potential Pareto improvement cannot, then, be achieved, and the project in question ought not to be admitted.

If the argument is accepted, however, the requirements of consistency might seem to be highly restrictive. Since an increase in the annual number of deaths can be confidently predicted in connection with a number of particular developments – those, for example, which contribute to an increase in ground and air traffic – such developments would no longer appear as economically feasible. For it would not surprise us to discover that, in ordinary circumstances,[12] no sum of money is large enough to compensate a man for the loss of his life.

11. Within the same broad context, and allowing for sufficient divisibility in the construction of such projects, the corresponding rule necessary to determine the optimal output of such projects – or, in short periods, the optimal output of the goods of the existing project – takes the simple form that

$$\sum_{j}^{n} v_j = 0,$$

where v_j is the CV of the jth person in response to a marginal increment in the size of the industry or (in the short period) the size of its output.

12. If a man and his family were so destitute and their prospects so hopeless that one or more members were likely to die of starvation, or at least to suffer from acute deprivation, then the man might well be persuaded to sacrifice himself for the sake of his family. But without dependents or close and needy friends, the inducement to sacrifice himself for others is not strong.

In conditions of certainty, the logic of the above proposition is unassailable. If, in ordinary circumstances, we face a person with the choice of continuing his life in the usual way or of ending it at noon the next day, a sum large enough to persuade him to choose the latter course of action may not exist. And, indeed, if the development in question unavoidably entailed the death of this specific person or, more generally, a number of specific persons, it is highly unlikely that any conceivable excess benefit over cost, *calculated in the absence of these fatalities*, would warrant its undertaking on the potential Pareto criterion.

It is never the case, however, that a specific person, or a number of specific persons, can be designated in advance as being those who are certain to be killed if a particular project is undertaken.[13] All that can be predicted, although with a high degree of confidence, is that out of a total of n members in the community an additional x members per annum will be killed (and, say, an additional ten x members will be seriously injured). In the absence, therefore, of any breakdown of the circumstances surrounding the additional number of accidents to be expected, the increment of risk of being killed imposed each year on any one member of the community can be taken as x/n (and $10x/n$ for the risk of being seriously injured). And it is this fact of complete ignorance of the identity of each of the potential victims that transforms the calculation. Assuming universal risk aversion,[14] the relevant sums to be subtracted from the benefit side are no longer those which compensate a specific number of persons for their certain death but are those sums which compensate each person in the community for *the additional risk* to which he is to be exposed.[15]

13. Cf. Schelling's remarks (1968, pp. 142–6).

14. Risk aversion is assumed throughout (unless otherwise stated) solely in the interests of brevity. If some people enjoy the additional risk, their CVs will be positive. In general, if the aggregate of the CVs for the additional risk is negative, which is the case for universal risk aversion, there is a subtraction from the benefit side. If, on the other hand, it was positive, there would be an addition to the benefit side.

15. In a most engaging and highly perceptive paper, Schelling (1968) divides the problem into three parts: (a) society's interest, (b) an economic interest (in which category a man's contribution to GNP is placed), and (c) a 'consumer's interest'. Discussing this third interest in connection with a lifesaving program, Schelling correctly poses the relevant question: what will people pay for a government program that reduces risk? (p. 142). But

In general, of course, every activity will have attached to it some discernible degree of risk (even staying at home in bed bears some risk of mishap – the bed might collapse, the wind might blow the roof in, a marauder might enter). Any change, from one environment to another, from one style of living to another, can be said to alter the balance of risk, sometimes imperceptibly, sometimes substantially. Only the dead opt out of all risk. Yet the actual statistical risk attaching to some activity may be so small that only the hypersensitive would take account of it. In common with all other changes in economic arrangements, there is some *minimum sensibile* beyond which an increment, or decrement, of risk will go unnoticed. More important, however, what is strictly relevant to the analysis is not the change in the statistical risk *per se* but the person's response, if any, to such a change. For the change in risk may go unperceived, and, if perceived, it may be improperly evaluated. Indeed, people do have difficulty in grasping the objective significance of large numbers and, where chance or risk is at issue, they are prone to underestimate it. One chance in 50,000 of winning a lottery, or of having one's house burned down, seems a better chance, or a greater risk, than it is in fact. If so, the existence of gambling and insurance by the same person is explicable without recourse to the ingenious Friedman-Savage hypothesis (1948).

The analysis which follows does not, however, depend upon the veracity of such conjectures. All the reader has to accept is the proposition that people's subjective preferences of the worth of a thing must be counted. In the market place, the price of a good or a 'bad' (such as labor input or other disutility) is fixed by the

---

being uneasy about the actual measurement of such a sum, and absorbed with other fascinating, though in the context irrelevant, considerations, he does not develop the analysis systematically. Indeed, he goes on later to discuss the value of certain and inescapable loss of life and comes up with the suggestion that college professors would be prepared to pay an amount equal to something between ten and a hundred times their annual income in order to save the life of one of their family. If one is interested solely in the conceptual measure, as I am here, one can make use of the notion of external effects to develop the analysis. Fromm's hypercritical comments (1968), on the other hand, make use of external effects, along with the difficulties of measuring, largely to cast doubt upon this valid part of Schelling's paper.

producer, and the buyer or seller determines the amount by reference to his subjective preferences. Where, however, the amount of a (collective) good or 'bad' is fixed for each person – as may be the case with a change in risk – a person's subjective preference can only determine the price he will accept or offer for it; in short, his CV. People's imperfect knowledge of economic opportunities, their imprudence and unworldliness, have never prevented economists from accepting as basic data the amounts people freely choose at given prices. Such imperfections cannot, therefore, consistently be invoked to qualify people's choices when, instead, their preferences are exercised in placing a price on some increment of a good or 'bad'. True, attempts to observe the change of magnitude when people adjust the price to the change in quantity – rather than the more common assumption that they adjust the quantity to the change in price – does pose problems of measurement. But the problems of measurement must not be allowed to obscure the validity of the concept.

Placed within the broadest possible context, then, any additional risk of death, associated with the provision of some new facility, takes its place as one of a number of economic consequences (including employment gains and losses, new purchase and sale opportunities, and the withdrawal of existing ones), all of which affect the welfare of each of the n members of the community.

We shall now consider four types of risk, two of them direct, or physical, risks, the remaining two being indirect, or derivative, risks.

First, there are the direct, or physical, risks that people *voluntarily* assume whenever they choose to buy a product or avail themselves of a service or facility. Inasmuch as such risks are evaluated by each jth person as a CV, equal say to r_{jj}^1, his benefit from the service or facility is estimated net of such risk; that is, after r_{jj}^1 has been subtracted from it. If smoking tobacco causes 20,000 deaths a year, no subtracting from the benefits, on account of this risk, need be entered in a cost-benefit analysis of the tobacco industry inasmuch as smokers are already aware that the tobacco habit is unhealthy. And if, notwithstanding their awareness, they continue to smoke, the economist has no choice but to assume that they consider themselves better off despite the risks. Indeed, the benefits to smokers, net of risk, that is, after subtracting the aggregate,

$$\sum_{j}^{n} r_{jj}^{1},$$

are reflected in the demand schedule for tobacco. Once the area under the demand curve has been estimated and used as an approximation of the benefit smokers derive from the use of tobacco, any further subtraction for such risks would entail double counting.

Another example will help clarify the principle and will extend the argument. In an initially riskless situation, the jth person's anticipated consumer's surplus on buying a new car can be expressed by

$$C = \int_{0}^{M} \{v(m) - g'(m)\}\, dm + g_{o} - P,$$

where $v(m)$ is the present discounted value of the maximum amounts he will pay (net of all operating costs) for each successive mile for which the car is to be used; $g'(m)$ is the derivative of $g(m)$, the present discounted value of the sum the car will fetch if sold after it has been driven m miles; g_{o} is the discounted present value of the car if he holds it over time without driving it at all; P is the original price of the car (including tax); and M is the total number of miles he expects to drive the car. If we observe that he buys the car, we infer that C_{j} is positive; that, in his own estimation, he is better off with the car than without it.

The introduction, now, of some personal risk associated with driving the car does not alter this inference.[16] Once he is aware of the additional element of risk in driving the car, the consequent

16. The nice distinction made by Schelling (1968, pp. 132–5) between loss of life and loss of livelihood is, possibly, meaningful, but difficult to capture. Given the 'conjuncture' of circumstances in which a man finds himself, there is, in principle, some amount of money that will just induce him to assume a particular risk of being killed. But it is hardly likely that he will be able to apportion that sum as between 'life' and 'livelihood' – and it is not necessary, in this analysis, that he should be able to do so.

reduction in the jth person's welfare is valued at the risk compensation r^1_{jj}. If, in spite of the additional risk, the jth person still offers to buy the car, we are compelled to infer that $(C_j - r^1_{jj}) > 0$; that is, his original consumer's surplus exceeds the risk compensation or, put otherwise, his consumer's surplus net *of risk* is positive. The evaluation of a new automobile plant will, therefore, disregard this type of risk, since the benefits are roughly equal to the aggregate of consumers' surplus net of risk. Similarly, a cost-benefit study of a highway project which is expected to increase the number of casualties need make no allowance for the expected loss of life provided, again, that this is the only type of risk. For in this case, also, the benefits to be measured are, ultimately, the maximum sums motorists are willing to pay for the new highway system in full cognizance of the additional risks they choose to assume.

Occasionally, as in the automobile example, the risk assumed by each person will depend upon the numbers availing themselves of the service or facility. Since the additional degree of risk generated by all the others are imposed on each one, in addition to the risk he would assume in the absence of all others, the analysis must extend itself to include 'external diseconomies internal to the industry'.[17] If we let r^1_{ij} stand for the risk-compensation sum required by the jth person for the risk imposed on him by the ith individual, the compensatory sums for the extra risks contributed by all other individuals is given by

$$\sum_i^n r^1_{ij} \quad (i \neq j).$$

Now, although these additional risks are imposed on the jth person, they can always be avoided by his refusal to avail himself of the new service or facility. If, however, he decides to avail himself of it, the economist cannot but assume that he believes he is better off with it than without it. Again, therefore, we must assume that

$$\left(C_j - \sum_i^n r^1_{ij} \right) > 0,$$

17. The distinction between external effects *internal* to the industry and those *external* to the industry is proposed in Mishan (1965).

where i now includes j so as to make provision also for the risk that person j would run if he alone enjoyed the new service or facility.[18] Aggregating over all n members, the net consumer's surplus is

$$\sum_{j}^{n} \left(C_j - \sum_{i}^{n} r_{ij}^1 \right),$$

which can be abbreviated to $C - R^1$.

Insofar, then, as additional risks associated with the service or facility are all *voluntarily* assumed, there is no call for intervention in the allocative solution to which the market tends. As for project evaluations, insofar as benefits are calculated by reference to estimates of consumers' surplus, no allowance need be made for additional risk of loss of life. For the sum each person is willing to pay for the services provided by the project is net of all the risks associated with them. However, once we turn from risks that can be voluntarily assumed to *involuntary* risks that cannot be avoided – or, rather, cannot be avoided without incurring expenses – special provision for them has to be made in any cost-benefit analysis.

The additional involuntary risks that are imposed on the community as a whole as a by-product of some specific economic

18. The external diseconomies of traffic risk are, therefore, treated exactly as the external diseconomies of traffic congestion. But, as distinct from the problem of estimating the excess benefit of a project of given size, the determination of an *optimal* traffic flow does require intervention by the economist in consequence of these mutual external diseconomies. For the question raised in determining an optimal traffic flow is no longer one of showing that for a given volume of traffic total benefits (*net* of risk and congestion) exceed total costs. The question now is to *choose* a volume of traffic so as to *maximize* excess benefit over cost, this being realized by equating marginal social benefit to marginal cost. The standard argument is then invoked, namely, that although the effects on all others of risk and congestion grow with each additional car, the jth, or marginal vehicle owner, in deciding whether to use the highway, considers only the term

$$\sum_{i}^{n} r_{ij}^1$$

(ignoring the similar congestion term), as indeed does each of the other members, that is, he takes account only of the costs to him of each of the n vehicles on the road, including his own. What he does *not* take into account

activity, and are, therefore, to be regarded as external diseconomies external to the industry, can be separated into three types. Although all three can be inflicted on the same person who could propose a single sum in compensation, it is useful to separate them, there being circumstances where only one or two types of risk are of any importance.

The *direct* involuntary risk of death that is inflicted on the jth person by some specific project can be compensated by the sum r_{jj}^2. For example, the establishment of a nuclear power station and the resulting disposal of radioactive waste materials is held to be responsible for an increase in the annual number of deaths. Again, if supersonic flights over inhabited areas are introduced as a regular service, we can anticipate an increase in the annual number of deaths, at least among the frail, the elderly, and among those suffering from heart ailments.

In addition to this primary risk, there is a secondary risk to which the jth person is exposed, which will arise in other instances. For example, in the absence of legal prohibition, an industry pours 'sewage' into the air and increases the incidence of death from a number of lung and heart diseases. Apart from those who are the direct victims of this activity, there will be a number of fatalities arising from infection through others. And this possibility of infection obviously increases the risk since, within a given area, every person becomes a source of risk to every other. In addition, therefore, to the sum r_{jj}^2 to compensate the jth person for the risk imposed on him even if he were the sole inhabitant, he requires also a sum

$$\sum_{i}^{n} r_{ij}^2 \quad (i \neq j)$$

is the effect he himself produces on each of the others by his decision to add his vehicle to theirs; which is to say, he ignores the cost

$$\sum_{i}^{n} r_{ji}^1 \quad (i \neq j),$$

the costs imposed on each of the intra-marginal vehicles by introducing his own ith vehicle. This latter term, therefore, represents the cost of those external diseconomies generated by the marginal vehicle, diseconomies that are internal to and absorbed by all intra-marginal vehicles, and which are properly attributable to the marginal vehicle in determining the optimal flow of traffic.

to compensate for the risk that each of the other $n-1$ persons imposes on him.

There does not seem to be any advantage, however, in upholding this distinction between primary and secondary physical risk. Where the risk of infection through others is acknowledged, it is difficult, if not impossible, to separate primary from secondary risk. In such cases the risk compensation required by each person covers both. We shall, therefore, employ the general term

$$\sum_{i}^{n} r_{ij}^2$$

for the jth person (which includes the term r_{jj}^2 for the risk he runs in the absence of others). Aggregating over the n members of the community this total risk compensation is to be valued at

$$\sum_{j}^{n} \sum_{i}^{n} r_{ij}^2,$$

which can be denoted by R^2.

There are, finally, the *indirect*, or derivative, risks arising from the general concern of each of the n persons with the physical risks, voluntary and involuntary, to which any of the others is exposed. This additional concern to which, in general, each member is prone (as a result of the additional physical risks run by others) has both a financial and a psychic aspect.

(*a*) *The financial aspect.* If, on balance, the death of the ith person improves the financial position of the jth person, the additional chance of i's death is a benefit to j, and the risk-compensatory sum r_{ij}^3 is therefore positive. This means that the jth person is willing to pay up to a given sum for the improved chance of his losing some dependent or inheriting some asset – or of inheriting it sooner.[19] If, on the other hand, the death of the ith person

19. It might, at first, appear that an asset which is transferred from the deceased to his beneficiaries cancels out, as it does in the L_1 or L_2 measure. But, if transfers are generally omitted from such calculations, it is simply because they take place between living persons: a transfer of \$10,000 from person A to person B implies that the sum of their CVs is zero. On our criterion there is neither gain nor loss. However, where the issue is no longer a voluntary transfer of wealth but the risk of an involuntary transfer through death, the case is different. If there is an increased risk of person B

would reduce j's real income, the sum r_{ij}^3 is negative; that is, the jth person would have to receive a sum of money to compensate him for the increased risk of suffering a reduction in his real income. Although the jth person's financial condition is likely to be affected by the death of only a few members of the community, his risk compensation, on this account, can be written in general as

$$\sum_{i}^{n} r_{ij}^3 \quad (i \neq j).$$

Bearing in mind that most of the terms in the sum will be zero, the total expression will be positive or negative as the increased risk of death run by others makes the jth person on balance better off or worse off.

For this financial risk to which the community as a whole is exposed, the total risk compensation is obtained by aggregating the above expression over the n members to give

$$\sum_{j}^{n} \sum_{i}^{n} r_{ij}^3 \quad (i \neq j),$$

which can be represented by R^3. This sum can, as suggested, be positive or negative according to the way the community as a whole expects to be made financially better off or worse off by the death of others.[20]

---

losing his life, the CV for that risk is negative; that is, there is some minimum amount of money which will restore his welfare. To person A, however, who cares nothing for B's person but expects to inherit B's vast estate, the increased risk to which B is now exposed is a benefit for which he is willing to pay up to some maximum sum.

20. Only in an economy in which income was wholly from human capital would the R^3 component be comparable with the L_2 measure. A figure for the latter could be got by subtracting the net *losses* to the surviving members, arising from the death of breadwinners, from the net *gains* to the surviving members, arising from the death of dependents. As for R^3, the better the information, and the more constant the relation between income and utility along the relevant range, the closer the figure would be to the aggregate of the actuarial values of the net expected gain or loss to each person. It is the existence of nonhuman assets, and the possibility of their transfer from deceased to survivors, that adds to the positive value of R^3 and raises it above the L_2 measure.

(b) *The psychic aspect.* It is convenient, as well as charitable, to suppose that this concern for the additional risks to which others are exposed entails a reduction in a person's welfare. Thus, the compensatory sum

$$\sum_{i}^{n} r_{ij}^{4} \quad (i \neq j)$$

for the jth person's increased risk of bereavement carries a negative sign, being the sum of money necessary to reconcile him to bearing the additional risk of death to which his friends and the members of his family are exposed.

The increased risk of bereavement to which the community as a whole is exposed is to be valued at a sum equal to the aggregate

$$\sum_{j}^{n} \sum_{i}^{n} r_{ij} \quad (i \neq j),$$

which sum is abbreviated to R^4.

Simplicity of exposition has restricted the analysis to an increase only in the risk of death. The qualifications necessary for the treatment of an increase also in the risk of injury and disease are too obvious to justify elaboration. Application of the above analysis to a *reduced* risk of death, and to a reduced risk of injury and disease, is perhaps slightly less obvious and it may reassure the reader if its symmetrical nature is briefly illustrated by an example. Just as an increase in the number of accidents and fatalities can be a by-product of some growth in economic activity, so also can a reduction in the number of accidents and fatalities. More familiar, however, is public investment designed primarily to reduce the incidence of disease, suffering, and death. And, although such activity is to be regarded as a collective good, the relationship between collective goods and external effects (which can be thought of as incidental, 'non-optional', collective goods and 'bads') is close enough to permit us to make use of our conceptual apparatus without significant modification.

Suppose, then, that the government has a scheme for purifying the air over a vast region, one which is expected to save 20,000 lives annually.[21] The costs of enforcing a clean-air act and of

21. Again, for simplicity of exposition we omit reference, in this example, to the reduction of suffering or the enjoyment of better health.

installing preventive devices needed has to be set against the above social benefits. In accordance with our scheme, they are to be evaluated as follows:

1. Since, in this example, the reduced risk of death is a collective good, and not an external economy that is internal to some specific economic activity (as there could be, say, in a development that promoted horticulture, regarded as a healthy occupation), there is no R^1 term. There is here no question of how much a person will pay for some market good after making allowance for the *incidental* reduction of risk. The only good in question here is the collective reduction of risk itself.

2. If the population of the area is 100 million, and the chance of dying from causes connected with air pollution is independent of age, location, occupation, physical condition, or other factors, the risk of death to each person in the region is reduced by 2/10,000. More generally, there is for the jth person a reduction of the risk of death from factors connected with air pollution (including infection by others suffering from air-pollution diseases) for which he is prepared to pay up to

$$\sum_i^n r_{ij}^2,$$

which, on our assumption of universal risk aversion, is positive. Aggregating over the n members, the total sum R^2 is, therefore, also positive.[22]

22. It is frequently alleged that at low levels risk can have a positive utility. (In the absence of 'income effects' one can, for example, hypothesize a curve relating the person's CV to increasing risk of death. Measuring risk on a horizontal axis, the CV curve is above it for low risk, and below it for all risk exceeding a critical level. As the probability of death rises toward unity, we should expect the curve to increase its rate of decline and become asymptotic to a vertical axis passing through the unity point.) But whether this is so, and the extent to which it is so, would seem to depend upon the activity associated with the risk. Driving at 100 miles per hour increases the risk of a fatal accident. And if some people choose gratuitously to drive at this speed, it is not simply in response to the additional risk *per se*. It is partly because a test of skill, physical courage, or manhood is involved. Even where skill is absent, as in playing Russian roulette, there is a certain bravado in openly flirting with death. On the other hand, it is hard to imagine a man deriving positive utility from the information that henceforth

3. A reduction in the risk of death for everyone implies, for the jth person, a reduction in the chance of his being financially worse off or better off in the future. The risk compensation

$$\sum_i^n r_{ij}^3 \quad (i \neq j)$$

can therefore be positive or negative. The greater the proportion of aggregate income arising from nonhuman capital, the more likely is the total sum R^3 to be negative for the reduced risk.

4. Finally, there is the reduced risk of the jth person's suffering bereavement over the future, the corresponding risk compensation

$$\sum_i^n r_{ij}^4 \quad (i \neq j)$$

being positive. The total sum R^4 will, therefore, also be positive.

Evaluation of the benefits of the government scheme is, then, to be based ultimately on the aggregate of maximal sums that all persons in the region affected are willing to pay for the estimated reduction of the risks of death, an aggregate which can be split usefully into three components, R^2, R^3 and R^4.

A word on the deficiencies in the information available to each person concerning the degree of risk involved. These deficiencies of information necessarily contribute to the discrepancies experienced by people between anticipated and realized satisfactions. For all that, in determining whether a potential Pareto improvement has been met, economists are generally agreed – either as a canon of faith, as a political tenet, or as an act of expediency – to accept the dictum that each person knows best his own interest. If, therefore, the economist is told that a person, A, is indifferent regarding not assuming a particular risk or assuming it along with a sum of money, V, then, on the Pareto principle, the sum

---

he is to be exposed – though anonymously, along with millions of others – to an increased risk of death, one over which he has no semblance of choice or control. The risk of increased infection by some new disease or by increased radioactive fallout would be examples. Nevertheless, the question of whether risk, at some levels, has a positive or a negative utility, in any particular case, is an empirical one and does not affect the formal analysis.

V has to be accepted as the relevant cost of his being exposed to that risk. It may be the case that, owing either to deficient information or congenital optimism, person A consistently overestimates his chances of survival. But once the dictum is accepted, as indeed it is in economists' appraisals of allocative efficiency, cost-benefit analysis has to accept V as the only relevant magnitude – this being the sum chosen by A in awareness of his relative ignorance.[23] Certainly all the rest of the economic data used in a cost-benefit analysis or any other allocative study, whether derived from market prices and quantities or by other methods of inquiry, is based on this principle of accepting as final only the individual's estimate of what an article is worth to him at the time the decision is to be made. The article in question may, of course, also have a direct worth, positive or negative, for persons other than its buyer or seller, a possibility which requires a consideration of external effects. Yet, again, on the above dictum, it is the values placed on this article by these other persons which will count. Thus, while it is scarcely necessary to urge that more economical ways of refining and disseminating information be explored, the economist engaged in allocative studies traditionally follows the practice of evaluating all social gains and losses solely on the basis of individuals' own evaluations of the relevant effects on their welfare, given the information they have at the time the decision is taken.

In sum, any expected loss of life or saving of life, any expected increase or reduction in suffering in consequence of economic activity, is to be evaluated for the economy by reference to the Pareto principle; in particular, by reference to what each member of the community is willing to pay or to receive for the estimated change of risk. The resulting aggregate of CVs for the community can be usefully regarded as comprised of four components and, of these, R^1 – which encompasses all the voluntary risks (where they exist) – can be ignored on the grounds that the benefit to

23. Person A, for example, may find himself disabled for life and rue his decision to take the risk. But this example is only a more painful one of the fact that people come to regret a great many of the choices they make, notwithstanding which they would resent any interference with their future choices.

each individual of the direct activity in question (often estimated as equal to the area under the demand curve) is already net of this risk.

The other involuntary components of risk – R^2, R^3, R^4 – cannot in general be ignored, though one can surmise that with the growth in material prosperity their magnitude will tend to grow. On the other hand, with the growth in the welfare state, and in particular with an increasingly egalitarian structure of real disposable incomes, the financial risk compensation, R^3, will tend to decline. The gradual loosening of family ties and the decline of emotional interdependence should cause the magnitude of the bereavement risk compensation, R^4, to decline also. In a wholly impersonal society in which, for any jth person, the loss of any member of the community is easily replaceable in j's estimation by many others, R^4 will tend to vanish; R^2, however, is wholly selfish in the sense that it depends on people's preference for staying alive. Until such time as a genetic revolution turns men into pure altruists, or pure automatons, ready, like some species of ants, to sacrifice themselves at a moment's notice for the greater convenience of the whole, it can be expected that R^2 will grow over time.

Before concluding, however, it should be emphasized that the basic concept introduced in this paper is not simply an alternative to, or an auxiliary to, any existing methods [24] that have been proposed for measuring the loss or saving of life. It is the only

24. It is far from impossible that society may choose to refer decisions in matters involving life and death to a representative body or committee and that a decision may be reached that differs from the one which would arise from the consistent application of cost-benefit techniques. Nevertheless, the economist is free to criticize the decision, to point out inconsistencies, and to discover what features, if any, warrant a departure from the Pareto criterion. Consistency, in this instance, requires that the expected change in risk associated with any contemplated scheme be evaluated by reference to the same principle as all other relevant economic gains and losses. To evaluate the welfare effect of risk on some other principle, say, by a voting procedure, entails the adding together of incommensurables. Thus, an implicit figure for the effect of risk on welfare attributable to a decision taken by a smaller group (or even by the whole group), by the method of counting heads, is added to a figure for the other economic effects which, using the Pareto principle, aggregates the valuation of each member determined on a CV basis.

economically justifiable concept. And this assertion does not rest on any novel ethical premise. It follows as a matter of consistency in the application of the Pareto principle in cost-benefit calculations.

Insofar as an immediate application of the concepts to the measurement of loss or saving of life is in issue, one's claims must be more muted. In the attempts to measure social benefits and losses, price-quantity statistics lend themselves better to the more familiar examples in which people choose quantities at given market prices than they do to examples in which people have to choose prices for the given quantities. For one can observe the quantities they choose, at least collectively, whereas one cannot generally observe their subjective valuations. In the circumstances, economists seriously concerned with coming to grips with the magnitudes may have to brave the disdain of their colleagues and consider the possibility that data yielded by surveys based on the questionnaire method are better than none, or better than data obtained by persisting with some of the current measures such as L_1 or L_2. In the last resort, one could invoke 'contingency calculations' (Mishan, 1969, p. 70) in order to determine, for example, whether the apparent excess benefit of a scheme (calculated in the absence of any allowance for the expected increase in fatalities and injuries) is likely or not to exceed any plausible estimate of the evaluation of the increased risk to which people are exposed.

In view of the existing quantomania, one may be forgiven for asserting that there is more to be said for rough estimates of the precise concept than precise estimates of economically irrelevant concepts. The caveat is more to be heeded in this case, bearing in mind that currently used and currently mooted measures of saving life or the loss of life – such as L_1, L_2, L_3 and L_4 – have no conceptual affinity with the Pareto basis of cost-benefit analysis.

References

DEVONS, E. (1961), *Essays in Economics*, Allen & Unwin.
EISNER, R., and STROTZ, R. H. (1961), 'Flight insurance and the theory of choice', *J. polit. Econ.*, vol. 69, no. 4, pp. 355–68.
FRIEDMAN, M., and SAVAGE, L. J. (1948), 'Utility analysis of choices involving risks', *J. polit. Econ.*, vol. 56, no. 4, pp. 279–304.
FROMM, G. (1965), 'Civil aviation expenditures', in R. Dorfman (ed.), *Measuring Benefits of Government Investment*, Brookings Institution.

FROMM, G. (1968), 'Comment on T. C. Schelling's paper "The life you save may be your own"', in S. B. Chase (ed.), *Problems in Public Expenditure Analysis*, Brookings Institution.

KNEESE, A. V. (1966), 'Research goals and progress toward them', in H. Jarrett (ed.), *Environmental Quality in a Growing Economy*, Johns Hopkins Press.

MARGLIN, S. (1963), 'The social rate of discount and the optimal rate of investment', *Quart. J. Econ.*, vol. 77, no. 1, pp. 95–111.

MISHAN, E. J. (1959), 'Rent as a measure of welfare change', *Amer. econ. Review*, vol. 49, no. 3, pp. 386–94.

MISHAN, E. J. (1965), 'Reflections on recent development in the concept of external effects', *Can. J. Econ.*, vol. 31, no. 1, pp. 3–34.

MISHAN, E. J. (1969), *Welfare Economics: An Assessment*, North-Holland.

NATH, S. K. (1969), *A Reappraisal of Welfare Economics*, Routledge & Kegan Paul.

RIDKER, R. G. (1967), *The Economic Costs of Air Pollution*, Praeger.

ROTHENBERG, J. (1961), *The Measurement of Social Welfare*, Prentice-Hall.

SCHELLING, T. C. (1968), 'The life you save may be your own', in S. B. Chase, Jr (ed.), *Problems in Public Expenditure Analysis*, Brookings Institution.

Part Three
The Social Time Preference Rate and the Social Opportunity Cost of Capital

The second hurdle in project appraisal is to find a way of comparing net benefits in one period and another. Feldstein surveys the general issue, arguing that market rates of interest are not an adequate guide to social time preference. In support of this view Sen puts forward a specific model, in which the welfare of the present generation is affected by what happens to its successors. This shows that, if people are less 'selfish' for their heirs than for themselves, they may underinvest if investment is left to the free market.

But, even if time preference were known, there remains the problem that public investment may displace private. If savings are sub-optimal the money cost of public investment will then understate its social opportunity cost. Marglin's celebrated article shows how in principle to deal with this problem. The displacement effects are not, however, easy to estimate. Harberger provides a method for estimating the displacement effects of public investment financed by borrowing, while Feldstein's recent paper points out that the opportunity cost of funds is not necessarily higher if they are raised by government borrowing than by taxation. Feldstein also argues strongly against the common practice of dealing with the opportunity-cost-of-capital problem by using a synthetic discount rate, which is a weighted average of the rate of return on private investment and the social time preference rate.

9 M. S. Feldstein

The Social Time Preference Rate

M. S. Feldstein, 'The social time preference discount rate in cost-benefit analysis',[1] *Economic Journal*, vol. 74, 1964, pp. 360–79.

Choosing between alternative time-streams of social benefits and costs is one of the most difficult and most important problems in the evaluation of public investment projects. The attention devoted to this subject in recent discussions of cost-benefit analysis [2] is justified by the practical realities of public investment decision-making. As an example of the numerous choices of this kind that arise in both the design and final selection stages, we need only recall the common problem of choosing between a technique of production that requires large capital investment but has low operating costs and one with the opposite profile of expenditure: nuclear versus conventional power, electric versus diesel railroads, etc.

Determining a project's admissibility requires comparing its annual net benefit time-stream with the time-stream of consumption that would have occurred if funds had not been used in the particular project. In selecting among admissible projects that are

1. I am grateful to J. S. Flemming, I. M. D. Little, W. M. Gorman and U. K. Hicks for comments on a previous draft. I have also benefited from the opportunity to discuss this subject with other members of the Oxford Cost-Benefit Seminar, especially C. D. Foster, P. D. Henderson, D. L. Munby and R. J. Van Noorden.
2. Eckstein (1957; 1958; 1961); Feldstein (1964); Hirshleifer, De Haven and Milliman (1960); Hitch and McKean (1960); Hufschmidt *et al.* (1961); Krutilla and Eckstein (1958); Kuhn (1962); Marglin (1962; 1963a, b and c); McKean (1958); Steiner (1959); Turvey (1963).

mutually exclusive for technical reasons (e.g. two different techniques for producing the same output) it is only in the rare (and trivial) case that one project dominates all others, i.e. has a greater net benefit in each year than that of every other project. In general, it is necessary to choose between time-streams with different durations and profiles. Except in cases of dominance, selecting among alternative projects requires assigning a single-value measure to each time-stream. This is the purpose of the 'interest-rate' or discount-rate calculations in public investment decision-making.

The most useful measure of a project's desirability is the present value of the net addition to consumption created by the project.[3] In the framework of present value investment rules, the discount-rate calculation defines a functional relationship that makes outputs at different points in time commensurable with each other by assigning to them equivalent present-values. In traditional capital theory a *single* interest rate equates the marginal time preference of savers with the marginal productivity of capital in investment. Today most economists have begun to recognize that in a mixed economy with market imperfections and multiple interest rates no single discount rate can be taken as a measure of *both* time preference and the productivity of capital. Nevertheless, much cost-benefit writing has been a search for such a single discount rate with normative significance for public expenditure decisions.[4]

Two types of discount rates have been advocated: social time preference (STP) and social opportunity cost (SOC). A social time preference function assigns current values to future consumptions: it is a normative function reflecting society's evaluation of the relative desirability of consumption at different points in time. The STP function need not take the form of a constant

3. For a discussion of the superiority of the present value approach to the use of any measure of yield or internal rate of return, see Hirshleifer *et al.* (1960, chs. 6 and 7). The appropriate method of calculating the present value of the addition to consumption created by a project and of using this for public investment decision-making under a number of different conditions of capital rationing is developed in Feldstein (1964).

4. This has been particularly true in government discussions. But see also the recent works by Hirshleifer *et al.* (1960), Kuhn (1962) and McKean (1958).

discount rate; the relation of an STP function to an STP rate is discussed in section III below. The social opportunity cost (SOC) is a measure of the value to society of the next best alternative use to which funds employed in the public project might otherwise have been put. In a perfectly competitive world the opportunity cost of these funds could be represented by the market interest rate; but in our economy no single interest rate or rate of return can fully measure the SOC of funds. The SOC depends on the source of the particular funds and *must also itself reflect the STP function*. It is best therefore to allow for the SOC of funds directly by placing a 'shadow price' on the funds used in the project and to make all inter-temporal comparisons with an STP rate or function.[5]

The search for a 'perfect' formula to specify the social time preference rate is futile. An STP function must reflect public policy and social ethics, as well as judgement about future economic conditions. Nevertheless, there is much to be gained by understanding why a social time preference rate is necessary and by examining the factors that must be considered in formulating such a rate.

In this paper we show that the STP function cannot be derived on the basis of existing market rates, but must be administratively determined as a matter of public policy. We then examine the characteristics of the STP function, its relation to an STP rate and the movement of the STP rate through time.

I Inapplicability of a 'perfect' market interest rate to public policy

The ubiquitous imperfections of the capital market[6] should be adequate reason for rejecting the use of any market interest rate in a public policy decision. Why, then, encumber ourselves with an investigation into the reasons why even the interest rate of a

5. For a development of this idea and a method of combining STP and SOC, see Feldstein (1964, especially section I). Earlier work on this subject was done by Otto Eckstein (1958; 1961), Peter Steiner (1959) and Stephen Marglin (1962; 1963c).

6. In particular, institutional imperfections impeding access to credit, the divergence between lending and borrowing rates, the interference of risk and uncertainty and related problems that give rise to the simultaneous existence of multiple interest rates.

'perfect' capital market would lack normative significance? First, some writers have argued that if a perfect market rate existed it would be appropriate for evaluating public investment projects.[7] Such an opinion would no doubt influence an economist's conception of an appropriate social time preference rate for use in the absence of perfect capital market conditions. Eckstein, for example, writes, 'I shall endeavour to present that set (of value judgements) which, in my view, most closely adheres to the principle of consumer sovereignty'.[8] This adherence to the 'consumer sovereignty' which a 'perfect' market rate would reflect may not accord with the characteristics of the social time preference rate we would otherwise accept. Second, considering the faults of a perfect market rate will demonstrate a number of defects inherent in the use of any market rate, or rate derived from market rates.

Pre-Keynesian theories considered the interest rate to be a price induced by the productivity of capital and required as payment for postponing consumption. Although the emphasis of economic theorists has shifted from this idea that the interest rate is an equilibrator of 'real' savings and investment schedules to the loanable funds and liquidity preference theories which emphasize the 'non-real' monetary nature of interest rate determination,[9] normative discussions of the role of the interest rate are still based on the old notion that the interest rate in a perfect capital market would equate the marginal productivity of capital and the marginal time preference of consumers to produce a Paretian social

7. R. N. McKean suggests that in the absence of capital rationing 'the market rate' should be used (1958, pp. 76–81). Otto Eckstein develops his theory of intertemporal welfare economics because the absence of a 'well-functioning capital market' prevents deriving these 'social value judgements ... directly from observable market behaviour' (1957, p. 75). Although Maurice Dobb cites F. J. Atkinson as espousing the view that 'the government should only invest ... as much as it can raise by the sale of bonds to individuals' (quoted from Dobb, 1960, p. 15), Atkinson himself is careful to explain that he attaches no normative significance to the proposition that a Socialist Government could allow the forces of a perfect capital market to determine the amount of investment by the public's willingness to absorb government bonds; he even comments, 'It may be that it would be *better* for the state to decide the rate of accumulation ... The validity of the norm of consumers' sovereignty is not discussed' (1948, p. 78).

8. Eckstein (1957, pp. 75–6).

9. Shackle (1961, pp. 209–54).

optimum. It is the application of this theory that we shall criticize.

Such an interest rate would acquire its usefulness for public decisions because it would also be the price that guided *private* investors to maximize their welfare over time. But even the interest rate of a perfect capital market is inadequate for this task. Unless all other assumptions of perfect competition are also fulfilled, this particular price will have no normative significance.[10] Further, individual savers must foresee their future incomes and wants, as well as the future prices of all goods. But the future income of each individual (or household) depends on the savings and investment decisions of society as a whole. The individual cannot possibly have the information he requires for rationally redistributing his income through time.[11] Similarly, although investors must know the marginal efficiency of capital in each private investment option, they may be unable to obtain such knowledge. The internal rate of return of a net revenue time-stream may be non-unique or even non-existent.[12] In addition, the revenue time-stream will depend on the investment decisions of other entrepreneurs: the individual investor, just as the individual saver, cannot have the information necessary for rational intertemporal decision-making.[13]

More importantly, even if a perfect market interest rate could guide private investors to maximize their welfare over time, it would not produce socially optimal investment decisions. A perfect market would equate *private* demand (investor's rate of return) and net supply (willingness to save) schedules; to produce socially optimal decisions, an interest rate would instead have to equate the social productivity of investment schedule with a politically determined saving supply schedule.

The private demand schedule for investment funds, even if it equalled the investor's internal rate of return, would not reflect the social productivity of capital. Investment enhances the pro-

10. Little (1957, p. 147). More generally, see Lipsey and Lancaster (1956, pp. 11–12).

11. The necessary interdependence of rational savings decisions is developed by Graaff (1957, pp. 103–5), and by Dobb (1960, pp. 17–18).

12. For a discussion of the ambiguity of the internal rate of return, see Hirshleifer (1958, pp. 329–52); Pritchford and Hagger (1958, p. 597) and Wright (1963, p. 329).

13. Again see Graaff (1957, pp. 103–5).

ductivity of labour and other factors of production, and, as a result, increases their income. This is a cost to the private investor, who calculates his rate of return net of payments to other factors. But to society as a whole, those increased factor incomes should be treated as a gain. The *social* rate of return on investment, i.e. the marginal output–capital ratio, may therefore be much greater than the private marginal efficiency of capital.[14] This difference is important not only for the micro-economic question of the optimal rate of national investment[15] but for the public micro-economic problems of benefit-cost analysis. Surprisingly, however, economists have universally ignored this distinction in benefit-cost discussions by taking the market rate of interest (or some other estimate of the marginal efficiency of private investment) as a measure of the social productivity of funds withdrawn from private investment.

In any case, for public investment decisions we may wish to reject the market-determined evaluation of future consumption in favour of a politically determined social time preference function. We may, in short, wish to replace the weights given to the opinions of individuals by the distribution of income and wealth with other weights, such as those given them in the ballot box. For this reason, Eckstein has argued for a discount rate lower than the market rate, reminding us that 'Our notion of efficiency is relative to a distribution of income'.[16] Further, the divergence of social time preference from market-expressed time preference need not reflect conflicting opinions of different people. An individual's own time preference may depend on whether he is acting alone

14. This point was raised by A. K. Sen in discussing the optimal rate of national investment (1961, p. 487). J. Tinbergen (1956, pp. 603–4) made the mistake of treating the private marginal efficiency of capital as equal to the marginal output–capital ratio; his error was indicated by Branko Horvat (1958, pp. 157–8). Mr John Flemming has pointed out to me that the private investors' demand schedule would not only be too low, but would show unequal bias for industries and investments; although a perfect capital market would assure that the private marginal efficiency of investment was equal in all investments, there is no theoretical reason why the marginal output–capital ratio should be so.

15. The rule for determining the optimal rate of national investment should be: invest until the social rate of return on investment equals that rate of interest which reflects society's willingness to postpone consumption.

16. Otto Eckstein (1958, p. 100).

or collectively. Sen[17] and Marglin[18] have suggested that individuals, in their public role as citizens, may be willing to save for future generations if others are also willing to do so. Public investment and consumption by future generations could therefore be treated as Samuelsonian 'public goods' which are 'psychically consumed by every member of the community'.[19] Using the Samuelson formulation, Marglin provides a mathematical proof that 'an individual's marginal time preference in collective saving *vs.* consumption decisions is not based on the same parameters ... as his marginal time preference in unilateral decisions.'[20]

II Public preference versus the 'public good'

In an unusual departure from the safety of their habitual domain to the unfamiliar territory of political theory, economists have argued about the proper political determination of the social time preference rate. As we have seen, the political process may be invoked because the market cannot express the 'collective' demand for investment to benefit the future and because we may prefer the weights of some political process to those of the marketplace. The first of these is a matter of facilitating action on which all might agree; the second is the familiar problem of allowing democratically determined redistribution to alter the outcome of the market process. But two other important questions remain: should the Government endeavour to provide for the future welfare of the current generation in a more rational way than they would themselves? What should the Government's attitude be towards future generations? In terms more familiar to the political theorist, they ask: should the Government act in the best interests of the public or should it do what the public wants? Is the Government's responsibility only to the current population or should it show a concern for the welfare of future generations greater than that which the current electorate would sanction?

Economists have long believed that individuals irrationally

17. A. K. Sen (1961, p. 488) discusses this as the 'Isolation Paradox'.
18. S. A. Marglin (1962, pp. 194–7).
19. S. A. Marglin (1963a, p. 104). More generally, see P. A. Samuelson (1954, pp. 387–9).
20. S. A. Marglin (1963a, p. 109).

discount future *pleasures* merely because of their futurity.[21] Should not the Government correct this error, the argument continues, by substituting its own interpretation of the 'public good' for the opinions of public preference expressed through the market or ballot-box? Thus, Pigou wrote that although 'our telescopic faculty is defective, and . . . we therefore see future pleasures, as it were, on a diminished scale, . . . (this) does not imply that any economic dissatisfaction would be suffered if future pleasures were substituted at full value for present ones' (1920, p. 25). Although Marshall showed that we cannot be certain whether or to what extent individuals actually do discount future *pleasures* as such,[22] a controversy has developed between those such as Ramsey, Dobb and Sen,[23] who would disregard personal preferences and substitute a 'more rational' government time preference, and other such as Eckstein, Bain, Tinbergen, and Marglin,[24] who would base the social time preference rate on public opinion.

An irrational preference for immediate pleasures need not be the reason that individuals introduce a pure time discount into

21. Böhm-Bawerk remarked as early as 1888 that 'to goods which are destined to meet the wants of the future, we ascribe a value which is really less than the true intensity of their future marginal utility.' E. V. Böhm-Bawerk (1888, p. 253). Marshall and Pigou called attention to this same phenomenon. A. Marshall (1920, pp. 100–10), A. C. Pigou (1920, pp. 24–30).

22. Marshall (1920, pp. 101–2, especially the footnotes).

23. Discussing the optimal rate of national saving, F. P. Ramsey refers to pure time preference discounting as 'a practice which is ethically indefensible and arises merely from weakness of the imagination' (1928, p. 543). Maurice Dobb's views are most recently expressed in *An Essay on Economic Growth and Planning* (1960, ch. 2). Sen rejects the 'psychological discount' as irrational in *Choice of Techniques* (1960, ch. 8).

24. Otto Eckstein seeks to base his intertemporal comparisons on 'the principle of consumer sovereignty' (1957, p. 75). Joe Bain states that the appropriate social discount rate 'expressed the consensus of the electorate' (1960, p. 315). Jan Tinbergen's optimum rate of saving reflects a 'psychological discount rate' (1956, pp. 604–5). Stephen Marglin dismisses the opinions of Pigou and Dobb as implying 'an authoritarian rejection of individual preferences with which we are unwilling to associate ourselves' (1962, p. 197). Again, on a later occasion, he comments, 'I, for one, do not accept the Pigovian formulation of social welfare . . . I want the government's social welfare function to reflect only the preferences of present individuals' (1963a, p. 97).

their decisions; a quite rational fear of death is sufficient explanation for positive personal discount rates.[25] But if government is 'the trustee for unborn generations as well as for its present citizens,' as Pigou has said (1920, p. 29), is not the mortality of individuals irrelevant for social time preference calculations? Some, like Pigou, Dobb, Holzman and Sen,[26] are willing to impose on the public a responsibility for the welfare of future generations; others, like Eckstein, Bain and Marglin,[27] believe that the interests of future generations should be recognized only to the extent that the current public sanctions them through the democratic process.

Our own view would be to allow administrative determination of the STP with whatever weight to the welfare of future generations these democratic administrators would allow. An administrative decision by an accountable government satisfies our notion of the requirement of democracy; democratic theory does not require that each decision represent a consensus, but that government action as a whole be acceptable to the electorate.

III The two-period STP function

Despite their general agreement that social decisions should not be made on the interest-rate rules appropriate for private investors, the critics of using market or opportunity cost discount rates are not agreed on the proper nature of social time preference discounting. We begin by examining the factors that should affect an administrative determination of an STP function between any two years; this is presented in terms of the indifference curve analysis developed by Irving Fisher. From this we shall see what a single STP rate implies and consider the *ex ante* determinacy

25. This is developed by Otto Eckstein (1961, pp. 456–9); and A. K. Sen (1961, p. 83).

26. A. C. Pigou (1920, pp. 24–30); M. Dobb (1960, p. 18). F. D. Holzman argues that true consumer sovereignty requires that the 'wishes' of consumers of the future be represented in the decision (1958, pp. 193–207). Similarly, A. K. Sen says that a democratic solution to an intertemporal problem is impossible if the opinions of all who are concerned must be considered (1961, p. 486).

27. Marglin is not opposed to the government providing 'education of today's citizens to the "rightful claims" of future generations' (1963a, pp. 97–8).

of the rate. In the final section we discuss two aspects of the multi-period problem: factors affecting the change of the STP rate through time and the length of the time horizon of the STP function.

Fisher's indifference-curve analysis

Fisher's indifference curve analysis of private investment decision-making provides a useful framework for describing an STP function and defining an STP rate.[28] For convenience, we first present the Fisher analysis in terms of an individual and then extend it to the problems of public investment.

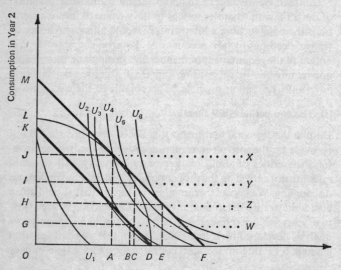

Figure 1

The two axes in Figure 1 indicate the amounts the investor consumes in each of two successive years. If he begins with no expected consumption in year 2, we may represent his situation

28. Fisher's original presentation is in *The Theory of Interest* (1930). For a discussion and development of Fisher's approach, still with respect to private investment, see Jack Hirshleifer (1958).

by a point such as D on the horizontal axis, indicating that he could consume D in year 1 and nothing in year 2. This would place him on indifference curve U_2. The line DK represents the borrowing-lending possibility line, equivalent to the budget line in consumer behaviour analysis. The slope of this line, say m, indicates the interest rate, i; $i = -(1+m)$. The individual may redistribute his consumption between the two years by moving to any point on this line. At point K he consumes nothing in year 1 and OK in year 2; but this places him on a lower indifference curve than before, U_1. The individual whose only way of redistributing consumption between the years is by lending and borrowing (i.e. who has no direct investment opportunities) reaches his highest accessible indifference curve by moving to point W; here he lends amount DB, consumes OB in year 1 and OG in year 2, and is on indifference curve U_3.

Curve DL indicates the real (i.e. physical) investment opportunities open to the investor. The slope of the curve indicates that the rate of transformation of present goods into future goods [29] decreases as the quantity of investment increases. If the investor follows the usual internal rate of return or present value rule he will invest the amount DA, bringing him to point X, where the marginal efficiency of capital is equal to the market interest rate. Here he will be on indifference curve U_4, consuming OA in year 1 and OJ in year 2. This is also the investment–consumption combination with maximum present value; the present value of the two-period consumption stream represented by point X is OF, the intercept of the interest rate line on the present year axis. It is obvious from the diagram that any other point on DL represents a lower present value.

Nevertheless, it is possible for the investor to reach higher indifference curves. If he invests DC, i.e. until the marginal efficiency of capital is equal to his marginal rate of substitution between consumption in years 1 and 2, he will be at point Y, on

29. This is the marginal efficiency of capital; since we are dealing with a two-period case, a unique internal rate of return may be calculated for each incremental pound of investment. In this case the present value and internal rate of return rules are also equivalent. For an amplification of the problem of a unique marginal efficiency of capital, see the discussions by Hirshleifer (1958) and J. F. Wright (1963).

indifference curve U_5, consuming OC in period 1 and OI in period 2. This is still not the optimal strategy. The investor reaches his highest attainable indifference curve by following the internal rate of return rule (i.e. investing DA) and *then borrowing the amount AE* along the borrowing-lending line MF.[30] This brings him to point Z on indifference curve U_6, consuming OE in period 1 and OH in period 2.

Applications to public investment. Although this solution is necessarily determinate only for the two-period case, it is worthwhile examining some analogies between this analysis and the problem of public investment.

Curve DL represents the social productivity of investment for society as a whole, the possible transformations of present goods into future goods. This is the basis of the social opportunity cost of funds diverted from private investment to public expenditure.

For the community as a whole, it is impossible to redistribute consumption through time by merely monetary borrowing–lending transactions;[31] lines such as KD and MF are therefore irrelevant for the public investment decision. This inability to redistribute the time stream of social benefits of public investment by borrowing and lending has extremely important consequences for benefit–cost analysis which are ignored by those economists who would disregard social time preference and concentrate exclusively on social opportunity cost. Because society cannot redistribute the consumption of outputs of the public investment through time, any test or measure of the desirability of a public investment is inadequate if it does not take into account the social time preference function, i.e. the relative 'weights' society places on consumption at different times in the future. Two net-benefit time streams *which differ in profile*, although they have the same unambiguous internal rate of return, are not necessarily equally desirable from society's point of view. A simple example will clarify this. Consider two possibilities of investing £100. One in-

30. This line is parallel to DK, indicating that the interest rate is the same.
31. This is strictly true only for a closed economy; but for the large developed countries with which we are concerned, net international borrowing or lending would not be significant.

vestment repays £200 after twelve years; the other repays £25,000 after a century. Both have internal rates of return of approximately 6 per cent. A private investor might be indifferent between the two options because he could sell his investment whenever he wished; in effect, he could borrow against the future output of the project. But society as a whole cannot sell or borrow in this way; it must evaluate the alternative investments in terms of their specific time profiles.[32] If society's time preference discount rate[33] is more than 6 per cent the £200 after twelve years is preferable to the £25,000 after a century; if society discounts consumption by less than 6 per cent the £25,000 is preferable.

Characteristics of the two-period function

The indifference curves in the Fisher diagram represent two-period STP functions. The slope of such an indifference curve at any point indicates society's marginal rate of substitution of present for future goods, the STP rate between the two years. If the slope of the curve at a particular point is n we can express the STP rate, d, as : $d = -(1+n)$. An STP *rate* is thus defined for each point in the consumption space in terms of the first derivative of an STP *function* at that point. This distinction between an STP function and an STP rate, although extremely important, is rarely recognized.[34]

Although Fisher's analytic technique provides a convenient framework for describing an STP function and defining an STP rate, it has never been used for this purpose. One reason may be the theoretical objections to extending Fisher's indifference curves

32. Thus, Tinbergen is misleading when he says, à propos the optimal rate of national saving and investment, 'There need not be, in principle, any difference between the choice an individual makes and the choice made for a whole nation' (J. Tinbergen, 1956, p. 603). Similarly, we cannot agree with Kuhn's statement, 'Time and interest problems arise in both public and private enterprise. By and large, the analytic treatment is identical.' (Tillo E. Kuhn, 1962, p. 102.) The idea that private investment methods are directly applicable to the public sector is also found in R. N. McKean (1958) and J. Hirshleifer *et al.* (1960).

33. The meaning of society discounting future consumption will be explored below; for now we treat it merely as the discounting algorithm.

34. Two exceptions are: J. Hirshleifer (1961, pp. 495 ff.); S. Marglin (1963a, footnote pp. 95–6). Neither of them, however, develops this point.

from individuals to society.[35] Nevertheless, the social indifference curve is not unfamiliar in the literature of public expenditure; in this context, Samuelson has gone even further than we propose to go and has used both social and individual indifference curves simultaneously.[36] There are, however, problems peculiar to using intertemporal social utility curves; we return to these below in our discussion of the utility function.

It is important to clarify our measurement of consumption, i.e. the units of the axes. First, we assume that goods in each period have the prices that would prevail in a perfect market in which relative price changes occurred but the absolute price level remained constant. The reason for dealing in terms of a constant absolute price level requires no further discussion. If we are to be able to discount the specific outputs of a public project at the STP rate we must recognize that the relative utility of these goods (vis à vis other goods at the same time) may change reflecting changes in scarcity, taste, etc.[37] To do this, we must assign to them prices which indicate their relative social utility at the time of their consumption. Allowing directly for changes in relative utility permits us to ignore the arguments for applying different STP rates to different types of publicly produced goods. Second, we may choose between measuring total consumption or *per capita* consumption; the choice is only a matter of convenience, since, whichever we choose, we adjust our definition of the social utility-consumption map accordingly. In order to consider the growth of consumption and population separately, we shall use the *total* consumption as our unit of measure.

Exogenous consumption change. We noted above that society's location in the consumption space and the first derivative of the indifference curve at that point together determine the STP discount rate. The location in the consumption space reflects the

35. On the 'impossibility' of constructing social indifference curves from individual indifference curves, see: P. A. Samuelson (1956, pp. 1–22); Kenneth Arrow (1951).

36. Paul A. Samuelson, op. cit., and also 1955, pp. 350–56.

37. Marshall recognized that the utility (to an individual) of *specific* commodities might change with time (1920, p. 101, especially the footnote). Later Hayek made this same point in his analysis of the relationship between the utility function and the interest rate; F. A. v. Hayek (1936, p. 45).

exogenously determined consumption level in the first year and the rate of growth during the two years. A positive rate of growth of consumption is indicated by a point lying above a 45° ray through the origin. If the indifference curves have the 'usual' properties of convexity higher growth rates imply higher STP rates.

To clarify this, we turn now to examine the factors which determine the shape of the social indifference curves: the social utility-consumption function, changes in population and the nature of the pure time discount, if any, that is imposed.

The social utility-consumption function. Precise definition of a utility-consumption function, capable of a normative evaluation of society's consumption through time, is obviously impossible. Even if we limited our aim to an ordinal function and ignored the distribution of consumption, we might still feel that changing population, tastes and levels of expectations presented insuperable problems of interpersonal and intertemporal comparison.[38] But impossibility is no excuse. Every intertemporal decision by government implies an underlying utility-consumption function; we turn therefore to examine the facets of this function which influence the social time preference rate.

Although we have stated our analysis in terms of total consumption, our basic belief is that the social consumption-utility function should reflect both total and *per capita* consumption. Previous writers have been far from unanimous on this subject. Ramsey safely evaded the problem by assuming that the population remained constant (1928, p. 544). Tinbergen (1956) and Chakravarty (1962, pp. 338–55) do not mention population in discussing the social consumption-utility functions that they employ, but their growth equations clearly indicate that they are thinking in terms of total consumption rather than consumption

38. Writers on social time preference have generally not been unaware of these problems. Some, such as Ramsey, assume that *ceteris* remain *paribus* F. P. Ramsey (1928, pp. 543–59). More appropriately, Sen recognizes that while these problems may frustrate exact specification of a social utility-consumption function, they do not preclude all consideration of the subject (1960, p. 84). Still others, like Dobb, use these Duesenberry-cum-Veblen effects as reason for completely abandoning the subject of intertemporal comparison (1960, pp. 19–22).

per capita. Eckstein (1957, pp. 65–81) explicitly introduces population growth and defines his social-welfare function strictly in terms of *per capita* consumption. Sen, while critical of Tinbergen's treatment, only commits himself to the comment that 'Even if the size of the population is assumed to be independent of our decision, the choice (of techniques) will be affected by the fact that social utility depends, among other things, upon consumption *per capita*' (1960, p. 85). We would go further than Sen in seeking a middle position between Tinbergen and Eckstein. Although *per capita* consumption may be the underlying determinant of social welfare, we will say that social welfare increases if a nation that enjoys a high standard of living maintains the level of *per capita* consumption while the population increases. More explicitly, in terms of a general social utility-consumption function, $U = f(P, C/P)$, where U is social utility, C is total consumption and P is population, we shall say

$$\frac{\partial U}{\partial (C/P)} > 0 \quad \text{and} \quad \frac{\partial U}{\partial P} > 0.^{39}$$

In terms of the Fisher indifference map,

$$\frac{\partial U}{\partial P} > 0 \quad \text{and} \quad \frac{\partial U}{\partial (C/P)} > 0$$

are necessary conditions for movement outwards along a ray through the origin to lead to higher indifference levels.[40]

The shape of the Fisher indifference curves will reflect the second-order properties of the social utility-consumption function, i.e. our assumptions about diminishing marginal utility of consumption. Although economists have long accepted proposi-

39. Note that $\partial U/\partial P > 0$ implies $\partial U/\partial C > 0$, i.e. social utility increasing when population increases with constant *per capita* consumption is equivalent to social utility increasing when total consumption increases. Throughout our discussion we ignore the cases of decreasing population and decreasing *per capita* consumption as practically unimportant.

40. If population remained constant, or if we redefined our measure of consumption in *per capita* terms, only

$$\frac{\partial U}{\partial (C/P)} > 0$$

would be necessary.

tions that rest on diminishing marginal utility of consumption by an individual, there is no reason to assert that increasing *total* consumption would have diminishing marginal utility, even if *per capita* consumption were constant. Our notion of a social-welfare function is insufficiently well defined to make this assertion; the ethical propositions on which such a judgement would have to rest have never received adequate consideration.[41] A recognition of our uncertainty would yield a more acceptable interim solution. We would be safer if we assumed decreasing marginal utility of *per capita* consumption

$$\left[\frac{\partial^2 U}{\partial (C/P)^2} < 0\right],$$

but remained sceptical about the marginal utility of increasing total consumption due to increasing population

$$\left[\frac{\partial^2 U}{\partial P^2} \leqslant 0\right].[42]$$

The usual indifference curve convexity properties require that $\partial^2 U/\partial C^2 < 0$; the stronger this inequality, the greater will be the convexity. Our second-order assumptions fulfil these conditions, except in the case where *per capita* consumption is constant and the population increases; here, unless $\partial^2 U/\partial P^2 < 0$, the indifference curves would be straight lines. As we noted above, convex indifference curves imply that the STP rate is an increasing function of the rate of growth of consumption. If we assume that $\partial^2 U/\partial P^2 = 0$, i.e. that there is no decreasing marginal utility of total consumption if *per capita* consumption remains constant, only the *per capita* consumption growth rate will influence the

41. Nevertheless, Tinbergen (1956) and Chakravarty (1962) both assume diminishing marginal utility of total consumption and define this relation without regard to population change. Eckstein goes further and implies that increasing total consumption has *zero* marginal utility when *per capita* consumption remains constant (1957, pp. 65–81).

42. Such scepticism would also be appropriate for attempts to formulate particular functions with decreasing marginal utility of consumption, e.g. Ramsey's asymptotic Bliss or the Tinbergen-Eckstein constant-elasticity consumption-utility function.

STP rate. If we allow that $\partial^2 U/\partial P^2 < 0$ both total and *per capita* consumption growth rates are significant.[43]

Pure time discount. In terms of the Fisher indifference map, discounting future consumption merely because of its futurity, i.e. discounting future utility as such, means that all points (except those on the horizontal axis) lie on lower-value indifference curves; this further implies that if a pure time discount exists at all consumption levels and growth rates the indifference curves are steeper at all points. The economists who have included pure time discount in formal models have implicitly assumed that the extent of this pure time discount is the same for all consumption levels and growth rates,[44] i.e. that the slope of the indifference curves is everywhere made steeper to the same degree. But society's impatience for current consumption may well reflect the level of well-being and the rate of progress; the first may be subsumed in the utility-consumption function, but the effect of the growth rate can only be reflected in the pure time discount. More important, the pure time discount may be a function of calendar time: the Government may reject a pure time preference in the near future (say, twenty to fifty years), but may impose an increasing one after that date to reflect a decreasing concern of the current electorate with the welfare of future generations.

IV The STP rate

A *single* STP rate is a measure of society's marginal rate of substitution of consumption in year $t+1$ for consumption in year t; more formally, d_t, the STP rate applicable between years t and $t+1$, may be defined: $d_t = \mathrm{MRS}_{t+1,t} - 1$. The STP rate is thus determined by the consumption level and growth rate (society's

43. This agrees with Eckstein's conclusion that higher growth rates of *per capita* consumption should imply higher STP discount rates (1957 and 1961). It also shows that this relationship need not rest on Eckstein's assumption that $\partial U/\partial P = 0$ (zero marginal utility of total consumption if *per capita* consumption is constant) but only requires $\partial^2 U/\partial P^2 = 0$ (*constant* marginal utility of total consumption if *per capita* consumption is constant). Further, we see that total as well as *per capita* consumption growth may influence the STP rate.

44. e.g. Tinbergen and Eckstein. They also assume that it remains constant through time.

location in the consumption space) and by the slope of the indifference curve at that point (which in turn reflects the social consumption-utility function, the rate of population growth and the pure time preference rate that is applied).

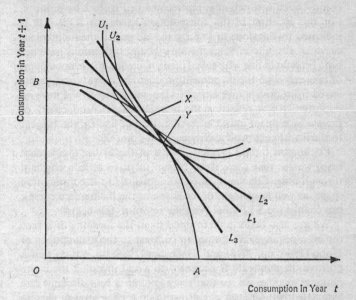

Figure 2

In an economy in which the total levels of both private and public investment were determined as a matter of national policy the location in the consumption space would be a point of tangency between the investment productivity curve and a social indifference curve. In Figure 2 this would occur at point X, where the social indifference curve U_2 is tangent to the investment productivity curve AB. Here the STP rate (as well as the marginal social productivity of investment) can be derived from the slope of line L_1, the tangent to the two curves at point X. But the Government may, for political as well as technical reasons, be unable to make private investment decisions conform to the STP discount rate; the marginal social productivity of private investment may therefore exceed the STP discount rate. In that case the Government can apply an STP rate (in combination with a measure of opportunity cost based on the marginal social productivity of private investment) only to its own investment decisions. Such a situation is represented in Figure 2 by point Y. For this location in the consumption space the STP rate is indicated by the slope of line L_2, the tangent to the indifference curve U_1 at point Y. Since private investment decisions have not been brought in line with social time preference, this is not a point of tangency with the investment productivity curve; funds transferred from private investment to the public sector will have an opportunity cost reflecting the marginal social productivity of private investment indicated by the slope of line L_3, the tangent to the investment productivity curve at point Y.[45]

Looking at the STP rate in terms of the Fisher indifference map, we see that there is no reason for it to remain constant through time. Changes in society's location in the consumption space, as well as changes in the shape of the indifference curves, can change the STP rate. We shall return to this below.

We are also better able to understand the meaning of a zero (or even negative) STP rate. In contrast to the assumptions of Dobb (1960, pp. 27–8) and Tinbergen (1956, pp. 604–5) that a positive discount rate is necessary to avoid investing the entire national income, we see that there is often a *zero* discount rate associated with at least one growth rate for the level of current consumption; for many points on the horizontal axis of the Fisher indifference map, there is a corresponding point vertically above it at which the slope of the social indifference curve is -1. Dobb and Tinbergen failed to see that the STP rate depends on the level of consumption and the rate of growth. If a nation reduces its consumption in order to invest more, the STP rate may rise. It is this, rather than the diminishing marginal productivity of investment, that precludes advice to invest the entire national income.[46] While we would expect that even in the absence of any

45. For a discussion of this problem and a method of calculating the opportunity cost 'shadow price' of funds transferred from private investment, see M. S. Feldstein (1964, especially section I).

46. Horvat, replying to Tinbergen's argument about the need for a positive discount rate, stated that the law of diminishing returns would prevent

pure time preference discount, the growth of *per capita* income would induce a positive STP rate, a zero or negative STP discount is not impossible.

A more serious question is whether the STP rate can be known in advance, and thus be available for use in the investment analyses or only emerges as a product of the investment decisions.[47] The STP rate appears at first both to determine and be determined by the Government's investment programme: the STP rate depends on society's location in the consumption space; but, subject to the condition that it must be on the investment-productivity curve, society's position in the consumption space reflects the amount of investment and thus ultimately the STP rate.[48] It seems from this that the STP rate cannot be known beforehand. An iterative method to solve for the optimum location on the investment productivity curve, and thus to yield simultaneously the amount of government investment, the marginal social productivity of private investment, and the STP rate, would no doubt be mathematically pleasing. It would, however, require that all projects be considered simultaneously, that the precise shape of the investment productivity curve be known and so forth. Extension of such a method to more than two periods would be of even more dubious practicability. In any case, its mathematical elegance would have little appeal to the administrator who requires a method for evaluating individual projects. Is there any way in which we might be able to know the STP rate in advance? Fortunately, although a precise *ex ante* estimate of the STP rate is not possible, for practical purposes there would be no harm in using such an advance estimate. The Government's range of total amounts of investment between which the Government may choose, i.e. the politically and econ-

investment of the total national income (1958, p. 158). But if the STP rate remained zero this would be true only if the marginal social productivity diminished to zero.

47. In somewhat different frameworks, Dobb (1960, p. 27) and Hirshleifer (1958, p. 329) argue that the investment criterion is itself a product of the analysis, and therefore cannot be available beforehand.

48. The STP rate determines the amount of public investment directly; private investment is affected by the taxation imposed to finance the programmes of public expenditure that are approved by calculations employing the STP rate.

omically feasible area in the consumption space, is very limited. Although we have not been able to say anything about the sensitivity of the STP rate to small changes in the consumption space location,[49] our uncertainty about the exact shape of the social indifference curves leads us to the conclusion that as long as the area of choice within which the Government may finally locate society is narrowly prescribed, we are safe to estimate the STP rate in advance. Our error in estimating the final location in the consumption space is likely to be no greater than the error which would be associated with an estimate of the STP rate after that location was known.

V The STP rate through time

The STP rate may vary through time if society's location in the consumption space changes or if the shapes or positions of the indifference curves do not remain constant.[50] Both of these are likely. We begin with the assumption that the social indifference map stays constant and examine the effects of changing consumption levels and growth rates. We then discuss the effects on the indifference map of changing the pure time preference discount rate.

Changes in the absolute level of consumption, even if its rate of growth remains constant, may alter the STP rate.[51] We have already seen that the properties we ascribed to the social utility-consumption function imply that the social indifference curves have the convexity properties associated with the second-order condition $\partial^2 U/\partial C^2 < 0$. The effect on the STP rate of a constant growth rate of *per capita* consumption will therefore depend on

49. Of course, for small enough movements along an indifference curve, the curve can be regarded as a straight line.

50. Julius Margolis has been the only writer to have suggested that the discount rate for evaluating public investment projects (not necessarily an STP rate) need not remain constant; he does not, however, develop the idea any further (1959, p. 102). Marshall and Böhm-Bawerk have suggested that individuals' time preferences vary with time; see the discussion in R. Strotz (1955–6, pp. 165–80).

51. This can, of course, happen if the rate of population growth changes. In our analysis this would imply a change in the social indifference map; we therefore ignore it at this point by assuming that the population growth rate remains constant, and is less than the growth rate of total consumption.

the function's third-order properties, i.e. on whether the marginal social utility of increasing consumption diminishes at a constant, accelerating or decelerating rate. In particular, the STP rate may increase through time as the level of consumption increases if the marginal utility of consumption diminishes at a sufficiently accelerating rate, i.e. if $\partial^3 U/\partial C^3 > 0$.

In terms of a social indifference map that remains constant through time, society's time path in the consumption space would be a single ray through the origin with a slope equal to 1 plus the rate of growth of consumption. The STP rate would remain constant only if the first derivative of every social indifference curve at its point of intersection with the growth ray was the same. This occurs, for example, in Ramsey's constant elasticity of marginal utility function (1928).

A changing rate of growth of consumption will cause society to digress from a straight-line time path through the consumption space. Given the assumed convexity properties, an increased growth rate (i.e. a vertical displacement in the consumption space) will produce a higher STP rate.[52]

52. The only exception would be if $\partial^3 U/\partial C^3 < 0$ to a great enough extent to counteract this.

References

ARROW, K. (1951), *Social Choice and Individual Values*, Wiley.

ATKINSON, F. J. (1948), 'Saving and investment in a socialist state', *Review econ. Stud.*, vol. 15.

BAIN, J. (1960), 'Criteria for undertaking water-resource developments', *Amer. econ. Review*, vol. 50.

BÖHM-BAWERK, E. VON (1888), *The Positive Theory of Capital*, trans. W. Smart, G. E. Stechert & Co., 1891.

CHAKRAVARTY, S. (1962), 'Optimal savings with finite planning horizon', *International Econ. Review*, vol. 3.

DOBB, M. (1960), *An Essay on Economic Growth and Planning*, Routledge & Kegan Paul.

ECKSTEIN, O. (1957), 'Investment criteria for economic development and the theory of intemporal welfare economics', *Quart. J. Econs.*, vol. 71, pp. 56–85.

ECKSTEIN, O. (1958), *Water Resource Development: The Economics of Project Evaluation*, Harvard University Press.

ECKSTEIN, O. (1961), 'A survey of the theory of public expenditure criteria', in J. M. Buchanan (ed.), *Public Finances: Needs, Sources and Utilization*, Princeton University Press.

FELDSTEIN, M. S. (1964), 'Net social benefit calculation and the public investment decision', *Oxford econ. Papers*, vol. 16, pp. 114–31.

FISHER, I. (1930), *The Theory of Interest*, Macmillan.

GRAAFF, J. DE V. (1957), *Theoretical Welfare Economics*, Cambridge University Press.

HAYEK, F. A. v. (1936), 'Utility analysis and interest', *Econ. J.*, vol. 46.

HIRSHLEIFER, J. (1958), 'On the theory of the optimal investment decision', *J. polit. Econ.*, vol. 66.

HIRSHLEIFER, J. (1961), 'Comment on Eckstein's survey of the theory of public expenditure criteria', in J. M. Buchanan (ed.), *Public Finances: Needs, Sources and Utilization*, Princeton University Press.

HIRSHLEIFER, J., DE HAVEN, J. C., and MILLIMAN, J. W. (1960), *Water Supply: Economics, Technology and Policy*, University of Chicago Press.

HITCH, C. J., and MCKEAN, R. N. (1960), *Economics of Defense in the Nuclear Age*, Harvard University Press.

HOLZMAN, F. D. (1958), 'Consumer sovereignty and the role of economic development', *Economia Internazionale*, vol. 11.

HORVAT, B. (1958), 'The optimum rate of saving: a note', *Econ. J.*, vol. 68.

HUFSCHMIDT, M. M., KRUTILLA, J., MARGOLIS, J., and MARGLIN, S. A. (1961), 'Report of panel of consultants to the Bureau of the budget on standards and criteria for formulating and evaluation Federal water resource developments', unpublished.

KRUTILLA, J. V., and ECKSTEIN, O. (1958), *Multiple Purpose River Development*, Johns Hopkins Press.

KUHN, T. E. (1962), *Public Enterprise Economics and Transport Problems*, University of California Press.

LIPSEY, R. G., and LANCASTER, K. (1956), 'A general theory of the second best', *Review of econ. Stud.*, vol. 24, pp. 11–32.

LITTLE, I. M. D. (1957), *A Critique of Welfare Economics*, 2nd edn, Oxford University Press.

MCKEAN, R. N. (1958), *Efficiency in Government Through Systems Analysis, with Emphasis on Water Resource Development*, Wiley.

MARGLIN, S. A. (1962), 'Economics factors affecting system design', in A. Maass *et al.*, *Design of Water Resource Systems*, Harvard University Press.

MARGLIN, S. A. (1963a), 'The social rate of discount and the optimal rate of investment', *Quart. J. Econ.*, vol. 77, no. 1, pp. 95–111.

MARGLIN, S. A. (1963b), *Approaches to Dynamic Investment Planning*, North-Holland.

MARGLIN, S. A. (1963c), 'The opportunity costs of public investment', *Quart. J. Econs*, vol. 77, pp. 276–89.

MARGOLIS, J. (1959), 'The economic evaluation of water resource development', *Amer. econ. Review*, vol. 69.

MARSHALL, A. (1920), *Principles of Economics*, 8th edn, Macmillan.

PIGOU, A. C. (1920), *Economics of Welfare*, 4th edn., Macmillan.

PRITCHFORD, J. D., and HAGGER, A. J. (1958), 'A note on the marginal efficiency of capital', *Economic Journal*, vol. 57.

RAMSEY, F. P. (1928), 'A mathematical theory of saving', *Econ. J.*, vol. 38.

SAMUELSON, P. A. (1955), 'Diagrammatic exposition of a theory of public expenditures', *Review of Economics and Statistics*, vol. 37.

SAMUELSON, P. A. (1956), 'Social indifference curves', *Quart. J. Econs.*, vol. 70.

SAMUELSON, P. A. (1957), 'The pure theory of public expenditure', *Review of Economics of Statistics*, vol. 36.

SEN, A. K. (1960), *Choice of Technique*, Blackwell.

SEN, A. K. (1961), 'On optimizing the rate of saving', *Econ. J.*, vol. 71.

SHACKLE, G. L. S. (1961), 'Recent theories concerning the nature and role of interest', *Econ. J.*, vol. 71.

STEINER, P. O. (1959), 'Choosing among alternative public investments in the water resource field', *Amer. econ. Review*, vol. 49.

STROTZ, R. (1955–6), 'Myopia and inconsistency in dynamic utility maximization', *Review econ. Stud.*, vol. 23.

TINBERGEN, J. (1956), 'The optimum rate of saving', *Econ. J.*, vol. 66.

TURVEY, R. (1963), 'Present value versus internal rate of return – an essay in the theory of the third best', *Econ. J.*, vol. 73.

WRIGHT, J. F. (1963), 'Notes on the marginal efficiency of capital', *Oxford econ. Papers*, vol. 15.

10 A. K. Sen

The Social Time Preference Rate in Relation to the Market Rate of Interest

A. K. Sen, 'Isolation, assurance and the social rate of discount',[1] *Quarterly Journal of Economics*, vol. 81, 1967, pp. 112–24.

Some of the recent discussions on the relationship between private and social rates of discount have been concerned with a special instance of a very general problem, being an extension of the two-person non-zero-sum game known as the 'prisoners' dilemma'.[2] In the first section of this paper the general nature of this problem will be studied, and it will also be shown that there is another problem close to this one with which it is sometimes confused, but which has a very different logical structure and involves different policy implications. In the remaining three sections the application of this general framework to the question of optimum savings and the social rate of discount will be examined, particularly in the light of some recent controversies.[3]

I The isolation paradox and the assurance problem

Consider a community of N individuals, each of whom must do one and only one of two alternatives, A and B. The payoff to each individual is a function of the actions of all individuals. Let the

1. This is a revised version of Working Paper no. 68 of the Committee on Econometrics and Mathematical Economics, University of California at Berkeley, May 1965.

2. Due to A. W. Tucker; see R. D. Luce and H. Raiffa (1958, sec. 5.4 and 5.5). See also M. Shubik (1964, chs. 20 and 23).

3. W. J. Baumol (1952); A. K. Sen (1961); S. A. Marglin (1963); G. Tullock (1964); Robert C. Lind (1964); D. Usher (1964); M. S. Feldstein (1964); A. C. Harberger (1964); E. S. Phelps (1965, ch. 4).

preference ordering of each individual satisfy the two following conditions: (1) given the set of actions off the others (no matter what they are), the individual is better of doing A rather than B; and (2) given the choice between everyone doing A and everyone doing B, each individual prefers the latter to the former.[4]

Given the two features noted of the preference pattern, certain results follow immediately. In particular the following three.

1. *Pareto-inferior outcome*: In the absence of collusion, each individual will prefer to do A rather than B, for no matter what the others do each is himself better off doing A. However, the outcome, viz. A by all, will be regarded as strictly worse by each than the alternative B by all. Thus the outcome is Pareto-inferior, and will be rejected by everyone in a referendum.[5]

2. *Strict dominance of individual strategy*: The atomistic result is completely independent of the individuals' expectations of other people's action. Irrespective of each person's expectations of the others' actions, each prefers to do A, i.e. the strategy of doing A strictly dominates over the alternative. Thus we do not have to make any assumption about the individual's behavior when faced with uncertainty and conflict, with which much of game theory is concerned.

3. *Need for enforcement*: Even if the policy of everyone doing B was adopted by resolution, this would not come about (assuming self-seeking) except through compulsory enforcement. Everyone would like the others to do B, while he himself does A, so that even if a contract is arrived at, it will be in the interest of each to break it.

4. If $i(x^i)$ stands for individual i pursuing strategy x^i, when x^i can be A or B, and if φ^i stands for the payoff to individual i in terms of his own welfare units, then

$$\varphi^i[1(x^1), 2(x^2), \ldots, i(A), \ldots, N(x^n)] > \varphi^i[1(x^1), 2(x^2), \ldots, i(B), \ldots, N(x^n)] \quad \mathbf{1}$$

and

$$\varphi^i[1(B), 2(B), \ldots, i(B), \ldots, N(B)] > \varphi^i[1(A), 2(A), \ldots, i(A), \ldots, N(A)]. \quad \mathbf{2}$$

5. It is possible to argue that the difference between the noncooperative equilibrium point and the collusive solution in this game corresponds precisely to Rousseau's distinction between 'the will of all' and the 'general will'. See Marglin (op. cit., p. 104, fn. 2). See also W. G. Runciman and A. K. Sen (1965); and R. R. Farquharson (1957–8).

It is easy to check that in the special case when there are only two individuals, the above corresponds exactly to the game of prisoners' dilemma. In fact with $N = 2$, the conditions **1** and **2** on the preference pattern give a complete strict ordering of the individuals over the entire field of possible outcomes, which consists of four alternatives.[6] We shall, however, stick to the N-person version, and call it the 'isolation paradox' (Sen, 1961, sec. 11).

The savings problem is only a special application of this. Suppose B stands for the policy of saving one more unit for the sake of the future of the community, and A for not doing it. Given the action of all others, each individual is better off not doing the additional unit of saving himself. Hence nobody will, but everyone would have preferred one more unit of saving by each than by none. This is the essence of the problem discussed by Marglin and myself.[7]

Consider now a somewhat different preference pattern. Let the individuals continue to hold **2**, but let **1** be modified. In the special case when everyone else does B, the individual now prefers to do B himself. Excepting this special case, the individual continues to prefer doing A to B no matter what the others do, *given* their action.[8]

This is a near-cousin of the isolation paradox, but differs from it in some of the main results. Result (2), i.e. strict dominance no longer holds. Expectations about other people's behavior must be brought in. If it is expected that the others will all do B, then this one would prefer to do B also; otherwise he may do A. Result (1) needs some modification also. If everyone has implicit faith in everyone else doing the 'right' thing, viz. B, then it will be in everyone's interest to do the right thing also. Then the outcome

6. A. K. Sen (1962, appendix to ch. 8). We have in this case:

$$\varphi^i[i(A), j(B)] > \varphi^i[i(B), j(B)] > \varphi^i[i(A), j(A)] > \varphi^i[i(B), j(A)]. \qquad \mathbf{3}$$

7. See Phelps (1965) for an illuminating discussion of this problem in the context of others involving growth and public savings.

8. Formally, we impose the restriction on **1** that

$$Not\,[x^1 = x^2 = x^3 = \ldots = x^n = B]. \qquad \mathbf{1^*}$$

And we supplement **1**, thus restricted, by

$$\varphi^i[1(B), 2(B), \ldots, i(B), \ldots, N(B)] > \varphi^i[1(B), 2(B), \ldots, i(A), \ldots, N(B)]. \qquad \mathbf{1.1}$$

need not be Pareto-inferior.[9] However, if each individual feels that the others are going to let him down, that is not do *B*, then he too may do *A* rather than *B*, and the outcome will be Pareto-inferior.

Result (3) does not hold any longer. Given that each individual has complete assurance that the other will do *B*, there is no problem of compulsory enforcement. Unlike in the case of the isolation paradox, it is not in the individual's interest to break the contract of everyone doing *B*. In this case assurance is sufficient and enforcement is unnecessary, and we shall refer to this case as that of the 'assurance problem'.

These two problems have often been confused with each other. Marglin's and my argument for the inoptimality of market savings is based on the assumption of a situation of the type of the isolation paradox. This problem, however, has been identified with Vickrey's analysis (1962) of 'the interdependence of the transfers of different donors', where 'an individual might be willing to make a gift to one of his fellows *if he knew* that others were doing so even if he would not make the gift on his own.'[10] This last is, however, a case of the assurance problem.[11] In our case an individual will not do the saving *even if* 'he knew that others were doing so', and this makes the inoptimality of the market result certain, which it is not in Vickrey's case.

The difference is a simple one when viewed in the context of game theory. In the assurance problem with which Vickrey is concerned,[12] everyone doing the 'right' thing, i.e. *B*, is an 'equilibrium point',[13] whereas in Marglin's case and in mine, this is

9. Note, however, that there is no guarantee that this will definitely not be Pareto-inferior. From **1**, **1.1** and **2**, we get an incomplete ordering for each individual, if $N > 2$.

10. Tullock (1964, p. 331); emphasis added.

11. The preference pattern corresponds to **1** subject to **1*** and **1.1**.

12. Vickrey goes into more complex cases also. He introduces the possibility that an individual donating a sum might induce others to do the same. This restricts condition **1** even more than in the assurance problem, with the individual preference for *A* over *B* being not only not applicable when *all* others do *B*, but also when, say, a certain suitably large fraction of the total group does *B*.

13. See Luce and Raiffa (1958, sec. 7.8). For the classic analysis of the meaning and the existence of equilibrium points, see J. F. Nash (1950).

definitely not so. Baumol's discussion of the optimum savings problem also fits in with the assurance problem, rather than with the isolation paradox, and it rests on an interdependence due to the indivisibility of public projects. The effect of trying to save alone for the sake of the future generation is 'negligible', so that the individual, though endowed with altruism, does not do this, 'except if he has grounds for assurance that others, too, will act in a manner designed to promote the future welfare of the community' (Baumol, 1952, p. 92). In the case of the isolation paradox, however, the individual will not do the saving *even with* the assurance.[14]

II Optimum savings

Consider now the following ordering of individual i. He attaches a weight of unity to his consumption today (simply a normalization assumption), β per unit to the consumption of his contemporaries, γ per unit to the consumption of his own heirs in the future, and a per unit to the consumption of the others in the future generation.[15] For each person, only one marginal choice is considered, viz. whether to increase the saving by one unit (B), or not to do it (A). Also, the future consumption is taken to be a one-shot affair, though this assumption can be easily relaxed without losing anything essential. The marginal rate of return on one unit of saving (i.e. one unit less of consumption) today is an increase in the consumption in the future by k units, where $k > 1$. The individual expects that a proportion λ of the fruits of his saving will accrue to his heirs, and the rest $(1-\lambda)$ to others in the future generation, when $0 \leq \lambda \leq 1$; we shall discuss presently

14. 'This possibility of the apparent paradox is present whenever his relative evaluation of others' consumption is such that he would prefer them to sacrifice some consumption for the future generations; and sacrificing something himself might, because of the indivisibility of the political decision, be the means of achieving this to a sufficient extent to over-compensate the loss that he would incur from his own act of sacrifice' (Sen, 1961, pp. 488–9). 'I am willing to abide by [the no-fix system], too, if this is the price I must pay for your adherence, although my first choice is that all of you abide by the no-fix system and I buy off the police force' (Marglin, 1963, p. 100).

15. These values can be interpreted as the relevant marginal utilities in the utility function of individual i, and can be taken as constant for small changes (see Marglin, 1963, p. 101).

the proper assumption about the value of λ. The individual figures that *given* the actions of other people today, the net gain $G(i)$ from one unit more of personal saving is the following

$$G(i) = [\lambda\gamma + (1-\lambda)a]k - 1. \qquad\qquad 4$$

If $G(i) > 0$, the individual i will clearly save the extra unit, i.e. do B. However, when we start with the amount of savings on which each has already made a decision (based on their atomistic calculation), and then consider the extra unit to be a tiny bit more, G clearly cannot be positive or they would not have been in atomistic equilibrium. Making the usual assumptions about well-behaved and continuously differentiable functions, we shall indeed find that in the atomistic equilibrium, $G = 0$ for every individual, which amounts to

$$[\lambda\gamma + (1-\lambda)a]k = 1. \qquad\qquad 5$$

Now, consider the possibility of a social contract of everyone (N in all) saving one more tiny unit, so that as evaluated by any individual the immediate loss is $1 + (N-1)\beta$, attaching the appropriate weights to the consumption of oneself and of one's contemporaries. This has to be set against the gain in the future. The total gain in physical terms is Nk for the future generation as a whole, and let the proportion of that enjoyed by one's own heirs be h; the appropriate assumptions for h will be discussed presently. However, the net gain $G(s)$ from the social contract, as viewed by any individual, will be of the general form

$$G(s) = Nkh\gamma + Nk(1-h)a - 1 - (N-1)\beta. \qquad\qquad 6$$

We can now examine what conditions have to be satisfied for the isolation paradox to hold. Note that 5 indicates the weak form of the preference relation 1. Since we are starting from an atomistic market equilibrium, people in isolation from the others do not want to save more than they are doing already. Strictly speaking they should be indifferent between A and B, since the net gain from the change is exactly nil, but we can assume that they prefer not to save when there is no net gain. For condition 2 to hold, we need $G(s) > 0$, i.e. everyone prefers B (saving) by each rather than A (not saving) by each.

$$Nk[h\gamma + (1-h)a] > 1 + (N-1)\beta. \qquad\qquad 7$$

When **7** is consistent with **5**, we have the isolation paradox holding, and people are willing to join in the contract to save but not do so individually. To get this result, the assumption that was made by Marglin and myself has been found to be unacceptable by many, viz. that individuals do not discriminate between their own heirs and the rest of the future generation, i.e. $\gamma = a$. As can be readily checked, exactly the same formula holds if $\lambda = h = 0$, i.e. if the fruits of my saving (both in individualistic saving and social contract) accrue to the future generation in general and not to my own heirs. Neither, I agree, is a good assumption, and it will be shown presently that neither is necessary. But before that, the consequence of this assumption, however bad, can be checked immediately. Then from **5**

$$k = \frac{1}{a}$$

and condition **7** reduces to

$$1 > \beta. \qquad \qquad \textbf{7.1}$$

The result is independent of the value of N, provided, of course, $N > 1$. It is quite reasonable to assume that $\beta < 1$, i.e. I value my consumption more than that of my other contemporaries.

In a closely-reasoned note on this problem, commenting on Marglin's paper, Lind has suggested an alternative set of assumptions. In effect, he assumes that the individual can pass on (if he chooses) all the fruits of his own saving to his own heir without any part of it going to others in the future generation. Then:

$$\lambda = 1, \qquad h = \frac{1}{N}, \quad \text{and} \quad k = \frac{1}{\gamma},$$

so that **7** reduces to

$$\frac{1}{\gamma} > \frac{\beta}{a}. \qquad \qquad \textbf{7.2}$$

We cannot be so sure that **7.2** will hold as **7.1**. If $1/\gamma > \beta/a$, the individuals will be willing to join the contract; and if $1/\gamma < \beta/a$, the individuals will not be willing to do so. Indeed, if the latter condition held, it would be easy to show that they will be prepared to join a contract to *reduce* savings; this too fits the isolation paradox, except it now runs the other way, with B standing for reducing the saving by one unit each, and A as before. In between these values lies the case where everything is fine with atomistic allocation, and the case of $1/\gamma = \beta/a$ can be seen to be one where my relative evaluation of your heir's consumption (a) and your consumption (β), exactly corresponds to your relative evaluation of your heir's consumption (γ) *vis-à-vis* your own 1. Lind finds this a 'reasonable' assumption.[16]

The difficulty with Lind's assumption of the balance of emotions is that it makes insufficient allowance for the personal nature of egoism. My egoism might not extend as much to my heirs *vis-à-vis* yours, as it applies to me personally *vis-à-vis* you. The longer the distance in time that we consider the more is this likely to be the case. So that $a/\beta > \gamma$, does not seem to be a particularly bad assumption. However, for the sake of argument, let us grant this balance of emotions, and assume that γ is exactly equal to a/β, no more and no less. There is the further question of $\lambda = 1$, which is the only case Lind discusses. If it is assumed that there is a gap between the marginal productivity of capital and the rate of interest, λ must be below 1.[17] But even when there is no such gap, in a society with taxation this will happen again. Even if we assume, in a competitive dream world, that no one is prevented from enjoying the full 'return' of his own investment through taxes, this does not rule out taxes, such as estate duties, that apply to unrequited transfers. And these too will make $\lambda < 1$. This is not to say that Marglin's and my assumption of $a = \gamma$, or alternatively, of $\lambda = 0$, is a good assumption, but neither is the other special case of $\lambda = 1$, with exactly balanced emotions. The natural question to ask is what happens when λ takes a value in between these extremes, i.e. when it is selected from the open interval] 0, 1[. The answer is that the condition for the isolation paradox remains *exactly* the same as with $\lambda = 0$. Lind's case of

16. Lind (1964, pp. 341–2, 345). In commenting on my *Economic Journal* paper on the subject, the same suggestion was made in a personal communication (dated 4 April 1962) by the late Sir Dennis Robertson.

17. In much of the literature on economic development, it is conventional to assume that the market wage rate is above the social opportunity cost of labor, which will also make $\lambda < 1$, since the marginal benefits to the owners of capital will fall short of the marginal benefits to the community. This is a sufficient assumption for $\lambda < 1$, but, of course, not necessary.

$\lambda = 1$ is the one exceptional value; the rest of the interval gives the same condition. This is shown below.

Let us assume first that in the case of the social contract to save more, my heir gets only λ part of my own savings, and nothing of other people's savings. In that case

$$h = \frac{\lambda}{N}. \hspace{6cm} 8.1$$

Then the required condition 7 reduces to

$$[\lambda\gamma + (N-\lambda)a]k > 1 + (N-1)\beta. \hspace{3cm} 7.3$$

In view of 5 and the Lindian balanced emotions ($\gamma = a/\beta$), this is equivalent to

$$\beta < 1. \hspace{6cm} 7.1$$

Precisely the same condition, as with $a = \gamma$, or with $\lambda = 0$.

Now, this assumption of my heir getting only λ part of the fruits of my savings in the social contract with other people's heirs getting the whole of the fruit of their savings *plus* $1 - \lambda$ part of the result of my saving, seems a poor one. Surely my heirs will do better than this from the social contract; they can expect to get a part of the $1 - \lambda$ portion of other people's savings that goes to future generations in general. But, if this is the case, 7.1 will be *a fortiori* sufficient for the isolation paradox, as can be readily checked from the fact that $\gamma > a$, since $\gamma = a/\beta$, and $\beta < 1$. If 7.1 is sufficient to induce me to join the contract even with the minimum share of my heirs, it is naturally sufficient if they get a higher share.

III The rate of discount

To derive the formula for the social rate of discount implicit in this, we have to specify the value of h more than working with its minimum magnitude. The symmetrical assumption is the following: each set of heirs get λ part of the results of their progenitor's savings, while $1 - \lambda$ goes to a general pool of the 'future generation', out of the total of which each set again gets $1/N$ portion. It is readily seen

$$h = \frac{1}{N}. \hspace{6cm} 8.2$$

And with this symmetrical sharing of the general pool, the social rate of discount (ρ) is given by exactly the same formula as that of Lind (except in the special case of $\lambda = 0$)[18]

$$\rho = \frac{1+(N-1)\beta}{\gamma+(N-1)a}-1. \qquad\qquad 9$$

Marglin's formula coincides with this only when $a = \gamma$, or when N is very large, which reduces this to $\beta/a - 1$, and also reduces Marglin's to the same value. However, the difference between the private and the social rate of discount continues to hold, except when the knife-edge balance happens to occur. This is the dual to the problem of the optimum rate of saving, and 7.1 can be seen to be sufficient for the social rate to be below the private rate of discount.

Representing the private rate of discount by π, it is seen from 5 and 9 that

$$\rho \lessgtr \pi,$$

according as

$$\frac{1+(N-1)\beta}{1+(N-1)a/\gamma} \lessgtr \frac{1}{\lambda+(1-\lambda)a/\gamma}. \qquad\qquad 10$$

Lind gets $\rho = \pi$; by assuming the balance of emotions $a/\gamma = \beta$, and that $\lambda = 1$. The more general set of conditions is given by taking 10 as an equality; there are pairs of values of (λ, γ) that satisfy this equality, of which Lind's is one. However, there is nothing at all in the market mechanism to guarantee that we shall indeed have one of these critical pairs holding. Of course, it *can* happen, but it will be an accidental outcome.

Marglin's case can be obtained from 10 by putting $a = \gamma$, a different balance of emotions. This reduces 10 to

$$\rho \lessgtr \pi, \quad \text{according as } \beta \lessgtr 1. \qquad\qquad 10.1$$

18. Lind points out that the assumption of identical individuals is quite crucial for this formulation, and indeed the existence of a social rate of discount.

We would get the same condition if $\lambda = 0$, and $h = 0$, when the social rate of discount is as given in Marglin.[19] Suppose, however, we grant (as in our discussion of the dual problem to this) that Lind's emotional balance holds; i.e., $a/\beta = \gamma$; then **10** becomes

$$\rho \lesseqgtr \pi, \quad \text{according as } \beta(1-\lambda) \lesseqgtr (1-\lambda). \tag{10.2}$$

The equality holds only in Lind's special case of $\lambda = 1$. For any other value of λ, **10.2** reduces into **10.1**. Thus, while $\lambda = 1$, and $\lambda = 0$, look like two extreme cases, they are not symmetrical in the generality of their respective results.

IV Rich they, poor us

Finally, the point has been raised[20] whether the isolation paradox in savings is at all likely to arise when it is borne in mind that the future generation is going to be a great deal more wealthy than the present generation. In the determination of the social rate of discount, this will undoubtedly be an important consideration. This can be checked readily by looking at **9**, where the wealth of the future generation will tend to make the values of γ and a relatively lower. However, will this affect the condition for the isolation paradox to hold? Not at all! It is seen from **7.1** and **7.2** that a proportionate fall in γ and a (the values attached to the consumption of the future generation) *vis-à-vis* the values attached to the consumption of members of the present generation, will not make any difference to the fulfilment of the conditions.

The explanation is simple; the fact that the future generation will be wealthier has already been taken into account in the atomistic allocation of resources, and the average wealth of the future generation *vis-à-vis* that of the present generation does not affect the *relative* profitability of atomistic allocation and the social contract. Indeed substituting the value of k from **5** into **7**, we find that **7** is equivalent to

$$\frac{N[h\gamma + (1-h)a]}{[\lambda\gamma + (1-\lambda)a]} > 1 + (N-1)\beta. \tag{7*}$$

19. Equation (13), Marglin (1963, p. 106).
20. Tullock (1964, pp. 333–5); Harberger (1964, sec. 4).

In this general condition a proportionate change in the values of γ and a would leave the fulfilment of the inequality entirely unchanged.

Exactly the same is true, naturally, in the dual to this problem, i.e. in the difference between the private and the social rate of discounts. A proportionate change in γ and a will leave condition 10 exactly the same, as is obvious from its form.

V Conclusions

In section I two specific problems concerning individual and social actions were studied. One, the isolation paradox, is an N-person extension of the two-person non-zero-sum game of the prisoners' dilemma. Here each individual has a strictly dominant strategy, and the pursuit of this by each produces an overall result that is Pareto-inferior. Individuals can do better than this by collusion, but the collusive solution requires enforcement.

The second, the assurance problem, which is sometimes confused with the first, has a different analytical structure and implies different policy questions. Here there is no strictly dominant strategy, and one of the equilibrium points in the non-cooperative game may be Pareto-optimal. Whether this will be the outcome of the noncooperative game or whether the outcome will be Pareto-inferior depends on what each individual expects about the others' action. To get out of the problem all that is necessary is that each individual is assured that the others are doing the 'right' thing, and then it is in one's own interest also to do the 'right' thing. No enforcement is necessary.

Marglin's and my discussion of the inoptimality of market savings corresponds to the isolation paradox, whereas that of Baumol, and of Vickrey (in the context of philanthropy), corresponds to the assurance problem. The distinction is important analytically as well as for policy decisions.

In the last three sections, Marglin's and my formulation of the problem of the inoptimality of market savings was examined as an application of the paradox of isolation. It should be conceded immediately that if one is ready to make some rather special assumptions, the problem can in fact be assumed away. Lind's conditions of balance ($\gamma = a/\beta$, and $\lambda = 1$) achieve this,[21] and, as we have seen, so does a family of pairs of values of (γ, λ). However, there is nothing in the market mechanism that will ensure this achievement. This inoptimality of the market mechanism, and the possibility of a social contract by which everyone will agree to do something he would not be ready to do individually, is not a surprising result when viewed in the context of games such as the prisoners' dilemma. It is a paradox only as an apparent one, as most paradoxes are. Even from the point of view of usual theories of optimum allocation through decentralized decisions, the result need not be viewed as particularly contrary, for the basis of it lies in an *external* concern for members of the future generation *vis-à-vis* of the present.

If the emotional balance of the type proposed by Lind is taken ($\gamma = a/\beta$), then the optimality of the market rate of saving and that of the market rate of discount are unlikely to hold in any economy that we know of. With this type of balanced emotions, the isolation paradox can be ruled out, as Lind does, by assuming $\lambda = 1$. Marglin's and my assumptions about people's concern for others ($\gamma = a$) differ from this, but if $\lambda = 0$ then, of course, the condition for the existence of the isolation problem is the same as with $\gamma = a$, no matter what emotional assumptions we make. While $\lambda = 1$ and $\lambda = 0$, represent two extreme cases, their positions are not symmetrical. In fact, for any value of λ in between these limits, i.e. from the open interval $]0, 1[$, the condition for the isolation paradox, with Lindian balanced emotions, will be exactly the same as with $\lambda = 0$, i.e. precisely the result we get from Marglin's and my assumptions.

Finally, the question of the future generation being, on the average, much richer than the present generation was studied as grounds for an objection that has been raised against the chances of the isolation paradox.[22] It was shown that a change in the

21. Lind's condition is not, of course, in conflict with the claim that 'this possibility of the apparent paradox is present whenever his relative valuation of others' consumption is such that he would prefer them to sacrifice some consumption for the future generations' (Sen, 1962, p. 488). With $\gamma = a/\beta$, and $\lambda = 1$, the condition is not met, and the consequence does not, naturally, follow. See also Marglin (1963, pp. 100–2).

22. Tullock (1964, pp. 333–5); Harberger (1964, sec. 4). Harberger has a further argument which we have not discussed. 'The third argument (c),

average wealth of the future generation *vis-à-vis* that of the present generation, bringing about a change in a and γ in the same proportion, leave the possibility of the isolation paradox completely unchanged.

---

best reflected by Sen and Marglin, smacks of charity. . . . My reaction to this is simple: any individual who wants to help others, and to make sure that his contribution is not dissipated, can do so by selecting one or more people of the present generation to help' (pp. 14–15). This seems a good way of working off one's irrepressible urge towards charity, but surely this need not cure the misallocation in the rate of saving.

References

BAUMOL, W. J. (1952), *Welfare Economics and the Theory of the State*, Harvard University Press.

FARQUHARSON, R. R. (1957–8), 'An approach to the pure theory of voting procedure', Ph.D. thesis, University of Oxford.

FELDSTEIN, M. S. (1964), 'The social time preference discount rate in cost-benefit analysis', *Econ. J.*, vol. 74, pp. 360–79.

HARBERGER, A. C. (1964), 'Techniques of project appraisal', Universities National Bureau of Economic Research, Conference on Economic Planning, mimeo. 27 and 28 November.

LIND, R. C. (1964), 'Further comment', *Quart. J. Econ.*, vol. 78, pp. 336–45.

LUCE, R. D., and RAIFFA, H. (1958), *Games and Decisions*, Wiley.

MARGLIN, S. A. (1963), 'The social rate of discount and the optimal rate of investment', *Quart. J. Econ.*, vol. 77, pp. 95–111.

NASH, J. F. (1950), 'Equilibrium points in *N*-person games', *Proceedings of the National Academy of Sciences*, vol. 36.

PHELPS, E. S. (1965), *Fiscal Neutrality Toward Economic Growth*, McGraw-Hill.

RUNCIMAN, W. G., and SEN, A. K. (1965), 'Games, justice and the general will', *Mind*, vol. 74.

SEN, A. K. (1961), 'On optimizing the rate of saving', *Econ. J.*, vol. 71, pp. 479–96.

SEN, A. K. (1962), *Choice of Techniques*, 2nd edn, Blackwell.

SHUBIK, M. (ed.) (1964), *Game Theory and Related Approaches to Social Behavior*, Wiley.

TULLOCK, G. (1964), 'The social rate of discount and the optimal rate of investment: comment', *Quart. J. Econ.*, vol. 78.

USHER, D. (1964), 'Comment', *Quart. J. Econ.*, vol. 78.

VICKREY, W. S. (1962), 'One economist's view of philanthropy', in F. G. Dickinson (ed.), *Philanthropy and Public Policy*, National Bureau of Economic Research.

11 S. A. Marglin

The Opportunity Costs of Public Investment

S. A. Marglin, 'The opportunity costs of public investment',[1]
Quarterly Journal of Economics, vol. 77, 1963, pp. 274–89.

Introduction

A previous article in this Journal (Marglin, 1963a) presented the thesis that external effects render an atomistic capital market inadequate for registering the time preferences of individuals. It followed that market-determined rates of investment and interest, even rates determined in a competitive market, need have no normative significance, and that the optimal level of investment for an economy is the level at which the marginal productivity of investment equals the marginal *social* rate of discount incorporating external effects, rather than the level at which the marginal productivity equals the market rate of discount determined by unilateral investment and saving decisions. The earlier essay concluded by pointing out that if the marginal social rate of discount is lower than the market rate for the operation of a

1. Discussions with many individuals (see the list at the beginning of Marglin, 1963a), especially Kenneth Arrow, Robert Dorfman, and Amartya Sen, have left their imprint on this essay, and I am grateful to them all. A summary of an earlier draft of this paper appears as part of chapter 4 of *Design of Water Resource Systems* (1962) by Arthur Maass and others. I should like to thank the Harvard University Press for permission to use material published under their imprimatur. A second version of this essay was presented to the 1961 Winter Meeting of the Econometric Society as part of a paper titled 'The social rate of discount and the opportunity costs of public investment'.

laissez-faire market,[2] then the impact of this result in a frictionless competitive model is that the community in its collective, political capacity properly sees to it – directly or indirectly – that some investment opportunities are exploited that have future returns too low to justify development by private individuals.

There are two ways of carrying out this injunction. The government can directly undertake public investment until further investment becomes marginal from the collective as well as unilateral point of view. Alternatively, the government can employ fiscal and monetary policy to induce private enterprise to exploit all opportunities for which the present value of the net benefits to society is positive at the marginal social rate of discount. Appropriate use of monetary operations to ensure plentiful and cheap credit, coupled with subsidies and differentiated tax rates, would make socially desirable opportunities privately desirable as well.[3] In either event the marginal social rate of discount would equal the marginal productivity of investment, and in the latter case at least the marginal social rate of discount would equal the market rate as well.

However, the first of these counsels of perfection is clearly not applicable to actual investment decisions, at least not in mixed enterprise economies like our own. For it takes no heed of the difference in the kinds of investment opportunities likely to be open to public and private development. In the United States the government does not allow itself to exploit most of the opportunities for which the future gain, when evaluated at a social rate of discount lower than market rates, justifies the present sacrifice; most of these opportunities, for better or worse, lie in the sector that in the present institutional structure has been marked off as 'private'.

Nor is the alternative counsel relevant. The government does not exercise the degree of control over the volume and mix of

2. This must be the case for the United States if there is any welfare content to the argument that our economy is not growing fast enough.

3. Indeed, if the economy were perfectly competitive, the government need only follow the suggestion advanced by Jack Hirshleifer, James C. De Haven, and Jerome Milliman in their recent study *Water Supply* (1960, ch. 6). The government is to drive the market rate down to the marginal social rate by means of monetary policy alone and employ fiscal policy simply to avoid the inflation that increased private investment would otherwise set off.

private investment through fiscal and monetary policy that would be necessary to ensure development of all socially desirable opportunities in the private sector. And it is not clear that capital markets are sufficiently competitive that the government *could* exercise the necessary degree of control over private investment even if it wished to – short of direct controls.

On the other hand, the boundary between the public and private investment sectors is not absolute in modern capitalistic economies. Government fiscal and monetary policies can and are used to encourage (or restrict) private investment. And the rate of public investment itself, as a result of deviations from the competitive model in the actual determination of private investment, can affect the rate of private exploitation of socially desirable investment opportunities.[4]

The potential displacement of private by public investment poses the problem of this essay: how should the planning of the class of investments that the government does undertake be affected by the existence of private investment opportunities that are (1) socially desirable by virtue of a discrepancy between the social rate of discount and the rate(s) of discount governing private investment and (2) displaced by public investment by virtue of the institutional structure?

The formal models

This is a problem of 'second best'. The optimal solution, undertaking *all* investment that has a positive present value at the social rate of discount is precluded by the institutional structure, and we consequently are faced with the necessity of choosing the best of

4. The extent to which the rate of private investment declines in response to increases in the rate of public investment will depend on the level of unemployment in the economy and the method of financing public investment. In situations of less than full employment of resources – especially long-run, structural unemployment characteristic of underdeveloped countries – public investment, in so far as it can be arranged to take up slack in the economy, need disturb private investment and private consumption somewhat less than in situations of full employment. And financing public investment by a tax on luxury goods would reduce private investment less than an equal amount of taxation on business profits – because of the importance of the availability of funds supplied internally by firms in determining their investment programs.

inferior combinations of public and private investment. Clearly, the goal in planning public investment should be to avoid displacing 'better' opportunities in the private sector.

This answer, however, simply shifts the ground of the question. The problem becomes one of deciding whether private investment offers better opportunities than public investment. 'Better' is easy to decide if, of two alternative investments entailing the same initial outlay, the benefits less operating costs for one are greater in every year than for the other. For example, if alternatives A and B both require the same initial outlay and their respective time streams of benefits less operating costs are as depicted in Figure 1, then we have no trouble identifying B as the superior investment.

But the question of superiority becomes difficult to resolve if the time streams intersect, as in the example of alternatives C and D in Figure 2. Here C is better only until t_0, after which D becomes superior. Or to put the problem another way, C has the higher net present value at rates of discount higher than some 'breakeven' rate r_0, and D has the higher net present value at rates lower than r_0. Which rate of discount is relevant for comparisons between public and private investment that compete for resources?

The answer to this question was sketched in embryonic form by Otto Eckstein (1958, pp. 101–3) and developed in a masterful paper by Peter Steiner (1959, p. 893). And the answer is remarkably straightforward. Since the marginal social rate of discount reflects the community's marginal weight on consumption at different times, the appropriate basis for comparison of alternative public and private investment is the present value of their net benefits to society evaluated at the marginal social rate of discount. Thus, in the planning of public investment, the present value of the social benefits of private investment that public investment displaces, evaluated at the marginal social rate of discount, supersedes the money cost of public investment as the measure of its true social cost. In other words, we plan public projects to maximize their net present value at the marginal social rate of discount, but, in evaluating the social cost of public investment, an opportunity cost reflecting the social value of utilizing resources in private investment replaces the money cost of the portion of the

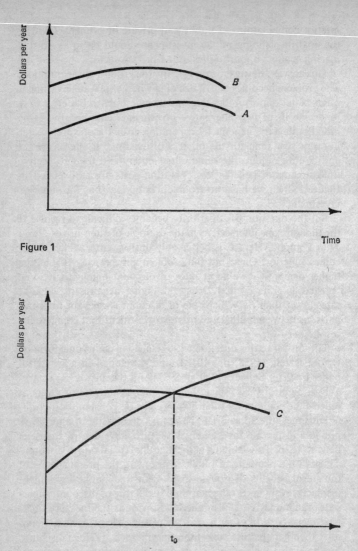

Figure 1

Figure 2

resources that comes from the private investment sector. Formally, for each public project we replace the objective function [5]

$$\int_0^\infty B(x, t)e^{-rt}\, dt - K(x) \qquad\qquad 1$$

where

1. x, the choice variable, represents the scale of the project,
2. t represents time,
3. $B(x, t)$ represents the benefit rate (net of operating costs) of the project as a function of project scale and time,
4. r represents the marginal social rate of discount, and
5. $K(x)$ represents the capital cost (as a function of scale)

by the objective function

$$\int_0^\infty B(x, t)e^{-rt}\, dt - aK(x), \qquad\qquad 2$$

where a represents the opportunity cost per dollar of public investment. The parameter a is a shadow price that replaces the nominal price of funds of one dollar per dollar. [6]

How is the opportunity cost parameter measured? As we have seen, two questions must be answered: (1) What portion of the resources required to undertake public investment come from the private investment sector? (2) What is the present value to the nation of the stream of benefits that displaced private investment would generate? These answers are, however, quite general.

5. This objective function is grossly oversimplified. For one thing, in this as in the previous essay, we assume perfect certainty. This assumption is made not in the belief that it mirrors the world, but rather in the belief that the discount rate and opportunity costs are inappropriate vehicles for reflecting uncertainty and hence that in a discussion of these aspects of the investment decision, perfect certainty is a legitimate simplifying assumption.

Another shortcoming of the objective function employed in this essay is that it is static, implying that the investment decision is a 'now or never' proposition. For a discussion of the dyamics of investment planning, see S. Marglin (1963b).

6. If the public investment objective function is constrained by a limited budget, the appropriate interpretation of a is as the value of budgetary slack.

To learn something of substance about the measurement of opportunity costs, we examine the relationship between public and private investment in a series of simplified models.

Measuring opportunity costs – model I

Suppose that private investment displaced by public investment yields annual benefits equal to ρ per cent of the original outlay in perpetuity. As the perpetual annual throw-off from a one dollar investment, ρ has a simple interpretation: it is the marginal productivity, or the marginal rate of return, of investment in the private sector. The parameter ρ, it should be emphasized, is assumed to measure the social benefits of private investment in units exactly comparable to the benefits $B(x, t)$ of public investment, and for many reasons this measure may differ from the private benefits of investment.[7] Moreover, we must assume that the annual throw-off ρ is consumed as it becomes available. Otherwise the real benefit stream alternative to the benefits of public investment is not the perpetuity of ρ per cent annually, but rather the benefit stream of the nominal alternative *plus reinvestment*.

We denote the amount of private investment displaced by each dollar of public investment by θ_1, this parameter being restricted by the inequality of $O \leqslant \theta_1 \leqslant 1$. We assume full employment of resources, so that the portion of the resources required to undertake public investment which does not come out of private investment comes out of private consumption.

With these assumptions the opportunity cost per dollar of public investment is

$$a_I = \theta_1 \frac{\rho}{r} + (1 - \theta_1). \qquad\qquad 3$$

Consider equation 3 term by term: ρ/r represents the social present value per dollar of private investment, and $\theta_1 \, \rho/r$ consequently represents the loss from displacement of private investment for each dollar of public investment; the second term $(1-\theta_1)$ is the portion of each dollar of public investment that displaces private

7. For a discussion of the measurement of benefits under two different objectives (increasing national income and improving the distribution of income), see A. Maass *et al.* (1962, ch. 2).

consumption and is therefore reckoned at face value. Alternatively, equation 3 can be rewritten as

$$a_I = \frac{\theta_1 \rho + (1-\theta_1)r}{r}. \qquad\qquad 4$$

The numerator can be thought of as the annual value of a dollar 'investment' in a 'perpetuity' split in the proportions θ_1 and $(1-\theta_1)$ between private investment with annual yield ρ and private consumption with annual yield r. The ratio of this sum to r is the present value of the 'perpetuity' at the discount rate r.

Expressions 3 and 4 define the minimum present value that the marginal dollar of public investment must earn to qualify for inclusion in a public investment program designed to maximize the present value, at the marginal social rate of discount, of the stream of benefits to society from investment in both the public and private sectors. If, for example, $r = 0.02$, $\rho = 0.05$, and $\theta_1 = 0.75$, then $a_I = 2.125$. That is, increments to the public investment program must show a present value of \$2.125 per dollar of outlay rather than simply a present value of \$1.00 per dollar.[8]

Measuring opportunity costs – model I'

In defining the returns from private investment, we emphasized that it was not the nominal throw-off that is important but the actual stream of consumption that the investment provides, taking reinvestment into account. The same holds true of public investment itself. Reinvestment of the benefits of public investment tends to offset any loss of benefits from private investment that results from diversion of resources to public investment.

To illustrate, suppose that a constant proportion θ_2, $0 \leqslant \theta_2 \leqslant 1$, of the benefits $B(x, t)$ of a public project are reinvested as they become available.[9] And suppose the yield from reinvestment is a

8. Note that if $\theta_1 = 1$, that is, if displacement of private investment is 'one for one', the second term of the right-hand side of equation 3 drops out and a_I becomes simply ρ/r, the present value of the displaced benefits of private investment. At the other extreme, if $\theta_1 = 0$, that is, if public investment entails no displacement of private investment, a_I reduces to one dollar per dollar, the value of present consumption displaced by each dollar of public investment.

9. The parameter θ_2 is thus a 'marginal propensity to invest' and $(1-\theta_2)$ is a 'marginal propensity to consume' – the quotation marks reflecting our

perpetuity with a continuous throw-off at the rate of ρ per cent of the amount reinvested. Under the assumption that this throw-off is consumed as it becomes available, the present value at time t of the benefit $B(x,t)$ is

$$V(x,t) = \int_t^\infty \theta_2 \rho B(x,t)e^{-r(u-t)}\,du + (1-\theta_2)B(x,t).\qquad 5$$

The first term on the right-hand side of equation 5 represents the present value at time t of the reinvested portion of the benefits and the second term the value of the portion that is immediately consumed at time t. If we perform the integration and combine terms, we have

$$V(x,t) = \frac{\theta_2 \rho + (1-\theta_2)r}{r}\,B(x,t).\qquad 6$$

The present value today of the entire stream of benefits of the public project, including reinvestment, is

$$\int_0^\infty V(x,t)e^{-rt}\,dt = \frac{\theta_2 \rho + (1-\theta_2)r}{r}\int_0^\infty B(x,t)e^{-rt}\,dt.\qquad 7$$

Thus, substituting the value of the opportunity cost parameter defined in equation 4, we replace the objective function for public projects 2 by the maximand

$$\frac{\theta_2 \rho + (1-\theta_2)r}{r}\int_0^\infty B(x,t)e^{-rt}\,dt - \frac{\theta_1 \rho + (1-\theta_1)r}{r}\,K(x).\qquad 8$$

Now multiplication of the objective function by a constant does not affect the composition or level of public investment. That is, the objective function 8 is equivalent to the objective function

$$\int_0^\infty B(x,t)e^{-rt}\,dt - \frac{\theta_1 \rho + (1-\theta_1)r}{\theta_2 \rho + (1-\theta_2)r}\,K(x).\qquad 9$$

---

earlier assumption that multiplier effects are cancelled out by fiscal and monetary policies which insure full employment regardless of the level of investment.

Since $B(x, t)$ gives the nominal benefit stream of the public project, expression 9 reflects the influence of reinvestment of the immediate throw-off of public investment entirely in the opportunity cost parameter. That is, we replace a_I by the parameter $a_{I'}$, where

$$a_{I'} = \frac{\theta_1 \rho + (1 - \theta_1) r}{\theta_2 \rho + (1 - \theta_2) r}. \qquad \qquad 10$$

Measuring opportunity costs – models II and II'[10]

The asymmetry in Model I' between the disposition of the throw-off of public and private investment between consumption and reinvestment is but thinly veiled behind the assumption that the perpetual yield of private investment, ρ, already takes into account whatever reinvestment there might be. And why stop with the reinvestment of the immediate throw-off on either the public or the private side? Why not allow for reinvestment of the throw-off from reinvestment, the reinvestment of the throw-off from reinvestment of the throw-off from reinvestment, *ad infinitum*?

Both modifications – explicit inclusion of reinvestment of the throw-off from private investment and continual reinvestment of a portion of all throw-off – are easily made. Consider private investment first. Let ρ denote, as before, the perpetual throw-off rate, and assume that the rate of reinvestment of all throw-off is θ_2, the rate of reinvestment of the immediate throw-off from public investment in Model I'. Then, if we denote by $S(t)$ the capital that would be accumulated at time t by private investment (and reinvestment) of an initial stock S_0, we have

$$S(t) = S_0 e^{\theta_2 \rho t}. \qquad \qquad 11$$

(This relationship follows directly from the differential equation

$$\dot{S}(t) = \theta_2 \rho S(t), \qquad \qquad 12$$

where $\dot{S}$ denotes the rate of change of S with respect to time). Now consumption at time t, $C(t)$, is given by the relationship

$$C(t) = (1 - \theta_2) \rho S(t) = (1 - \theta_2) \rho S_0 e^{\theta_2 \rho t}. \qquad \qquad 13$$

10. The prime superscript will be used consistently to distinguish models which reflect reinvestment of the throw-off from public investment from those that do not.

The present value $V(t)$ at $t = 0$ of the consumption stream $C(t)$ is

$$V(0) = \int_0^\infty C(t)e^{-rt}\,dt = (1-\theta_2)\rho S_0 \int_0^\infty e^{(\theta_2\rho - r)t}\,dt. \qquad 14$$

If we assume that $\theta_2\rho$ is less than r, the integral in equation 14 converges, and in place of equation 14 we have

$$V(0) = \frac{(1-\theta_2)\rho}{r-\theta_2\rho}\,S_0. \qquad 15$$

If we continue to denote the ratio of displaced private investment to public investment by θ_1, then $S_0 = \theta_1 K(x)$ and the displacement of consumption by $K(x)$ dollars of public investment at $t = 0$ is $(1-\theta_1)K(x)$. Hence the opportunity cost of one dollar of public investment ($K(x) = 1$) becomes

$$a_{II} = \frac{\theta_1(1-\theta_2)\rho}{r-\theta_2\rho} + (1-\theta_1)$$

$$= \frac{(1-\theta_1)r - (\theta_2-\theta_1)\rho}{r-\theta_2\rho}. \qquad 16$$

A similar argument can be made with regard to the throw-off of public investment. If the throw-off is continually divided between consumption and reinvestment in the proportion $1-\theta_2$ to θ_2, the present value at time t of the consumption stream generated by the benefit $B(x,t)$ is

$$V(x,t) = \theta_2(1-\theta_2)\rho\,B(x,t)\int_t^\infty e^{(\theta_2\rho - r)(u-t)}\,du + (1-\theta_2)B(x,t)$$

$$= \left[\frac{\theta_2(1-\theta_2)\rho}{r-\theta_2\rho} + (1-\theta_2)\right]B(x,t)$$

$$= \frac{r(1-\theta_2)}{r-\theta_2\rho}\,B(x,t). \qquad 17$$

The present value today of the public investment becomes

$$\int_0^\infty V(x,t)e^{-rt}\,dt - a_{II}K(x)$$

$$= \frac{(1-\theta_2)r}{r-\theta_2\rho}\int_0^\infty B(x,t)e^{-rt}\,dt - \frac{(1-\theta_1)r-(\theta_2-\theta_1)\rho}{r-\theta_2\rho}\,K(x). \qquad 18$$

The equivalent objective function, derived by multiplying equation 18 through by $(r-\theta_2\rho)/(1-\theta_2)r$, is

$$\int_0^\infty B(x,t)e^{-rt}\,dt - \frac{(1-\theta_1)r-(\theta_2-\theta_1)\rho}{(1-\theta_2)r}\,K(x). \qquad 19$$

That is, the opportunity cost parameter reflecting displacement with continuous reinvestment of a portion of all throw-off is

$$a_{II'} = \frac{(1-\theta_1)r-(\theta_2-\theta_1)\rho}{(1-\theta_2)r}. \qquad 20$$

Evaluation of each dollar of cost at $a_{II'}$ dollars is equivalent to reflection of reinvestment of the throw-off from public investment in the computation of benefits.

Measuring opportunity costs – models III and III'

One might object to the assumption that the throw-off from each dollar of investment and reinvestment is grudgingly released at the rate ρ in perpetuity. The logical structure underlying the evaluation of opportunity costs does not depend at all on the assumption that capital is 'locked in' in perpetuity, and in this section we examine the consequences of exchanging this assumption for the assumption that the full amount of an investment made at time t, as well as the 'interest' ρ, is available to the investor at time $t+1$ for consumption or reinvestment. To derive the opportunity cost parameters a_{III} and $a_{III'}$ under the new rules, it is helpful to replace the objective function 2 by the discrete analogue[11]

$$\sum_{t=0}^{\infty} \frac{B_t(x)}{(1+r)^t} - a\,K(x). \qquad\qquad 21$$

Suppose we look at private investment first. Let ρ now denote the rate at which capital grows between two adjacent periods. As before ρ represents the marginal productivity of investment, but now investment is assumed to yield its entire fruit at the end of one period rather than at the perpetual rate ρ; that is, private investment of one dollar today makes $(1+\rho)$ dollars available for consumption or reinvestment a year hence and yields no benefits thereafter. The parameter θ_2 is defined, as before, as the percentage of throw-off that is reinvested, but now throw-off includes the return of capital as well as the interest premium ρ. The parameter θ_1 continues to measure the rate at which public investment displaces private investment originally.

With these assumptions each dollar of public investment displaces $(1-\theta_1)$ dollars of private consumption immediately, that is, at $t = 0$. The remaining θ_1 dollars displaces private investment which would provide a throw-off of $\theta_1(1+\rho)$ dollars next year, at $t = 1$. By assumption the portion $(1-\theta_2)$ of this throw-off, or $(1-\theta_2)\theta_1(1+\rho)$ dollars, would be consumed as it became available, and the portion $\theta_{2'}$ or $\theta_2\theta_1(1+\rho)$ dollars in all, would be reinvested. The reinvested portion would grow to $\theta_2\theta_1(1+\rho)^2$ dollars by year two, and of this immediate consumption would take $(1-\theta_2)\theta_2\theta_1(1+\rho)^2$ dollars and reinvestment $\theta_2\theta_1(1+\rho)^2$ dollars.

If we trace out the entire consumption stream that one dollar of public investment would displace, we have

$$\underset{t=0}{(1-\theta_1)},\ \underset{t=1}{(1-\theta_2)\theta_1(1+\rho)},\ \underset{t=2}{(1-\theta_2)\theta_1\theta_2(1+\rho)^2},$$

$$\underset{t=3}{(1-\theta_2)\theta_1\theta_2^2(1+\rho)^3},\ldots,\ \underset{t=t}{(1-\theta_2)\theta_1\theta_2^{t-1}(1+\rho)^t},\ldots. \qquad 22$$

---

11. We substitute a discrete model for the continuous model because we wish to allow arbitrarily large percentages of throw-off to be consumed in arbitrarily small periods of time after the throw-off becomes available. In the continuous model this would imply arbitrarily large *rates* of consumption, which are not tractable.

The present value of this stream evaluated at the marginal social rate of discount gives the opportunity cost parameter

$$a_{III} = (1-\theta_1)+\frac{(1-\theta_2)\theta_1}{\theta_2} \sum_{t=1}^{\infty} \frac{\theta_2^t(1+\rho)^t}{(1+r)^t}.$$

23

The summation on the right-hand side of equation 23 is geometric, and it converges if $\theta_2(1+\rho) < 1+r$. We shall assume this to be the case. Equation 23 then becomes

$$a_{III} = \frac{(1-\theta_1)(1+r)-(\theta_2-\theta_1)(1+\rho)}{(1+r)-\theta_2(1+\rho)}.$$

24

The parallel argument for reinvestment of the throw-off of public investment gives the following formula for the present value at time t, $V_t(x)$, of the consumption stream generated by the benefit $B_t(x)$ at time t:

$$V_t(x) = (1-\theta_2)B_t(x) \sum_{u=t}^{\infty} \frac{\theta_2^{u-t}(1+\rho)^{u-t}}{(1+r)^{u-t}}$$

$$= \frac{(1-\theta_2)(1+r)}{(1+r)-\theta_2(1+\rho)} B_t(x).$$

25

The present value of the benefits from public investment becomes

$$\sum_{t=0}^{\infty} \frac{V_t(x)}{(1+r)^t} - a_{III} K(x)$$

$$= \frac{(1-\theta_2)(1+r)}{(1+r)-\theta_2(1+\rho)} \sum_{t=0}^{\infty} \frac{B_t(x)}{(1+r)^t}$$

$$- \frac{(1-\theta_1)(1+r)-(\theta_2-\theta_1)(1+\rho)}{(1+r)-\theta_2(1+\rho)} K(x).$$

26

Just as we replaced the objective functions 9 and 13 by the equivalent maximands 10 and 19, so can we replace the objective function 26 by the expression

$$\sum_{t=0}^{\infty} \frac{B_t(x)}{(1+r)^t} - \frac{(1-\theta_1)(1+r)-(\theta_2-\theta_1)(1+\rho)}{(1-\theta_2)(1+r)} K(x).$$

27

We have now reflected reinvestment and displacement in a single opportunity cost parameter

$$a_{III'} = \frac{(1-\theta_1)(1+r) - (\theta_2-\theta_1)(1+r)}{(1-\theta_2)(1+r)}. \qquad 28$$

Comparison of the models

The following table summarizes the opportunity cost formulas in a manner designed to facilitate comparisons among them:

Table 1

$a_I = \dfrac{(1-\theta_1)r + \theta_1\rho}{r}$	$a_{I'} = \dfrac{(1-\theta_1)r + \theta_1\rho}{(1-\theta_2)r + \theta_2\rho}$
$a_{II} = \dfrac{(1-\theta_1)r + (\theta_1-\theta_2)\rho}{r - \theta_2\rho}$	$a_{II'} = \dfrac{(1-\theta_1)r + (\theta_1-\theta_2)\rho}{(1-\theta_2)r + (\theta_2-\theta_2)\rho}$
$a_{III} = \dfrac{(1-\theta_1)(1+r) + (\theta_1-\theta_2)(1+\rho)}{(1+r) - \theta_2(1+\rho)}$	
	$a_{III'} = \dfrac{(1-\theta_1)(1+r) + (\theta_1-\theta_2)(1+\rho)}{(1-\theta_2)(1+r) + (\theta_2-\theta_2)(1+\rho)}$

We need not dwell on the formal relationships among the six parameters, for these relationships are clear from inspection of the table. For example, $a_{II'}$ turns out to be $a_{I'}$ with $\theta_2\rho$ subtracted from both the numerator and the denominator.

Regardless of which model is employed, reinvestment of the benefits of public investment reduces the opportunity cost; the denominators in the right-hand column of Table 1 exceed the corresponding denominators in the left-hand column (provided $\rho > r$), hence the ratios in the right-hand column of 'primed' models are each less than the corresponding ratios on the left. The ratio of the displacement coefficient θ_1 to the reinvestment coefficient θ_2 determines whether the opportunity cost is equal to, greater than, or less than unity in the primed models incorporating reinvestment of public investment benefits. It is clear that if $\theta_1 = \theta_2$, then the opportunity cost parameters $a_{I'}$, $a_{II'}$, and $a_{III'}$ all reduce to the nominal cost of one dollar per dollar. Displacement and reinvestment cancel each other out in this case and can be ignored. If public investment leads to proportionally more original displacement than reinvestment ($\theta_1 > \theta_2$), then the primed opportunity cost parameters are each greater than unity, and if the reinvestment rate exceeds the displacement rate ($\theta_1 < \theta_2$), the parameters $a_{I'}$, $a_{II'}$, and $a_{III'}$ fall below unity.

The numerical value of the opportunity cost is sensitive to the assumption employed about the throw-off of displaced investment and reinvestment, as the following comparison reveals. If we employ the parameter values

$$\rho = 0{\cdot}05,$$
$$\theta_1 = 0{\cdot}75,$$
$$\theta_2 = 0{\cdot}25,$$
$$r = 0{\cdot}02,$$

we obtain these results:

$$a_I = 2{\cdot}125, \qquad a_{I'} = 1{\cdot}54,$$
$$a_{II} = 4{\cdot}00, \qquad a_{II'} = 2{\cdot}00,$$
$$a_{III} = 1{\cdot}02, \qquad a_{III'} = 1{\cdot}01.$$

The actual value of the opportunity cost for any given social rate of discount is, of course, an empirical matter. In our models there are only three parameters (other than r) to be estimated, but this is surely a result of oversimplification, not a description of the world. Once we drop the assumption that displacement and reinvestment rates θ_1 and θ_2 are constant throughout the economy, it becomes clear that the values of these parameters depend on the distribution of the costs and benefits. Moreover the reinvestment rate for the benefits of private and public investment may not be the same; the distribution of the benefits from public investment may differ from the distribution of the benefits from private investment, if for no other reason than that the government may be able to recapture more of the benefits from public investment through user charges and the like than it can recapture from private investment in the form of income and other taxes. Within the private sector, the rates of displacement and reinvestment will be positively correlated with the disposition to invest and negatively correlated with the ability and willingness to borrow funds of those who bear the costs and enjoy the benefits of public investment.[12]

Similarly, ρ is not constant throughout the economy. In fact the distribution and quality of investment opportunities vary widely within the private sector and between the private and public sectors, and realistic attempts to measure opportunity costs must reflect this variance.

A step in the direction of realism then would be to replace the single private investment sector by n sectors (for example, manufacturing, construction, transportation and the like). For illustrative purposes, consider the effect of this elaboration on the simplest version of the opportunity cost parameter.

$$a_l = \frac{\theta_1 \rho + (1-\theta_1)r}{r}. \qquad\qquad 11$$

Expression 11 reflects displacement alone, on the assumption that the consumption stream generated by displaced investment is a perpetuity. To replace the two-sector (investment and consumption) model of the private economy with an $(n+1)$-sector (n investment sectors plus one consumption sector) model, all we need do is regard θ_1 and ρ as n-vectors – the typical elements of which θ_{1l} and ρ_l, represent respectively the marginal displacement by public investment of investment in sector i and the annual value of the benefit stream from investment in sector i – and replace $1-\theta_1$ by $1-\Sigma_l \theta_{1l}$. A similar modification can be made for reinvestment of the throw-off of public investment.

We are now in a position conveniently to relax the assumption that resources are fully utilized. Unemployed resources can be regarded as an additional investment 'sector'. The n-vectors θ_1 and ρ are replaced by $(n+1)$-vectors. The annual throw-off from unemployed resources, denoted ρ_{n+1}, is zero. The parameter $\theta_{1,n+1}$

12. The influence of the willingness and ability of cost-bearers and beneficiaries to borrow on displacement and reinvestment rates may not be at once apparent: to the extent this willingness and ability are present, cost-bearers and beneficiaries are not dependent on decreases in the level of public investment or increases in benefits to supply funds for the exploitation of investment opportunities.

reflects the extent to which each dollar of public investment simply takes up slack in the economy.[13]

Conclusion

We tried to show in the paper cited at the beginning of this essay that individuals' marginal time preferences in the context of collective saving v. consumption decisions may well differ from their marginal time preferences in the context of unilateral decisions. The impact of this result in a frictionless competitive model is simply that *laissez-faire*-determined rates of investment and interest lose any normative significance they might otherwise have. The optimal rates of investment and interest are those for which the marginal productivity of investment is equated to the marginal social time preference rather than to the marginal private time preference. But in the imperfectly competitive environment in which investment decisions are actually made, policy prescriptions become more complicated. If private investment decisions are made in terms of a marginal time preference different from that governing public investment decisions, the opportunity costs to which imperfections give rise must be reflected in the evaluation of public investment. Symmetrically, public investment planning must reflect the benefits from reinvestment of the throwoff of all investment – public and private – at rates of return different from the marginal social rate of discount.

The models presented in this paper express opportunity cost as a function of displacement, reinvestment, and yield rates under a variety of assumptions whose most common denominator is the degree to which they oversimplify the measurement problem.

13. Differences in the values of θ_{1i} and ρ_i have obvious implications for the formulation of fiscal policy to achieve the goal of maximization of the present value of benefits throughout the economy evaluated at the marginal social rate of discount. To keep opportunity costs as low as possible, resources diverted to public use should be drawn from the private sectors in which the ρ_i have the smallest values. That is, the combination of tax and debt financing of public expenditure should be designed, insofar as choice exists, to minimize $\theta_1 \circ \rho$. Similarly, differences in the values of θ_2 and ρ among various classes of beneficiaries of public investment will affect the composition of the public investment program. The program will be weighted in favor of projects whose benefits go to groups with higher reinvestment coefficients and superior investment opportunities.

Therefore if one accepts the foregoing analysis, the next step is empirical measurement of the extent to which public investment displaces private investment, as well as empirical measurement of the shape of the benefit streams of the displaced investment.[14] Equally important is the measurement of the rates of reinvestment of the throw-off from investment and the measurement of the shapes of the benefit stream from reinvestment.

14. The pioneering efforts to measure these magnitudes, albeit in a different framework of analysis, are the studies of J. Krutilla and O. Eckstein (1958, ch. 4), and G. Reuber and R. Wonnacott (1961). For a preliminary attempt to attach numbers to θ_1 and ρ in the framework of analysis of this paper, see M. Hufschmidt, J. Krutilla and J. Margolis, with assistance of S. Marglin (1961).

References

ECKSTEIN, O. (1958), *Water Resource Development*, Harvard University Press.

HIRSHLEIFER, J., DE HAVEN, J. C., and MILLIMAN, J. (1960), *Water Supply*, University of Chicago Press.

HUFSCHMIDT, M., KRUTILLA, J., MARGOLIS, J., and MARGLIN, S. (1961), *Standards and Criteria for Formulating and Evaluating Federal Water Resources Development*, mimeo. Report of Panel of Consultants to the Bureau of the Budget, Washington DC.

KRUTILLA, J., and ECKSTEIN, O. (1958), *Multiple-Purpose River Development*, Johns Hopkins Press.

MAASS, A. *et al.* (1962), *Design of Water Resource Systems*, Harvard University Press.

MARGLIN, S. A. (1963a), 'The social rate of discount and the optimal rate of investment', *Quart. J. Econ.*, vol. 77.

MARGLIN, S. A. (1963b), *Approaches to Dynamic Investment Planning*, North Holland.

REUBER, G., and WONNACOTT, R. (1961), *The Cost of Capital in Canada*, Resources for the Future, Washington DC.

STEINER, P. (1959), 'Choosing among alternative public investments in the water resource field', *Amer. econ. Review*, vol. 49, pp. 893–916.

12 A. C. Harberger

The Opportunity Costs of Public Investment
Financed by Borrowing

Excerpt from A. C. Harberger, 'Professor Arrow on the social discount
rate', in G. G. Somers and W. D. Wood (eds), *Cost-Benefit Analysis of
Manpower Policies, Proceedings of a North American Conference*, Industrial
Relations Centre, Queens University, Kingston, Ontario, 1969, pp. 81–8.

In this section I briefly sketch an alternative conceptual framework for measuring the social rate of discount. In it, the discount
rate is obtained by tracing through the effects of additional
government borrowing on various classes of investment and saving. The resulting figure for the social rate of discount is a weighted average of the marginal rates of productivity of capital in the
various sectors from which investment is displaced, and of the
marginal rates of time preference applicable to the various groups
(if any) whose saving is stimulated (through higher interest rates)
by the additional government borrowing.

We approach the problem indirectly, considering first the social
opportunity cost of an input into a public-sector project, the
private use of which is subject to a tax; second, the social opportunity cost of foreign exchange under both uniform and diverse
tariff treatment of various classes of imports; and only then the
social opportunity cost of public funds. This indirect approach
will reveal that essentially the same methodology is applicable to
all three cases, thus reinforcing its credibility when it is applied to
the discount rate problem.

The social opportunity cost of an input

Let $S(P)$ be the total supply of the input in question, and
$D[P(1+t)]$ be the total private-sector demand. The net-of-tax
price is P, and t is the rate at which the use of the input by the

private sector is taxed. Following the established convention of cost-benefit analysis that a competitive demand price reflects the value of the commodity to the purchaser, and a competitive supply price reflects the value of the commodity to the seller, we can say that the social opportunity cost of an additional unit of the commodity taken by the government will be a weighted average of P and $P(1+t)$, the weights depending on the relative impact of added government demand in stimulating additional production of the input on the one hand and in displacing its private-sector use on the other. The weights can be derived from the identity

$$G \equiv S(P) - D[P(1+t)],$$
1

by differentiating with respect to G, which refers to government demand. This yields

$$\frac{\partial S}{\partial G} = \frac{\partial S}{\partial P}\frac{\partial P}{\partial G} = \frac{S'}{S' - D'(1+t)} = \frac{\varepsilon}{\varepsilon - \eta(D/S)}$$

$$-\frac{\partial D}{\partial G} = \frac{-\partial D}{\partial P}\frac{\partial P}{\partial G} = \frac{-D'(1+t)}{S' - D'(1+t)} = \frac{-\eta(D/S)}{\varepsilon - \eta(D/S)},$$
2

where ε and η (defined as < 0) are the elasticities of supply and demand for the good. The social opportunity cost of the input, P_s, is obtained using these weights

$$P_s = \frac{\varepsilon P - \eta(D/S)P(1+t)}{\varepsilon - \eta(D/S)}.$$
3

The social opportunity cost of foreign exchange

For this case we assume the country in question to have no influence over the world prices of its exports or its imports. This permits the aggregation of heterogeneous commodities, with the common unit of account being the 'dollar's worth' at world market prices. If X represents private-sector exports, M private-sector imports, N net demand on the part of the public sector for foreign exchange, E the exchange rate, and t the uniform *ad valorem* duty on private-sector imports, then **1** is replaced by

$$N \equiv X(E) - M[E(1+t)],$$
4

and **3** becomes

$$E_s = \frac{\varepsilon E - \eta(M/X)E(1+t)}{\varepsilon - \eta(M/X)},$$
5

where E_s is the social opportunity cost of foreign exchange and ε and η here refer to the elasticities of the private sector's supply of exports and of its demand for imports, respectively.

Assuming now that there are several categories of imports, each struck by a different tariff rate t_i, 4 must be replaced by

$$N \equiv X(E) - \sum_i M_i[E(1+t_i)], \qquad\qquad 4'$$

and 5 becomes

$$E_s = \frac{\varepsilon E - \sum_i \eta_i (M_i/X) E(1+t_i)}{\varepsilon - \sum_i \eta_i (M_i/X)}. \qquad\qquad 5'$$

Here the social opportunity cost of foreign exchange is a weighted average of the exchange rate governing exports, and of the internal values that a dollar's worth of foreign exchange produces when spent on imports in the various categories. The weights are the fractions in which an extra dollar of net government demand for foreign exchange will be reflected in increased exports on the one hand and in reduced imports of the various categories on the other.

The social opportunity cost of capital

In most modern economies the effective weight of taxation of income from capital varies substantially among sectors. Let us assume that the rate of return i, defined to be after such taxes as corporation income and property taxes but before personal income tax, is equalized in all lines of investment, through the operation of market forces. The marginal productivity of capital will accordingly be different in the various lines of activity, being equal to $\rho_j = i/(1-t_j)$, where t_j is the average rate at which such levies as corporation income and property taxes, taken together, strike the income from capital in sector j. At the same time, although savers by assumption all receive the same rate of return, i, before personal income taxes, their after-tax rates of return will differ as among marginal tax rate brackets. Hence we can express the marginal rate of time preference of savers in the kth tax bracket as $r_k = i(1-t_k)$.

Using S_k to denote private saving by individuals in the kth tax bracket, I_j to denote private investment in the jth sector, and B to denote net government borrowing, we have, as the counterpart of **4'**,

$$B \equiv \sum_k S_k[i(1-t_k)] - \sum_j I_j[i/(1-t_j)] \qquad\qquad 6$$

and as the counterpart of **5'**,

$$i_s = \frac{\sum_k \varepsilon_k(S_k/S)r_k - \sum_j \eta_j(I_j/S)\rho_j}{\sum_k \varepsilon_k(S_k/S) - \sum_j \eta_j(I_j/S)}. \qquad\qquad 7$$

Here ε_k refers to the elasticity of supply of savings with respect to their rate of yield, by individuals in the kth tax bracket, η_j refers to the elasticity of the investment schedule of the jth sector with respect to the cost of capital, and S denotes total private savings. The savings and investment schedules are defined at the full employment level of income.

In words, **7** says that the social opportunity cost of capital will be a weighted average of the marginal rates of time preference of the various categories of savers, and of the rates of marginal productivity of capital in the various sectors. The weights are proportional to the extents to which the various types of saving increase and the various types of investment decrease when new net borrowing occurs in the capital market. In the model just sketched, which assumes that the net yield i, after other but before personal income taxes, is the same in all sectors, **7** measures not only the social opportunity cost of public borrowing, but also that of any net increment to private borrowing (i.e. an upward shift of any of the I_j schedules). In this case the I_j and S_k schedules should be defined not including the shift, and the shift itself, ΔI_j, replaces B in **6**. By the same token, i_s as measured in **7** represents both the social yield of any autonomous increment in private savings (i.e. rightward shift in any of the S_j schedules), and also the potential social yield of any increase in taxes, as well as the social opportunity cost of any increment in government expenditures. The analogy with the foreign exchange market is useful here. What we defined as E_s in subsection III (b) above [not included here] is not only the social opportunity cost of public expenditures of foreign exchange, it is also the social opportunity cost of private expenditures of foreign exchange and at the same time the social opportunity yield of increments of foreign exchange, regardless of whether they are generated in the public or private sector.

Advantages in the i_s approach

The advantages of this approach, as I see them, are the following:

1. The basic data from which estimates of i_s are generated can in principle be obtained from market observations. In the case treated above, where a single interest rate i rules throughout the capital market, these observations are simply the after-personal-tax rates of return on saving r_k, in each tax bracket, and the before-tax rates of return, ρ_j, on capital in each sector. When a more complicated case is treated, in which there is a whole gamut of interest rates reflecting all kinds of variations in riskiness, in preferences concerning asset types, etc., the basic data needed are the rate of return i_g on government bonds, plus a weighted average of the distortions (taxes in our example, but monopoly profits and external effects in general can also be incorporated) prevailing in the various sectors and affecting the various income brackets.[1] Though there are unquestioned practical problems connected with the estimation of these magnitudes, there can be no question that the discount rate i is in principle related and responsive to market phenomena.

1. Defining $\delta_k = r_k - i$, and $\delta_j = \rho_j - i$, 7 can be re-expressed as

$$i_s = i + \frac{\sum_k \varepsilon_k (S_k/S)\delta_k - \sum_j \eta_j (I_j/S)\delta_j}{\sum_k \varepsilon_k (S_k/S) - \sum_j \eta_j (I_j/S)} ; \qquad 7'$$

when the assumption of a single interest rate i, is dropped, the equation corresponding to 7' contains i_g in place of i. The interpretation of δ_k and δ_j also changes in this case, becoming $r_k - i_k$ and $\rho_j - i_j$ respectively, i_k being the before-personal-tax yield required to elicit the marginal unit of savings from the kth income bracket, and i_j the expected rate of return, before personal taxes but after other ones, which is required to obtain voluntary financing for the marginal unit of investment in sector j. These modifications are discussed in detail in section II of 'On measuring the social opportunity cost of public funds', to be published in *Proceedings* of the December 1968 Meeting of the Water Resources Research Committee, Western Agricultural Research Council. The entire approach is also presented there much more fully than is possible here.

2. The procedures used to obtain i_s are fully consistent with the tenets that underlie cost-benefit analysis as such. I take these to be (a) competitive supply price measures marginal private opportunity cost, (b) competitive demand price measures marginal private benefit, and (c) the Hicks-Kaldor principle of potential compensation is accepted. In particular, defining i_s^t as the social opportunity cost of using funds for the period between $t-1$ and t, it can be shown that a rate of return of i_s^t, on a project with costs only in $t-1$ and benefits only in t, would be just barely sufficient to compensate all parties affected by the government's borrowing the required funds in year $t-1$ and effectuating the corresponding compensations in year t.[2] The principle thus developed for the case of a one-year project can readily be extended to cover all projects.

This result is a matter of some importance. For, so long as i_s^t reflects at one and the same time the social rate of discount applied to benefits, and the social rate of return obtainable from private savings, the so-called reinvestment problem disappears, since the discounted value of the income stream produced by a given amount of savings is necessarily equal to that amount.

In saying that the reinvestment problem disappears, I do not mean to assert that there can never be circumstances where consideration of it would be important. Rather, I say that so long as one accepts the three basic tenets of cost-benefit analysis set out above, the 'natural' measure of the social discount rate is i_s, and that when i_s is used, no reinvestment problem will emerge, nor will any problem of the shadow pricing of investible funds. Put another way, the occasions on which a reinvestment problem is really unavoidably present are at the same time occasions which

2. The discounting in cost-benefit analysis should in principle be at a rate which can vary through time. If discounting is done to year 0 (the initiation of a project), this implies that the costs and benefits of year j should be divided by

$$\prod_{t=1}^{j} (1+i_s^t).$$

This also emphasizes the fact that the most important uses of cost-benefit analysis are forward-looking. Past data on observed yields on capital are relevant, but only because they provide us with experience to help us reach judgements concerning their likely trend in the future.

call for some deviation from one or more of what I have called the basic tenets of cost-benefit analysis.

3. The approach underlying i_s, and the measure itself, take existing distortions amply into account. They thus seem far more suited to the way cost-benefit problems appear in real-world situations than do approaches which implicitly posit optimization.

One may question, however, whether the i_s measure does not build in too great a degree of rigidity in the pattern of distortions. Is it not, in a sense, too fatalistic about the possibilities of reducing or eliminating distortions? I think that the answer is no. In the first place, the values of i_s' projected for future years may embody any desired set of changes in the pattern of distortions. The corporation income tax may be projected to decline, the personal tax to rise, etc. No limits are in principle imposed on the analyst – but the ultimate test is the realism of his projections.

There is a second way in which the approach in question can be defended against the charge of excessive rigidity or 'fatalism' regarding distortions. For although the analysis builds in distortions, it also throws out strong signals as to the changes in the pattern of distortions that would most improve the economy. For example, suppose that the highest sectoral marginal productivity of capital, ρ_j, is 15 per cent in the corporate sector (as distinct from the housing and unincorporated business sectors) of the economy, and that the lowest marginal rate of time preference, r_k, is 3 per cent, in the highest personal income tax bracket. The social rate of discount, i_s, must necessarily lie between these two extremes. Obviously, whether or not i_s is used, the prospect of obtaining funds at a social cost of 3 per cent, and putting them to use with a social yield of 15 per cent, is very appealing indeed. If we leave tax rates unchanged, we cannot accomplish this, for the market, not the borrower, dictates what investments will be foregone and what savings will be stimulated as a consequence of additional public borrowing. However, if the government reduces somewhat the highest personal tax rate, it will thereby generate a certain increment of saving by the affected group. It can then borrow these incremental savings without affecting the interest rate, and hence without influencing the saving of other income groups. By the same token, lending by the government to the private capital market would without tax rate changes affect investment in all sectors. However, if the government lowers somewhat the corporation income tax, additional investible funds will be demanded by the corporate sector at the same interest rate as before. The government can therefore under such circumstances lend the relevant amount of funds to the corporate sector, financing the additional investment there – without affecting investment in other sectors of the economy.

If policy-makers obey the implicit signals emitted by the approach underlying i_s, they will obviously at each point in time reduce the highest sectoral taxes t_j and the highest bracket personal taxes t_k. The end result of this procedure is the complete elimination of corporate, property, and personal income taxes. What would replace them? In theory, perhaps, the proverbial head tax, with no distorting properties at all. But in practice some combination of a value-added tax of the consumption type and a progressive consumption-expenditure tax of the type advocated by Kaldor would be a more plausible alternative. Such taxes have a certain (probably very mild) distorting effect on the labor-leisure choice, but otherwise they are neutral as among goods and services and as between saving and consumption. Given that they can provide any desired degree of progression in the tax structure, economic theory leads us naturally to prefer a system based on them to the present pattern of personal income, corporate, and property taxes. Thus, when the methodology underlying i_s is used for the purpose of seeking reform, rather than sticking with given or sluggishly changing tax rates, it leads to conclusions that follow directly from economic theory. Whatever degree of fatalism may be implied by an analyst's assuming that the tax structure will not change much or rapidly over time must therefore (assuming he is right) be attributed to the realities of political life – not to the i_s methodology!

13 M. S. Feldstein

The Inadequacy of Weighted Discount Rates

Excerpt from M. S. Feldstein, 'Financing in the evaluation of public expenditure', written for a forthcoming volume of essays in honour of Richard A. Musgrave, edited by W. L. Smith.

Public expenditures are financed by user charges, taxation and public debt. The mix of financing affects the total social cost of any project and should therefore influence the choice among projects. The purpose of the current essay is to examine the relation between the sources of finance and the value of public projects. The first section derives a general framework for public project evaluation that reflects the three sources of finance. Section 2 provides a critique of a widely advocated alternative approach, discounting net benefits by a weighted average of interest rates (Baumol, 1969; Eckstein, 1968; Harberger, 1968a and b; Joint Economic Committee, 1968; Ramsey, 1969; Usher, 1969). The inadequacy of this approach is shown to result from its failure to separate the problem of opportunity cost measurement from the problem of intertemporal aggregation. To emphasize this, the section presents several special decision problems in which this discounting technique gives answers that are clearly incorrect. The third section considers the important problem of debt financing and derives a measure of the social cost of financing a project by debt creation. Finally, section 4 (not reproduced) discusses the role of user charges and modifies the traditional rules for optimal public sector pricing.

To focus attention on the resource allocation implications of the sources of finance, the following six assumptions will be made unless otherwise indicated: (1) Resources are fully employed and prices are stable. (2) Small redistributions of income leave social welfare unchanged. (3) All magnitudes are known with certainty. (4) Commodity markets are perfect so that market prices reflect social costs. (5) There are no collection costs or deadweight losses associated with tax revenues. (6) There is no external borrowing. Although relaxing these assumptions might alter the specific result in any particular decision, it would not change the basic principles discussed in this paper. The expenditure evaluation algorithm presented in the next section provides an appropriate framework within which to make the generalizations that would be needed to deal with these additional problems.

1 Social time preference and the opportunity cost of public spending

It is now generally agreed that public expenditure projects should be evaluated by discounting the difference between appropriately measured benefits and costs. A project is admissible ('worth doing') if its present value is positive; among mutually exclusive alternatives, the project with the highest present value is preferable.[1,2] If the rate of private investment were socially optimal, the benefits and costs of public projects could be discounted at the marginal rate of return on private investment. As Irving Fisher showed, in a perfect capital market this rate would measure both the opportunity cost of foregone private investment and the rate of time preference of all individuals. The sources of finance for public projects, i.e. the proportions that come from private investment and private consumption, would therefore be irrelevant. But the presence of corporation and personal income taxes implies

1. These criteria must be modified if there is a constraint on the budget or specific inputs; I return to this below.

2. Although valuing projects by the *ratio* of discounted benefits and costs provides an equivalent criterion of admissibility (i.e. the benefit–cost ratio exceeds one if and only if the present value is positive), the benefit–cost ratio cannot be used to choose among mutually exclusive alternatives. Any benefit–cost ratio can be substantially raised by reclassifying a 'cost' as a 'reduction in benefits'; such classification decisions are arbitrary and do not affect the present value of a project. The benefit–cost ratio, like the internal rate of return, also biases the choice in favor of small projects with high yields; see Feldstein and Flemming (1964).

that society's marginal rate of transformation between present and future consumption exceeds the corresponding marginal rate of substitution of individual savers. In this 'second-best' situation, there is no single interest rate that can represent both time preference and opportunity cost.

A variety of solutions to this problem have been advocated. Some economists would ignore the return on private investment and discount at a time preference rate. Others would ignore time preference considerations and discount at the rate of return on private investment. Both approaches disregard the source of finance for marginal public projects. In contrast, a number of writers have suggested that the source of finance be reflected by using a weighted average of different rates with the weights reflecting the incidence of taxation or government borrowing.[3] All of these methods are unsatisfactory because they try to use a single 'price' – the rate of discount – when two quite different prices are needed: the relative value of future consumption in terms of current consumption,[4] and the relative value of current private investment in terms of current consumption. The first price corresponds to the rate of time preference. The second price, the opportunity cost of private investment, exceeds one in a second best economy in which the marginal rate of transformation between future and present consumption exceeds the marginal rate of substitution. The shadow price algorithm described below is an appropriate framework for combining these measures of time preference and opportunity cost. Before discussing this algorithm, it will be useful to consider briefly the notion of social time preference.

Social time preference

The social time preference (STP) rate is a normative measure of the relative value of present and future consumption. More specifically, the social marginal rate of substitution between consumption at time t and at time $t-1$ is equal to $1+d_t$, where d_t is the STP discount rate between those two years. For simplicity, the STP rate is generally assumed to remain constant through time.

3. Section 2 provides a detailed critique of this method.
4. More accurately, a separate such price for consumption at each future date.

At a theoretical level, the time preference rate can be calculated in terms of the rate of growth of per capita consumption, the elasticity of the marginal utility function, and the extent of pure time preference (i.e. the discounting of future *utility*) if any.[5]

More operationally, each individual's rate of time preference is equal to his 'marginal' borrowing–lending rate. If the capital market functions properly, every individual has the same rate of time preference; differences in observed interest rates reflect differences in the uncertainty, liquidity, or marketability of loans. In the absence of consumption externalities (Sen, 1957; Marglin, 1963a) and paternalistic considerations (Feldstein, 1964b), this common rate of individual time preference is also the social rate of time preference.[6]

It is instructive to consider a special case in which it is clear that present values calculated at the social time preference rate should be the basis for an expenditure decision, i.e. an application in which the return on private investment and the method of finance are irrelevant. To abstract from the problems that will be considered in more detail later, assume that the government wishes to choose between two mutually exclusive projects, both of which are clearly worth doing, both of which would last ten years, both of which would have the same costs in each year and both of which would be financed in the same way. The projects differ only in the time streams of benefits: the first project produces relatively more benefits during the early years and the second project produces relatively more benefits during the later years. For both projects, the benefits are provided to consumers without charge and represent a net addition to consumption. Since the cost and finance streams are the same, choosing between the two projects is equivalent to choosing between two consumption streams. Since only consumption is involved, the STP rate is the appropriate rate at which to discount the two benefit streams. Neither

5. This type of intertemporal aggregation is now common in optimal growth theory. For discussions in the context of project evaluation, see Arrow and Kurz (1970), Eckstein (1961) and Feldstein (1965).

6. If the capital market functions poorly so that individuals have different marginal rates of time preference, a single social rate of time preference cannot be defined. The effects of the project on each individual must, in principle, be aggregated (discounted) separately. Even if capital markets are perfect this problem arises if marginal tax rates are not equal.

the rate of returns on private investment nor the source of finance is relevant. Of course, if the costs of the two projects were different, the opportunity cost of the funds would be important in choosing between the projects but only because of its effect on the cost of the project and not because it changes the present value of the benefits.

A second example in which only the STP rate is relevant can help to clarify its more general role. Assume now that the government's problem is to decide whether a particular project is worth doing rather than to choose between projects. The special feature of the current problem is that all of the government's expenditures on the project will be financed by a combination of taxes and user charges whose effect is to reduce consumption but leave investment unchanged. The project can therefore be described as a substitution of one consumption stream (the benefits of the project) for another consumption stream (foregone to pay for it). The benefits and costs should therefore be evaluated by discounting at the STP rate.

The shadow price algorithm

The last example suggests an approach to the more general problem of evaluating projects when the method of financing involves a reduction of both private investment and consumption. A dollar of private investment today results, directly and indirectly, in a future stream of consumption. The present value of this stream, discounting at the STP rate, is the opportunity cost of foregone investment expressed in terms of equivalent consumption. In a 'second-best' world in which the rate of return on private investment exceeds the STP rate, this opportunity cost price exceeds one; i.e. a dollar of private investment has greater value than a dollar of private consumption.[7] Let S denote the shadow price

7. The actual opportunity cost of private investment will reflect not only the STP rate and the rate of return on private investment but also the rate of taxation and the rate at which profits are reinvested. For the simplest case in which all net profits are consumed and all tax receipts are redistributed as transfer payments that are completely consumed, the opportunity cost is the ratio of the rate of return on private investment to the STP rate. These ideas are latent in early papers by Eckstein (1957), Galenson and Leibenstein (1955), and Steiner (1959) and developed more fully in Feldstein (1964a) and Marglin (1963b).

of a dollar of foregone private investments; reducing private investment by one dollar is therefore equivalent to reducing private consumption by S dollars. In addition, let the incidence of the marginal tax [8] be such that a proportion p of the funds raised by taxes would otherwise have been invested and the remaining $1-p$ proportion would have been consumed.[9] This implies that a dollar of funds raised by such taxes has a value of $pS+1-p$ dollars of consumption. By valuing the funds transferred from the private sector in this way we have essentially solved the problem of measuring opportunity cost; since all transfers from the private sector are now expressed in 'equivalent dollars of consumption', they can be aggregated by discounting at the STP rate.

An example will illustrate this procedure. Consider a project that lasts T years, producing benefits b_t in year t and incurring costs c_t. If the benefits are distributed to consumers without charge and all of the costs are reflected in market payments, the deficit of the project in year t is c_t. If this deficit is financed by a tax that reduces investment by pc_t and consumption by $(1-p)c_t$, and if the shadow price of investment (S) remains unchanged, the value of the project is given by

$$V = \sum_{t=0}^{T} \frac{b_t - [pS+(1-p)]c_t}{(1+d)^t}, \qquad 1$$

i.e. by the discounted difference between the consumption benefits and the consumption equivalent of the costs, discounting at the STP rate. The project is worth doing if V exceeds zero.

A somewhat more general statement of this shadow price investment algorithm is preferable. The description of any project should recognize not only the costs (c_t) and benefits (b_t) but also the project's cash expenditures (e_t) and user charge (sales) revenues (r_t).[10,11] The project deficit in year t is thus $e_t - r_t$. Let the

8. The problems of debt finance are considered below.
9. I shall assume throughout the paper that $0 < p < 1$ even though it would be possible to have $p < 0$ if a tax on companies were shifted more than 100 per cent.
10. Cash expenditures (e_t) may differ from social costs (c_t) if the project employs otherwise unemployed workers or imposes negative externalities for which it need not pay.
11. For simplicity it will be assumed that all sales are to final consumers,

proportion of this project deficit financed by taxes be q_t and the proportion by the issuance of additional public debt be $1-q_t$. The consumption equivalent of a dollar transferred by taxes has been shown to be $pS+1-p$. Section 3 will derive a measure of the consumption equivalent of a dollar transferred by debt issuance; for now let this merely be denoted by $D+1$.

The net contribution of the project in year t is thus equal to the benefits $[b_t]$ minus the user charge revenues paid by consumers $[r_t]$ plus the transfer payments to consumers [12] $[e_t-c_t]$ minus the 'consumption equivalent value' of the funds transferred by taxation $[(pS+1-p)q_t(e_t-r_t)]$ and by debt issuance $[(D+1)(1-q_t)(e_t-r_t)]$. Equation 1 can therefore be replaced by

$$V = \sum_{t=0}^{T} \frac{b_t-r_t+(e_t-c_t)-[(pS+1-p)q_t+(D+1)(1-q_t)](e_t-r_t)}{(1+d)^t}.$$

2

By rearranging terms, this can be written more simply as

$$V = \sum_{t=0}^{T} \frac{(b_t-c_t)-(S-1)pq_t(e_t-r_t)-D(1-q_t)(e_t-r_t)}{(1+d)^t}.$$

3

Until section 3 we shall ignore the role of debt finance and assume that $q_t = 1$ for all years. Equation 3 then becomes

$$V = \sum_{t=0}^{T} \frac{(b_t-c_t)-(S-1)p(e_t-r_t)}{(1+d)^t}.$$

4

Here b_t-c_t is the 'real' net benefit of the project in year t, e_t-r_t is the cash deficit, and $p(e_t-r_t)$ is the reduction in private investment. Since $S-1$ is the *excess* opportunity cost of investment in comparison to consumption, equation 4 is equivalent to deducting from each year's 'real' net benefit the additional cost of the

---

that such sales reduce other consumption by an equal amount, and that the income in kind of the project has no effect on saving. These assumptions are relaxed in Feldstein (1964a).

12. Or, if $c_t > e_t$, minus the social costs of the projects not reflected in payments.

deficit in that year and their discounting to the present.[13] Since the quantities in equation 2 (and therefore in equations 3 and 4) are in forms of 'equivalent consumption', the STP rate is the appropriate rate for discounting.

Although discounting is at the time preference rate, the method of financing and the rate of return on private investment are reflected in the calculation through p and S. A tax on high income savers or on corporations would imply a higher p than a payroll or general excise tax. A higher return on private investment would, *ceteris paribus*, imply a higher value of S. This extra shadow price $[p(S-1)]$ on funds transferred from the private sector essentially prevents the government from replacing private investments with high returns by public investments of lower value.

Because V is a present value, a project is worth doing if $V > 0$ and, among mutually exclusive projects, the project with the highest V is to be preferred. The problem of a single budget (or other) constraint is easily solved in this framework. Let V_i be the value of the ith project and R_i the amount of the constrained input (e.g. current expenditure, c_0) that it uses. Then it is possible to find an additional shadow price, k, for the constrained input that can be used to select an optimal set of projects according to the following rules: (1) a project is admissible if $V_i > kR_i$ and (2) between two mutually exclusive admissible projects, project i is preferable if $(V_i - V_j) > k(R_i - R_j)$. For some value of k, this procedure produces the maximum sum of V's without exceeding the input constraint.

2 The inadequacy of discounting by a weighted average of rates

Section 1 stressed the need for two types of prices in project evaluation: a price of funds transferred from the private sector (which in turn implies a price of foregone investment) and a price of future consumption, both prices being stated in terms of current consumption. The notion of two separate prices to measure

13. Note that if $S = 1$, the term $(S-1)p(e_t - r_t)$ of equation 3 vanishes and the value of the project does not depend on the size or source of finance of the deficit. S equals one only if the STP rate is equal to the rate of return on private investment; i.e. the source of finance is only relevant because of the second-best divergence between the STP and the return on private investment.

opportunity cost and time preference is no doubt strange to economists who are accustomed to theoretical models of the economy in which a single interest rate performs both functions. Perhaps this explains why a number of economists have advocated evaluating public projects by discounting benefits and costs at either the rate of return earned on private investment (on the argument that it 'dominates' time preference considerations) or some weighted average of the return earned on private investment and the rate that measures savers' time preference. The current section summarizes the different arguments for using a 'simple discount rate algorithm' (in contrast to a method that combines discounting with an opportunity cost shadow price) and shows why this method is inadequate.

All of the simple discount rate algorithms evaluate projects by

$$V' = \sum_{t=0}^{T} \frac{b_t - c_t}{(1+i)^t} \qquad\qquad 5$$

and differ only in the way that i is defined and measured. The expenditures and cash receipts are ignored in the problem even though they, and not b_t and c_t, influence the extent to which private investment may be affected.

Several economists, including Hirshleifer, Milliman and De Haven (1961; 1960) and Mishan (1967a and b), have advocated disregarding time preference completely and defining the discount rate (i in equation 5) as the rate of return on private investment. They argue as follows: since the resources used in any public expenditure project could have been invested in the private sector where they could have earned a yield of i, public projects should not be undertaken unless they will obtain an equal yield. This argument reflects a basic ambiguity in the notion of opportunity cost. Economic textbooks often define opportunity cost as 'the value of resources in the best alternative use to which those resources *could* be put.' This is the definition implicit in the argument above. In fact, the actual opportunity cost of any resources is their value in the alternative use to which they *would* have been put. The two coincide in a perfectly functioning economy: if resources are not used in one activity they *would* be used in the most valuable alternative in which they *could* be used. But it is the very essence of the second-best problem that resources that could be invested with greater value are instead consumed. The economists who advocate discounting by the return on private investment fail to distinguish between the 'ideal opportunity cost' (what *could* be done with the resources) and the 'predictive opportunity cost' (what *would* be done with them).[14]

A much more widely held view is that the second-best problem can be recognized and the sources of finance taken into account by defining the discount rate (i) to be a weighted average of different rates of return. The Joint Economic Committee (1968) has recently recommended that a procedure of this type be adopted in government decision-making. The approach was first suggested by Krutilla and Eckstein (1958) who estimated opportunity cost of funds raised through different marginal tax changes by calculating a weighted average of company rates of return and of the interest rates paid and received by households; the weights were based on their estimates of the immediate incidence of the taxes.[15] Harberger (1968a) seems to agree in principle with this general approach but has a different measurement strategy. By assuming that all marginal finance is by debt issue, he avoids the difficulties and ambiguities of estimating tax incidence. The issuance of public debt raises the interest rate, implying less investment and perhaps more saving. The new government revenue can be divided into an amount that would have been consumed and an amount that would have been invested in the same ratio as the interest impact on consumption and investment: $|\partial C/\partial r|$ to $|\partial I/\partial r|$, where r is 'the' market rate of interest. Harberger therefore proposes that the project evaluation discount rate (i) be a weighted average of the gross rate of return on investment and the net rate of interest received by savers with the weights equal to $|\partial I/\partial r|$ and $|\partial C/\partial r|$. Although Baumol's (1968) original position was ambiguous – he presented arguments for discounting by the return on private investment but concluded that the correct social dis-

14. Diamond and Mirrlees (1960) have shown that, in an economy with *optimal excise and income taxation*, public and private investments should be discounted at the same rate. Their analysis has no implication for the current problem if such optimal taxes cannot be assumed to prevail.

15. In a recent statement to the Joint Economic Committee in support of this method, Eckstein (1968) indicated that on theoretical grounds he would prefer a method that is generally similar to the shadow price investment algorithm.

count rate must somehow reflect time preference as well – he has more recently (1969) been convinced by a comment on his paper by Ramsey (1969) that projects should be evaluated by a discount rate that is a weighted average of gross rates of return on investment and net yields to savers.

The argument for discounting at a weighted average of discount rates has also been developed from a different viewpoint. By explicit utility maximization in a two-period model, Diamond (1968) has derived the rule that the marginal rate of transformation in public sector production between present and future output should equal a weighted average of the marginal rate of transformation in private production and the marginal rate of substitution of consumers.[16] This is equivalent to the conclusion that the marginal rate of return on public investment should equal a weighted average of the return to private investment and the time preference rate. This result cannot be generalized to more than two periods. A weighted average of interest rates is equal to a weighted average of present values in a two-period model but not more generally. With only two periods, there is no future reinvestment to be taken into account. Moreover, even in the two-period model the rule is only applicable to deciding the appropriate margin for public investment and provides no guide to the optimal amount of public consumption.

Rather than presenting a detailed critique of the specific arguments for discounting by a weighted average rate, I will consider four special decision problems in which any such proceedings would give a very different and clearly inferior answer than the shadow price algorithm. These special cases point to general weaknesses in any method that does not (1) explicitly recognize the size of the cash deficit; (2) include a shadow price for funds transferred from the private sector; and (3) discount benefits at the STP rate.

Public sector consumption: *current benefits and costs*

The discount rate technique is often advocated on the grounds that it correctly represents the opportunity cost of funds trans-

16. See Usher (1969) for a similar derivation, also restricted to the two-period case. Diamond is careful to note that the result is misleading if the restriction to a two-period model is dropped.

ferred from the private sector to the public sector and therefore prevents the undertaking of public projects that reduce private investment without creating sufficient benefits in the public sector. It is useful therefore to consider a case in which the discount rate technique obviously fails and would permit inefficient public spending.

Consider the simplest of all projects: one which occurs in the current period only. The benefits are b_0 and the costs c_0; the receipts and expenditures are r_0 and e_0. Substitution into equation 5 shows that the discount rate technique would approve such a project if $b_0 > c_0$. The rate of discount is irrelevant and the amount of funds transferred from private investment is not taken into account. In contrast, the shadow price algorithm would approve the project only if

$$(b_0-c_0)-p(S-1)(e_0-r_0) > 0. \qquad\qquad 6$$

In words, the net benefits (b_0-c_0) must not only be positive but must be large enough relative to the deficit (e_0-r_0) to warrant the reduction in private investment. Only if private investment is not decreased by the project $(p = 0)$ is $b_0 > c_0$ sufficient to make the project worth doing. The shadow price algorithm thus reflects the method of financing and provides an appropriate measure of the private sector opportunity cost. In contrast, the discount rate technique completely ignores foregone private investment in this case! This failure to reflect opportunity cost adequately is a result of trying to measure opportunity cost with a *discount rate* instead of a *shadow price*.

The special decision problem treated in this example is of great practical importance. Most public spending does not involve long-lived capital investment. Public expenditure decisions are frequently made for a single year or for relatively few years in the future. Even in programs stretching over many years, marginal changes for each current year should be considered. Moreover, the example points to an obvious weakness that affects the evaluation of long-lived investments as well. The important point is the distinction between measuring the opportunity cost and making appropriate intertemporal comparisons of benefits: a shadow price is the appropriate method for the former and an STP discount rate for the latter.

Equal costs and different benefits

Consider the problem (which was mentioned in section 1) of choosing between two admissible projects with different benefit streams but the same time streams of costs, deficits and financing. The choice between the projects should obviously depend only on the relative desirability of the benefit streams since, whatever the amount and value of foregone private investment and consumption, it is the same for both projects. Since the benefits are consumed, the appropriate method of aggregating each benefit stream into a single measure is by discounting at the STP rate. The project with the higher present value of benefits when discounted at the STP rate should be chosen.

This is the criterion implied by the shadow price algorithm but not by the discount rate technique (unless i is also the STP rate and does not reflect a different return on private investment). Identifying the benefits of the first and second project by b_t^1 and b_t^2, the shadow price investment algorithm indicates a preference for project 1 over project 2 if

$$\sum_{t=0}^{T} \frac{b_t^1 - c_t - p(S-1)(e_i - r_t)}{(1+d)^t} > \sum_{t=0}^{T} \frac{b_t^2 - c_t - p(S-1)(e_t - r_t)}{(1+d)^t}. \qquad 7$$

This obviously simplifies to

$$\sum_{t=0}^{T} \frac{b_t^1}{(1+d)^t} > \sum_{t=0}^{T} \frac{b_t^2}{(1+d)^t} \qquad 8$$

as required. In contrast, the discount rate algorithm implies that project 1 is preferable if and only if

$$\sum_{t=0}^{T} \frac{b_t^1 - c_t}{(1+i)^t} > \sum_{t=0}^{T} \frac{b_t^2 - c_t}{(1+i)^t} \qquad 9$$

or, equivalently,

$$\sum_{t=0}^{T} \frac{b_t^1}{(1+i)^t} > \sum_{t=0}^{T} \frac{b_t^2}{(1+i)^t}. \qquad 10$$

Since i is presumably greater than d, the discount rate algorithm would be biased in favor of short-lived projects.

This example emphasizes that only the STP rate is relevant for the intertemporal aggregation of benefits. Although the assumption of identical costs and mix of financing is crucial to the conclusion that the return on private investment and the source of finance can be ignored in the current case, that assumption is irrelevant to the conclusion that *benefit streams* should be compared in terms of the STP rate alone.

Self-financing projects

If a project has no deficit in a particular year, i.e. if $e_t = r_t$, no funds are transferred from private investment that year. A project that is self-financing in every year is simply a substitution of a publicly provided consumption stream for an alternative private consumption stream. In that case, only the STP rate is relevant for evaluating the project; the return on private investment is of no importance.

More generally, a project may be described as self-financing even if it does have a deficit in some years if the discounted value of the cash surpluses equals the discounted value of the cash deficits. In the special case of a project that is self-financing when the surpluses and deficits are discounted at the STP rate, i.e. when

$$\sum_{t=0}^{\pi} (e_t - r_t)(1+d)^{-t} = 0,$$

it is easily shown that the source of finance and the return on private investment are irrelevant. This follows from rewriting the basic shadow price algorithm (equation 4) as

$$V = \sum_{t=0}^{T} \frac{b_t - c_t}{(1+d)^t} - p(S-1) \sum_{t=0}^{T} \frac{e_t - r_t}{(1+d)^t}, \qquad \textbf{11}$$

and noting that the second sum is zero. Such a project is worth doing if the net benefits ($b_t - c_t$) have a positive present value when discounted at the STP rate. Because the simple discount rate algorithm evaluates a project by discounting at a rate higher than the STP rate, it may reject long-lived projects that are actually worth doing. More generally, this example points to the weakness of the discount rate algorithm in failing to reflect sales revenues (or user charges) and the sizes of the annual deficits and surpluses.

Choice of technique

An important practical problem is the choice between alternative techniques of producing the same set of benefits. The shadow price algorithm shows that in general project 1 is better than project 2 if

$$\sum_{t=0}^{T} \frac{b_t^1 - c_t^1 - p(S-1)(e_t^1 - r_t^1)}{(1+d)^t} > \sum_{t=0}^{T} \frac{b_t^2 - c_t^2 - p(S-1)(e_t^2 - r_t^2)}{(1+d)^t}. \qquad 12$$

The choice of technique problem is characterized by the equality of benefits and revenues in each year, i.e. $b_t^1 = b_t^2$ and $r_t^1 = r_t^2$ for all t. If in addition the annual expenditures are adequate measures of social cost (i.e. $e_t^1 = c_t^1$ and $e_t^2 = c_t^2$ for all t), the inequality in **11** reduces to

$$\sum_{t=0}^{T} \frac{c_t^1}{(1+d)^t} < \sum_{t=0}^{T} \frac{c_t^2}{(1+d)^t}. \qquad 13$$

In choosing among alternative techniques, the size of the deficits, the source of finance and the opportunity cost of private investment can be ignored even though they differ between the two projects. All that is relevant is the present value of the costs, discounting at the STP rate. Because the simple discount rate algorithm would choose between techniques by comparing the present value of costs discounted at a higher rate (i) it would bias the choice toward inefficient projects with higher long-run costs.[17,18]

These four examples show important decision problems in which a simple discount rate algorithm with any fixed weighted

17. For additional discussion of the choice of technique problem, see Feldstein (1970).

18. Arrow (1966; 1970) has presented a different type of special case in which S is irrelevant and project evaluation depends only on the STP rate. This result reflects his special assumptions about taxes, the savings induced by benefits and the absence of sales revenues. Given these assumptions, the result is equivalent to the shadow price investment algorithm. For further details, see Feldstein (1970).

average interest rate (i) gives misleading advice. To repeat what was stated above, they also point to the weakness of any method that does not explicitly recognize the size of the cash deficit, include a shadow price for funds transferred from the private sector and discount benefits at the STP rate. The two problems – opportunity cost measurement and intertemporal aggregation – must be kept separate if correct choices are to be made.

3 Implications of debt finance

The analysis in section 1 discussed the shadow price algorithm on the assumption that the project deficits in each year are financed by an increase in taxes. This is an unduly restrictive assumption. The issuance of additional public debt is a particularly important source of marginal finance. The separation of taxation and expenditure decisions in the legislative process implies that new capital expenditures are generally financed as a deficit even if the operating costs of the projects induce higher tax rates in the future.[19] As Musgrave (1959) has explained, the use of debt creation to finance current costs that yield future benefits is an appropriate application of the benefit principle of finance.

The logic of the shadow price algorithm has implications about debt financing that are worth careful examination. In a previous discussion of public investment criteria (Feldstein, 1964a), I incorrectly stated that debt financing should be reflected in the shadow price algorithm by using a high value of p (the proportion of private sector funds that would otherwise have been invested). This would, I argued, reflect the fact that the additional public debt would raise the interest rate, reducing private investment but having a very small effect on saving. Musgrave took a similar position in stating that 'public investment is more likely to "qualify" if tax financed, where withdrawal is more largely from consumption than if loan financed, where withdrawal is more largely from investment' (1969, p. 802). This is also the implication of Harberger's (1968a) procedure of evaluating the opportunity cost of debt by weighting the gross yield on investment and the net rate paid by savers by the relative impacts on investment and saving of a rise in the interest rate. All of us were wrong in

19. See Harberger (1968a) for further reasons why debt finance is particularly important in practice.

failing to take into account the fact that a debt financed expenditure necessarily implies future payments to service or repay the debt. It is therefore incorrect to treat the debt as equivalent to a tax with the same immediate incidence. In particular, in certain circumstances debt financing can actually increase the value of the project.

This section shows how debt financing should be incorporated into the shadow price algorithm. For simplicity, I shall assume that saving is completely interest inelastic and shall ignore the liquidity effects of portfolio composition on interest rates. As elsewhere in this paper, a fully-employed, closed economy is assumed.[20]

Section 1 showed that the value of a project in which the deficits are financed by both tax and debt is

$$V = \sum_{t=0}^{T} \frac{(b_t - c_t) - q_t p(S-1)(e_t - r_t) - (1 - q_t)D(e_t - r_t)}{(1+d)^t}, \qquad 14$$

where q_t is the proportion of the project deficit financed by taxation, p is the proportion of tax revenue that would otherwise have been invested, $p(S-1)$ is the *excess* cost of a dollar of tax finance (i.e. the excess over an equal reduction in consumption) and D is the *excess* cost of a dollar of debt finance.[21] The problem of evaluating debt financed expenditure will therefore be solved when we have evaluated D, the excess cost per dollar of debt financing.

It is simplest and probably most realistic to consider the case of a 'perpetual' bond, i.e. to assume that when actual bonds mature they are refinanced by a new issue of debt and not paid by tax revenues.[22] The assumption that saving is not sensitive to the interest rate implies that the issuance of government debt concurrently reduces private investment by an equal amount. A one dollar debt issue therefore has an equivalent consumption

20. The problems of debt issue by state and local governments and of external finance are therefore not considered. See Feldstein (forthcoming).
21. Recall that $D+1$ was defined as the total cost of a dollar of debt finance.
22. The method of extending the results to the case in which the debt is fully repaid after a finite period will be clear from the discussion.

cost of S dollars *in the year of issue*. If the interest rate on government debt is $100r$ per cent, the government must pay r dollars as interest payment in each subsequent year. To make these interest payments, the government taxes and borrows r dollars. Let θ be the proportion of these funds obtained by taxation and $1-\theta$ the proportion obtained by additional debt issue; for simplicity, these proportions are assumed to remain constant. Finally, let σ be the proportion of marginal interest income that bond holders save and $1-\sigma$ the proportion that they consume.

In each year after the issuance of the bond the government imposes additional taxes with a cost of $r\theta[pS+1-p]$. Using the notation that D is the *excess* cost of a dollar of debt finance and therefore that $D+1$ is its total cost, the cost of the induced debt issue may be written $r(1-\theta)(D+1)$. The total cost of the annual debt finance is therefore $r\{\theta[pS+1-p]+(1-\theta)(D+1)\}$. Against this must be set the benefits of the debt finance the increased consumption $[r(1-\sigma)]$ and the value of the increased investment $[r\sigma S]$. The net cost of the annual debt finance is therefore

$$r\{\theta[pS+1-p]+(1-\theta)(D+1)-(1-\sigma)-\sigma S\} =$$
$$r\{(\theta p-\sigma)(S-1)+(1-\theta)D\}.$$

Since this annual cost is measured in terms of equivalent consumption, the perpetual stream may be discounted to the present at the STP rate d to yield $(r/d)\{(\theta p-\sigma)(S-1)+(1-\theta)D\}$. Adding to this the value of reduced investment at the time that the debt is issued (S) gives the following expression for the social cost of a dollar of public debt:

$$(D+1) = S+ \frac{r}{d}\{(\theta p-\sigma)(S-1)+(1-\theta)D\}. \qquad 15$$

Solving explicitly for D, the excess cost of a dollar of debt, yields [23]

$$D = \frac{[d+r(\theta p-\sigma)](S-1)}{d-r(1-\theta)}. \qquad 16$$

23. This method of presentation hides the fact that D may not have a finite value. If the annual interest payments are financed by creating new debt ($\theta = 0$), the addition to the debt grows at the rate r. Since r is presumably greater than the STP rate d, the discounted increase in the size of the debt is infinite. This implies that D cannot be both constant and finite. More specifically, equations 15 and 16 are only valid if the convergence condition $d > r(1-\theta)$ holds.

Equation **16** shows that there are only two cases in which debt finance is equivalent to a tax that reduces investment, i.e. in which $D = S-1$.[24] There is first the trivial case in which the debt pays no interest and is therefore (disregarding distribution) no different from a tax. More generally, $D = S-1$ for $r \neq 0$ if and only if $1-\sigma = \theta(1-p)$, i.e. when bondholders' marginal propensity to consume $1-\sigma$ equals the proportion of the interest payments raised by taxes that reduce consumption. Stated more simply, a debt issue is equivalent to a tax on investment only when future tax and interest payments do not alter the amount of investment.

The special case in which all interest payments are financed by tax increases is of particular interest. Writing D_1 to denote the excess cost of the debt when $\theta = 1$, equation **16** implies

$$D_1 = (S-1)\left[1+\frac{r}{d}(p-\sigma)\right].\qquad\qquad 17$$

Since $r \geqslant d$, the cost of the debt exceeds the cost of an equal reduction in investment whenever $p > \sigma$, i.e. whenever future interest payments reduce investment and raise consumption. It is perhaps more likely that the opposite is true, i.e. that the future taxes levied to pay the interest fall more heavily on consumption (implying a low value of p) while bondholders have a high marginal propensity to save (high σ). In this case, the excess cost of the debt will be less than of a tax falling on investment and may even be negative. More specifically, $\sigma-p > d/r$ implies that D_1 is negative, i.e. that debt finance has a lower social cost than a tax on consumption even though the debt issue leads to an equal concurrent reduction in investment. It is even possible that, because of future induced increases in investment, the current issuance of debt is a positive benefit; i.e. $D_1+1 < 0$ whenever $\sigma-p > (d/r)[S/(S-1)]$.

More generally, equation **16** implies that the social cost per dollar of debt finance lies between the cost of reducing consumption and the cost of reducing investment whenever $1-\theta < \sigma-\theta p < d/r$. The social cost of debt finance is less than the equivalent reduction in consumption ($D < 0$) when $\sigma-\theta p > d/r$. Finally, whenever $D < -1$, a condition which can be satisfied by various

24. Recall that the current analysis assumes that saving is completely interest inelastic.

realistic combinations of the parameters, the debt finance is actually a positive benefit.

Summary

This paper has analysed several aspects of the relation between the sources of finance and the value of public sector projects. Section 1 provided the framework for the analysis, the shadow price algorithm. The next section explained why the opportunity cost of public expenditure cannot be represented by any weighted average of discount rates. In the common case of projects that involve only current expenditure and benefits, the discount rate approach makes no allowance at all for the excess social cost of foregone private investment. The special problems of debt finance were examined in section 3. The analysis as a whole has stressed that the value of any public expenditure depends on the extent to which it is financed by user charges, by different types of taxation and by the issuance of public debt.

References

ARROW, K. J. (1966), 'Discounting and public investment criteria', in A. V. Kneese and S. C. Smith (eds), *Water Research*, Johns Hopkins Press.

ARROW, K. J., and KURZ, M. (1970), *Public Investment, the Rate of Return and Optimal Fiscal Policy*, Johns Hopkins Press.

BAUMOL, W. J. (1968), 'On the social rate of discount', *Amer. Econ. Review*, vol. 58, pp. 788–802.

BAUMOL, W. J. (1969), 'On the discount rate for public projects', in Joint Economic Committee (ed.), *The Analysis and Evaluation of Public Expenditures: The PPB System*, vol. 1, pp. 489–504, U S Government Printing Office.

DIAMOND, P. (1968), 'The opportunity cost of public investment: comment', *Quart. J. Econ.*, vol. 82, pp. 682–8.

DIAMOND, P., and MIRRLEES, J. (1968), 'Optimal taxation and public production', MIT working paper, no. 22, May.

ECKSTEIN, O. (1957), 'Investment criteria for economic development and the theory of intertemporal welfare economics', *Quart. J. Econ.*, vol. 71, pp. 56–85.

ECKSTEIN, O. (1961), 'A survey of the theory of public expenditure criteria', in J. M. Buchanan (ed.), *Public Finances: Needs, Sources and Utilization*, Princeton University Press.

ECKSTEIN, O. (1968), 'Statement', in *Hearings Before the Sub-committee on Economy in Government of the Joint Economic Committee of the Congress of the United States*, US Government Printing Office.

FELDSTEIN, M. S. (1964a), 'Net social benefit calculation and the public investment decision', *Oxford Econ. Papers*, vol. 16, pp. 114–31.

FELDSTEIN, M. S. (1964b), 'The social time preference discount rate in cost benefit analysis', *Econ. J.*, vol. 74, pp. 360–79.

FELDSTEIN, M. S. (1965), 'The derivation of social time preference rates', *Kyklos*, vol. 18, pp. 277–86.

FELDSTEIN, M. S. (1970), 'Choice of technique in the public sector: a simplification', *Econ. J.*, vol. 20.

FELDSTEIN, M. S. (forthcoming), 'Cost-benefit analysis of aid-financed projects', volume of essays in honour of Lady Ursula Hicks.

FELDSTEIN, M. S., and FLEMMING, J. S. (1964), 'The problem of time, stream evaluation', *Bulletin of the Oxford University Institute of Econs. and Stats.*, vol. 26, pp. 79–85.

GALENSON, W., and LEIBENSTEIN, H. (1955), 'Investment criteria, productivity and economic development', *Quart. J. Econ.*, vol. 69, pp. 343–70.

HARBERGER, A. (1968a), 'The social opportunity cost of capital: a new approach', paper presented at the Annual Meeting of the Water Resources Research Committee, December.

HARBERGER, A. (1968b), 'Statement', in *Hearings Before the Sub-committee on Economy in Government of the Joint Economic Committee of the Congress of the United States*, US Government Printing Office.

HIRSHLEIFER, J. (1961), 'Comment on Eckstein's survey', in J. M. Buchanan (ed.), *Public Finances: Needs, Sources and Utilization*, Princeton University Press.

HIRSHLEIFER, J., *et al.* (1960), *Water Supply: Economics, Technology and Policy*, University of Chicago Press.

Joint Economic Committee, U.S. Congress (1968), *Economic Analysis of Public Investment Decisions: Interest Rate Policy and Discounting Analysis*, US Government Printing Office.

KRUTILLA, J., and ECKSTEIN, O. (1958), *Multiple Purpose River Development*, Johns Hopkins Press.

MARGLIN, S. A. (1963a), 'The social rate of discount and the optimal rate of investment', *Quart. J. Econ.*, vol. 77, pp. 95–111.

MARGLIN, S. A. (1963b), 'The opportunity costs of public investment', *Quart. J. Econ.*, vol. 77, pp. 274–89.

MISHAN, E. J. (1967a), 'A proposed normalization procedure for public investment criteria', *Econ. J.*, vol. 77, pp. 777–96.

MISHAN, E. J. (1967b), 'Criteria for public investment: some simplifying suggestions', *J. polit. Econ.*, vol. 75, pp. 139–46.

MUSGRAVE, R. A. (1959), *The Theory of Public Finance*, McGraw-Hill.

MUSGRAVE, R. A. (1969), 'Cost-benefit analysis and the theory of public finance', *Journal of Economic Literature*, vol. 7, pp. 797–806.

RAMSEY, D. D. (1969), 'On the social rate of discount comment', *Amer. Econ. Review*, vol. 59, pp. 919–24.

SEN, A. K. (1957), 'A note on Tinbergen on the optimum rate of saving',
  Econ. J., vol. 67, pp. 745–8.
STEINER, P. O. (1959), 'Choosing among alternative public investments
  in the water resource field', *Amer. econ. Review*, vol. 49, pp. 893–916.
USHER, D. (1969), 'On the social rate of discount: comment', *Amer.
  Econ. Review*, vol. 59, pp. 924–9.

Part Four
The Treatment of Risk

Should risky returns to public projects be valued at less than
the expected (average) value of those returns? Many people
have argued that they should, since this is how a private
investor would view them. But Arrow and Lind argue that, if
the returns are spread over a large number of taxpayers, the
risk can, in the limit, be ignored. However, if there are
individuals who face returns that could vary substantially
relatively to their incomes, risk cannot be ignored. Dorfman
puts forward various ways in which it can be handled in this
case.

14 K.J.Arrow and R.C.Lind

Uncertainty and the Evaluation of
Public Investment Decisions

K. J. Arrow and R. C. Lind, 'Uncertainty and the evaluation of public
investment decisions', *American Economic Review*, vol. 60, 1970, pp.
364–78.

The implications of uncertainty for public investment decisions
remain controversial. The essence of the controversy is as follows.
It is widely accepted that individuals are not indifferent to uncertainty and will not, in general, value assets with uncertain returns
at their expected values. Depending upon an individual's initial
asset holdings and utility function, he will value an asset at more
or less than its expected value. Therefore, in private capital markets, investors do not choose investments to maximize the present
value of expected returns, but to maximize the present value of
returns properly adjusted for risk. The issue is whether it is appropriate to discount public investments in the same way as private
investments.

There are several positions on this issue. The first is that risk
should be discounted in the same way for public investments as it
is for private investments. It is argued that to treat risk differently
in the public sector will result in overinvestment in this sector at
the expense of private investments yielding higher returns. The
leading proponent of this point of view is Jack Hirshleifer.[1] He
argues that in perfect capital markets, investments are discounted
with respect to both time and risk and that the discount rates
obtaining in these markets should be used to evaluate public
investment opportunities.

1. J. Hirshleifer (1965, 1966) and Hirshleifer, J. C. De Haven and J. W.
Milliman (1960, pp. 139–50).

A second position is that the government can better cope with uncertainty than private investors and, therefore, government investments should not be evaluated by the same criterion used in private markets. More specifically, it is argued that the government should ignore uncertainty and behave as if indifferent to risk. The government should then evaluate investment opportunities according to their present value computed by discounting the expected value of net returns, using a rate of discount equal to the private rate appropriate for investments with certain returns. In support of this position it is argued that the government invests in a greater number of diverse projects and is able to pool risks to a much greater extent than private investors.[2] Another supporting line of argument is that many of the uncertainties which arise in private capital markets are related to what may be termed moral hazards. Individuals involved in a given transaction may hedge against the possibility of fraudulent behavior on the part of their associates. Many such risks are not present in the case of public investments and, therefore, it can be argued that it is not appropriate for the government to take these risks into account when choosing among public investments.

There is, in addition, a third position on the government's response to uncertainty. This position rejects the notion that individual preferences as revealed by market behavior are of normative significance for government investment decisions, and asserts that time and risk preferences relevant for government action should be established as a matter of national policy. In this case the correct rules for action would be those established by the appropriate authorities in accordance with their concept of national policy. The rate of discount and attitude toward risk would be specified by the appropriate authorities and the procedures for evaluation would incorporate these time and risk preferences. Two alternative lines of argument lead to this position. First, if one accepts the proposition that the state is more than a collection of individuals and has an existence and interests apart from those of its individual members, then it follows that government policy need not reflect individual preferences. A second position is that markets are so imperfect that the behavior

2. For this point of view, see P. A. Samuelson and W. Vickrey (1964).

observed in these markets yields no relevant information about the time and risk preferences of individuals. It follows that some policy as to time and risk preference must be established in accordance with other evidence of social objectives. One such procedure would be to set national objectives concerning the desired rate of growth and to infer from this the appropriate rate of discount.[3] If this rate were applied to the expected returns from all alternative investments, the government would in effect be behaving as if indifferent to risk.

The approach taken in this paper closely parallels the approach taken by Hirshleifer, although the results differ from his. By using the state-preference approach to market behavior under uncertainty, Hirshleifer demonstrates that investments will not, in general, be valued at the sum of the expected returns discounted at a rate appropriate for investments with certain returns.[4] He then demonstrates that using this discount rate for public investments may lead to non-optimal results, for two reasons. First, pooling itself may not be desirable.[5] If the government has the opportunity to undertake only investments which pay off in states where the payoff is highly valued, to combine such investments with ones that pay off in other states may reduce the value of the total investment package. Hirshleifer argues that where investments can be undertaken separately they should be evaluated separately, and that returns should be discounted at rates determined in the market. Second, even if pooling were possible and desirable, Hirshleifer argues correctly that the use of a rate of discount for the public sector which is lower than rates in the private sector can lead to the displacement of private investments by public investments yielding lower expected returns.[6]

For the case where government pooling is effective and desirable, he argues that rather than evaluate public investments differently from private ones, the government should subsidize the more productive private investments. From this it follows that to treat risk differently for public as opposed to private investments would only be justified if it were impossible to transfer the ad-

3. For this point of view, see O. Eckstein (1961) and S. Marglin (1963).
4. Hirshleifer (1965, pp. 523–34); (1966, pp. 268–75).
5. Hirshleifer (1966, pp. 270–75).
6. Hirshleifer (1966, pp. 270–75).

vantages of government pooling to private investors. Therefore, at most, the argument for treating public risks differently than private ones in evaluating investments is an argument for the 'second best'.[7]

The first section of this paper addresses the problem of uncertainty, using the state-preference approach to market behavior. It demonstrates that if the returns from any particular investment are independent of other components of national income, then the present value of this investment equals the sum of expected returns discounted by a rate appropriate for investments yielding certain returns. This result holds for both private and public investments. Therefore, by adding one plausible assumption to Hirshleifer's formulation, the conclusion can be drawn that the government should behave as an expected-value decision-maker and use a discount rate appropriate for investments with certain returns. This conclusion needs to be appropriately modified when one considers the case where there is a corporate income tax.

While this result is of theoretical interest, as a policy recommendation it suffers from a defect common to the conclusions drawn by Hirshleifer. The model of the economy upon which these recommendations are based presupposes the existence of perfect markets for claims contingent on states of the world. Put differently, it is assumed that there are perfect insurance markets through which individuals may individually pool risks. Given such markets, the distribution of risks among individuals will be Pareto optimal. The difficulty is that many of these markets for insurance do not exist, so even if the markets which do exist are perfect, the resulting equilibrium will be sub-optimal. In addition, given the strong evidence that the existing capital markets are not perfect, it is unlikely that the pattern of investment will be Pareto optimal. At the margin, different individuals will have different rates of time and risk preference, depending on their opportunities to borrow or to invest, including their opportunities to insure.

There are two reasons why markets for many types of insurance do not exist. The first is the existence of certain moral hazards.[8] In particular, the fact that someone has insurance may alter his

7. Hirshleifer (1966, p. 270).
8. For a discussion of this problem see M. V. Pauly (1968) and Arrow (1968).

behavior so that the observed outcome is adverse to the insurer. The second is that such markets would require complicated and specialized contracts which are costly. It may be that the cost of insuring in some cases is so high that individuals choose to bear risks rather than pay the transaction costs associated with insurance.

Given the absence of some markets for insurance and the resulting sub-optimal allocation of risks, the question remains: How should the government treat uncertainty in evaluating public investment decisions? The approach taken in this paper is that individual preferences are relevant for public investment decisions, and government decisions should reflect individual valuations of costs and benefits. It is demonstrated in the second section of this paper that when the risks associated with a public investment are publicly borne, the total cost of risk-bearing is insignificant and, therefore, the government should ignore uncertainty in evaluating public investments. Similarly, the choice of the rate of discount should in this case be independent of considerations of risk. This result is obtained not because the government is able to pool investments but because the government distributes the risk associated with any investment among a large number of people. It is the risk-spreading aspect of government investment that is essential to this result.

There remains the problem that private investments may be displaced by public ones yielding a lower return if this rule is followed, although given the absence of insurance markets this will represent a Hicks-Kaldor improvement over the initial situation. Again the question must be asked whether the superior position of the government with respect to risk can be made to serve private investors. This leads to a discussion of the government's role as a supplier of insurance, and of Hirshleifer's recommendation that private investment be subsidized in some cases.

Finally, the results obtained above apply to risks actually borne by the government. Many of the risks associated with public investments are borne by private individuals, and in such cases it is appropriate to discount for risk as would these individuals. This problem is discussed in the final section of the paper. In addition, a method of evaluating public investment decisions is developed that calls for different rates of discount applied to different classes of benefits and costs.

Markets for contingent claims and time-risk preference[9]

For simplicity, consider an economy where there is one commodity and there are I individuals, S possible states of the world, and time is divided into Q periods of equal length. Further suppose that each individual acts on the basis of his subjective probability as to the states of nature; let π_{is} denote the subjective probability assigned to state s by individual i. Now suppose that each individual in the absence of trading owns claims for varying amounts of the one commodity at different points in time, given different states of the world. Let $\bar{x}_{isq}$ denote the initial claim to the commodity in period $q+1$ if state s occurs which is owned by individual i. Suppose further that all trading in these claims takes place at the beginning of the first period, and claims are bought and sold on dated commodity units contingent on a state of the world. All claims can be constructed from basic claims which pay one commodity unit in period $q+1$, given state s, and nothing in other states or at other times; there will be a corresponding price for this claim, $p_{sq}(s = 1,\dots, S; q = 0,\dots, Q-1)$. After the trading, the individual will own claims x_{isq}, which he will exercise when the time comes to provide for his consumption. Let $V_i(x_{i1,0},\dots, x_{i1,Q-1}, x_{i2,0},\dots, x_{iS,Q-1})$ be the utility of individual i if he receives claims $x_{isq}(s = 1,\dots, S; q = 0,\dots, Q-1)$. The standard assumptions are made that V_i is strictly quasi-concave $(i = 1,\dots, I)$.

Therefore each individual will attempt to maximize

$$V_i(x_{i1,0},\dots, x_{i1,Q-1}, x_{i2,0},\dots, x_{iS,Q-1}) \qquad 1$$

subject to the constraint

$$\sum_{q=0}^{Q-1}\sum_{s=1}^{S} p_{sq} x_{isq} = \sum_{q=0}^{Q-1}\sum_{s=1}^{S} p_{sq} \bar{x}_{isq}.$$

Using the von Neumann-Morgenstern theorem and an extension

9. For a basic statement of the state-preference approach, see Arrow (1964).

by Hirshleifer,[10] functions $U_{is}(s = 1, \ldots, S)$ can be found such that

$$V_i(x_{i1,0}, \ldots, x_{iS,Q-1}) = \sum_{s=1}^{S} \pi_{is} U_{is}(x_{is0}, x_{is1}, \ldots, x_{iS,Q-1}).\qquad 2$$

In equation 2 an individual's utility, given any state of the world, is a function of his consumption at each point in time. The subscript s attached to the function U_{is} is in recognition of the fact that the value of a given stream of consumption may depend on the state of the world.

The conditions for equilibrium require that

$$\pi_{is} \frac{\partial U_{is}}{\partial x_{isq}} = \lambda_i p_{sq}\qquad 3$$

$$(i = 1, \ldots, I; s = 1, \ldots, S; q = 0, \ldots, Q-1),$$

where λ_i is a Lagrangian multiplier.

From 3 it follows that

$$\frac{p_{sq}}{p_{rm}} = \frac{\pi_{is}(\partial U_{is}/\partial x_{isq})}{\pi_{rm}(\partial U_{ir}/\partial x_{irm})}\qquad 4$$

$$(i = 1, \ldots, I; r, s = 1, \ldots, S; m, q = 0, \ldots, Q-1).$$

Insight can be gained by analysing the meaning of the prices in such an economy. Since trading takes place at time zero, p_{sq} represents the present value of a claim to one commodity unit at time q, given state s. Clearly,

$$\sum_{s=1}^{S} p_{s0} = 1$$

since someone holding one commodity unit at time zero has a claim on one commodity unit, given any state of the world. It follows that p_{sq} is the present value of one commodity at time q, given state s, in terms of a certain claim on one commodity unit at time zero. Therefore, the implicit rate of discount to time zero on returns at time q, given state s, is defined by $p_{sq} = 1/(1+r_{sq})$.

Now suppose one considers a certain claim to one commodity unit at time q; clearly, its value is

$$p_q = \sum_{s=1}^{S} p_{sq}$$

10. J. von Neumann and O. Morgenstern (1964), and Hirshleifer (1965, pp. 534–6).

and the rate of discount appropriate for a certain return at time q is defined by

$$\frac{1}{1+r_q} = \sum_{s=1}^{S} \frac{1}{1+r_{sq}} = \sum_{s=1}^{S} p_{sq}. \qquad 5$$

Given these observations, we can now analyse the appropriate procedure for evaluating government investments where there are perfect markets for claims contingent on states of the world.[11] Consider an investment where the overall effect on market prices can be assumed to be negligible, and suppose the net return from this investment for a given time and state is $h_{sq}(s = 1, \ldots, S; q = 0, \ldots, Q-1)$. Then the investment should be undertaken if

$$\sum_{q=0}^{Q-1} \sum_{s=1}^{S} h_{sq} p_{sq} > 0, \qquad 6$$

and the sum on the left is an exact expression for the present value of the investment. Expressed differently, the investment should be adopted if

$$\sum_{q=0}^{Q-1} \sum_{s=1}^{S} \frac{h_{sq}}{1+r_{sq}} > 0. \qquad 7$$

The payoff in each time-state is discounted by the associated rate of discount. This is the essential result upon which Hirshleifer bases his policy conclusions.[12]

Now suppose that the net returns of the investment were (a) independent of the returns from previous investment, (b) independent of the individual utility functions, and (c) had an objective probability distribution, i.e. one agreed upon by everyone. More specifically, we assume that the set of all possible states of the world can be partitioned into a class of mutually exclusive and collectively exhaustive sets, E_t, indexed by the subscript t such that, for all s in any given E_t, all utility functions U_{is} are the same for any individual i ($i = 1, \ldots, I$), and such that all production conditions are the same. Put differently, for all s in E_t, U_{is} is the same for a given individual, but not necessarily for all individuals.

11. The following argument was sketched in Arrow (1966, pp. 28–30).
12. Hirshleifer (1965, pp. 323–34).

At the same time there is another partition of the states of the world into sets, F_u, such that the return, h_{sq}, is the same for all s in F_u. Finally, we assume that the probability distribution of F_u is independent of E_t and is the same for all individuals.

Let E_{tu} be the set of all states of the world which lie in both E_t and F_u. For any given t and u, all states of the world in E_{tu} are indistinguishable for all purposes, so we may regard it as containing a single state. Equations 3 and 5 and the intervening discussion still hold if we then replace s everywhere by tu. However, $U_{is} = U_{itu}$ actually depends only on the subscript, t, and can be written U_{it}. From the assumptions it is obvious and can be proved rigorously that the allocation x_{isq} also depends only on t, i.e. is the same for all states in E_t for any given t, so it may be written x_{itq}. Finally, let π_{it} be the probability of E_t according to individual i, and let π_u be the probability of F_u, assumed the same for all individuals. Then the assumption of statistical independence is written

$$\pi_{itu} = \pi_{it}\pi_u. \qquad 8$$

Then 3 can be written

$$\pi_{it}\pi_u\frac{\partial U_{it}}{\partial x_{itq}} = \lambda_i p_{tuq}. \qquad 9$$

Since p_{tuq} and π_u are independent of i, so must be

$$\frac{\pi_{it}(\partial U_{it}/\partial x_{itq})}{\lambda_i};$$

on the other hand, this expression is also independent of u and so can be written u_{tq}. Therefore,

$$p_{tuq} = u_{tq}\pi_u. \qquad 10$$

Since the new investment has the same return for all states s in F_u, the returns can be written h_{uq}. Then the left-hand side of 6 can, with the aid of 10, be written

$$\sum_{q=0}^{Q-1}\sum_{s=1}^{S}h_{sq}p_{sq} = \sum_{q=0}^{Q-1}\sum_{t}\sum_{u}h_{uq}p_{tuq}$$

$$= \sum_{q=0}^{Q-1}\left(\sum_{t}\mu_{tq}\right)\sum_{u}\pi_u h_{uq}. \qquad 11$$

But from **10**

$$p_q = \sum_{s=1}^{S} p_{sq} = \sum_t \sum_u p_{tuq}$$

$$= \left(\sum_t \mu_{tq} \right) \left(\sum_u \pi_u \right) = \sum_t \mu_{tq}, \qquad \textbf{12}$$

since of course the sum of the probabilities of the F_us must be 1. From **11**,

$$\sum_{q=0}^{Q-1} \sum_{s=1}^{S} h_{sq} p_{sq} = \sum_{q=0}^{Q-1} \frac{1}{1+r_q} \sum_u \pi_u h_{uq}. \qquad \textbf{13}$$

Equation **13** gives the rather startling result that the present value of any investment which meets the independence and objectivity conditions, equals the expected value of returns in each time period, discounted by the factor appropriate for a certain return at that time. This is true even though individuals may have had different probabilities for the events that governed the returns on earlier investments. It is also interesting to note that each individual will behave in this manner so that there will be no discrepancy between public and private procedures for choosing among investments.

The independence assumption applied to utility functions was required because the functions U_{is} are conditional on the states of the world. This assumption appears reasonable, and in the case where U_{is} is the same for all values of s, it is automatically satisfied. Then the independence condition is simply that the net returns from an investment be independent of the returns from previous investments.

The difficulty that arises if one bases policy conclusions on these results is that some markets do not exist, and individuals do not value assets at the expected value of returns discounted by a factor appropriate for certain returns. It is tempting to argue that while individuals do not behave as expected-value decision-makers because of the nonexistence of certain markets for insurance, there is no reason why the government's behavior should not be consistent with the results derived above where the allocation of resources was Pareto optimal. There are two difficulties with this line of argument. First, if we are to measure benefits and costs in terms of individuals' willingness to pay, then we must treat risk in accordance with these individual valuations. Since individuals do not have the opportunities for insuring assumed in the state-preference model, they will not value uncertainty as they would if these markets did exist. Second, the theory of the second best demonstrates that if resources are not allocated in a Pareto optimal manner, the appropriate public policies may not be those consistent with Pareto efficiency in perfect markets. Therefore, some other approach must be found for ascertaining the appropriate government policy toward risk. In particular, such an approach must be valid, given the nonexistence of certain markets for insurance and imperfections in existing markets.

The public cost of risk-bearing

The critical question is: What is the cost of uncertainty in terms of costs to individuals? If one adopts the position that costs and benefits should be computed on the basis of individual willingness to pay, consistency demands that the public costs of risk-bearing be computed in this way too. This is the approach taken here.

In the discussion that follows it is assumed that an individual's utility is dependent only upon his consumption and not upon the state of nature in which that consumption takes place. This assumption simplifies the presentation of the major theorem, but it is not essential. Again the expected utility theorem is assumed to hold. The presentation to follow analyses the cost of risk-bearing by comparing the expected value of returns with the certainty equivalent of these returns. In this way the analysis of time and risk preference can be separated, so we need only consider one time period.

Suppose that the government were to undertake an investment with a certain outcome; then the benefits and costs are measured in terms of willingness to pay for this outcome. If, however, the outcome is uncertain, then the benefits and costs actually realized depend on which outcome in fact occurs. If an individual is risk-averse, he will value the investment with the uncertain outcome at less than the expected value of its net return (benefit minus cost) to him. Therefore, in general the expected value of net benefits overstates willingness to pay by an amount equal to the cost of risk-bearing. It is clear that the social cost of risk-bearing will depend both upon which individuals receive the benefits and pay the costs and upon how large is each individual's share of these benefits and costs.

As a first step, suppose that the government were to undertake an investment and capture all benefits and pay all costs, i.e. the beneficiaries pay to the government an amount equal to the benefits received and the government pays all costs. Individuals who incur costs and those who receive benefits are therefore left indifferent to their pre-investment state. This assumption simply transfers all benefits and costs to the government, and the outcome of the investment will affect government disbursements and receipts. Given that the general taxpayer finances government expenditures, a public investment can be considered an investment in which each individual taxpayer has a very small share.

For precision, suppose that the government undertook an investment and that returns accrue to the government as previously described. In addition, suppose that in a given year the government were to have a balanced budget (or a planned deficit or surplus) and that taxes would be reduced by the amount of the net benefits if the returns are positive, and raised if returns are negative. Therefore, when the government undertakes an investment, each taxpayer has a small share of that investment with the returns being paid through changes in the level of taxes. By undertaking an investment the government adds to each individual's disposable income a random variable which is some fraction of the random variable representing the total net returns. The expected return to all taxpayers as a group equals expected net benefits.

Each taxpayer holds a small share of an asset with a random payoff, and the value of this asset to the individual is less than its expected return, assuming risk aversion. Stated differently, there is a cost of risk-bearing that must be subtracted from the expected return in order to compute the value of the investment to the individual taxpayer. Since each taxpayer will bear some of the cost of the risk associated with the investment, these costs must be summed over all taxpayers in order to arrive at the total cost of risk-bearing associated with a particular investment. These costs must be subtracted from the value of expected net benefits in order to obtain the correct measure for net benefits. The task is to assess these costs.

Suppose, as in the previous section, that there is one commodity, and that each individual's utility in a given year is a function of his income defined in terms of this commodity and is given by $U(Y)$. Further, suppose that U is bounded, continuous, strictly increasing, and differentiable. The assumptions that U is continuous and strictly increasing imply that U has a right and left derivative at every point and this is sufficient to prove the desired results; differentiability is assumed only to simplify presentation. Further suppose that U satisfies the conditions of the expected utility theorem.

Consider, for the moment, the case where all individuals are identical in that they have the same preferences, and their disposable incomes are identically distributed random variables represented by A. Suppose that the government were to undertake an investment with returns represented by B, which are statistically independent of A. Now divide the effect of this investment into two parts: a certain part equal to expected returns and a random part, with mean zero, which incorporates risk. Let $\bar{B} = E[B]$, and define the random variable X by $X = B - \bar{B}$. Clearly, X is independent of A and $E[X] = 0$. The effect of this investment is to add an amount $\bar{B}$ to government receipts along with a random component represented by X. The income of each taxpayer will be affected through taxes and it is the level of these taxes that determines the fraction of the investment he effectively holds.

Consider a specific taxpayer and denote his fraction of this investment by s, $0 \leqslant s \leqslant 1$. This individual's disposable income, given the public investment, is equal to $A + sB = A + s\bar{B} + sX$. The addition of sB to his disposable income is valued by the individual at its expected value less the cost of bearing the risk associated with the random component sX. If we suppose that each taxpayer has the same tax rate and that there are n taxpayers, then $s = 1/n$, and the value of the investment taken over all individuals is simply $\bar{B}$ minus n times the cost of risk-bearing associated with the random variable $(1/n)X$. The central result of this section of the paper is that this total of the costs of risk-bearing goes to zero as n becomes large. Therefore, for large values of n the value of a public investment almost equals the expected value of that investment.

To demonstrate this, we introduce the function

$$W(s) = E[U(A+s\bar{B}+sX)] \quad (0 \leqslant s \leqslant 1).$$ **14**

In other words, given the random variables A and B representing his individual income before the investment and the income from the investment, respectively, his expected utility is a function of s which represents his share of B. From **14** and the assumption that U' exists, it follows that

$$W'(s) = E[U'(A+s\bar{B}+sX)(\bar{B}+X)].$$ **15**

Since X is independent of A, it follows that $U'(A)$ and X are independent; therefore

$$E[U'(A)X] = E[U'(A)]E[X] = 0,$$

so that

$$W'(0) = E[U'(A)(\bar{B}+X)]$$
$$= \bar{B}E[U'(A)].$$ **16**

Equation **16** is equivalent to the statement

$$\lim_{s \to 0} \frac{E[U(A+s\bar{B}+sX)-U(A)]}{s} = \bar{B}E[U'(A)].$$ **17**

Now let $s = 1/n$, so that equation **17** becomes

$$\lim_{n \to \infty} nE\left[U\left(A+\frac{\bar{B}+X}{n}\right) - U(A)\right] = \bar{B}E[U'(A)].$$ **18**

If we assume that an individual whose preferences are represented by U is a risk-averter, then it is easily shown that there exists a unique number, $k(n) > 0$, for each value of n such that

$$E\left[U\left(A+\frac{\bar{B}+X}{n}\right)\right] = E\left[U\left(A+\frac{\bar{B}}{n}-k(n)\right)\right].$$ **19**

or, in other words, an individual would be indifferent between paying an amount equal to $k(n)$ and accepting the risk represented by $(1/n)X$. Therefore, $k(n)$ can be said to be the cost of risk-bearing associated with the asset B. It can easily be demonstrated that

$\lim_{n \to \infty} k(n) = 0$, i.e. the cost of holding the risky asset goes to zero as the amount of this asset held by the individual goes to zero. It should be noted that the assumption of risk aversion is not essential to the argument but simply one of convenience. If U represented the utility function of a risk preferrer, then all the above statements would hold except $k(n) < 0$, i.e. an individual would be indifferent between being paid $-k(n)$ and accepting the risk $(1/n)X$ (net of the benefit $(1/n)\bar{B}$).

We wish to prove not merely that the risk-premium of the representative individual, $k(n)$, vanishes, but more strongly that the total of the risk-premiums for all individuals, $nk(n)$, approaches zero as n becomes large.

From **18** and **19** it follows that

$$\lim_{n \to \infty} nE\left[U\left(A + \frac{\bar{B}}{n} - k(n)\right) - U(A)\right] = \bar{B}E[U'(A)]. \qquad \textbf{20}$$

In addition, $\bar{B}/n - k(n) \to 0$, when $n \to \infty$. It follows from the definition of a derivative that

$$\lim_{n \to \infty} \frac{E[U\{A + \bar{B}/n - k(n)\} - U(A)]}{\bar{B}/n - k(n)} = E[U'(A)] > 0. \qquad \textbf{21}$$

Dividing **20** by **21** yields

$$\lim_{n \to \infty} [\bar{B} - nk(n)] = \bar{B} \qquad \textbf{22}$$

or $\quad \lim_{n \to \infty} nk(n) = 0.$ \qquad \textbf{23}

The argument in **21** implies that $\bar{B}/n - k(n) \neq 0$. Suppose instead the equality held for infinitely many n. Substitution into the left-hand side of **20** shows that $\bar{B}$ must equal zero, so that $k(n) = 0$ for all such n, and hence $nk(n) = 0$ on that sequence, confirming **23**.

Equation **23** states that the total of the costs of risk-bearing goes to zero as the population of taxpayers becomes large. At the same time the monetary value of the investment to each taxpayer, neglecting the cost of risk, is $(1/n)\bar{B}$, and the total, summed over all individuals, is $\bar{B}$, the expected value of net benefits. Therefore, if n is large, the expected value of net benefits closely approximates the correct measure of net benefits defined in terms of willingness to pay for an asset with an uncertain return.

In the preceding analysis, it was assumed that all taxpayers were identical in that they had the same utility function, their incomes were represented by identically distributed variables, and they were subject to the same tax rates. These assumptions greatly simplify the presentation; however, they are not essential to the argument. Different individuals may have different preferences, incomes, and tax rates; and the basic theorem still holds, provided that as n becomes larger the share of the public investment borne by any individual becomes arbitrarily smaller.

The question necessarily arises as to how large n must be to justify proceeding as if the cost of publicly-borne risk is negligible. This question can be given no precise answer; however, there are circumstances under which it appears likely that the cost of risk-bearing will be small. If the size of the share borne by each taxpayer is a negligible component of his income, the cost of risk-bearing associated with holding it will be small. It appears reasonable to assume, under these conditions, that the total cost of risk-bearing is also small. This situation will exist where the investment is small with respect to the total wealth of the taxpayers. In the case of a federally sponsored investment, n is not only large but the investment is generally a very small fraction of national income even though the investment itself may be large in some absolute sense.

The results derived here and in the previous section depend on returns from a given public investment being independent of other components of national income. The government undertakes a wide range of public investments and it appears reasonable to assume that their returns are independent. Clearly, there are some government investments which are interdependent; however, where investments are interrelated they should be evaluated as a package. Even after such groupings are established, there will be a large number of essentially independent projects. It is sometimes argued that the returns from public investments are highly correlated with other components of national income through the business cycle. However, if we assume that stabilization policies are successful, then this difficulty does not arise. It should be noted that in most benefit-cost studies it is assumed that full employment will be maintained so that market prices can be used to measure benefits and costs. Consistency requires that this assumption be retained when considering risk as well. Further, if there is some positive correlation between the returns of an investment and other components of national income, the question remains as to whether this correlation is so high as to invalidate the previous result.

The main result is more general than the specific application to public investments. It has been demonstrated that if an individual or group holds an asset which is statistically independent of other assets, and if there is one or more individuals who do not share ownership, then the existing situation is not Pareto-efficient. By selling some share of the asset to one of the individuals not originally possessing a share, the cost of risk-bearing can be reduced while the expected returns remain unchanged. The reduction in the cost of risk-bearing can then be redistributed to bring about a Pareto improvement. This result is similar to a result derived by Karl Borch. He proved that a condition for Pareto optimality in reinsurance markets requires that every individual hold a share of every independent risk.

When the government undertakes an investment it, in effect, spreads the risk among all taxpayers. Even if one were to accept that the initial distribution of risk was Pareto-efficient, the new distribution of risk will not be efficient as the government does not discriminate among the taxpayers according to their risk preferences. What has been shown is that in the limit the situation where the risk of the investment is spread over all taxpayers is such that there is only a small deviation from optimality with regard to the distribution of that particular risk. The overall distribution of risk may be sub-optimal because of market imperfections and the absence of certain insurance markets. The great advantage of the results of this section is that they are not dependent on the existence of perfect markets for contingent claims.

This leads to an example which runs counter to the policy conclusions generally offered by economists. Suppose that an individual in the private sector of the economy were to undertake a given investment and, calculated on the basis of expected returns, the investment had a rate of return of 10 per cent. Because of the absence of perfect insurance markets, the investor subtracted from the expected return in each period a risk premium and, on the basis of returns adjusted for risk, his rate of return is 5 per cent.

Now suppose that the government could invest the same amount of money in an investment which, on the basis of expected returns, would yield 6 per cent. Since the risk would be spread over all tax-payers, the cost of risk-bearing would be negligible, and the true rate of return would be 6 per cent. Further, suppose that if the public investment were adopted it would displace the private investment. The question is: Should the public investment be undertaken? On the basis of the previous analysis, the answer is yes. The private investor is indifferent between the investment with the expected return of 10 per cent, and certain rate of return of 5 per cent. When the public investment is undertaken, it is equivalent to an investment with a certain rate of return of 6 per cent. Therefore, by undertaking the public investment, the government could more than pay the opportunity cost to the private investor of 5 per cent associated with the diversion of funds from private investment.

The previous example illustrates Hirshleifer's point that the case for evaluating public investments differently from private ones is an argument for the second best. Clearly, if the advantages of the more efficient distribution of risk could be achieved in connection with the private investment alternative, this would be superior to the public investment. The question then arises as to how the government can provide insurance for private investors and thereby transfer the risks from the private sector to the public at large. The same difficulties arise as before, moral hazards and transaction costs. It may not be possible for the government to provide such insurance, and in such cases second-best solutions are in order. Note that if the government could undertake any investment, then this difficulty would not arise. Perhaps one of the strongest criticisms of a system of freely competitive markets is that the inherent difficulty in establishing certain markets for insurance brings about a sub-optimal allocation of resources. If we consider an investment, as does Hirshleifer, as an exchange of certain present income for uncertain future income, then the misallocation will take the form of under-investment.

Now consider Hirshleifer's recommendation that, in cases such as the one above, a direct subsidy be used to induce more private investment rather than increase public investment. Suppose that a particular private investment were such that the benefits would be a marginal increase in the future supply of an existing commodity, i.e. this investment would neither introduce a new commodity nor affect future prices. Therefore, benefits can be measured at each point in time by the market value of this output, and can be fully captured through the sale of the commodity. Let $\overline{V}$ be the present value of expected net returns, and let V be the present value of net returns adjusted for risk where the certainty rate is used to discount both streams. Further, suppose there were a public investment, where the risks were publicly borne, for which the present value of expected net benefits was P. Since the risk is publicly borne, from the previous discussion it follows that P is the present value of net benefits adjusted for risk. Now suppose that $\overline{V} > P > V$. According to Hirshleifer, we should undertake the private investment rather than the public one, and pay a subsidy if necessary to induce private entrepreneurs to undertake this investment. Clearly, if there is a choice between one investment or the other, given the existing distribution of risk, the public investment is superior. The implication is that if a risky investment in the private sector is displaced by a public investment with a lower expected return but with a higher return when appropriate adjustments are made for risks, this represents a Hicks-Kaldor improvement. This is simply a restatement of the previous point that the government could more than pay the opportunity cost to the private entrepreneur.

Now consider the case for a direct subsidy to increase the level of private investment. One can only argue for direct subsidy of the private investment if $V < 0 < \overline{V}$. The minimum subsidy required is $|V|$. Suppose the taxpayers were to pay this subsidy, which is a transfer of income from the public at large to the private investor, in order to cover the loss from the investment. The net benefits, including the cost of risk-bearing, remain negative because while the subsidy has partially offset the cost of risk-bearing to the individual investor, it has not reduced this cost. Therefore, a direct public subsidy in this case results in a less efficient allocation of resources.

We can summarize as follows: It is implied by Hirshleifer that it is better to undertake an investment with a higher expected return than one with a lower expected return. (See 1965. This proposition is not in general valid, as the distribution of risk-bearing is critical. This statement is true, however, when the costs of risk-bearing associated with both investments are the same. What has been shown is that when risks are publicly borne, the costs of risk-bearing are negligible; therefore, a public investment with an expected return which is less than that of a given private investment may nevertheless be superior to the private alternative. Therefore, the fact that public investments with lower expected return may replace private investment is not necessarily cause for concern. Furthermore, a program of providing direct subsidies to encourage more private investment does not alter the costs of risk-bearing and, therefore, will encourage investments which are inefficient when the costs of risk are considered. The program which produces the desired result is one to insure private investments.

One might raise the question as to whether risk-spreading is not associated with large corporations so that the same result would apply, and it is easily seen that the same reasoning does apply. This can be made more precise by assuming there were n stockholders who were identical in the sense that their utility functions were identical, their incomes were represented by identically distributed random variables, and they had the same share in the company. When the corporation undertakes an investment with a return in a given year represented by B, each stockholder's income is represented by $A + (1/n)B$. This assumes, of course, that a change in earnings was reflected in dividends, and that there were no business taxes. Clearly, this is identical to the situation previously described, and if n is large, the total cost of risk-bearing to the stockholders will be negligible. If the income or wealth of the stockholders were large with respect to the size of the investment, this result would be likely to hold. Note that whether or not the investment is a large one, with respect to the assets of the firm, is not relevant. While an investment may constitute a major part of a firm's assets if each stockholder's share in the firm is a small component of his income, the cost of risk-bearing to him will be very small. It then follows that if managers were acting in the interest of the firm's shareholders, they would essentially ignore risks and choose investments with the highest expected returns.

There are two important reasons why large corporations may behave as risk averters. First, in order to control the firm, some shareholder may hold a large block of stock which is a significant component of his wealth. If this were true, then, from his point of view, the costs of risk-bearing would not be negligible, and the firm should behave as a risk averter. Note in this case that the previous result does not hold because the cost of risk-bearing to each stockholder is not small, even though the number of stockholders is very large. Investment behavior in this case is essentially the same as the case of a single investor.

The second case is when, even though from the stockholder's point of view, risk should be ignored, it may not be in the interest of the corporate managers to neglect risk. Their careers and income are intimately related to the firm's performance. From their point of view, variations in the outcome of some corporate action impose very real costs. In this case, given a degree of autonomy, the corporate managers, in considering prospective investments, may discount for risk when it is not in the interest of the stockholders to do so.

Suppose that this were the case and also suppose that the marginal rate of time preference for each individual in the economy was 5 per cent. From the point of view of the stockholders, risk can be ignored and any investment with an expected return which is greater than 5 per cent should be undertaken. However, suppose that corporate managers discount for risk so that only investments with expected rates of return that exceed 10 per cent are undertaken. From the point of view of the stockholders, the rate of return on these investments, taking risk into account, is over 10 per cent. Given a marginal rate of time preference of 5 per cent, it follows that from the point of view of the individual stockholder there is too little investment. Now suppose further that the government were considering an investment with an expected rate of return of 6 per cent. Since the cost of risk-bearing is negligible, this investment should be undertaken since the marginal rate of time preference is less than 6 per cent. However, in this case, if the financing were such that a private investment with a 10 per cent expected rate of return is displaced by the public investment, there is a loss because in both cases the risk is distributed so as to make the total cost of risk-bearing negligible. The public investment should be undertaken, but only at the expense of consumption.

The actual allocation of risk

In the idealized public investment considered in the last section, all benefits and costs accrued to the government and were distributed among the taxpayers. In this sense, all uncertainty was borne collectively. Suppose instead that some benefits and costs of sizeable magnitudes accrued directly to individuals so that these individuals incurred the attendant costs of risk-bearing. In this case it is appropriate to discount for the risk, as would these individuals. Such a situation would arise in the case of a government irrigation project where the benefits accrued to farmers as increased income. The changes in farm income would be uncertain and, therefore, should be valued at more or less than their expected value, depending on the states in which they occur. If these increases were independent of other components of farm income, and if we assume that the farmer's utility were only a function of his income and not the state in which he receives that income, then he would value the investment project at less than the expected increase in his income, provided he is risk averse. If, however, the irrigation project paid out in periods of drought so that total farm income was not only increased but also stabilized, then the farmers would value the project at more than the expected increase in their incomes.

In general, some benefits and costs will accrue to the government and the uncertainties involved will be publicly borne; other benefits and costs will accrue to individuals and the attendant uncertainties will be borne privately. In the first case the cost of risk-bearing will be negligible; in the second case these costs may be significant. Therefore, in calculating the present value of returns from a public investment a distinction must be made between private and public benefits and costs. The present value of public benefits and costs should be evaluated by estimating the expected net benefits in each period and discounting them, using a discount factor appropriate for investments with certain returns. On the other hand, private benefits and costs must be discounted with respect to both time and risk in accordance with the preferences of the individuals to whom they accrue.

From the foregoing discussion it follows that different streams of benefits and costs should be treated in different ways with respect to uncertainty. One way to do this is to discount these streams of returns at different rates of discount ranging from the certainty rate for benefits and costs accruing to the government and using higher rates that reflect discounting for risk for returns accruing directly to individuals. Such a procedure raises some difficulties of identification, but this problem does not appear to be insurmountable. In general, costs are paid by the government, which receives some revenue, and the net stream should be discounted at a rate appropriate for certain returns. Benefits accruing directly to individuals should be discounted according to individual time and risk preferences. As a practical matter, Hirshleifer's suggestion of finding the marginal rate of return on assets with similar payoffs in the private sector, and using this as the rate of discount, appears reasonable for discounting those benefits and costs which accrue privately.

One problem arises with this latter procedure which has received little attention. In considering public investments, benefits and costs are aggregated and the discussion of uncertainty is carried out in terms of these aggregates. This obscures many of the uncertainties because benefits and costs do not in general accrue to the same individuals, and the attendant uncertainties should not be netted out when considering the totals. To make this clear, consider an investment where the benefits and costs varied greatly, depending on the state of nature, but where the difference between total benefits and total costs was constant for every state. Further, suppose that the benefits and costs accrued to different groups. While the investment is certain from a social point of view, there is considerable risk from a private point of view. In the case of perfect markets for contingent claims, each individual will discount the stream of costs and benefits accruing to him at the appropriate rate for each time and state. However, suppose that such markets do not exist. Then risk-averse individuals will value the net benefits accruing to them at less than their expected value. Therefore, if net benefits accruing to this individual are positive, this requires discounting expected returns at a higher rate than that appropriate for certain returns. On the other hand, if net benefits to an individual are negative, this requires discounting expected returns at a rate lower than the certainty rate. Raising the rate of discount only reduces the present value of net benefits when they are positive. Therefore, the distinction must be made not only between benefits and costs which accrue to the public and those which accrue directly to individuals, but also between individuals whose net benefits are negative and those whose benefits are positive. If all benefits and costs accrued privately, and different individuals received the benefits and paid the costs, the appropriate procedure would be to discount the stream of expected benefits at a rate higher than the certainty rate, and costs at a rate lower than the certainty rate. This would hold even if the social totals were certain.

Fortunately, as a practical matter this may not be of great importance as most costs are borne publicly and, therefore, should be discounted using the certainty rate. Benefits often accrue to individuals, and where there are attendant uncertainties it is appropriate to discount the expected value of these benefits at higher rates, depending on the nature of the uncertainty and time-risk preferences of the individuals who receive these benefits. It is somewhat ironic that the practical implication of this analysis is that for the typical case where costs are borne publicly and benefits accrue privately, this procedure will qualify fewer projects than the procedure of using a higher rate to discount both benefits and costs.

References

ARROW, K. J. (1964), 'The role of securities in the optimal allocation of risk-bearing', *Review econ. Stud.*, vol. 31, pp. 91–6.
ARROW, K. J. (1966), 'Discounting and public investment criteria', in A. V. Kneese and S. C. Smith (eds), *Water Research*, Johns Hopkins Press.
ARROW, K. J (1968), 'The economics of moral hazard: further comment', *Amer. econ. Review*, vol. 58, pp. 537–8.
BORCH, K. (1960), 'The safety loading of reinsurance', *Skandinavisk Aktuarietid-Skrift*, pp. 163–84.
ECKSTEIN, O. (1961), 'A survey of the theory of public expenditure', and 'Reply', in J. M. Buchanan (ed.), *Public Finances: Needs, Sources and Utilization*, Princeton University Press, pp. 493–504.
HIRSHLEIFER, J. (1965), 'Investment decision under uncertainty: choice – theoretic approaches', *Quart. J. Econ.*, vol. 79, pp. 509–36.
HIRSHLEIFER, J. (1966), 'Investment decision under uncertainty: applications of the state preference approach', *Quart. J. Econ.*, vol. 80, pp. 252–77.

HIRSHLEIFER, J., DE HAVEN, J. C., and MILLIMAN, J. W. (1960), *Water Supply: Economics, Technology and Policy*, University of Chicago Press.

MARGLIN, S. (1963), 'The social rate of discount and the optimal rate of investment', *Quart. J. Econ.*, vol. 77, pp. 95–111.

PAULY, M. V. (1968), 'The economics of moral hazard: comment', *Amer. econ. Review*, vol. 58, pp. 531–7.

SAMUELSON, P. A., and VICKREY, W. (1964), 'Discussion', *Amer. econ. Review Proceedings*, vol. 59, pp. 88–96.

VON NEUMANN, J., and MORGENSTERN, O. (1964), *Theory of Games and Economic Behavior*, 2nd edn, Wiley.

15 R. Dorfman

Decision Rules under Uncertainty

Excerpt from R. Dorfman, 'Basic economic and technologic concepts: a general statement', in A. Maass *et al.*, *Design of Water Resource Systems*, Harvard University Press, 1962, pp. 129–58.

Uncertainty enters into economic decisions whenever the consequences of a decision cannot be foretold with confidence, which is to say almost always. Both in practical affairs and in theorizing about them, it is frequently expedient to ignore uncertainty – to act as if consequences could be predicted accurately – in order to simplify problems. By and large this is the course we have followed up to this point. But in design and operating decisions the results of which are influenced by chance or unknown factors, such as the whims of the weather, this simplification is clearly untenable. Therefore we must analyse decision-making in circumstances where uncertainty is taken explicitly into account, and for this purpose we turn to decision theory, a new discipline being developed largely by statisticians.

Decision theory

A decision problem can be visualized as follows. A choice is to be made among a number of alternative courses of action. The practical consequences of adopting any particular course depend not only on the choice made but also on other data, called with purposeful vagueness 'the state of nature', which cannot be known at the time the choice is made. Therefore the decision must be based on three types of consideration: (1) some judgement as to the likelihood of nature being in each of its possible states,

(2) predictions as to the consequences of each course of action assuming that nature is in each of its possible states, and (3) evaluations of the desirability of each possible outcome of the situation.

To illustrate these concepts, let us suppose that a reservoir used for both irrigation and flood protection is full at the beginning of the flood season, and that only one type of flood occurs in the region. (Of course, at the beginning of the flood season one cannot predict whether or not a flood will occur.) The allowable decisions are to spill one-third of the water in the reservoir, spill two-thirds of it, or spill all of it. Table 1 shows the physical consequences of

Table 1 **Physical consequences of decisions in text example: reservoir used for both irrigation and flood protection**

| Decision | Flood | | No flood | |
	Harvest (10^3 bu)	Flood damage (10^3 dollars)	Harvest (10^3 bu)	Flood damage (10^3 dollars)
Spill one-third	950	250	1000	0
Spill two-thirds	600	100	650	0
Spill all	200	0	200	0

each permissible decision in each of the two possible states of nature, flood or no flood. To compress the two dimensions of these consequences into one to facilitate comparisons, we assume that the crop is worth $0.40 a bushel and thus derive the monetary consequences of each decision-state contingency,[1] shown in Table 2.

1. It should be noted that the method employed in this illustration for adding the benefits from flood control to the benefits from other purposes such as irrigation is different from that used elsewhere in this book. Here we subtract flood damages incurred from irrigation benefits, whereas elsewhere flood damages prevented (that is, flood damages that would occur if the reservoir were not used for flood protection minus actual flood damages) are added to the benefits from other sources. Thus, where our figures for benefits under the assumption that a flood would occur are 130, 140, and 80, depending on the decision on spill, the level of benefits under the other method of measurement would be 380, 390, and 330. This difference in method of computation does not affect the ranking of alternatives or the difference in the monetary consequences of any two decisions.

Table 2 Monetary consequences of decisions in text example

| | Returns (10³ dollars) | |
Decision	Flood	No flood
Spill one-third	130	400
Spill two-thirds	140	260
Spill all	80	80

From Table 2 it is seen that the monetary consequences of spilling all the water are inferior to those of spilling two-thirds, whether or not a flood occurs. Such a decision is said to be 'dominated' or 'inadmissible', and an obvious principle of decision theory is that all dominated decisions can be discarded forthwith. They are analogous to the inefficient points we encountered in discussing production theory.

The choice between the other two decisions is much more difficult. If a flood is in the offing, two-thirds of the water should be spilled, otherwise only one-third. But whether or not a flood impends is precisely what cannot be known at the time the decision has to be made.

The maximin-returns principle. One plausible decision would be to release two-thirds of the contents of the reservoir, on the grounds that this act would assure a return of at least $140,000 whatever happens. The underlying principle invoked here is that each alternative should be evaluated by the minimal return that it guarantees, and the one with the highest guarantee should be adopted. This principle is known as the 'maximin-returns principle' and is one of the most frequently advocated bases for decisions under uncertainty.

It suffers from two serious defects. In the first place, it is exceedingly conservative and pays no attention to the potentialities of a decision in any circumstances except the worst possible ones for that decision. In the present illustration, the maximin-returns decision would not be very appealing if floods are rare, for then its consequence would be to accept returns of $260,000 in many years when $400,000 are attainable in order to avoid losses of $10,000 during a few years.

The other defect is that this principle can lead to illogical behavior. This can be seen by considering a modification of the problem. Suppose that if no flood occurs, insect damage amounting to $135,000 will be sustained no matter how much water is released. Since the release decision will have no effect on the insect damage, one feels that this additional datum should not influence the release decision. But it does influence decisions based on the maximin-returns principle. Table 3 shows the mone-

Table 3 **Monetary consequences of decisions in text example, allowing for insect damage**

Decision	Returns (10^3 dollars)	
	Flood	No flood
Spill one-third	130	265
Spill two-thirds	140	125
Spill all	80	−55

tary returns of the three permissible decisions allowing for the predaciousness of the insects. The maximin-returns principle now instructs us to release only one-third of the water, thus securing a guaranteed return of $130,000 and avoiding the possibility of only $125,000. If the insect damage had been estimated at $125,000, the maximin-returns policy would have been to release two-thirds. Thus it appears that decisions based on the maximin-returns principle are influenced by irrelevant considerations.[2]

The minimax-risk principle. To avoid this objection, most decision theorists recommend an alternative decision criterion based on

2. We did not really need to drag the insects into the story. The same paradoxical behavior would result if a flood-relief agency stood ready to pay an indemnity of $135,000 to the members of the water district in case of flood, irrespective of the release policy followed. This alternative supposition perhaps makes clearer the reasons for the paradox. Either modification of the problem makes the consequences of a flood less serious as compared with the consequences of no flood, and therefore reduces the need to guard against them. Even though the paradox is explicable, it is damaging; for the fact remains that neither the insect damage nor the indemnity alters the differential consequences of the three decisions in either possible state of nature. Therefore it seems illogical for them to alter the relative desirability of the three decisions.

the idea that a decision should take the fullest possible advantage of the potentialities of a situation. Where uncertainty prevails, these potentialities are unknown, but we can analyse them in the following manner. Releasing one-third of the water will secure the maximum possible return if no flood impends but will result in a return $10,000 below the maximum possible in the alternative state of nature. Thus that decision exposes the water district to the risk of a loss of $10,000. On the other hand, releasing two-thirds of the water will secure the maximum attainable return if it is a flood year at the risk of sacrificing potential returns of $140,000 ($400,000 minus $260,000) if it is a no-flood year. In a sense, then, releasing two-thirds is the riskier alternative since it has the potentiality of falling farther short of the actual returns permitted by the situation.

To generalize these ideas, define the risk of any combination of a decision and a state of nature by the excess of the maximum return attainable in that state of nature over the return that actually results from the given decision in that state of nature.[3] Thus the risks in an uncertain situation can be computed from a table of returns by subtracting each return from the highest figure in its column. The risks for our example are given in Table 4. It seems reasonable to choose the alternative for which the

Table 4 **Risk table for text example**

| | Risk (10^3 dollars) | |
Decision	Flood	No flood
Spill one-third	10	0
Spill two-thirds	0	140
Spill all	60	320

maximum possible risk, defined in this way, is as small as possible. This criterion is called the 'minimax-risk principle'. In this case it recommends releasing one-third of the water. Since a risk table computed from Table 3 will be identical with the one computed from Table 2, the minimax-risk principle is free of the distorting effect of irrelevant circumstances.

3. Later on we shall use the word 'risk' in a different sense, but until further notice it will have the meaning just given.

The minimax-risk principle is a bit more sophisticated and less intuitive than the maximin-returns principle, so perhaps one more word should be written in its behalf. It is based on the notion that the absolute magnitudes of the returns in the two states of nature are useful only to determine how earnestly we should hope that one or the other will prevail. But they are irrelevant to any practical decision, which should depend only on the comparative consequences of the various alternative decisions. The subtraction involved in computing risks has the effect of canceling out the absolute levels attributable to the various states of nature and placing them all on the same footing, so that the consequences of each decision as compared with the maximum attainable in the circumstances are no longer obscured. In our example the minimax-risk decision assures a return within $10,000 of the maximum possible, whatever happens. To be sure, this return may be only $130,000 in an adverse state of nature, but this low result is the cost of a flood, not to be attributed to the decision.

Whether or not we have made the minimax-risk principle seem plausible, we now have to confess that it too suffers from a logical defect. We have just seen that, according to this principle, releasing one-third of the water is preferable to releasing two-thirds. Now suppose that another alternative becomes available. Rather than try to conjecture as to its nature, let us just call it decision X and suppose that it yields a return of $300,000 if a flood occurs and $50,000 if not. Adding this alternative to the data of Table 2, we obtain Table 5. The evaluation of the returns

Table 5 **Returns and risks of four alternatives in text example**

Decision	Returns (10^3 dollars)		Risks (10^3 dollars)	
	Flood	No flood	Flood	No flood
Spill one-third	130	400	170	0
Spill two-thirds	140	260	160	140
Spill all	80	80	220	320
Decision X	300	50	0	350

to the three original alternatives is unaltered, but the values of the risks are radically different. In fact, the minimax-risk criterion now recommends releasing two-thirds (maximum risk = $160,000) instead of releasing one-third (maximum risk = $170,000). The new alternative has reversed our choice between the old two, in spite of the fact that it is inferior to both of them in terms of the criterion. (The maximum risk for decision X is $350,000, greater than for any other alternative.) This, surely, is illogical behavior.

We have demonstrated that both the maximin-returns and the minimax-risk principles can lead to illogical behavior and consequently must violate some fundamental axiom of rational choice. Rigorous scrutiny from the standpoint of formal logic indeed shows this to be the case. These are by no means the only principles that can be devised for decision-making under uncertainty, although they are probably the two most popular ones. For example, an optimistic decision-maker might advocate a maximax principle, selecting the alternative whose maximum return is as great as possible. But, just as in our two previous cases, skeptically-minded critics have found a logical defect in every proposal thus far advanced for making decisions without forming a judgement of the relative likelihood of the various states of nature. Furthermore, there seems to be no logical basis for preferring any of these principles over any other. It seems fair to conclude that no satisfactory basis for decision can be found that does not invoke judgements concerning the likelihoods of the various states of nature. We turn now to the question of how such judgements can be incorporated into the decision process.

Probabilistic approach. Judgements about the likelihoods of various states of nature are expressed by assigning probabilities to them, making use of whatever statistical evidence and other information is available at the time the decision is to be made. These probabilities are therefore relative to the state of information on the decision date. To define the probability of any state of nature, we conceive of all instances with the given state of information and define the probability as the proportion of those instances in which nature turns out to be in the given state.[4]

4. The very concept of the probability of a state of nature raises philosophical difficulties that are at present controversial. One difficulty is that at any given time nature is in some particular state, unknown to be sure, and there is no question of probability about it. As Einstein said, 'God does not play at dice'. Another line of objection is that the concept is not operational.

The probabilities of the various states of nature can be applied to each decision to arrive at a probability distribution of the consequences of that decision. For example, if the probabilities of flood and no-flood are judged to be 0·4 and 0·6, the probability distribution of the consequences of releasing one-third of the water would be $130,000 with the probability 0·4 and $400,000 with the probability 0·6. In general, the probability to be assigned to any outcome of a particular decision is the sum of the probabilities of all the states of nature that give rise to that outcome when the particular decision is taken.

The choice among decisions, then, amounts to the choice among the probability distributions of outcomes associated with them. Of course, it is more difficult to choose among a number of probability distributions of outcomes than among a number of definite outcomes, but it is by no means a sophisticated or rare accomplishment. In fact, every businessman, government administrator, and housewife performs it many times a day. A common and important example is the decision as to whether to insure a risk (automobile collision, flood, warehouse fire, or the like) and if so, how fully. The purchase of insurance converts a situation in which there is a small probability of a great loss into one with a certainty of a small loss (the premium) plus a small probability of a middling loss (the uninsured or uninsurable part of the risk).

The considerations involved in choosing among probability distributions can be illustrated by analysing Table 2, assuming particular probabilities for the two states of nature. The augmented data, assuming probabilities of 0·4 and 0·6 for flood and no-flood respectively, are given in Table 6. The reader may have

---

It does not give rules for deciding which data are relevant and therefore to be included in the 'state of information', and except in artificially contrived cases there will never occur two instances in which the state of information is identical. And even if a number of instances of sufficiently identical information have occurred, past experience is only a rough indicator of the proportion of future times in which various states of nature will actually occur. The approach taken in the text is just a rough-and-ready cut through this morass. In the context of our example, the two possible states of nature are that a flood is impending and that it is not. The probabilities in question are simply the proportions of the time that one would expect to be right or wrong if one predicted that there would be a flood on the basis of available evidence and standard methods of prediction.

Table 6 **Probability distributions of the outcomes of three decisions in text example**

Decision	Return (10^3 dollars)		Weighted average return (10^3 dollars)
	Flood	No flood	
Spill one-third	130	400	292
Spill two-thirds	140	260	212
Spill all	80	80	80
Probability	0·4	0·6	

either of two reactions to this table. One is that the additional data have solved everything. If one-third of the water is released, an average return of $292,000 will result; if two-thirds, only $212,000; therefore one-third should be released. We shall discuss this conclusion at length below.

The other possible reaction is that the added data have solved nothing. Releasing one-third of the water still offers the enticement of a $400,000 return offset by the risk of returning only $130,000; releasing two-thirds still guarantees a larger minimum at the cost of reducing the maximum. How is one to evaluate these contingencies, even given the probability estimates?

The answer is almost immediately apparent. A listing of outcomes and their associated probabilities is not the only way to describe a probability distribution, and for the purpose of choosing among distributions it is not the best way. For this reason, among others, probability distributions are often described by their moments instead of by the outcome probabilities themselves.

The first moment of a probability distribution, often called the expected value or mathematical expectation (two misnomers), is defined by the formula $\mu = \Sigma_i p_i x_i$, where x_i is the value of the ith possible outcome and p_i is the probability of its occurrence. The second moment, called also the variance or the square of the standard deviation, is defined by $\mu_2 = \sigma^2 = \Sigma_i p_i (x_i - \mu)^2$ and the nth moment is given by $\mu_n = \Sigma_i p_i (x_i - \mu)^n$.

It is often said that the first moment, μ, is the most important characteristic of a probability distribution and therefore a very useful summary of the array of probabilities that comprise it.

This assertion is justified as follows. Suppose that an insurance company or fund undertakes to assume the risks resulting from an uncertain situation by making a guaranteed payment of g dollars to the people exposed to the risk and keeping for itself the actual outcome of the situation, x_i dollars. Then the central-limit theorem, which is perhaps the most fundamental result of mathematical probability, asserts that in a long series of such contracts (1) if $g < \mu$ the insurance company is almost certain to receive more than it pays out, (2) if $g > \mu$ the insurance company is almost certain to pay out more than it receives and, indeed, to go bankrupt, (3) if $g = \mu$ it is impossible to predict whether the insurance company will pay out more or less than it receives. Thus in a sense μ, the mathematical expectation, is a fair certainty equivalent to the proceeds of the risky situation; it is the only amount which in a long series of such undertakings is not certain to average out at either more or less than the actual result.

While this reasoning has some appeal, there is legitimate question about its applicability to actual situations where the number of replications is small (often only one) and where no guarantee fund is actually established. The expected value does measure the 'central tendency' of the probability distribution in the sense we have described, but there are other useful measures of central tendency too, for example, the mode (the outcome with a probability at least as great as that of any other) and the median (roughly, the outcome which has a 0·5 probability of being exceeded).

The second most important characteristic of a probability distribution is the degree of uncertainty, that is, the spread of the possible outcomes around their expected value. This is measured by the second moment. The first two moments together are often considered to contain most of the essential information about a probability distribution, and we shall discuss below some proposals for choosing among probability distributions that make use of only these two moments. Some alternative measures of the degree of uncertainty are the average deviation and the inter-quartile range, discussed in standard statistics texts.

The third moment measures the asymmetry of the probability distribution, and the fourth and higher moments measure other more esoteric characteristics. All the moments together constitute as complete a specification of the probability distribution as the list of probabilities itself.[5] In addition, as we have just seen, they have considerable intuitive appeal as summary indicators of the main characteristics of the distribution. Table 7 gives statistics

Table 7 **Statistics of outcome distributions in text example, computed from the first few moments**

Decision	Expected value μ	Variance σ^2	Standard deviation σ	μ_3/σ^3	μ_1/σ^4
Spill one-third	292	17,500	132	−0·41	1·17
Spill two-thirds	212	3460	59	−0·41	1·17
Spill all	80	0	0	—	—

computed from the first few moments of the three possible decisions in our example. Because there are only two possible states of nature, only the first two moments differ in this instance.

Although a complete description of a probability distribution requires all its moments, much of the information and most of the intuitive significance is contained in the first two. For this reason most practicable proposals for choice among probability distributions fall into two broad classes: those that employ only the first moment (that is, choose the distribution with the highest possible expected value) and those that employ only the first two. We now consider the first, and simpler, of these proposals.

Expected-value approach. In the first place, it is clear that in a comparison between two decisions the one that gives rise to the

5. If the uncertain situation has k possible outcomes, then it is a matter of elementary algebra to see that if the first $k-1$ moments are known or, for that matter, any $k-1$ moments, then the probabilities of the k outcomes can be computed. If the probability distribution is continuous, so that an infinite number of outcomes is possible, then it is a very difficult theorem, but true, that knowledge of all the moments is equivalent to knowledge of the probability distribution itself. It is for this reason that we are justified in saying that an uncertain situation can be described fully by the moments of the probability distribution of its outcomes. These are not the only means used for describing probability distributions. For some purposes, for example, the generating function or the characteristic function (the Laplace and Fourier transforms of the probability distribution, respectively) are more useful than either the distribution itself or its moments.

higher expected value is not invariably to be preferred. Expected value, after all, is only a mathematical artifact; there is nothing compelling about it. The most familiar example of situations in which it is considered reasonable to choose an alternative that does not have the highest possible expected value is provided by insurance. An individual contemplating insurance of some risk, say collision damage to his automobile, faces two alternatives. If he decides not to insure, his expected disposable income for a year will be his expected income from other sources minus the expected value of collision damage to his car. If he insures, his expected disposable income will be his expected income from other sources minus the insurance premium. Since insurance premiums are invariably greater than the expected value of the losses insured against, in order to cover the expenses and profits of insurance companies, the expected disposable income will be smaller if insurance is taken out than if it is not. Nevertheless, people do insure; they knowingly choose the alternative with smaller expected value. From this we see that it is quite reasonable to give up some expected value in order to reduce uncertainty, that is, in order to reduce the standard deviation of the distribution of outcomes.

There are certain circumstances, however, in which the expected value alone is an adequate basis for choice among alternatives. Most trivially, this is the case when all the alternatives have approximately the same spread or standard deviation of outcomes. A more important case that leads to the same result is where the decision-maker is in the position of an insurance company. We shall call this the case of 'actuarial risk'. Actuarial risk arises when the decision to be made is one of a large number of similar, and independent, decisions and when major importance attaches to the average or over-all result of all the decisions.[6]

In the water-resource field actuarial risk can arise in at least two ways. First, an agency such as the Soil Conservation Service may construct a large number of relatively small projects. It

6. Note the asymmetry between the rational behavior of the insurer and the insured. The insured reduces the expected value of his net benefits when he takes out insurance, and may be behaving rationally when he does so, but the rational policy for the insurer, who has the advantage of pooling numerous risks, is to maximize his expected net benefits.

would like to choose and design them so that each year the aggregate net benefits arising from its program, per dollar expended, are as large as possible. We shall now show that such an agency should design each project so as to obtain the maximum expected net benefits per dollar expended, without regard to any other characteristic of the probability distribution of net benefits. Let n be the number of projects undertaken by the agency, x_i the actual net benefits of the ith project, and y_i the cost of the ith project. We assume that the benefits x_i are independent random variables but that the costs y_i are known.[7] The agency is supposed to be concerned with its aggregate benefits per dollar, or $A = \Sigma x_i / \Sigma y_i$. The expected value and variance of A are $E(A) = \Sigma Ex_i / \Sigma y_i$ and $\sigma_A^2 = \Sigma \sigma_i^2 / (\Sigma y_i)^2$, where σ_i^2 is the variance of the net benefits of the ith project. Now the variance of A is small if the number of projects is large, as can be seen most readily by writing $\bar{\sigma}^2$ for the average variance, averaged over all projects, and $\bar{y}$ for the average cost of a project. Replacing the sums in the formula for σ_A^2 by these symbols, we have $\sigma_A^2 = n\bar{\sigma}^2 / (n\bar{y})^2 = (1/n)(\bar{\sigma}^2 / \bar{y}^2)$, which clearly decreases as n increases provided only that $\bar{\sigma}$ does not grow in proportion to n. Since, therefore, the variance of A is very small when n is large, we can be assured[8] that the actual realized value of A will be close to its expected value. But the expected value of A depends only on the expected values of the net benefits resulting from the individual projects. This argument is simply an application of the law of averages.

Actuarial risks can also arise in conjunction with a single project if the net benefits in the individual years of its life are independent random variables, and if we are more concerned with the average net benefits of the project over its lifetime than with the net benefits in particular years. The argument is similar to the one just presented.

The third circumstance in which the expected value suffices as a basis for choice among probability distributions or the decisions that give rise to them is suggested by decision theory. Clearly it is

7. This last assumption is not necessary, but simplifies the algebra considerably.

8. The assurance is provided by 'Tchebycheff's inequality', which asserts that for any probability distribution that has a finite standard deviation σ, the probability that an observation will fall q or more units away from the mean is at most σ^2/q^2. See, for example, H. Cramer (1955, pp. 81–2).

easy to choose among probability distributions if the expected value is an adequate measure of desirability, but otherwise it is substantially more difficult. Decision theory responds to this fact by asserting that if the various outcomes in the returns table are measured properly, the expected value will be an adequate measure of desirability and the problem of choosing among alternatives can be solved. Let us consider the rationale of this position.

In Tables 1 and 2 the outcomes of the various possible combinations of decision and state of nature are expressed in terms of physical and monetary results. The underlying idea of decision theory, however, is that we are not really interested in these results *per se*, but rather in the utilities that they provide. Thus we construct a table of returns, called a 'payoff table', in which the entries are not physical or monetary quantities but the utilities corresponding to them – the easy affluence of a bountiful year, the pain and disruption of a heavy flood, or the sober prosperity of an average crop. Estimating these utilities is naturally a bit of a problem, but the technique is as follows.

To set up a scale, we choose two results arbitrarily, say $100,000 and $300,000, and define a utility of zero as that yielded by a return of $100,000 and a utility of 100 as that resulting from a return of $300,000. Thus we can write $u(100) = 0$, $u(300) = 100$. Now we have to determine the utilities of all other possible returns consistently with these two values. By way of example, let us consider a return of $260,000. We can present the members of the water district with a series of options as in Table 8.

In this table, option 0 is a certainty of $260,000, the result the utility of which we wish to evaluate. The other options involve uncertainty. They offer returns of $100,000 and $300,000, whose utilities we have already established by definition, with the varying probabilities listed in the lower part of the table. Clearly option 1, which amounts to $100,000 for certain, is inferior to option 0, and option 11, which offers $300,000 for certain, is preferable to option 0. It is highly plausible to assume that somewhere between options 1 and 11 we can find one that is indifferent to option 0, although we may have to interpolate some additional options if, for example, option 0 is preferred to option 9 but option 10 is preferred to option 0.

Table 8 **Options for estimating the utility of a return of $260,000**

Option	Returns (10^3 dollars)	
0	260	260
All other	100	300
	Probabilities of returns of –	
	100×10^3 dollars	300×10^3 dollars
1	1·0	0·0
2	0·9	0·1
3	0·8	0·2
⋮	⋮	⋮
9	0·2	0·8
10	0·1	0·9
11	0·0	1·0

Let us suppose that it turns out that option 10 is indifferent to option 0. Then a return of $260,000 is the 'certainty equivalent' of a 0·1–0·9 chance of returns of $100,000 and $300,000, respectively. Now since option 10 and option 0 are indifferent, their utilities are the same. Up to this point these utilities, although equal, have been undefined; but let us now define the utility of an uncertain event like option 10 to be the expected value of the utility that will result from adopting it. Making the calculation, we find

$$u(\text{option 10}) = 0·1u(100)+0·9u(300)$$
$$= 0·1(0)+0·9(100) = 90, \qquad\qquad 1$$

which is also the utility of the certain return of $260,000. Thus $u(260) = 90$.

The calculation of the utility of a yield outside the range of the two arbitrarily established values is slightly different. We illustrate it by calculating the utility of $400,000 in Table 9. The main difference between this table and Table 8 is that we now take a yield of $300,000 as our certain outcome and a yield of $400,000, whose utility we wish to ascertain, as one of the outcomes of the uncertain options. Suppose that option 10 in this table is indifferent to option 0. Then, by the same definitions and reasoning,

$$u(\text{option 10}) = u(300) = 0·13u(100)+0·87u(400). \qquad\qquad 2$$

Table 9 Options for estimating the utility of a return of $400,000

Option	Returns (10^3 dollars)	
0	300	300
All other	100	400
	Probabilities of returns of –	
	100×10^3 dollars	400×10^3 dollars
1	1·00	0·00
2	0·90	0·10
3	0·80	0·20
⋮	⋮	⋮
9	0·20	0·80
10	0·13	0·87
11	0·10	0·90
12	0·00	1·00

Since $u(100)$ and $u(300)$ are known, we can solve for $u(400)$ to obtain $u(400) = 100/0·87 = 115$.

As these calculations indicate, once utilities have been assigned to two outcomes, the utilities of all other outcomes can be derived from them by some introspection followed by a simple calculation. The advantage of this procedure, as von Neumann and Morgenstern have shown,[9] is that under some very plausible axioms if utilities are computed in this manner, the utility of any uncertain situation equals the expected value of the utilities of the possible outcomes. We shall make use of this fact in a moment, but first note that although a bit shocking – it says that any two uncertain situations with the same mathematical expectation of utility are indifferent, even though the range of possible outcomes in one situation is much greater than the range in the other – this conclusion should not be surprising, since it is just an extension of the definition of our utility scale.

To apply these concepts to the problem presented by Tables 1 and 2, we assume that we have ascertained the utilities corresponding to the physical and monetary consequences in those tables, and so deduce Table 10. The final column is now the basis

9. von Neumann and Morgenstern (1947); Dorfman, Samuelson and Solow (1958).

of an unambiguous choice. Since the utility of any decision is the expected value of the utilities to which it can give rise, we see that the best decision is to release one-third of the water in the reservoir. This is decision theory's solution to the problem of planning under uncertainty. Its essence lies in converting from physical units to utility units. Its virtue is that after this conversion a choice can be made among a number of alternatives simply by comparing the mathematical expectations of the utilities of their outcomes.

Table 10 **Utility payoff table for text example of reservoir used for both irrigation and flood protection**

Decision	Utility in case of Flood	No flood	Expected value of utility
Spill one-third	30	115	81
Spill two-thirds	37	90	68·8
Spill all	−23[a]	−23[a]	−23[a]
Probability	0·4	0·6	

[a] These negative utilities do not mean that a harvest of 200,000 bushels or a return of $80,000 has a 'disutility' of 23 units, but simply that the utility of this outcome is 23 units below that of the outcome that was assigned arbitrarily a utility of zero.

It must be recognized that decision theory has provided the most thoroughgoing and profound analysis thus far achieved of the problem of reaching decisions under uncertainty, and that one must give serious consideration to the results of research in this area. For this reason we have presented its main tenets fully and fairly. Nevertheless, we feel that at the present stage of development its conclusions cannot be applied to decisions in the water-resource field. For this there are several reasons.

First, decision theory does not so much solve the difficulties as shift their locale. It makes deciding among alternatives easy at the cost of requiring us to determine a scale of utilities in a particular way. To appreciate the severity of this requirement, try to visualize a water-district meeting at which government experts try to ascertain the sense of the meeting with respect to a long list of options like those in Tables 8 and 9. In effect, this approach replaces the problem of choosing among the actual alternatives with a number of artificial-choice problems, each of which is simpler than the actual one (which is to the good) but also more artificial (which is to the bad).

The second objection to the decision-theory approach pertains more to principle. It assumes that there is no cost of uncertainty *per se*. This is implicit in the postulate that all options with the same expected utility are indifferent regardless of the spread of possible results. To see where the cost of uncertainty has its impact, consider Table 6 again. If two-thirds of the water is released, the members of the district can count on returns of at least $140,000 whatever happens and can plan their affairs with the assurance that funds to this extent will be forthcoming. But if only one-third of the water is released, the members are assured of only $130,000. Under no circumstances can they undertake obligations costing $292,000, still less $400,000. Their arrangements must provide for the possibility of the least favorable outcome. This consideration indicates that any income expected with assurance is more valuable, because it can be utilized more fully, than that same income resulting from an uncertain situation.

Another way to see the same point is to turn to Table 8 or 9 and suppose that one of the conditions of the choice is that the chooser will not be informed for several months whether the right- or the left-hand column is to be applicable. This delay is of no consequence if he chooses option 0, but in every other option the utility of the more favorable result is diminished by the fact that no firm plans for employing it can be made. The utility of any physical or monetary option depends not only on the possible outcomes and their probabilities, but also on the promptness with which the result of the choice will be known. The procedure given for evaluating the utilities of options makes no allowance for this fact. Thus in equation 1 the symbol $u(300)$ stands for the utility of $300,000 received as the favorable outcome of an uncertain situation, whereas in equation 2 the same symbol denotes the utility of $300,000 for certain. It is illegitimate to assume, as we have done, that these two utilities are the same.

Since a substantial delay in learning the results of uncertain situations is inherent in the uncertainties encountered in water-resource planning, the technique of utility scaling will tend to yield unduly high estimates of certainty equivalents by ignoring the cost of uncertainty. This is regrettable because, as we have said, where the techniques of decision theory apply, uncertain alternatives can be ranked simply by computing the expected values of their consequences, measured in utility units; if decision theory cannot be applied, a judgement must somehow be made as to whether an alternative with higher expected value but more uncertainty is or is not preferable to one with lower expected value and lower uncertainty. There seem to be no well-established rules for making such judgements. Nevertheless, since such judgements must be made, we turn to the discussion of a number of expedients that seem to be useful for the purpose.

More traditional approaches

There are three time-honored approaches to the problem of uncertainty that occur repeatedly in the literature of economics although, as we shall see, all are too vague to constitute usable solutions to the problem.

Certainty equivalents. The simplest, and vaguest, is the concept of a 'certainty equivalent'. The idea is that to every uncertain situation there corresponds some riskless one that is indifferent to it. For example, consider the situation resulting from releasing one-third of the water in the reservoir, as in Table 6. The members of the water district presumably would prefer that situation to a guaranteed yield of $130,000 but, at the other extreme, would prefer a guaranteed yield of $400,000 to the uncertain situation. Between these two extremes there must be some guaranteed yield, perhaps $250,000, which would content them just as well as the risky situation. This is its certainty equivalent. Where a choice is to be made among a number of uncertain situations, the one with the highest certainty equivalent should be selected.

This concept is clearly close to the one we used in deriving the von Neumann utility function but is free of its defect of introducing an artificial intermediate choice. However, it really begs the question at issue, since the problem of ascertaining certainty equivalents is simply the problem of evaluating uncertain situations in thin disguise, and what we are seeking is a rational basis for solving either of these problems.

Gambler's indifference map. A somewhat more elaborate version of the uncertainty equivalent is the 'gambler's indifference map'. Suppose, for simplicity, that all that matters in an uncertain situation is the expected value and the standard deviation of its probability distribution. Then the essence of any uncertain situation can be represented by a point on a graph with axes that measure expected value and standard deviation. Each of the crosses in Figure 1 represents an uncertain situation in this

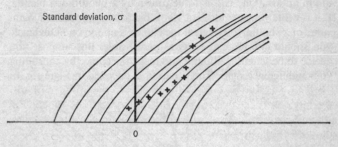

Figure 1 Representation of an uncertainty situation by a gambler's indifference map

manner. This form of diagram derives its name from the curved lines that have been drawn in, each of which connects a family of expected-value–standard-deviation pairs that are indifferent to one another; as we move along any of these lines, the increase in expected value is just sufficient to compensate for the increase in standard deviation or riskiness. The shape of these lines is purely hypothetical; all one can feel confident of *a priori* is that they slope upward to the right. If the crosses represent a number of alternatives from which one is to be selected, the one marked *A* should be chosen, since it lies on a more desirable indifference curve than any of the others. The certainty equivalent of any uncertain situation can be read from a gambler's indifference map by tracing back the indifference curve on which its expected-value–standard-deviation point lies until the curve reaches the axis of abscissas. Thus a gambler's indifference map is a device for determining certainty equivalents. It has, however, more predictive content than the certainty-equivalent concept itself, because once the indifference map for an individual or group has been determined, the certainty equivalent of any new risky situation can be ascertained by plotting its first two moments on the map.

Unfortunately, it is generally impracticable to establish gambler's indifference maps, and, besides, the concept contains a fundamental logical inconsistency which is disclosed by the following example. Suppose that P white balls and Q black balls are in an urn. One ball is to be drawn by a blindfolded blonde. If it is white you get x dollars, if it is black you get nothing. What value of x should you select if the choice is up to you? Obviously you should choose x as large as permissible. But suppose you decide to be scientific about it and make the choice by consulting your indifference map. The situation is depicted in Figure 2. In

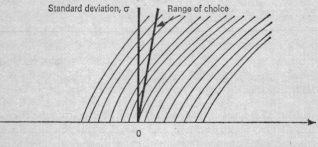

Figure 2 Gambler's indifference map for the paradoxical problem

drawing this diagram, we assume that the slopes of the indifference curves are everywhere positive. The line representing the range of choice is computed from the formulas for the expected value and standard deviation of this chance event as functions of x, which are

$$\mu = \text{expected value} = x\left[\frac{P}{P+Q}\right]$$

and $\quad \sigma = \text{standard deviation} = x\sqrt{\frac{PQ}{(P+Q)^2}}$

or $\quad \sigma = \mu\sqrt{\frac{Q}{P}}.$

By choosing a large enough ratio of black balls to white, we can make the range-of-choice line as steep as desired. In particular it can be made steeper than any of the indifference curves, as drawn. But when this is done, the point on the line that touches the most preferable indifference curve attainable corresponds to $x = 0$, which we already know to be the least desirable point on the line. Hence the use of indifference curves has led to a nonsensical recommendation. This shows that, more generally speaking, an analysis based on the principle of the gambler's indifference map can lead to the adoption of an inadmissible alternative.

Risk-discounting. The third traditional expedient for dealing with uncertainty in economics is 'risk-discounting'. In this approach the certainty equivalent to a risky venture is computed by multiplying the expected value of the outcome by a factor between zero and one which is proportionately smaller as the risk is higher. A typical risk-discount factor is $1/(1+c\sigma)$, where σ denotes the standard deviation of outcomes and c is a behavioral constant which we shall consider in a moment. By this discount formula, if the expected net benefits of a plan are denoted by μ, its risk-discounted net benefits, or certainty equivalent, is $\mu/(1+c\sigma)$. Differentiating this formula shows readily that $c/(1+c\sigma)$ is the percentage increase in expected net benefits necessary to compensate for a one-unit increase in the standard deviation of the outcome distribution, so that c expresses the additional enticements required to compensate for additional risks.

The risk-discounting approach has the formal merit that it fits in very well with ordinary interest-discounting when, as is frequently the case, time streams of net benefits are at issue. Indeed it is a quite common presumption in economics that the rate of return payable by a risky loan or venture must be greater than the rate payable by a safe loan. For example, one would expect that normally the yields on common stocks would be greater than those on high-grade bonds. Thus in computing the present value of the benefits anticipated from a risky venture, one might apply a rate of discount of the form $r+c\sigma$, where r is the rate of interest on a very safe investment and $c\sigma$ is a risk premium which increases in proportion to σ. Of course, a more elaborate function of the standard deviation might also be used and is frequently preferred to the simple linear one. This device has the effect of sharply reducing the present value of net benefits expected with uncertainty in the remote future, while it reduces the present value of early-maturing benefits only mildly. The logic of this differential treatment (which, it should be noted, does not depend on the fact that the standard deviations of anticipated benefits may increase with distance) is open to some question.

Efforts to overcome defects of traditional approaches. The short-coming common to all three of these traditional approaches to the problem of uncertainty is that they contain no hint of how rationally to adjust expected values for uncertainty – for example, of how to determine the parameter c of the risk-discount formula. There have been a number of attempts to fill this gap, of which we shall mention two.

In some uncertain situations there is a discontinuity in the list of outcomes such that some possible outcomes are considered catastrophically bad, while the others range from mildly bad on up. In such cases an appealing basis for choice is to select the alternative that has the smallest probability of a disastrous outcome. For example, using the data of Table 6, if a yield of $130,000 or less is considered catastrophic, this principle would recommend spilling two-thirds of the contents of the reservoir; for with this decision the probability of reaching the disaster level is zero, while with either of the other alternatives it is 0·4. If the disaster level is $140,000 or greater, however, the first two alternatives are indifferent, and the same is true if the disaster level is less than $130,000. This example shows that this basis for decision disregards a great deal of information about each alternative; indeed, it utilizes only a single point in its probability distribution.

An approximation to the disaster-level approach can be based upon the expected value and standard deviation of the outcome distribution. Let μ_i and σ_i denote the expected value and standard deviation, respectively, of the probability distribution corresponding to the ith alternative, and let D be the disaster level. Then, generally speaking, the probability of a result as bad as the disaster level is a decreasing function of $(\mu_i - D)/\sigma_i$. Therefore one can minimize the probability of experiencing the disaster level by choosing the alternative for which this ratio is as large as possible. Under this approach the indifference curves are the loci of (μ, σ) satisfying $(\mu - D)/\sigma =$ constant. Figure 3 illustrates such

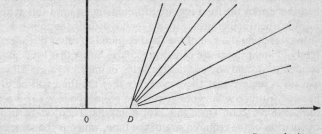

Figure 3 Gambler's indifference map for minimizing the probability of disaster, where D represents the disaster level

an indifference map. Note the peculiarity that all (μ, σ) points have the same certainty equivalent, namely D. Thus the disaster-minimization approach implies and determines a gambler's indifference map on rational grounds.

It can, however, lead to ridiculous results. Let us apply it, for example, to the data of Table 7 with a disaster level of $100,000. The critical ratio for releasing one-third of the water is 1·45, for releasing two-thirds of the water it is 1·90, but for releasing all the water it is infinite. The last alternative wins handsomely, although we know it to be inadmissible.

Another method for deducing a gambler's indifference map from rational considerations has been suggested by H. A. Thomas, Jr, specifically for application to the design of water-resource systems. This approach stems from the idea that the net benefits yielded by any installation are the present value of its gross benefits minus the present value of its costs, where the costs include the cost of any uncertainties inherent in the project. The crux of the method is the device for measuring the cost of uncertainty. Imagine that at the time the system is constructed an equalization fund is established with the understanding that in any year when actual benefits fall short of expected benefits the fund will be used to make up the difference, while in any year when actual benefits exceed expected benefits the excess will be used to replenish the fund. Thus, provided that the fund is adequate, the users of the project will receive precisely the expected benefits in every year. This device converts a risky situation into a fully insured one. The cost of the uncertainty is then just the size of the fund required to obliterate it, and this statement is true whether or not such a fund is actually established.

In estimating the size of the fund required to offset the uncertainty of any project, we cannot, of course, insist that it be large enough to sustain any imaginable string of unlucky years. All we can do is require that the probability that the fund will be exhausted within the time horizon of the project be low, say 5 per cent or 1 per cent. Once this probability has been established, calculation of the required size of the fund, which is the same as the cost of the uncertainty, is a purely actuarial problem, although a difficult one. When the size of the fund has been computed for each alternative design, it can be added to the construction and operating costs, and that design can be adopted for which the excess of expected net benefits over total costs, calculated in this way, is greatest.

If some plausible simplifying assumptions are made, it can be shown that the size of the fund required to hold the probability of exhaustion down to any specified level is proportional to the standard deviation of the distribution of outcomes in a single year. Specifically, the formula for the net benefits B of a project is approximately

$$B = \mu - \frac{v_\alpha \sigma}{\sqrt{(2r)}},$$

where μ is the present value of the expected benefits minus the present value of expected costs, v_α is the normal deviate with probability a of being exceeded, a is the specified probability that the fund will be exhausted, σ is the standard deviation of the single-year outcome distribution, and r is the rate of interest earned by the equalization fund. The second term in this formula is the cost of the uncertainty. Since all designs with the same value of B are indifferent, in terms of a gambler's indifference map the indifference curves are straight lines with slope $\sqrt{2r}/v_\alpha$, as shown in Figure 4.

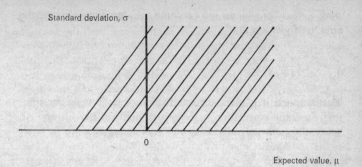

Standard deviation, σ

0

Expected value, μ

Figure 4 Gambler's indifference map for the equalization fund method

To illustrate this approach, let us apply it to the data of Table 7 assuming an interest rate of 4 per cent and an exhaustion probability of 0·05. Then $\sqrt{2r} = 0·283$, $v_\alpha = 1·645$, and the cost of uncertainty is $5·8\sigma$. For the three plans considered, these costs are approximately $765,000, $342,000, and zero, respectively. Converting to an annual basis by taking 4 per cent of each and subtracting from the annual expected values shown in the table gives approximately $261,000, $198,000, and $80,000 for the annual net benefits of the three plans, allowing for the cost of uncertainty. Releasing one-third of the water in the reservoir is clearly the best policy.

Multiperiod decision problems

At this stage it will be useful to take account of the fact that a decision is likely to have consequences that extend over a considerable period of time. A decision regarding the capacity of a reservoir, for example, is of this nature. The consequences of such a decision are not a single yield but rather a sequence of yields, one for each year of the life of the project. These yields will not be exactly predictable, but each will be a random variable with a probability distribution that depends on the original decision (for example, as to the size of the reservoir), as well as on other factors.

Any particular stream of yields can be reduced to a present value by applying a discount factor. If r denotes the rate of interest used in discounting, y_t denotes the yield in the tth year, and T years are taken into account, the present value of the stream of yields u is

$$u = \sum_{t=1}^{T} \frac{y_t}{(1+r)^t}.$$

Furthermore, if $\bar{y}_t$ is the expected value of y_t, σ_t^2 is its variance, and δ_{st} is the correlation between the yields in the sth and tth years, the expected value $E(u)$ and variance σ_u^2 of u are

$$E(u) = \sum_{t=1}^{T} \frac{\bar{y}_t}{(1+r)^t}$$

and

$$\sigma_u^2 = \sum_{s=1}^{T} \sum_{t=1}^{T} \frac{\delta_{st}\sigma_s\sigma_t}{(1+r)^{s+t}}.$$

If the present value of the yields is all that matters, a plausible simplification (although somewhat dangerous, as we shall see below), then $E(u)$ and σ_u for each plan can be graphed on an indifference map and the most favorable plan chosen, just as before. If the correlations between yields in different years are small and T is sufficiently large, things are even simpler. In that case σ_u will be small in relation to $E(u)$, and $E(u)$ itself is sufficient to determine the optimal plan. This is the case of actuarial risk.

The assumption that the present value of an income stream is all that concerns the recipients, while plausible, is not innocuous. For example, even in an income stream with a high present value the variances of some of its components may be so great that a run of bad luck for a few years will endanger the solvency of the recipients. In such a case the risk of insolvency at some stage has to be taken into account, and Thomas' device for measuring it by estimating the required size of a disaster-insurance fund becomes necessary.

One characteristic of uncertain time streams that we have not yet taken into account is that they afford enough time for decisions to be revised. This simultaneously decreases their riskiness and complicates the analysis. An essential feature of uncertain time streams is that at least some of the decisions that have to be made can be postponed until relevant data have been accumulated. In the case of our irrigation district, for example, it may be necessary to decide on the capacity of the reservoir once and for all, but thereafter the amount of water to be released in each month, or in even shorter periods, need not be decided until information is available on the current contents of the reservoir, short-run predictions of inflow, and so on. Thus an element of sequential decision-making enters the problem. To be sure, these sequential decisions typically relate to operating procedure rather than to design,[10] but the criterion for appraising a design must be the yields it will afford when managed by a good operating procedure. One might even say that the best design is the one that permits use of the best possible operating procedure.

The analysis of operating procedures or sequential decision problems, which has a large literature under such headings as inventory theory, queuing theory, and dynamic programming, is too technical and elaborate to be discussed here at any length.[11] The central problem is whether resources available at present (water, in our context) should be used in the current period or saved for later employment. The most promising line of attack is to divide the entire future history of the undertaking into a sequence of periods, each of some convenient length like a month or a year. The number of periods may be either finite or infinite.

The analysis then proceeds by considering time horizons of different length. If the horizon is only one period long, the problem is of a familiar sort. A little notation will be helpful at this stage. Let R denote the quantity of resources available at the beginning of the period and z the quantity used. There will be some functional relationship between the benefits yielded and the quantity of resources used; denote it by $f_1(z)$. The one-period problem, then, is to choose the value of z that makes $f_1(z)$ as large as possible where the range of permissible choices of z depends

10. Sequential decision-making often enters design problems more directly, as when the construction of a system will be spread out over a considerable period of time. Then the exact timing and design of the later units need not be decided when construction of the first units is begun, but the early units should be planned so that the later components can be added efficiently and economically when they appear desirable. For further discussion of stage construction and related possibilities, see chapter 4 [not included here]

11. These matters, especially queuing theory, are discussed further in chapter 14 [not included here].

on R. Now the optimal z and the corresponding net benefits are both functions of the resources available, so we may denote the maximum attainable net benefits in a single period by $f_1^*(R)$, a function of the quantity of resources available. As we shall see, this function is fundamental to the solution of the multiperiod problem.

With this background we can advance to the two-period case. Let us suppose again that R units of resources are available at the outset and z_1 units are used in the first period. Then the benefits during the first period are $f_1(z_1)$, and the resources available at the beginning of the second period will be $R - z_1$ plus the quantity of resources received during the first period. Denote the quantity of resources received by x_1, and assume that it is a random variable. Then the second period begins with resources amounting to $R - z_1 + x_1$ and, utilizing the concepts introduced in the preceding paragraph, we see that the maximum attainable benefits in the second period are $f_1^*(R - z_1 + x_1)$.

To find the present value of net benefits for both periods together, discount the second period's benefits at an appropriate rate of interest r, and add to the first period's benefits to obtain $f_1(z_1) + [f_1^*(R - z_1 + x_1)]/(1 + r)$. Unfortunately this formula cannot be evaluated at the time that the first period's utilization must be determined, since x_1 generally will not be known at that time. Its expected value can be computed, however, and the expected value of the benefits of the two periods together corresponding to a use of z_1 units in the first period is

$$f_2(z_1) = f_1(z_1) + \frac{E f_1^*(R - z_1 + x_1)}{1 + r},$$

where E denotes expected value. If x_1 has the probability distribution $p(x_1)$, then

$$E f_1^*(R - z_1 + x_1) = \int_{-\infty}^{\infty} f_1^*(R - z_1 + x_1) p(x_1) \, dx_1$$

and
$$f_2(z_1) = f_1(z_1) + \int_{-\infty}^{\infty} \frac{f_1^*(R - z_1 + x_1) p(x_1) \, dx_1}{1 + r}.$$

This formula says that the net benefits in two periods, if R units of resources are available initially and z_1 units are used in the first period, is the sum of two parts. The first part is the net benefits yielded by z_1 units used in the first period; the second is the discounted expected value of the maximum net benefits attainable in the second period. The first part is a basic datum of the problem, the one-period production function. The second part is an integral, or sum, involving a given probability distribution and a function $f_1^*(R-z_1+x_1)$ that has been determined by analysis of the one-period case. Thus we can find the permissible value of z_1 that maximizes the sum. It will depend on R, of course, and so will the maximum value of the sum, which we can now denote by $f_2^*(R)$.

In the three-period case the only decision that has to be made at the outset is again the value of z_1, the quantity of resources to be used in the first period. As before, the expected benefits resulting from any choice of z_1 can be written

$$f_3(z_1) = f_1(z_1) + \frac{Ef_2^*(R-z_1+x_1)}{1+r},$$

where the second term uses the function that was determined in the analysis of the two-period case. Thus we can proceed recursively and write for the t-period case with initial resources R

$$f_t(z_1) = f_1(z_1) + \frac{Ef_{t-1}^*(R-z_1+x_1)}{1+r},$$

where $f_t(z_1)$ is the net benefit in t periods resulting from the use of z_1 units of resources in the first period and optimal use of resources in the $t-1$ periods remaining. Since the second term was determined in the preceding step, the maximum attainable net benefits for the t periods is the maximum of this function with respect to z_1 and can be denoted by $f_t^*(R)$.

The foregoing exposition has assumed that the single-period net-benefit function is the same for all the periods considered. This assumption has served merely to simplify the notation a bit, but now we shall make a substantive use of it. We have repeatedly remarked that in each case the optimal value of z_1 is a function of the available resources R. If z_1^* is this optimal value, we can denote this relationship by $z_1^* = g_t(R)$, introducing the subscript because the function will be different, in general, for different time horizons. But if the successive periods are identical, it can be shown[12] that the functions $g_t(R)$ gradually change less as t increases, and approach some limiting function $g(R)$. This function, $g(R)$, is then the optimal operating procedure – the relationship between first-period releases and available resources – for a long or infinite time horizon. With luck, the ultimate function $g(R)$ is approached fairly quickly in the first few iterations so that it is not necessary to repeat the analysis just sketched 50 times for a 50-year horizon, or 600 times for a 600-month horizon.

In principle, this method of solution is sound and appealing; in practice, the required computations are very difficult to carry out, especially if some of the functions are stochastic. In general, therefore, this mode of analysis is more useful for formulating problems and guiding intuition than for actually deriving solutions.

Loss functions. In view of these difficulties a much simpler approach is used frequently in the following chapters to allow for some of the uncertainties that enter into designing water-resource installations for use over many periods. This approach consists in dividing the actual benefits yielded each year into two parts, a 'normal benefit' and a 'loss'. The normal benefit is the benefit obtained when the quantity of water for which the project was designed is available and used. The loss is the discrepancy between the normal benefit and the actual benefit which results when the quantity of water available departs from the design amount. Since the consequences of a water shortage are in general more marked than those of a surplus, the emphasis in this concept is on the loss side; but it should be kept in mind that when water is more abundant than it normally is, the 'loss' can be negative.

The reason for distinguishing between normal benefits and losses is that the normal amount of water and discrepancies from it affect benefits in different ways. The installations of both a water project and its customers are designed to make use of a certain amount of water, expected to be available in most years. Neither the project nor its customers are prepared to take full advantage of any overage that may occur, and the customers in particular stand to suffer losses when the water supply falls short of the amount required for normal operations. The relationship

12. See R. Bellman (1957, ch. 4).

between the amount of the loss and the discrepancy between the actual water availability and the normal quantity will be referred to as the 'loss function'.

As an illustration of a loss function suppose that irrigation water is worth $6 per acre foot when supplied in the amount planned for and that, on this basis, laterals are installed, land cleared, and other measures taken. Suppose also that when installations and improvements are made and the anticipated volume of water is not forthcoming the losses amount to $12 per acre foot of deficiency. If, however, the water supply in any year is superabundant, let us say that the additional benefits are worth only $1 per acre foot. Then if Y_n denotes the normal supply of water for which the irrigation system was designed and Y_t is the actual supply in the tth year, we may summarize these data by the benefit formula:

Benefit in year $t = 6Y_n - 12(Y_n - Y_t)^+ + (Y_t - Y_n)^+,$

where we use the notation $(y)^+ = \max(0, y)$. In this formula $6Y_n$ is the normal benefit and $12(Y_n - Y_t)^+ - (Y_t - Y_n)^+$ is the loss function.

More generally, using the same notation, we can write

$B(Y_n, Y_t) = N(Y_n) - L(Y_n - Y_t),$

indicating that the normal benefits N depend on Y_n alone, the loss L depends on the difference between Y_n and Y_t, and the actual benefits B depend on both Y_n and Y_t. The expected benefits $B_{\exp}$ are then

$B_{\exp}(Y_n, Y_t) = N(Y_n) - L_{\exp}(Y_n - Y_t).$

Generally speaking, the expected loss $L_{\exp}(Y_n - Y_t)$ will be an increasing function of two factors: the excess of Y_n over the expected value of Y_t, and the standard deviation of Y_t. The introduction of the loss function, therefore, has the effect of diminishing estimated benefits in response to variability and consequently makes some allowance for this aspect of uncertainty. Because of its relative simplicity, this concept will be used many times in the present volume.

One final word about uncertainty. In the latter part of this discussion we have assumed that although precise results of decisions could not be foretold, their probability distributions were known or could be estimated with tolerable accuracy. This may be the case where the uncertainty results from physical phenomena, like hydrologic conditions, concerning which adequate records and experience are available. It is not likely to be so if, for instance, the uncertainty is generated by economic or political phenomena. If the probability distributions resulting from different decisions are not known, we are thrown back on the conundrums considered earlier in this discussion. Then, as we say, it is by no means clear how to formulate an objective function or measure of merit, let alone how to find its maximum, and rational decision-making becomes very difficult indeed.

In this long discussion of decision-making under uncertainty we have been compelled to point out flaws and shortcomings in every solution that has been proposed. One would hope that this will not always be the case, and that some day satisfactory solutions will be found to this pervasive and fundamental problem. At present, however, the problem of uncertainty is clouded by uncertainty.

References

BELLMAN, R. (1957), *Dynamic Programming*, Princeton University Press.
CRAMER, H. (1955), *The Element of Probability*, Wiley.
DORFMAN, R., SAMUELSON, P. A., and SOLOW, R. M. (1958), *Linear Programming and Economic Analysis*, McGraw-Hill.
VON NEUMANN, J., and MORGENSTERN, O. (1947), *Theory of Games and Economic Behavior*, Princeton University Press, 2nd edn; 3rd edn, 1953.

Part Five
The Treatment of Income Distribution

If constraints exist that prevent the optimal redistribution of
income by cash transfers, the income distribution aspects
of projects cannot be ignored. Weisbrod puts forward one
possible method for valuing benefits and costs accruing to
different groups in the community.

16 B. A. Weisbrod

Deriving an Implicit Set of Governmental Weights
for Income Classes

B. A. Weisbrod, 'Income redistribution effects and benefit-cost analysis',
in S. B. Chase, Jr. (ed.), *Problems in Public Expenditure Analysis*,
The Brookings Institution, 1968, pp. 177–209.

What can economics – as a science – say about whether a particular government expenditure program is or is not desirable? Welfare economics – the branch of economics concerned explicitly with the application of economics to policy issues – divides the question into two analytically separate parts: (1) is the program economically 'efficient', and (2) are the income-redistributive effects (if any) 'desirable'? For reasons that will be discussed shortly, advice given by economists to decision-makers tends to be restricted to questions of the first type. At the same time, actual decisions do, and should, also reflect answers to questions of the second type. As a result, economists often are disappointed that their advice carries little weight, and decision-makers are disappointed that economists do not provide more complete advice.

The state of affairs just sketched forms the background for this paper, which concentrates on the proper role of distributional considerations in a benefit-cost framework. In so doing, however, the paper necessarily touches on a number of other complex issues that cannot be resolved here. One is the relevance of the benefit–cost ratio in determining whether a project should be undertaken. This and other issues of appropriate investment criteria have been discussed elsewhere.[1] The use of such ratios here is not intended as support for them under all circumstances.

1. See, for example, Hirshleifer (1958, pp. 329–52); and McKean (1958).

The paper is in three sections. The first considers the conceptual case for integrating income-distributional effects and allocative-efficiency effects in the evaluation of public expenditure projects. The second and third sections present some methods by which this might be achieved. Empirical approaches are set forth and utilized in an illustrative manner, in the hope that if any are promising, additional analytic work will be undertaken and additional data gathered to implement them.

Efficiency and equity: a case for their integration

The distinction between 'efficiency' and 'equity' is often analytically useful, but it is nonetheless arbitrary. If efficiency were viewed broadly as measurable by the difference between all the advantages (benefits) and all the disadvantages (costs) of a program, the equity or distributional effects of an expenditure program could be viewed as a subset of the 'grand-efficiency' effects. To the extent that equity effects were favorable, they could, in principle, be included in the benefits of the program, and to the extent they were unfavorable they could be included among the costs. The problem, of course, is placing a value upon such favorable or unfavorable effects so that they will be commensurable with other costs and benefits. To date, valuation of distributional effects of public expenditure programs has eluded economists, although it cannot be said that many attempts have been made to deal with the issue in recent decades.[2]

Distributional-equity effects are by no means the only conceptually relevant program effects that raise severe problems of valuation. The valuation of a human life – important in the analysis of benefits from health, flood control, and highway safety programs – is also a very thorny matter, as is the valuation of the 'psychic' benefits from education or manpower retraining

2. The conceptual relevance of distributional effects has been pointed out by various writers, although there has been little empirical work. Otto Eckstein notes that 'one of the criteria on which a project must be judged, and which benefit-cost analysis disregards altogether, is the redistribution of income which a project brings about'. (See Eckstein, 1961a, p. 17.) Robert H. Haveman has dealt intensively and quantitatively with the geographical-income distribution effects of water resource projects. (See Haveman, 1965.) Nearly ten years ago John Krutilla provided estimates of the distribution,

programs. Yet economists have not refused to grapple with the human life problem, and progress is being made.[3] Neither should distributional effects be neglected simply because economists are not ready to deal with them neatly.

If 'costs' and 'benefits' are regarded as synonyms for 'advantages' and 'disadvantages' – as they should be – then it is clear that there is no logical basis for the separation of efficiency from equity. Moreover, the conventionality of the distinction, while it does have its uses, has had the unfortunate effect of directing research away from the identification and measurement of distributional equity – and has perversely imparted the connotations of 'economic' and 'scientific' to efficiency questions, and 'noneconomic' and 'nonscientific' to equity considerations. It has thereby provided a misleading rationale for neglect of both theoretical and empirical research into the latter type of problem.

To be sure, the efficiency-equity distinction, though it has no compelling logical foundation, can be defended on pragmatic grounds. Standards of distributional equity may be changeable over time, variable among people at any given point in time, and in any event difficult to discover. Thus it may have been wise research strategy for economists to avoid them. On the other hand, perhaps the time has come for a reappraisal of the strategy. There is no doubt that the efficiency-equity division is extremely

---

both among income classes and geographic regions, of a particular river basin project's costs and benefits. '. . . although we have concentrated on questions of economic efficiency, we cannot ignore the redistributive consequences and the issues which these raise in terms of equity.' John V. Krutilla and Otto Eckstein (1958, p. 200). Chapters 7 and 8 of the volume deal, respectively, with the distributions of costs and of gains expected from development of the Willamette River in Oregon. See also McKean (1958, esp. pp. 206–8 and 240–43), where some indications of the effects on regional wealth distribution of two specific water projects are presented. In general, McKean preferred 'to have the cost-benefit measurements shed light on efficiency in th[e] *limited sense*, [while having] . . . further exhibits shed light on redistributional effects.' *Ibid.*, p. 133; italics added.

For an excellent treatment at the conceptual level of ways by which distributional factors might be taken into account by decision makers, see Stephen A. Marglin (1962, esp. pp. 78–81).

3. Thomas Schelling (1968) deals with the valuation of reduced mortality rates. Among other attempts to value human life are Louis Israel Dublin and A. J. Lotka (1930); J. R. Walsh (1935); and Burton A. Weisbrod (1961).

valuable as a device for breaking a complex problem into more manageable parts. Economists have simply neglected to put the parts back together.

Until means are developed for valuing distributional effects, their importance to policy makers makes it clear that economists who undertake or advise about benefit-cost analyses should at least spell out and discuss the forms of redistributive effects of a program, even if the end product of the research fails to place a value (positive or negative) on those effects.

There is some evidence that congressional appropriations actually do reflect recognition of one type of distributional effect – the geographic impact of federal expenditures. Robert Haveman recently examined the twenty-nine water resource projects out of 150 authorized in 1960 that received appropriations in the succeeding appropriation bill. He points out that 'if the budget of 133 million dollars which was committed to the twenty-nine projects . . . was allocated most efficiently . . . no project having a benefit–cost ratio of less than 1·8 would be chosen . . .'.[4] Actually, eleven projects with lower ratios, involving $69 million, were chosen. Projects from particular geographic regions seemed to be selected in spite of relatively low measures of efficiency.

Notwithstanding the clear theoretical relevance of distributional effects, it is the exceptional benefit-cost analysis – regardless of type of project – that considers them explicitly.[5] Indeed, according to a recent survey of the literature on benefit-cost analysis, it almost seems wrong to consider distributional effects: 'In other words, we have to eliminate the purely transfer or distributional items from a cost-benefit evaluation . . .' (Prest and Turvey, 1965, p. 688). Elsewhere in the paper, however, the authors recognize that ' . . . when the authorities . . . do clearly care about income distribution . . . the analyst will have to set out not only total costs and benefits but also the costs and benefits for those particular groups whose economic welfare is of interest to the decision-maker' (p. 701).

4. Haveman (1965, p. 49; also tables 2 and 4, pp. 44, 48).
5. In two papers presented at the first Brookings Institution conference on government expenditures, references were made to the desirability of taking distributional considerations into account. See Jerome Rothenberg (1965, p. 294) and Burton Weisbrod (1965, pp. 136–7).

They go on to say that concern about distributional effects can be taken into account, at least formally, by introducing constraints (restrictions). Thus, they suggest that net benefits may be maximized 'subject to constraints on benefits less costs of particular groups' or, alternatively, net gains to a particular group may be maximized 'subject to a constraint relating to total benefits and costs'.[6]

There are two objections to either proposal. First, neither approach suggests what the form of constraints ought to be. Second, neither approach focuses attention on trade-offs between better distributional effects and greater economic efficiency.

It is for these reasons that the present paper urges greater efforts to develop weights for various groups of people so that benefits (and costs) of a distributional sort can be integrated with those of a real (or economic efficiency) sort. Such a development of what was termed above a 'grand-efficiency' measure would permit choosing between projects of which one had better distributional consequences and the other was more efficient in the narrow sense of the term.

The possibility that considerations of economic efficiency and distributional equity might be integrated – that is, stated in commensurable terms such that sacrifices in one could be compared with improvements in the other – was discussed by Stephen Marglin as another way, in addition to using constraints, to introduce the objective of income-distributional effects into a criterion of choice. Although he did not attempt to cope with the matter operationally, he pointed out that if policy-makers indicated their willingness 'to sacrifice efficiency for redistribution . . . planners would formulate designs to maximize a weighted sum of redistribution and efficiency, the weights representing the pre-assigned values of the opportunity costs' (Marglin, 1962, p. 79). This 'weighted sum' is precisely what is termed in this paper 'grand efficiency', and the 'opportunity costs' are the indicators of relative importance of a marginal dollar to each group – that is, the 'weights' referred to above.

Is there a theoretical justification for leaving distributional considerations out of project evaluations? Several alternative

6. *ibid*. Also see Marglin (1962) for discussions of these approaches.

explanations may be given for the traditional disregard of distributional effects.

1. The marginal utility of income is taken to be essentially equal for all people, and so, as a consequence, a dollar of additional income is equally valuable to all people, as is the burden of an additional dollar of cost.

2. The effect of any one project on the distribution of income is considered inconsequential, or the overall distributional effects of all projects are thought to be neutral, and may therefore be disregarded.

3. Economists, as scientists, are unwilling to make any explicit assumptions regarding the relative importance of a marginal dollar of benefits (or of costs) to different people. This reticence, which I regard as the primary explanation of the disregard for distributional effects, means that the implicit assumption has been that the marginal importances are all equal – that is, a dollar's worth of marginal income or cost has been given an equal weight (equal to one) regardless of the people who received that benefit or who bore the cost. This implicit assumption cannot bear scrutiny, however, and economists have simply made it for convenience.

4. Finally, one often encounters the view that any 'adverse' distributional effects of a given project can be undone – without costs – by means of a pure redistributional project and that any 'favorable' distributional effects are obtainable also without cost by means of a pure redistributional project. In other words, the assumptions are that the distribution of income (1) *can* be easily altered independently of any real-resource-using project, and (2) that it *will* be so altered if the occasion warrants. It follows, therefore, that any distributional effects of such a project may be disregarded in an analysis of the desirability of undertaking the project. This is, of course, essentially a statement of the Hicks-Kaldor position regarding the conditions under which a policy may be regarded as increasing economic welfare – a position which represented an attempt to separate the production aspects of economic policy from their distributional by-products.[7]

7. J. T. Hicks (1940); Nicholas Kaldor (1939). For a useful brief

The present paper is not the place for a detailed critical review of the development of modern welfare economics. Suffice it to say that whatever may be said in favor of this argument for separating distributional effects from efficiency and basing policy only on the latter, it is clearly unacceptable if pure, lump-sum transfers of income are not costless to undertake. If pure transfer projects do involve costs – administrative or political[8] – any unfavorable income-distributive by-product of a government investment project can be costly to undo, while any favorable effects will bring savings in the costs of an equivalent pure-redistribution project.

There is little to be gained by arguing whether economists are right or not in shunting income distribution considerations aside and concentrating efforts on so-called allocative-efficiency considerations. The fact remains that distributional considerations are relevant to political leaders and others in decision-making positions.[9] Therefore, when economists disregard these distributional considerations, they should not be surprised to find that their advice is not necessarily fully heeded by decision-makers. If economists refuse to examine distributional aspects of government expenditure programs – whether because the task is difficult or because, as some argue, this takes them outside the bounds of economics – they will retard the development of positive models for predicting actual political-economic behavior, and

summary of the theoretical welfare economics literature on this and related issues involving specification of the nature of the social welfare function to be optimized, see Otto Eckstein (1961b, pp. 440–45) and the sources cited therein.

8. For example, from a political standpoint, large direct transfers of income might not be acceptable even though the equivalent effects occurring as by-products of government investment projects were. As Marglin has noted, 'the community may not find it wholly satisfactory to achieve a given redistribution by simply transferring cash from one individual to another, even if this is administratively possible . . . the size of the economic pie and its division may not be the only factors of concern to the community – the method of slicing the pie may also be relevant' (1962, p. 63).

9. Jesse Burkhead's observation of several years ago warrants repetition: 'The public decision-maker does not proceed on the assumption that social goods are consumed equally by all. His assumption is quite the opposite – namely, that all government programs have distributional consequences....' 'Comment' on Roland N. McKean (1961, p. 362).

they will retard development of normative decision rules for determining appropriate choices.

An attempt to bring consideration of distributional factors into the mainstream of discussions regarding benefit-cost analyses seems, therefore, a worthwhile endeavor. Ideally – although the ideal is currently very far from realization – both distributional-equity considerations and allocative-efficiency considerations would be evaluated in commensurable terms so that every expenditure project would be evaluated in terms of grand efficiency.[10] The third section of this paper presents a possible technique by which a full integration of allocative efficiency and distributional equity could be approached. This involves estimation of a social welfare function – a functional form and a set of weights to translate changes in the well-being of individual persons into changes in the well-being of the group.

Since realization of this ideal is surely far in the future, we shall first consider, in the next section, a device that would facilitate consideration of distributional effects within a benefit-cost framework, even though it would fall short of the ideal measure, which is conceptually superior but operationally far more demanding.

The separate presentation of distributional effects

A useful, though modest, step in the direction of introducing distributional considerations explicitly into benefit-cost analyses would be for economists to supplement estimates of the total costs and benefits of a project with indications of how those totals are divided among the population.[11] If the distributional effects of a project are to be made explicit, however, there must be a decision concerning which distributional dimensions are worthy of consideration. There are numerous criteria by which the

10. Although a grand-efficiency measure would facilitate choice among competing government expenditure projects – that is, would aid in the allocation of a budget of predetermined size – it would not be directly helpful for determining the optimal size of that budget. Additional information first must be obtained about the distributional effects of private expenditures. It is certainly improper to base decisions on a comparison of the grand efficiency of government projects with the narrower allocative efficiency of private projects.

11. McKean has urged this approach. (See 1958, pp. 206–8, 240–43.

distributions could be categorized: income, age, race, sex, region, family size, religion and educational level cover only some of the more familiar ones.[12]

Two related questions – the first positive, the second normative – may be posed in this regard.

Which distributional criteria *do* decision-makers regard as relevant?

Which distributional criteria *should* they consider?

Insofar as the two questions have different answers, this paper concentrates on the first. However, a thorough inquiry into this question would be a major study, perhaps involving perusal of the stated legislative considerations and the justifications offered for a large number of diverse public expenditure programs. Short of undertaking such an investigation, it is suggested that four criteria receive most frequent note by political decision-makers in the Congress and administrative agencies; discussions of the desirability of aiding various segments of the population most often indicate concern about *income* groups, *age* groups, *racial* groups, and *geographic* areas. Thus, it would be useful to show how the benefits (and costs) of each project would be divided among these various groupings.[13]

Detailed subdivision of these groups is possible. However, whereas the resulting detail might be interesting and useful, the cost of obtaining the information would grow geometrically with respect to the number of subclasses, and the difficulty of showing the information would grow accordingly. Data presented for each of six income classes, six age classes, eight regions, and two races or colors would require a table with nearly 600 cells, and adding one more racial class would increase the number of cross-classifications by 50 per cent.

12. In principle, the distributions of both costs and benefits are of interest; however, in this paper emphasis is placed on the analysis of benefits. Since most expenditures may be regarded as financed by general revenue, the distribution of costs will tend to vary less among projects than will the distribution of benefits, and for this reason the benefit side seems more challenging. Nearly everything that is said about benefits, however, will also apply to costs.

13. It may be argued by some that of these groupings only income ought to count. Perhaps so, but this normative viewpoint aside, it seems clear that other groupings are, in fact, of interest to government decision-makers.

As a pragmatic compromise between the desire for full information and the cost of obtaining and displaying it, Table 1 is proposed as a basis for discussion. Two issues are involved in its evaluation: (1) the choice of major variables – age, region, income, color; and (2) the degrees of subdivision. The proposition is that if, in addition to data on aggregate real benefits (and costs), data were obtained on the distribution of those benefits from each project and were shown in such a table, the work of decision-makers would be facilitated. Both absolute and percentage distributions might be helpful. In considering this, or any other, general-purpose tabulation, one must recognize that no classificatory scheme will be perfectly satisfactory for all program areas.[14]

Table 1 Benefits of – project, by age, income, region, and color of beneficiary

Region and age	Income $0–$2999		Income $3000–$9999		Income $10,000 and over		Total
	White	Nonwhite	White	Nonwhite	White	Nonwhite	
North							
0 to 18 years							
19 to 64 years							
65 years and over							
South							
0 to 18 years							
19 to 64 years							
65 years and over							
West							
0 to 18 years							
19 to 64 years							
65 years and over							
Total							

The data to fill even this modest a table will rarely be fully available, and often not even partially. However, the feasibility of the approach, slightly modified, is illustrated by Tables 2 and 3, which display one possible estimate of the distribution of recrea-

14. The paper by James T. Bonnen (1968) uses a tabular presentation of benefit distributions of the general type proposed here.

Table 2 **Annual recreational benefits, Beaver Creek State Park, Ohio, project, by age, income, region, and color of beneficiary**

Region and age	Income $0–$2999		Income $3000 and over		Total
	White	Nonwhite	White	Nonwhite	
North					
0 to 18 years	$19,800	$2400	$59,400	$3100	$84,800 (39%)
19 to 64 years	27,300	3100	81,800	4000	116,200 (53%)
65 years and over	4100	300	12,300	400	17,100 (8%)
South					
0 to 18 years					
19 to 64 years					
65 years and over					
West					
0 to 18 years					
19 to 64 years					
65 years and over					
Total	51,200	5800	153,500	7500	219,000
Percentage of total	24	3	70	3	100

Note: Total annual recreational benefits are $219,000. *Beach Erosion Control Study of Ohio Shore Line of Lake Erie Between Vermilion and Sheffield Lake Village*, H. Doc. 229, 83 Cong. 1 sess. (1953). The distribution is arrived at by assuming that persons in the two counties (Lorain and Erie) nearest the park share in the benefits according to their proportion of the population, based on the 1960 U S Census. Figures are rounded and may not add to totals.

tional benefits from two water resource projects. They suggest, for example, that the Beaver Creek project is far more helpful, in terms of percentage of total benefits, to low-income persons in general, and to low-income children in particular, than is the Hammonasset project. However, as the notes to the tables make clear, the basis for this conclusion is a very questionable procedure for allocating aggregate benefits among population groups. It is rarely true that project benefits are actually distributed only to persons living in the vicinity, or that each such person benefits

Table 3 **Annual recreational benefits, Hammonasset State Park, Connecticut, project, by age, income, region, and color of beneficiary**

Region and age	Income $0-$2999		Income $3000 and over		Total
	White	Nonwhite	White	Nonwhite	
North					
0 to 18 years	$4800	$800	$48,500	$2100	$56,200 (36%)
19 to 64 years	7300	1000	74,300	2700	85,400 (55%)
65 years and over	1300	100	12,900	200	14,500 (9%)
South					
0 to 18 years					
19 to 64 years					
65 years and over					
West					
0 to 18 years					
19 to 64 years					
65 years and over					
Total	13,400	2000	135,700	5000	157,000
Percentage of total	9	1	87	3	100

Note: Total annual recreational benefits are $157,000. *Beach Erosion Control Study of Connecticut Shore Line Area 2, Hammonasset River to East River,* H. Doc. 474, 81 Cong. 2 sess. (1950). The distribution is arrived at by assuming that persons throughout the state share in the benefits according to their proportion of the population, based on the 1960 Census. The state-wide proportions were used here because the report points out that the park's drawing area includes most of the state. Figures are rounded and may not add to totals.

equally. Clearly, more study of this problem is needed. Especially helpful would be some empirically verified generalizations concerning the distribution of benefits according to type of project.

When useful estimates of the distribution of real benefits from a project cannot be obtained, an alternative may exist – namely, to show how much of the project expenditures were allocated for the benefit of each group in the table. This approach – measuring benefits by expenditures – is used in our national product accounting to estimate the contribution of the government sector. It is far from ideal, but there may be no better alternative at the time a decision is required. When applied to the distributional framework under discussion, it implies that each group receives benefits in proportion to the costs incurred on its behalf. Where costs are not divisible – the public goods case – this might be interpreted to mean that each group receives benefits equal or proportional to the fraction of total beneficiaries (users?) which members of this group constitute. Thus, the geographic distribution of benefits from a highway might be tentatively estimated from information on total costs and the fraction of total vehicle-miles (passenger-miles) traveled on the highway by people in each region, state, county, income group, age class, and so on. Similarly, the racial distribution of benefits from an education project might be estimated from information on the fraction of whites and of nonwhites participating in the project. The implicit assumption that all beneficiaries benefit equally is, however, certainly an oversimplification.

Displaying information on the distribution of a project's real costs and benefits, while useful, does not provide all the information on distributional effects that is relevant to the decision-maker. In addition, he would wish to know who the secondary or indirect gainers and losers were. For example, if the real benefits from two competing projects of equal cost were realized by high-income persons, but the additional real incomes were spent on the services of low-income persons in the case of project 1 but not in the case of project 2, then project 1 might be regarded as distributionally superior. Accordingly, that project could receive a higher priority even though it was less 'efficient', in the narrow sense.

Such thinking may be implicit in the decision by the Congress in 1965 to spend additional money on resource development in Appalachia as part of an antipoverty program. It was true that the incidence of 'poverty' was perhaps 50 per cent greater in Appalachia than in the United States as a whole, but it was also true that the poor were a clear minority even in Appalachia, and in addition it seemed clear that the real benefits would not accrue to the poor. Rather, the direct beneficiaries would probably include interstate truckers, who would benefit from reduced costs on the new roads, and relatively well-paid construction workers, who would be employed building the roads.

Even so, the secondary re-spending effects might well tend to benefit the poor to a greater degree than would have been the case if similar projects had been undertaken in more prosperous regions, simply because there were relatively more poor people in Appalachia.

Tracing these secondary effects through input and output markets is no mean task. Tracing them further according to region, income class, and so on, compounds problems at a geometric rate. Yet if we permit ourselves to be visionary there is no need to give up hope. Some success has already been achieved in the development of input-output tables, and more can be expected. In the meantime, judgements may have to suffice where empirical data would be preferable. Even so, agreement that judgements about the character of secondary distributional effects are relevant would itself be significant.

Apart from the cost of obtaining information, there seems to be no justification for disregarding the distributions of either the real or secondary effects. To disregard them is to assume implicitly that their importance is zero. However, real effects and secondary effects are in general not directly additive.

Integrating efficiency and equity

The method proposed in the preceding section would seem to be a useful device for showing certain distributional consequences of government programs. However, it falls short of the goal of introducing distributional effects into the benefit-cost framework in a manner that makes them commensurable with allocative-efficiency effects. The display method is a device for assisting decision-makers to allocate resources in a manner they regard as desirable, but it neither provides a basis for forecasting how resources actually will be allocated by the public sector, nor helps prescribe how they ought to be allocated.

To obtain full integration of distributional and allocative-efficiency considerations into a grand-efficiency measure – which would facilitate consideration of both actual and desirable marginal rates of substitution (trade-offs) between efficiency and equity – a Social Welfare Function (S W F) is required. This would set forth a relationship between the economic welfare of each member of the society and the economic welfare of the society as a whole.

In a democratic society the assumption may be made that the combined interests of the individual members of society constitute the interest of the 'society' – there being no such entity as the State, with its own separate interests. This being the case, the generalized Bergson S W F might be assumed,

$$W = f(w_1, w_2, \ldots, w_n),\qquad\qquad 1$$

where W is an indicator of total economic welfare and subscripts refer to specific individuals.

A further specification of the S W F might be as follows

$$W = w_1 + w_2 + \ldots + w_n.\qquad\qquad 2$$

Economic welfare of the whole society depends on the summation of individuals' economic welfare.

Moving toward the operational level, equation 2 might be rewritten in differential form, thereby directing attention to *changes* in economic welfare, and the changes might be measured by the product of the change in income (y) of each person and the importance ($a, b, c, \ldots, m$) attached (by him?) to that change in income. Thus

$$dW = a(dy_1) + b(dy_2) + \ldots + m(dy_n).\qquad\qquad 3$$

The change in aggregate economic welfare is the sum of the weighted changes in income for each person. This form of the S W F implies that there exist no interdependencies in utility. That is, $a(dy_1)$, the change in economic welfare attributed to person 1, is assumed to be independent of the change in economic welfare attributed to person 2, and so forth. The reasonableness of this assumption is open to some question.

At this point the problem of estimating dW becomes essentially one of estimating values of the weights $a, b, \ldots, m$ – these being, in effect, marginal utilities of income for each person.[15] The following discussion suggests a method by which relative values for these weights may be inferred from observed governmental actions. The assumption is made that governmental actions are

15. If one believes that the S W F used implicitly by decision-makers is not of the form indicated in equation 3 – perhaps being nonlinear, or involving interaction terms – or involves variables other than income in an important way, one can specify an alternative form, and then set out to estimate the weights for each group of beneficiaries, in the manner discussed below. The form presented above is suggested as a reasonable simplification of reality in the interest of operational feasibility.

undertaken if, but only if, they will increase W – that is, if $dW > 0$ (abstracting from uncertainty). In such a situation it may be possible to deduce the distributional weights $a, b, \ldots, m$ – as those weights are seen implicitly by government decision-makers – with the aid of additional assumptions that government decision-makers (legislators, administrators) are rational and fully informed about the consequences of their actions.[16]

Suppose there is a project 2, which receives priority over project 1, of equal cost, even though the real benefits from project 1 are greater *when a dollar's worth of additional income receives a weight equal to unity regardless of who receives it.* Given the specified assumptions, it follows that if project 2 is preferred nonetheless, then it must produce benefits that would be found to be at least as large as those from project 1 if appropriate differential weights were attached to the income received by each beneficiary.

What weights do governmental decision-makers actually attach? Or what weights are implied by their behavior in choosing among alternative expenditures?

Knowledge of these implicit weights would be of *normative* value – one could confront the question whether the decision-maker's implied valuations of the marginal utilities of income for various persons deviate significantly from more generally held views regarding the relative importance of aiding various people. Moreover, knowledge of the implicit weights would be of *positive* value – they could be used in forecasting future government expenditure choices among projects with differing distributional (as well as allocative-efficiency) effects.

In setting forth the following revealed behavior approach for inferring distributional weights, I shall first discuss it at a rather abstract level, making a number of simplifying assumptions. Later I shall attempt to implement the approach – in a very limited and, I must emphasize, a very tentative way. Even if the approach is deemed promising, there is no doubt that a good deal of additional effort is required to make it operational and useful.

16. The latter assumption is especially questionable. However, as techniques of benefit-cost analysis are refined and data systems improved, information of the required types will become increasingly available.

The model

Consider the following circumstances: a government decision-maker or agency has open to it at a particular moment of time a number of specific investment projects, not all of which can be funded. Assume that all projects are of equal cost, as determined by the decision-maker. (This assumption is not essential, and will be dropped later.) Assume further that the decision-maker finds that total benefits, excluding distributional considerations, differ among projects. Next, assume that if all projects were ranked in decreasing order of total real benefits, it would be found that some project was undertaken even though some other project higher on the list was not. Finally, assume that prior theorizing suggests that for projects of 'this type' (education, or highway, or water resource projects) certain distributions of benefits are relevant but others are not. For example, recalling the discussion in the preceding section about types of population groups, perhaps decision-makers are concerned only with the distribution of benefits between whites and nonwhites, and between families with annual incomes under and over $3000.

Thus, whereas in general there are m groups of beneficiaries from each prospective project, in this case m would equal 4: poor whites, nonpoor whites, poor nonwhites, and nonpoor nonwhites. For each project j, the total benefits, B_j, may be divided into these m components where subscripts to the left denote the particular group – for instance, $1 =$ poor white, $2 =$ poor nonwhite – and subscripts to the right denote the project. Thus,

Project 1: $\quad _1B_1 + {_2}B_1 + \ldots + {_m}B_1 \equiv B_1$ \hfill 4

Project 2: $\quad _1B_2 + {_2}B_2 + \ldots + {_m}B_2 \equiv B_2$ \hfill 5

Project 3: $\quad _1B_3 + {_2}B_3 + \ldots + {_m}B_3 \equiv B_3$ \hfill 6

$\quad\vdots$

Project n: $\quad _1B_n + {_2}B_n + \ldots + {_m}B_n \equiv B_n.$ \hfill 7

Each of the n projects must be selected so as to fulfill specific conditions. Project 1 is, by definition, the most profitable project that was not undertaken. All other $(n-1)$ projects listed are those meeting two conditions: they are less profitable than project 1 – that is, $B_2, \ldots, B_n < B_1$ – and yet they were undertaken. (At this stage in the analysis projects are assumed to be undertaken instantaneously. More will be said about this later.)

If it is assumed – for now – that the B_j include *all* benefits regarded by the decision-maker as relevant to the determination of the project's economic efficiency, then there seem to be two possible explanations for the failure to undertake a project that is more profitable than some project that was in fact undertaken: (1) mistakes or irrationality, and (2) considerations of distributional effects such that some projects that were less 'efficient' than others were regarded as 'better' (in an ethical sense) distributionally.

Any behavior can be explained, of course, as a product of error, irrationality, or accident. Yet such explanations for government expenditure patterns hardly seem applicable generally. If, instead, the second explanation – that distributional effects received weight in the decision process – is accepted, then the analysis can proceed. Specifically, it is possible to derive a set of weights that would make it rational to have selected the particular projects that were undertaken and to have rejected project 1.[17] With reference to the system of equations above, this requires assuming that, once distributional consequences are recognized, the resulting adjusted benefits, $B_2^*, B_3^*, \ldots, B_n^*$, are at least as great as B_1.

Thus, equations 4–7 may be rewritten as follows, where the coefficients, $a, b, \ldots, p$, are weights indicating the relative importance of a marginal dollar of benefits for the specified population group.

Project 1: $a_1 B_1 + b_2 B_1 + \ldots + p_m B_1 \equiv B_1^* = B_1$ **4***

Project 2: $a_1 B_2 + b_2 B_2 + \ldots + p_m B_2 \equiv B_2^* \geqslant B_1$ **5***

Project 3: $a_1 B_3 + b_2 B_3 + \ldots + p_m B_3 \equiv B_3^* \geqslant B_1$ **6***
$\vdots$

Project n: $a_1 B_n + b_2 B_n + \ldots + p_m B_n \equiv B_n^* \geqslant B_1.$ **7***

17. It is true that the proposed approach deduces weights in a 'residual' fashion, ascribing to distributional considerations all choices that deviate from allocative efficiency. This is unquestionably an oversimplification. However, through time, the ability to determine the allocative efficiency of projects will improve, and the capacity for dealing quantitatively with 'intangible' effects will grow; in the process it will become increasingly true

At this point it will be useful to consider 4*–7* in equation, rather than inequality, form – an approach which implies that projects 2, 3,..., n are thought to be just as good as, but not better than, project 1, in the grand-efficiency sense. Later, this assumption will be reconsidered.

This system of equations is or is not soluble for the weights a, b, etc., depending on the number of unknowns, m (which in this model is the number of classes of beneficiaries) and the number of equations, n (that is, the number of relevant projects, as defined earlier).

First, consider the case in which $m = n$. In this case, and assuming that the equations are independent, the coefficients (weights) are just identified; solution of the equations yields estimates of the implicit relative importance attached by decision-makers to an additional dollar of benefits to each of the various groups of beneficiaries.

However, the number of unknowns (pertinent beneficiary groups) may exceed the number of equations (relevant projects). In that case, what can be learned about implicit distributional weights? Two approaches might be followed.

1. The number of unknowns could be arbitrarily reduced. For example, the number of income classes or geographic classes could be cut, or the distinction between benefits to whites and nonwhites could be eliminated, and so on. Although this would not be ideal, since one might wish to produce a set of weights covering a larger number of groups of beneficiaries, it may still be worthwhile to learn something about the weights for these groups. Yet there are possible dangers in such an approach, for each weight will be affected – in some way that is not easily discernible – if the number of groups is altered.[18]

2. Alternatively, if the number of unknowns is excessive, some additional constraints on them may be assumed. For example, if there were groupings of the poor and the nonpoor, in the North and in the South, then it might be assumed that whatever the

---

that distributional considerations – which people receive the benefits and which bear the costs of projects – will constitute the primary reason why expenditure decisions deviate from the dictates of allocative efficiency.

18. 'Altered', that is, from the number that prior theorizing suggests is relevant for the decision-making process.

relative weights were in the North for the poor *vis-à-vis* the non-poor, the same ratio held in the South. Or the differences between the weights might be assumed to be equal in both regions.

Now consider the case in which the number of equations exceeds the number of unknowns, leading to over-identification of the weights. In this situation one could estimate the weights that 'approximately' solve all the equations, by computing, for example, least-squares estimates of them.

It should be noted, in review, that the number of equations or inequalities in the system is determined by the number of projects fulfilling the previously stated conditions, and the number of unknowns is determined by the population groupings deemed relevant. There is no reason to expect equality of the two. Neither is there reason to desire equality, although if the number of unknowns is excessive, estimation of the weights requires establishing additional assumptions (constraints).

Even if the system of equations can be used to estimate distributional weights, the question remains whether the distributional variables, or classes, have been specified correctly. There is, in principle, no limit to the number of ways in which total benefits from a project can be divided. In general, for each such division there is some set of weights that will satisfy the equations. Whether we have set forth 'correctly' the variables (groups of people) that (1) are actually taken into account by decision-makers, or that (2) are regarded as important by the society in general, are matters warranting further study.[19]

So far the assumption has been made that each of the n com-

19. Another approach for inferring distributional weights – one suggested by Otto Eckstein – would use effective marginal income tax rates to measure the government's notion of the relative marginal utilities of income for various people. See Eckstein (1961b, p. 448). Recently, Robert Haveman has attempted to apply Eckstein's suggestion to decisions in the water resource field (1965). This approach could be regarded as a special case of our more general framework, the latter allowing for the consideration of population groupings other than those based on income level.

The Eckstein approach could be used to complement the information about weights that is being proposed in this paper, although, as noted above, it would provide no direct help with respect to the distributional weights for population groupings based on social characteristics other than income. Moreover, regardless of which marginal tax rates were accepted as *norms* of public policy, it remains to be determined whether expenditure decisions

peting projects is of equal cost. If that assumption is dropped, the foregoing procedure for estimating distributional weights must be modified somewhat. If project costs were unequal we might expect that if ordinary economic efficiency were the only consideration, those projects would be undertaken which promised the greatest return relative to cost, assuming no capital-rationing. This would suggest that decision-makers would undertake the projects with the largest net present values, rates of return, benefit–cost ratios, or whatever other measure of efficiency they regarded as appropriate.

In the illustration that follows, the benefit–cost ($B–C$) ratio was the measure of economic efficiency used by the government agency involved. Thus, we would expect that in the absence of restraints imposed by capital rationing and project indivisibilities, projects with the highest $B–C$ ratios would be selected. But, whatever the measure of allocation efficiency, the model presented above requires the assumption that the apparently less efficient projects that were undertaken are – in the grand-efficiency sense – at least as efficient as the most efficient project not undertaken. If the $B–C$ ratio is used, this requires that the B^* on the right sides of expressions 4*–7* be greater than or equal to what the total benefits from each project would be if the $B–C$ ratio for that project equalled the ratio for project 1. That is, the B^* terms should at least equal not B_1, but $B_1(C_j/C_1)$, the cost ratio, C_j/C_1, being an adjustment factor.[20]

The model applied

Now that the model has been generalized to projects differing in level of cost as well as in level and distribution of real benefits, we are in a position to use it.

---

reflect those norms and thus whether our ability to predict public expenditure actions will be aided by knowledge of those norms. Here again the distinction between normative and positive uses for distributional weights should be emphasized.

Another way to determine the distributional weights that decision-makers use is the direct route: ask them. My own preference – as reflected in this paper – is for examining what people do rather than what they say, although detailed questioning of knowledgeable honest decision-makers may be fruitful.

20. Recall that in expressions 4*–7* it had been assumed that all projects were of equal cost. Thus, all $C_j/C_1 = 1$.

The following is presented simply as an illustration of how the model might be applied. No significance is attached to the numerical results. The input data, involving water resource projects, are seriously faulty in a variety of ways that require no elaboration.[21] On the other hand, to the extent that these faults – such as the use of an excessively low discount rate – are not recognized as faults by decision-makers, we may neglect them as explanations for any departures of actual choices from those implied by the measure of economic efficiency adopted – which, in this case, was the benefit–cost ratio.

Table 4 Costs and benefits of four water resource projects, and order of undertaking

Project	Total costs (C)	Total benefits (B)	B–C ratio	Order undertaken
1. Scarboro River, Me.[a]	$392,635	$1,225,021	3·12	4
2. Russian River, Calif.[b]	13,424,956	29,936,849	2·23	2
3. Charlotte Harbor, Fla.[c]	226,104	391,160	1·73	3
4. Corning, N.Y.[d]	3,300,000	5,577,000	1·69	1

[a] *Report on Survey of Scarboro River, Maine, between Prouts Neck and Pine Point*, H. Doc. 69, 81 Cong. 1 sess. (1949), p. 11.

[b] *Report on Survey of Russian River, California*, H. Doc. 585, 81 Cong. 2 sess. (1950), p. 79.

[c] *Report on Charlotte Harbor, Florida*, H. Doc. 186, 81 Cong. 1 sess. (1949), p. 20.

[d] *Report on Monkey Run Creek, Corning, New York*, H. Doc. 305, 81 Cong. 1 sess. (1949), p. 26.

Table 4 presents data on total costs and benefits for each of four prospective water resource projects that were considered by the Corps of Engineers in 1950. The project numbered 1 is seen to have the highest B–C ratio; however, projects 2–4 were undertaken before project 1. That fact is taken as evidence – for the purpose of illustrating the model – that projects 2–4 would be found to have B–C ratios at least equal to that of project 1 *if* the benefits accruing to various population groups were weighted in the manner that decision-makers regarded as appropriate.

21. Weaknesses in the project-evaluation procedures of the Corps of Engineers have been discussed extensively by Eckstein (1961b) and McKean (1958).

For this illustration the total benefits from each project were divided into only four classes. These were benefits to: white persons with annual incomes under $3000, whites with incomes of $3000 or more, nonwhites with incomes under $3000, and non-whites with incomes of $3000 or more. Since the distributions of total benefits from each project among the four groups were not known, they were assumed arbitrarily to be the same as the distributions of the total population in 1959 in the state where the project was located. Thus, if 40 per cent of the people in the state were white with annual incomes of $3000 or more, then 40 per cent of the project's total benefits were assumed to accrue to this group. (The assumed percentage distributions of benefits for each of the four projects are given in Table 5.) No defense of this

Table 5 **Percentage distribution of benefits from four water resource projects, by color of beneficiary and income**

	White		Nonwhite	
	Income under $3000 (Group I)	Income $3000 and over (Group II)	Income under $3000 (Group III)	Income $3000 and over (Group IV)
Project				
1. Scarboro River, Me.	36·2	62·8	0·7	0·3
2. Russian River, Calif.	24·0	67·0	3·5	5·5
3. Charlotte Harbor, Fla.	28·7	53·3	12·0	6·0
4. Corning, N.Y.	4·3	86·9	1·3	7·5·

Sources: Percentages are arbitrarily assumed to coincide with the percentage of the groups in the population of each state. For the population data, see US Bureau of the Census, *US Census of Population: 1960, General Social, and Economic Characteristics, Florida*, PC (1)-11C, p. 155, Table 65; *Maine*, PC (1)-21C, p. 95, Table 65; *California*, PC (1)-6C, p. 251, Table 65; and *New York*, PC (1)-34C, p. 229, Table 65.

procedure will be attempted. It is to be hoped that in the future more effort will be expended to learn how benefits from public expenditures are distributed, so that such crude procedures will not be needed.

Substituting the data for these four projects in the model of expressions 4*–7* (see above, p. 412), with the right side adjusted for differences in project costs, as discussed above, and then normalizing by dividing each equation by its right side, gives the following:

Project 1: $0{\cdot}360a + 0{\cdot}630b + 0{\cdot}007c + 0{\cdot}003d = 1$ **8**

Project 2: $0{\cdot}172a + 0{\cdot}479b + 0{\cdot}025c + 0{\cdot}039d \geqslant 1$ **9**

Project 3: $0{\cdot}161a + 0{\cdot}294b + 0{\cdot}066c + 0{\cdot}033d \geqslant 1$ **10**

Project 4: $0{\cdot}023a + 0{\cdot}470b + 0{\cdot}007c + 0{\cdot}041d \geqslant 1.$ **11**

If the elements on the left sides of expressions **9**, **10**, and **11** are assumed to add precisely to 1, simultaneous solution of the four equations produces these results:

$a = -1{\cdot}3$ (a is the coefficient, or weight, for whites with incomes under \$3000 per year – Group I)

$b = 2{\cdot}2$ (b is the coefficient, or weight, for whites with incomes of \$3000 or more per year – Group II)

$c = 9.3$ (c is the coefficient, or weight, for nonwhites with incomes under \$3000 per year – Group III)

$d = -2{\cdot}0$ (d is the coefficient, or weight, for nonwhites with incomes of \$3000 or more per year – Group IV).

The discovery that the implicit weights are unequal indicates – subject to the heroic assumption that all benefits relevant to allocative efficiency have been measured adequately – that a dollar of project benefits was being valued differently depending on who was expected to receive those benefits. The discovery that some of the implicit weights are negative indicates that the benefits accruing to those particular groups (I and IV in the illustration) were not merely disregarded but were treated implicitly as disadvantages (or costs) of the various projects. Only the benefits to groups II and III received (implicitly) positive weights, and benefits to the latter group received more than four times as much weight per dollar as benefits to the former group.

The reasons for this, or any other, pattern of relative weights are an interesting matter which goes beyond the scope of this paper. The ubiquitous, but hard to define and measure, 'political considerations' provide a ready 'explanation' of sorts. Another possible explanation is that the benefits *per person* differed among groups, and so perhaps those benefits that were most concentrated received the highest (or the lowest) weights.[22] Although this explanation warrants investigation in general, it is not valid for the illustration presented above, since the method of estimating the distribution of benefits assumed implicitly that benefits *per capita* were equal for all beneficiaries.

It was pointed out earlier that the theory described above actually implies that equations 5*–7* and 9–11 are either equations or inequalities, with their left sides being *at least* equal to their constant terms. In solving for the weights *a*, *b*, *c*, and *d*, the strong assumption of equality was made first. This assumption will now be relaxed in order to examine the resulting sensitivity of the estimated weights.

The procedure employed involves increasing the constant terms above those in equations 9–11 by, alternatively, 5 per cent, 10 per cent, and 20 per cent. This is equivalent to saying that the left sides of expressions 9, 10, and 11 are not equal to, but greater than, unity: in other words, the *B–C* ratios for projects 2–4 – *after* adjustment for distributive effects – were, alternatively, 5, 10, and 20 per cent greater than the ratio for project 1 (the highest *B–C* ratio project that was not undertaken). To illustrate: expression 9 was turned into the inequality

$$0 \cdot 172a + 0 \cdot 479b + 0 \cdot 025c + 0 \cdot 039d = 1 \cdot 05 > 1 \cdot 00. \qquad 12$$

The values for the implied weights (or marginal utilities of income) – *a*, *b*, *c*, *d* – derived by this method are presented in Table 6. The top row shows the initial results, previously presented, while succeeding rows give the weights implied by assum-

Table 6 **Distributional weights under four assumptions regarding benefit–cost ratios**

B–C ratio assumed for projects 2–4, as proportion of B-C ratio for project 1	Weights			
	a	*b*	*c*	*d*
1·00	−1·3	2·2	9·3	−2·0
1·05	−1·3	2·2	9·4	−0·7
1·10	−1·3	2·2	9·6	+0·5
1·20	−1·3	2·2	9·9	+3·0

22. This hypothesis was suggested by Julius Margolis.

ing that the adjusted *B–C* ratios – adjusted for distributional considerations – for projects 2–4 are each 5, 10, and 20 per cent greater than the (3·12) ratio for project 1.

These results – while applying only to the set of four projects in the illustration – seem noteworthy. Weights *a*, *b*, and *c* are remarkably stable over the *B–C* range considered (3·12–3·74), and while weight *d* is far more volatile, it does change monotonically, as do *a*, *b*, and *c*. Taking the entire set of weights, we can say that if it is assumed that the 'adjusted' *B–C* ratios for projects 2–4 are at least equal to, but not more than 20 per cent greater than, that for project 1, then the implied values for *a*, *b*, *c*, and *d* are as follows

$$a = -1 \cdot 3,$$
$$b = +2 \cdot 2,$$
$$+9 \cdot 9 \geqslant c \geqslant +9 \cdot 3,$$
$$+3 \cdot 0 \geqslant d \geqslant -2 \cdot 0.$$

If this degree of sensitivity of the weights to the assumed *B–C* ratios is not greatly exceeded by what is found in subsequent applications of this model, then it would appear that the model can be useful in producing estimated ranges of implied distributional weights. Regardless of the *B–C* ratio assumed in the illustration, it was found that $c > b > a$, that $c > d$, and that a dollar of benefits to low-income nonwhites received implicitly the heaviest weight.

With respect to further analysis of sensitivity of the model, I wanted to learn whether relatively small errors in determining the distribution of measured benefits would have substantial effects on the estimated weights. If they would not, then in order to derive the weights it would not be necessary to take great pains in accurately assessing the distribution of measured benefits.

Tests could be made of the effects of many different magnitudes and directions of measurement errors. Only a few are considered here, and the results are in Table 7. In that table, case 2 assumes that of the total measured benefits from each project, 1 per cent too little had been estimated to accrue to groups III and IV (the groups whose weights are *c* and *d*) in each project, while 1 per cent too much had been allocated to groups I and II. Throughout the various cases examined, the assumption was retained that the adjusted *B–C* ratios for projects 2–4 were equal to (but not greater than) that of project 1.[23]

Table 7 Effects on distributional weights of changes in the allocation of measured benefits

	Weights			
Allocation of measured benefits	*a*	*b*	*c*	*d*
1. Original distribution	−1·3	2·2	9·3	−2·0
2. Groups I and II, +1 percentage point Groups III and IV, −1 percentage point[a]	−1·1	2·2	9·1	−0·6
3. Groups I and II, −1 percentage point Groups III and IV, +1 percentage point[a]	−1·3	2·1	9·2	−1·9
4. Groups I and III, +1 percentage point Groups II and IV, −1 percentage point[a]	−1·5	2·3	9·8	−4·7
5. Groups I and III, −1 percentage point Groups II and IV, +1 percentage point[a]	−1·2	2·2	9·1	−0·7
6. Group I, +5 percentage points[b] Group II, −5 percentage points[b] Groups III and IV, unchanged	−1·3	2·1	9·2	−1·9
7. Group I, −5 percentage points[b] Group II, +5 percentage points[b] Groups III and IV, unchanged	−1·1	2·2	9·1	−6·3

[a] For project 1, the change was 0·2 percentage point, rather than 1·0 point. The reason is that the percentage of benefits shown (in Table 5) for group IV in the case of project 1 is only 0·3.

[b] For project 4, the change was 4 percentage points, rather than 5. The reason is that the percentage of benefits shown (in Table 5) for group I in the case of project 4 is less than 5.

Cases 2–5, involving various 1 percentage point shifts among

23. The original estimated distributions of benefits for each of the four projects appear in Table 5, above. A glance at this table discloses that a 1 percentage point change in the amount of benefits allocated to the non-white groups (III and IV) constitutes a rather sizable percentage change. For example, with respect to project 2, it amounts to approximately a 20–30 per cent change.

the four beneficiary groups, produced the following ranges for the implied distributional weights

$$-1 \cdot 1 \geqslant a \geqslant -1 \cdot 5,$$
$$+2 \cdot 3 \geqslant b \geqslant +2 \cdot 1,$$
$$+9 \cdot 8 \geqslant c \geqslant +9 \cdot 1,$$
$$-0 \cdot 6 \geqslant d \geqslant -4 \cdot 7.$$

Cases 6 and 7 examine the effects of a much larger, 5 percentage points, shift of the benefits among groups I and II in all four projects. In all of the cases considered the implicit distributional weights appear to vary only within rather narrow bounds, and in no case did a sign change. This comparative insensitivity of the weights to systematic errors in allocating benefits is a finding that is favorable to the use of the model.

Before considering any further the usefulness of distributional weights, an explanation is in order for the operational measure of whether a project is or is not 'undertaken'. Project 1 in Table 4 was selected as one which was 'undertaken' later than the other three projects, even though it had a higher B–C ratio.

The simplifying assumption was made earlier that projects are undertaken instantaneously. If they were, then an unambiguous statement would be possible regarding whether – at a point in time – some particular project was bypassed in favor of some others. However, realistically, such an assumption must be modified. This is especially clear with regard to water resource projects which often are ten years or more in construction.

One approach for determining when a project was undertaken would involve the date at which it was *started*.[24] For projects constructed over multi-year periods, however, this can be a questionable procedure, since the time pattern of expenditures may vary considerably among projects. Thus, one project may have been started before another, but the latter may have been completed first. It would seem that in the present context of attempting to infer decision-makers' social welfare function (distributional weights), we should be interested in the entire time pattern of expenditures, not simply in the starting date of projects.

24. Such a measure was used by Haveman (1965).

An alternative procedure, adopted in the present paper for developing the illustration above, does look, *ex post*, at the full-time pattern of expenditures on each project. Defined rigorously below, it measures an average time at which all of the expenditures on a project were undertaken. For each project, j, on which an expenditure was considered (that is, for which benefit-cost information was available at a given time – 1950 in the illustration), the following statistic, U_j, was calculated as a measure of how quickly that project was undertaken:

$$U_j = \sum_{t=0}^{T} \frac{_jP_t}{(1+r)^t}, \qquad\qquad 13$$

where $_jP_t$ is the percentage of total expenditures on project j that were made in year t, and r is the rate of discount (5 per cent was used in the illustration above). At the limit, if 100 per cent of the expenditures on a project, j, were incurred instantaneously at the time in 1950 when the benefit-cost information became available on the various projects, then that U_j would equal 1, since $_jP_t =$ 100 per cent and all expenditures would have been made at $t = 0$. The further any U_j is from 1 (that is, the closer it comes to zero), the later the project was regarded as having been 'undertaken'.

U_j was calculated for each project that was authorized by the Congress in 1950, and this measure was compared with the benefit–cost ratios to determine whether projects with relatively low ratios were undertaken before projects with higher ratios.[25] Thus, in Table 4 the statistic, U, for projects 2–4, was larger than that for project 1.

The proposed measure of when a project was undertaken is not offered as ideal for all purposes. Even its usefulness in the present context is questionable insofar as the time pattern of project expenditures reflects factors other than choices by government decision-makers.[26] In any event, the acceptance, rejection, or

25. The contrast between the results of this method and the method of using starting dates can be considerable. For example, among nine water resource projects investigated, the rank correlation coefficient of the two methods was actually negative, -0.2.

26. Robert Haveman has argued that the time pattern of expenditures is determined principally by the contractor.

modification of the proposed method for dating a project is a matter separate from the major objective and approach of this section of the paper. The concern here is with a methodology for inferring distributional weights. The method suggested requires some device for dating each project, but does not require any particular device.

Let us return now to the meaning of the weights deduced above in the illustration. These weights provide a sufficient explanation for the observed choice of projects 2, 3 and 4 over project 1. They do not, however, provide a necessary explanation – at least not unless a number of assumptions are made: namely, that (1) the variables selected have been correctly and fully specified – that is, implicitly if not explicitly, decision-makers regard these and only these population groupings, and no other variables, as relevant, and in the linear form indicated above; (2) decision-makers act so as to maximize total benefits (grand efficiency) – including benefits from an 'improved' distribution of income – for any given total costs incurred; [27] (3) total costs and benefits (except for those of a distributional sort) are known for each alternative project; (4) project-cost indivisibilities, together with an arbitrary constraint on the expenditure budget (in this case, for water projects), do not dictate selection of projects simply because the projects are small; (5) choices among projects and the timing of expenditures are not affected by exogenous factors such as legal difficulties in obtaining property rights, or changes in estimates of costs or benefits subsequent to a project being initiated.

It is clear that all of these assumptions are rarely if ever fulfilled entirely. How far they are from being fulfilled, and how important it is for each one to be completely fulfilled, are matters requiring further study. The following conclusion does seem quite warranted, in any case.

Even if this general grand-efficiency approach for inferring the distributional weights used implicitly by decision-makers is

27. Choices based on benefit–cost *ratios*, used by the Corps of Engineers, are not necessarily consistent with maximization of net benefits. However, if the decision-makers (such as the Corps, or the Congress) act as though such choices are consistent, then it should be possible to infer weights in the decision-maker's social welfare function from observed behavior, provided the other assumptions listed here are fulfilled.

appealing conceptually, to make it operational will require additional empirical study of the total real benefits from projects and the distribution of those benefits. Thus, caveats on the use of the approach are clearly in order. At present, quantitative estimates of benefits from particular projects (whether on education, highways, or anything else) are seldom made, and even less often is the distribution of those benefits investigated.[28] Moreover, the quantitative work that is currently being done is often incomplete in the sense that some forms of benefits (and costs) are not evaluated. For example, recreational benefits, in the water resources area, and benefits from increased length of life, in the areas of health, highway and airway safety, and so on, need more attention.

As long as some forms of benefits (and costs) are recognized but not evaluated explicitly, we cannot be certain to what extent the procedure presented above for estimating distributional weights actually measures those weights and to what extent it reflects the implicit valuations of the nonmeasured effects. This problem does plague us at present, given the state of empirical benefit-cost work. Yet the importance of the problem may or may not be great, depending on how much the unmeasured benefits and costs differ among competing projects.

The day is distant when we will be fully successful in uncovering the distributional weights and obtaining consensus on their validity. Yet the goal does seem worthy and attainable. At the normative level, determination of distributional weights would make explicit the weights being used implicitly in the social welfare function, provided that the general form of the function and the variables (groupings) in it have been specified correctly. This would be useful in directing attention to the question of whether 'society in general' is or is not satisfied with that social welfare function and with the relative weights being attached implicitly to the benefits (or costs) realized by various population groups.

28. The same is probably true of costs. In part this is a function of the existence of real costs that are not reflected by governmental expenditures – for example, relocation costs of homeowners displaced by highway construction – and in part a function of our very imperfect understanding of the incidence of the taxes used to finance even those project costs that are reflected in governmental expenditures.

At the positive level, discovery of these distributional weights could aid in forecasting government expenditure decisions, as the significance attached by decision-makers to distributional factors became better understood. In addition, it would assist decision-makers; insofar as they remained satisfied with the weights in their implicit social welfare function, they could then rely more on relatively formal procedures and less on informal judgements.

Also, at the positive level, this method of inferring distributional weights from revealed behavior may be useful in testing for the existence and extent of compromise ('log-rolling'?) in political decision-making. Evidence of such compromise would be the finding of significantly divergent distributional weights for given variables when various decisions – perhaps at different points in time or with respect to different sets of project alternatives – were examined. For example, if a relatively high weight for benefits in the North (*vis-à-vis* the South) were implied by one set of decisions, while a relatively low weight were implied by another, this might be regarded as an indication of compromise, and the ratio of the differing weights might be regarded as an index of its degree. The differing weights also might reflect other factors such as new information or a change in policy goals (that is, a change in the implicit social welfare function).

The possibility that weights may differ when deduced from decisions made at various times, by various decision-makers, and in various program areas, provides a basis for some interesting researchable questions. Do the weights (marginal utilities of income) vary? Systematically? Do some particular groups of beneficiaries consistently receive relatively high or low weights? What are the average weights for particular groups over time and across programs?

The approach presented in this section would shed light on the question whether, and in what ways, decision-makers take into account the distributional effects as well as the economic efficiency of alternative expenditure projects. The discovery that a dollar's worth of benefit (or cost) receives a different weight in decisions depending on who receives (or bears) it would seem to support the hope expressed earlier in the paper that a grand-efficiency measure of the 'profitability' (or desirability) of a project can be developed. Integrating considerations of economic efficiency and distributional equity, such a measure would amount to specifying the social welfare function that is being used – implicitly, perhaps – by decision-makers. It may or may not be a S W F which 'society' approves, but that too is worth knowing.

Summary

The traditional separation in economics of economic efficiency from distributional equity has great merit for a science that wishes to avoid, or at least minimize, its use of ethically controversial axioms. It is understandable, therefore, that economists engaged in benefit-cost studies have directed attention to economic efficiency. With distributional concerns aside, 'efficiency' involves only the rather noncontroversial ethic of Pareto optimality – a project being efficient if total benefits exceed total costs, for in that case everyone, at least theoretically, could be made better off if the project were undertaken.

The present paper has sought to direct attention to means by which economists can assist in improving the quality of decisions on public expenditures by confronting the issue of a project's distributional effects in addition to its allocative-efficiency effects. One device, presented in the second section, would be to determine and then display how the total benefits (and costs) of each project would be divided among various population groups, defined in such terms as income, age, sex, and geographic location – groupings that are presumably relevant to decision-makers. Such information would require no value judgements by economists regarding how income should be divided.

Another device, presented in the third section, would deduce the value judgements concerning the distribution of income that are implied by decision-makers' choices. By exposing these distributional weights, we can focus attention on the question of their ethical acceptability, even if, as economists, we refrain from answering the question. In addition, we may be better able to forecast government expenditure decisions.

References

BONNEN, J. T. (1968), 'The distribution of benefits from cotton price supports', in S. B. Chase, Jr (ed.), *Problems in Public Expenditure Analysis*, Brookings Institution.

DUBLIN, L. I., and LOTKA, A. J. (1930), *The Money Value of a Man*, Ronald Press.

ECKSTEIN, O. (1961a), *Water-Resource Development: The Economics of Project Evaluation*, Harvard University Press.

ECKSTEIN, O. (1961b), 'A survey of the theory of public expenditure criteria', in J. M. Buchanan (ed.), *Public Finances: Needs, Sources and Utilization*, Princeton University Press.

HAVEMAN, R. (1965), *Water Resource Investment and the Public Interest*, Vanderbilt University Press.

HICKS, J. R. (1940), 'The valuation of the social income', *Economica*, May, pp. 105–24.

HIRSHLEIFER, J. (1958), 'On the theory of optimal investment', *J. polit. Econ.*, vol. 67.

KALDOR, N. (1939), 'Welfare propositions of economists and interpersonal comparisons of utility', *Econ. J.*, September, pp. 549–52.

KRUTILLA, J. V., and ECKSTEIN, O. (1958), *Multiple Purpose River Development*, Johns Hopkins Press.

MCKEAN, R. N. (1958), *Efficiency in Government Through Systems Analysis*, Wiley.

MCKEAN, R. N. (1961), 'Evaluating alternative expenditure programs', in J. M. Buchanan (ed.), *Public Finances: Needs, Sources and Utilization*, Princeton University Press.

MARGLIN, S. A. (1962), 'Objectives of water-resource development: a general statement', in A. Maass *et al.*, *Design of Water-Resource Systems*, Harvard University Press.

PREST, A. R., and TURVEY, R. (1965), 'Cost-benefit analysis: a survey', *Econ. J.*, vol. 75, pp. 683–735.

ROTHENBERG, J. (1965), 'Urban renewal programs', in R. Dorfman (ed.), *Measuring Benefits of Government Investments*, Brookings Institution.

SCHELLING, T. (1968), 'The life you save may be your own', in S. B. Chase, Jr. (ed.), *Problems in Public Expenditure Analysis*, Brookings Institution.

WALSH, J. R. (1935), 'Capital concept applied to man', *Quart. J. Econ.*, vol. February, pp. 255–85.

WEISBROD, B. A. (1961), 'The valuation of human capital', *J. polit. Econ.*, October, pp. 425–36.

WEISBROD, B. A. (1965), 'Preventing high school dropouts', in R. Dorfman (ed.), *Measuring Benefits of Government Investments*, Brookings Institution.

Part Six
The Case of the Third London Airport

The *Roskill Report* on the Third London Airport was probably
the most ambitious cost-benefit analysis ever undertaken. As a
first step their research team provided a draft cost-benefit
exercise, which was then subjected to detailed criticism and
discussion in public hearings as well as to academic comment.
Mishan's article, written at this stage of the proceedings, not
only explains but criticizes the Commission's valuation of
noise and other items and questions whether an extra airport
is needed at all.

Having considered the criticisms, the Commission produced
its report. They included a revised cost-benefit analysis, in
which the short-listed sites were still ranked in the order:
Cublington, Thurleigh, Nuthampstead and Foulness (see map
overleaf). The Report also discussed each site from a qualitative
point of view. However, by this stage the key issue was whether
Foulness, the only seaside location, was preferable to an
inland site. The Commission concluded against it and in favour
of Cublington, one member, Professor Buchanan, dissenting.
The government finally chose Foulness. Owing to its method
of proceeding the Commission's report does not provide a
self-contained reading and instead we include a
specially-written paper describing the Commission's approach
prepared in his private capacity by Flowerdew, who was
formerly the Commission's Deputy Director of Research.

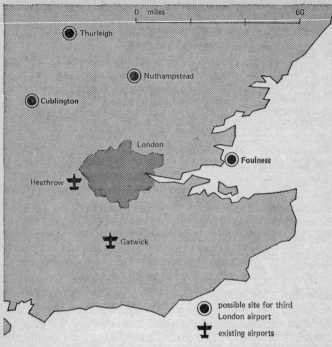

Short-listed sites for the Third London Airport

17 A. D. J. Flowerdew
Choosing a Site for the Third London Airport:
the Roskill Commission's Approach

A. D. J. Flowerdew, 'Choosing a site for the third London airport: the Roskill Commission's approach', specially written for this volume, 1972.

The Roskill Commission's terms of reference were 'to inquire into the timing of the need for a four-runway airport to cater for the growth of traffic at existing airports serving the London area, to consider the various alternative sites and to recommend which site should be selected'. The Commission's work lasted two and a half years, cost over a million pounds and is documented in a report and nine volumes of papers and proceedings. It was notable for including the largest research project undertaken by a Commission of Inquiry, the most far-reaching cost-benefit study carried out anywhere in the world and an unprecedented degree of public participation in the inquiry process. This short paper, which concentrates on the cost-benefit aspects of the choice of site, cannot hope to do justice to all the issues involved. Its purpose is to explain the approach, summarize the results and discuss some of the more important methodological considerations.

Criteria

The principle of valuation adopted by the Commission was to value the effects of the airport by reference to the values of those who would be directly affected by it. If the effect is beneficial, the value required is what the person affected would just be willing to pay for it; if it is adverse the value required is that which he would just be willing to accept in compensation. If all the effects of the airport are valued in this way, and the sum of the benefits

exceeds the sum of the costs, it should be possible for the beneficiaries to compensate fully all those who have been made worse
off while remaining better off themselves. Of course in practice
they will not normally do so. This means that the distribution of
costs and benefits between gainers and losers may be important
as well. If it is possible to identify a category of losers with serious
net costs, it might be desirable to compensate them from government funds rather than select an alternative with smaller net
benefits but fewer uncompensated losers.

Correct assessment of all costs and benefits resulting from a
new airport would of course be an impossible task. Any calculations of total net benefits can therefore be no more than a guide
to the right recommendation. The material which was considered
by the Commission fell into four groups:

1. the results of the cost-benefit study carried out on what the
Commission felt were the best assumptions.
2. Sensitivity tests showing the effect of varying the assumptions
made in the cost-benefit study.
3. Breakdowns of costs and benefits by the groups of people
affected.
4. Descriptive evidence on those items which had not been valued
as part of the study.

The process of reaching a recommendation based on these four
kinds of material was not and probably could not be systematized.
So the cost-benefit approach did not substitute for the exercise
of judgement. Rather it made clear exactly which issues required
the use of judgement and provided a framework within which
empirical evidence and analysis could be used to inform that
judgement.

Methodology

Figure 1 shows the outline study procedure, with approximate
timings. It was designed to ensure the maximum of public participation and included many public hearings, the last of which
was devoted to testing the evidence of the Commission's Research
Team and of others who had produced evidence on behalf of
various interested parties.

The methodology that was used was designed to fit this procedure. In order to produce a short-list quickly for detailed study an approximate cost-benefit method was devised and gradually refined as the original long list of seventy-eight sites was progressively reduced to fifteen sites, from which the short-list of four were chosen – Cublington, Foulness, Nuthampstead and Thurleigh.

The next stage involved the choice for each site of the best exact location, runway orientation and choice of flight-paths, so that the Commission could publish information from which local people could assess the impact on their lives of the new airport. This was to form the basis of the Stage II Local Hearings. The optimization also involved an approximate cost-benefit study, taking into account land and construction costs, noise costs, air-traffic control problems, effects on defence establishments and effects of runway orientation on airport usability in high cross-wind conditions.

At the same time a methodology for assessing whether and where a third London airport was required was being worked out and applied. The starting date of the new airport is of course an important input into the cost-benefit study.

The cost-benefit analysis for comparing sites could now be tackled. Figure 2 illustrates the main components of the study and the most important interactions between them. The effects taken into account in the study come under six main heads: planning, noise, aviation issues, airport design and construction, surface access and defence. I shall examine them in turn. Estimating the costs and benefits for each involves essentially three stages:

  (i) measuring the impact of the airport,
 (ii) forecasting how the people affected will react, and
(iii) assessing the costs and benefits associated with their reaction.

Planning

The planning effects of a new airport can be analysed in three categories:

  (i) effect of the site and fixed access links,
 (ii) effect of noise, and
(iii) effects of urban and industrial growth.

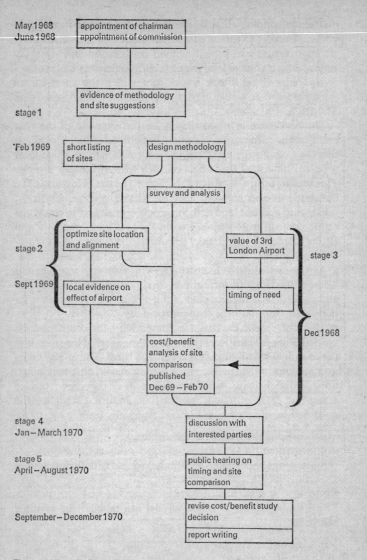

May 1968	appointment of chairman	
June 1968	appointment of commission	

stage 1 — evidence of methodology and site suggestions

Feb 1969 — short listing of sites / design methodology

survey and analysis

stage 2 — optimize site location and alignment

stage 3 — value of 3rd London Airport

Sept 1969 — local evidence on effect of airport

timing of need

Dec 1968

cost/benefit analysis of site comparison published Dec 69 – Feb 70

stage 4 Jan – March 1970 — discussion with interested parties

stage 5 April – August 1970 — public hearing on timing and site comparison

September – December 1970 — revise cost/benefit study decision

report writing

Figure 1 Roskill Commission—procedures

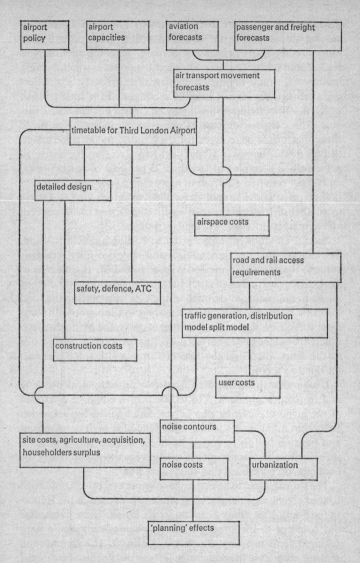

Figure 2 Cost-benefit study (site choice) – simplified structure diagram

The effects of noise are discussed below. The main difficulty in costing site acquisition is that it will almost certainly require some kind of compulsory purchase procedure. Thus the amount paid for the land will not necessarily reflect the prices at which existing landowners would willingly relinquish their property. The difference between the market price of a house and the least price at which the householder will sell may be termed householder's surplus. The Commission carried out a survey in areas similar to those that would be required for the airport, and attained a high response rate. Just over 10 per cent had zero surplus, nearly 50 per cent had a surplus of less than 25 per cent of market price, and 25 per cent had a surplus of more than 55 per cent. 8 per cent said no price would be enough for them to agree to sell and move to another district – in the cost-benefit study a cost of 200 per cent above market price was attributed to these.

Special attention was also given to costing agricultural land. The market value of agricultural land may not fully reflect its value to the country. Professor Wibberley and Mr Boddington of Wye College carried out a study for the Commission in which they made an approximate estimate of the cost of replacing the food losses by increasing production elsewhere in the country. In some cases this cost will be lower than the market value of the land; the difference will be due in part to the private or social amenity value to the landowner, and the loss of this amenity value was also included as a cost.

Urban growth was studied from two aspects: local planning and regional planning. Up to 65,000 people could be employed at the airport, requiring new urban development for about ten times that number. A site had to be found for such development and the sites had to be compared to see whether any significant differences in cost or benefit existed between them. Ultimately the Commission concluded that there were not.

The sites also had to be examined to see whether they conformed to the current regional planning strategy proposed in the Report of the South-East Study Team under Dr Burns. Three of the sites did conform to the strategy; one (Nuthampstead) would have required some not very drastic modifications. The Commission took no account of the possible benefits or disbenefits of industrial growth around the different sites, taking the view that they could not foresee future Government policy on allowing industrial expansion in the South-East.

Noise

The Commission studied the costs of aircraft noise on homes, schools, hospitals, public buildings, commerce and industry and recreation. In this paper I shall discuss only the model for estimating costs of aircraft noise on homes.

To measure aircraft noise, the Commission used the Noise and Number Index. This is an index which takes into account both the number of aircraft heard per day and the average loudness of the noise. It was derived from a social survey carried out by McKonnell in the area around Heathrow; loudness and duration of noise and the number of aircraft were correlated with the subjective reactions of the people affected and the NNI gave the best fit. NNI values can be plotted in a map in the form of contours. The Commission used contours going down to thirty-five NNI which cover the main areas of nuisance. Figure 3 shows the Heathrow NNI contours on 1967, and Figure 4 shows the Commission's estimated contours for Foulness with four operational runways. Forecasting NNI requires a forecast of the noise produced by the aircraft that will be in service, the number using each flight path and the extent to which they may deviate from the flight path. The Commission used a computer program developed for this purpose by the Board of Trade Directorate of Operational Research and Analysis.

People whose homes are affected by aircraft noise may be made worse off in three different ways: They may suffer depreciation of their property (D); if they move away to escape the noise they may lose householders' surplus (S); and if they remain they may suffer on account of the noise (N). The cost of noise on homes may therefore be assessed by (i) forecasting the number of people who move away because of noise, the number who move away for other reasons (for whom S is zero) and the number who remain, and (ii) estimating the values for D, S and N.

Property depreciation estimates were obtained from a survey of estate agents around Heathrow and Gatwick, who estimated the likely difference in property values between otherwise identical houses affected by varying degrees of noise nuisance. Their esti-

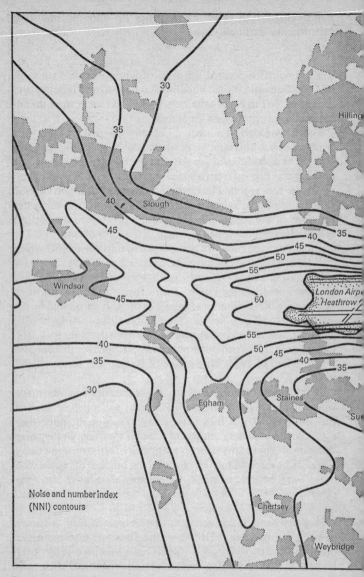

Figure 3 The noise disturbance caused by a single aircraft is measured in PNdB. But the number of aircraft heard is important too, and the Noise and Number Index (NNI) was devised in 1961 to combine these two factors. The contours on this map show the situation around Heathrow averaged over the summer of 1967 (day-time). Social surveys

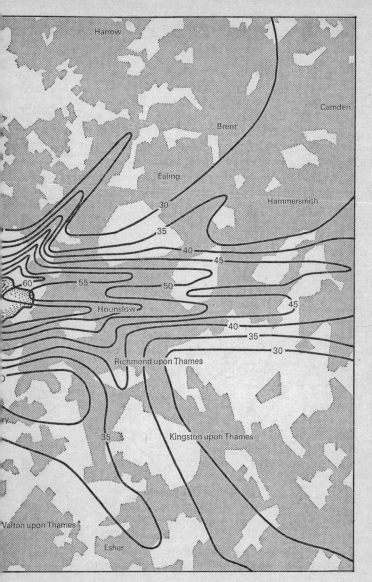

Harrow

Camden

Brent

Ealing

Hammersmith

30

35

40

45

60

55

50

45

Hounslow

40

35

30

Richmond upon Thames

45

Kingston upon Thames

35

Walton upon Thames

Esher

have shown that the average person regards the annoyance as 'slight' at 31 NNI, 'moderate' at 44 NNI and 'considerable' at 60 NNI. The results of a new social survey are now being processed.

Source: Board of Trade, *Action Against Aircraft Noise,* 1969

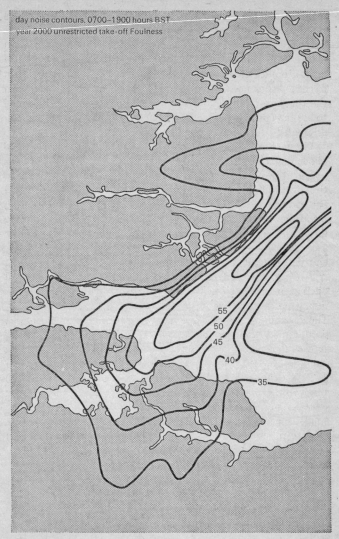

day noise contours, 0700–1900 hours BST
year 2000 unrestricted take-off Foulness

55
50
45
40
35

Figure 4 Estimated contours for Foulness
Source: Commission on the Third London Airport, *Report*

mates were subsequently verified by data on house transactions supplied by the Inland Revenue. Depreciations of up to 29 per cent were obtained; they were generally higher in the area around Gatwick, probably because those looking for houses in the country areas around Gatwick are more likely to place a high premium on freedom from noise from any source, including aircraft, than those living around Heathrow. The Commission therefore decided to use the Gatwick depreciation as a basis for estimating depreciation at the four third London airport sites.

The method for calculating householders' surplus was described above under planning.

The noise nuisance cost N was obtained in the form of a statistical distribution. Consider a person wishing to sell his house which has just become subject to some nuisance. He will have to bring his asking price down to attract potential purchasers to replace those who are put off by the nuisance. The people who will be attracted by the price reduction will be those for whom $N < D$, and the people put off by the nuisance will be those for whom $N > D$. So to attain the same potential market, the seller will pitch his price reduction at the median value of the noise distribution, when those for whom $N < D$ equal those for whom $N > D$. The distribution about the median was estimated by using a table produced by the Committee on the problem of noise, which showed the number of people with a given noise annoyance score (an index devised from their attitude survey) related to the NNI level. It is thus possible for each NNI level to assess the median annoyance score. At each price range this median annoyance score can now be related to the estimated depreciation so that the annoyance scores can all be given cash values. The distribution of annoyance scores for each NNI band is thus converted into a distribution of cash values. So for each NNI band and price level, we can estimate a distribution of noise nuisance cost. For example, the low price houses in the 35–40 NNI band had a distribution: £0–39 per cent, £200–33 per cent, £500–28 per cent while the high price houses in the 55 NNI+ band had a distribution: £0–8 per cent, £500–3 per cent, £2000–15 per cent, £4000–74 per cent.

The equation of D to the median of the noise nuisance distribution was criticized by several of those who gave evidence at the

Stage V Hearings. These argued that depreciation would depend upon the relative supply of noisy and quiet property. The British Airports Authority, whose consultant took this view, however, had a survey carried out asking people directly what compensation they would accept for noise, with results broadly in agreement with those obtained using the median assumption. Nevertheless the Commission decided that the range of uncertainty justified their taking three assumptions, equating D to the median, the upper quartile and the lower quartile of the noise nuisance distribution.

Given values of D, S and N, the two latter being defined as distributions, it remains to forecast the number who will incur each cost. Those who move away for reasons other than noise and hence incur D were forecast by projecting existing migration trends. The remaining population is assumed to choose whichever option minimizes their total cost, leaving if $S+D < N$ and remaining if $N < S+D$.

Average noise costs per household vary according to the proportions in the high noise bands and in each price range, but give an idea of a typical order of magnitude. They work out a little under £1000. The number of people affected by noise was 95,000 at Nuthampstead and from 20,000–30,000 at the other three sites. About 700,000 households are currently within the 35 NNI contour of Heathrow.

Aviation issues

The factors analysed under this heading include airspace movement costs, reflecting the differences in aircraft miles flown to reach the main airways from each site, air traffic control – analysis of possible interference between airports as a result of too many points where flight paths intersect, safety and interference with private flying. They do not require detailed comment here. Foulness poses extra safety problems, both as a shallow-water coastal site and from its position on the main flight path for migrating birds. But this is a question of costing tangible items such as the use of hovercraft for search and rescue operations and the probable damage to jet engines from ingesting birds, rather than anticipating extra fatalities at Foulness.

Airport design and construction

Although some of the inland sites, notably Cublington, involve formidable amounts of earth-moving and Foulness is a reclamation project on a massive scale, cost estimates for construction were relatively uncontroversial and did not greatly vary from site to site. The difference between Foulness and the other sites would have been greater if Foulness's construction timetable had not been postponed relative to the other sites, because of the Commission's assumption that Luton airport would continue to operate. This assumption also reduces the surface access and noise costs to Foulness, though it means that noise costs at Luton also need to be taken into account. The overall effect is to minimize the total costs attributed to Foulness.

The possibility of a deep-water sea port raises the problem of joint costs, since the dredging for the sea port could be used for reclamation of the airport site, and the same access system might be used for both. Detailed analysis showed that possible savings were small and because of the considerable uncertainty about the desirability of a port project at this site, the Commission did not consider that any benefit should be attributed to Foulness from this source.

Surface access

Since a new airport is first and foremost a major transport investment it is not surprising that access costs should be a key factor in evaluation. The main items to be considered are:

(a) the costs of constructing fixed access links,
(b) variable costs of travel to and from each airport,
(c) travel time, and
(d) consumer surplus benefits from generated travel.

To estimate items (b), (c) and (d) requires forecasting the origins and destinations of air travellers, the extent to which their trips will be affected by airport accessibility and the way in which these trips will be allocated between the available airports. Item (c) requires an estimate of the values passengers place on their time.

The Commission's traffic generation model was based on relating current accessibility to available airports around London (Heathrow and Gatwick) weighted by the number of passengers (to reflect the range of services offered) to the number of people who fly. There is a fairly close relationship between accessibility and propensity to fly and this was used to adjust the traffic forecasts to the accessibility of the different airport systems that would be available with each choice of third London airport. By the year 2000 the Cublington system was expected to generate about 7 per cent more traffic than the Foulness system. The value placed on these generated trips was calculated as it usually is in transportation studies, at half the cost difference (if 100 more people fly as a result of a saving in access cost of £1, their average benefit is assumed to be 50p).

Traffic was distributed between airports using a gravity model. The formula is

$$T_{ij} = \frac{O_i D_j F_{ij}}{\sum_j D_j F_{ij}},$$

where T_{ij} = trips between zone i and airport j,
O_i = trips generated in zone i,
D_j = trips attached to airport j,
F_{ij} = is a function of the cost of travel between i and j,

defined as

$$F_{ij} = \exp(-\lambda_p C_{ijp}) \cdot C_{ijp}^{-n_p} + \exp(-\lambda_r C_{ijr}) \cdot C_{ijr}^{-n_r},$$

where C_{ijp} is the behavioural cost of travel between i and j using public transport, C_{ijr} is the same using private transport, and the λ's and n's are parameters obtained from analysis of current travel patterns. If the distribution formula results in $\Sigma_i T_{ij} = D_j$ exceeding the capacity of airport j, then a cost penalty is added at airport j so as to ensure that the number of trips attracted is reduced to the airport's capacity. Behavioural costs include both the marginal monetary costs facing travellers (fares for those using public transport) and time values. When the cost differences between the airport systems came to be evaluated an adjustment had to be made for the difference between behavioural and resource costs, resource costs excluding transfer payments such as petrol tax and profits to public transport operators.

The research team followed the Ministry of Transport's approach to time valuation in separating business travel time from leisure travel time and in the general method of calculation. Business time was related to salary levels plus overheads; a higher figure than the Ministry's results because air passengers' salaries are higher. Leisure time was estimated from the results of a substantial number of empirical studies into the choices of travellers when they are in a position to choose to pay more to save travel time. Most of these studies relate to commuters' behaviour, but some are based on holiday traffic. The value attached to travel time is also found to be related to salary levels, as one would expect.

Both business and leisure time values were heavily criticized at the Stage V hearings, on a variety of grounds. On business time, for instance, it was argued that travel time saved would not in practice be spent on productive work. The evidence on leisure time was thought not to be relevant to air travellers, who might, especially on package tours, be thought to regard travel time as part of their holiday. The Commission decided to carry out calculations on a high and low time value, the high value being slightly above the research team's initial estimate and the low value being about half of it.

The differences in passenger user costs (including items (b), (c) and (d) but not (a) above) between Cublington and Foulness were £207 million on the high time values and £167 million on the low time values. Since the high time values are between two and three times the low values, the difference between the sites excluding time values altogether is likely to be around £130–£140 million.

Defence

At Foulness the only significant defence problem is the need to find another site for the complex of Ministry of Defence establishments at Shoeburyness and in Foulness Island. However the army's range located there is likely to have to move whichever site is selected due to the growth in air traffic over the Thames Estuary, though of course the move can be postponed considerably for the inland sites. All the inland sites will interfere significantly with the present pattern of operation for military airfields either in East Anglia or in the Oxford area, and very considerable costs would be involved in replacing those airfields by other facilities. These costs were estimated for the Commission by the Ministry of Defence.

Discounting

Costs and benefits were discounted at 10 per cent, the Treasury test discount rate for use on cost-benefit studies, to the year 1982. The reason for discounting to 1982 rather than 1970, say, was that the Commission wanted to be able to weigh differences in measured cost and benefits against unvalued items such as the effect on wildlife or the countryside. These effects will not start until the airport is in operation and so costs discounted to today's date (about 1/3, at 10 per cent, of their values in 1982) cannot meaningfully be compared with them.

Some of the values attached to intangible items are related to income and consequently must be expected to rise in real terms as real incomes rise. Because of this the Commission assumed a 3 per cent growth in the value of leisure time and a 5 per cent growth in the cost of noise nuisance.

Results

Table 1, taken from the Commission's report, gives the final assessment of costs and benefits for each site, expressed as differences from the lowest cost site, for both time values and the median noise assumption. Outstandingly important is the very large surface access cost against Foulness. Other very significant items are the cost penalty against Nuthampstead for noise, and the heavy defence cost penalty at Thurleigh, which requires the extension of controlled air space deep into East Anglia. Cublington has, by contrast, no very serious cost penalties compared with the other sites.

The Commission had to consider first what significance should be attached to these quantitative results and secondly what weight to give to other, unquantified, factors.

Error analysis

Possibilities of error in any analysis as complicated as this are immense, even though greatly reduced by the process of public scrutiny and testing of evidence. No single approach is likely to do full justice to the problem. Four kinds of uncertainty may be distinguished, each of which require somewhat different treatment.

1. Uncertainty about specific assumptions either of forecast or valuation
(e.g. Will Luton remain open with Foulness; should foreigners' costs and benefit be included?),

2. Uncertainty about assumptions which affect the magnitude of costs for all sites rather than their relativity between sites
(e.g. errors in the traffic forecasts),

3. Uncertainty about key valuation parameters
(e.g. time and noise costs), and

4. Random errors in estimating costs and benefits of any site.

Type (1) uncertainty was treated by sensitivity analysis. About 100 such sensitivity analyses were carried out. None showed Foulness as the cheapest site, although each of the inland sites could come out at lowest cost with some assumptions. Type (2) uncertainty it is not necessary to analyse in detail, except to confirm that these errors do not in fact affect the relative costs and benefits. For type (3) uncertainty a complete permutation seemed desirable; since there were two assumptions on time and three on noise this resulted in six estimates of inter-site differences. All produced the same ranking except that on low time and high noise values Foulness tied with Nuthampstead for the most expensive site. Type (4) uncertainty was treated by estimating the probable errors independently for each pair of sites and each row of the table. The research team calculated the cost difference 'margin of error' large enough to have a 95 per cent chance of indicating a real difference (say two standard errors). This figure was £40 million as between any pair of inland sites and £55 million between an inland site and Foulness. Even with these high errors, the difference between Cublington and all other sites was significant for each combined assumption about noise and time. Thurleigh was significantly superior to Nuthampstead in five out of six cases and to Foulness in all. But Nuthampstead was only significantly better than Foulness in two out of the six cases; high time values and middle or low noise values.

Unquantified items

Plenty of significant effects of the airport are not reflected in the cost-benefit analysis. Among those which have received a lot of

Table 1 Differences from lowest cost site (£ million discounted to 1982)

		Cublington		Foulness		Nuthampstead		Thurleigh	
Row		*High Time Values*	*Low Time Values*	*High Time Values*	*Low Time Values*	*High Time Values*	*Low Time Values*	*High Time Values*	*Low Time Values*
1	Airport construction	18			32	14			0
2	Extension of Luton			0	18		0		0
3	Airport services	23	22			17	17	7	
4	Meteorology	5		0	0		2		1
5	Airspace movements	0	0	7	5	35	31	30	26
6	Passenger user costs	0	0	207	167	41	35	39	22
7	Freight user costs		0		14	5			1
8	Road capital		0		4	4			5
9	Rail capital		3		26	12			0
10	Air safety		0		2	0			0
11	Defence	29			0	5			61
12	Public scientific establishments		1	0	0	21			27
13	Private airfields		7	0	0	13			15
14	Residential conditions (noise, off-site)	13			0	62			5

15 Residential conditions (on site)		11		0		8		6
16 Luton noise costs		0		11		0		0
17 Schools, hospitals and public authority buildings (including noise)		7		0		11		9
18 Agriculture		0		4		9		3
19 Commerce and industry (including noise)		0		2		1		2
20 Recreation (including noise)		13		0		7		7
Aggregate of inter-site differences (costed items only) high and low time values	0	0	197	156	137	128	88	68

Source: Commission on Third London Airport, Report, p. 119.

public attention are such things as the fate of the Brent geese at Foulness, Stewkley Parish Church at Cublington, the prospect of better employment opportunities in the area around Thurleigh or the need to redraw the regional plan to accommodate Nuthampstead. Some of these of course are special pleading. It requires a vivid imagination to see and assess the benefits of 'a regenerative process reaching right back to the heart of London where the East End butts against the city' which Professor Buchanan saw as one of the major advantages of Foulness. But many of these points are of real local significance, even if they have rather similar effects at each site. It may be that there is a shortage of attractive countryside for the enjoyment of Londoners; but there is also a shortage of attractive coast-line. The ecological loss at Cublington may be less dramatic than at Foulness, but it exists none the less.

Ultimately these factors have to be assessed against each other and compared with what has been quantified. The Commission's conclusion was that, whatever the advantages might be for these unquantified items in favour of Foulness, it should not be valued as highly as the quantified differential among both costs and benefits of £150–£200 million. This conclusion was not shared by Professor Buchanan, who did not wholly accept the results of the cost-benefit analysis. Nor was it accepted by the Government who attributed their choice of Foulness to 'environmental' reasons. This was a popular decision and a popular reason; indeed it is likely that the larger the cost penalty against Foulness, the more popular would have been the decision to choose it – for by implication the Government would have been placing an even higher value on the environment. Of course the fallacy lies in trying to value an absolute quality before it has been measured or assessed. It makes no sense to speak of a value of noise, or defence, or accessibility unless we can say how much noise, what kind of defence or what units accessibility is measured in. A cost-benefit analysis is in part an attempt to include environmental costs and other externalities within the framework of a quantitative study. Before the Commission began its work it was widely believed that aircraft noise was the most significant environmental effect of a new airport, and the work of the research team and others fully justified the importance of noise as a factor in airport location. It is of course possible that other environmental factors could be of as much, or more, significance in the choice of a site; for example the intrusion of the airport upon an area of outstanding natural beauty, or a major architectural monument. In the Commission's judgement nothing of this importance was at stake. In the absence of further evidence, each must judge for himself. But he should also consider what other goods, environmental, social or tangible could be paid for with £150–£200 million.

18 E. J. Mishan

What is Wrong with Roskill?

E. J. Mishan, 'What is wrong with Roskill?,'[1] *Journal of Transport Economics and Policy*, vol. 4, no. 3, pp. 221–34, 1970.

The Papers and Proceedings of the Commission on the Third London Airport run to nine volumes, covering between them the first three stages of the Commission's planned procedure. Under review here is the seventh volume, pertaining to stage III.[2] It runs to over 500 pages, and embodies both the method of approach and the quantitative assessment of the Commission's research team led by Mr F. P. Thompson, an economist formerly employed in the Ministry of Transport. I doubt whether an economist who, like myself, has had no hand in the writing of this volume could become familiar with all the aspects discussed in less than a couple of months of uninterrupted study. Nor would he be able to check all the calculations in less than about six months, and then with a goodly amount of research assistance. Since I can claim only to have perused a number of chapters – though I believe they are the more important chapters – the over-all impressions left on me have to be regarded as provisional only. Some of the more critical judgements, however, in particular those in parts 3 and 4, are put forward with less reservation, since they were reached only after a close scrutiny of the text. And the more general reflections at the end of this review depend neither on my over-all impressions of the Report nor on the more critical findings. They arise

1. I am very much indebted to Mr A. Flowerdew for prior discussion and to Mr D. L. Munby for later comments on a first draft of this paper.
2. Commission on the Third London Airport (1970).

from a consideration of the relevance of such cost-benefit evaluations for the world we are living in.

1 Cost or cost-benefit

It may be useful first to remind the reader of the limitations of cost-benefit techniques. As everyone knows, a cost-benefit analysis purports to measure in money terms all the benefits and all the costs to be expected over the future of some mooted project, and to admit the project if the sum of the benefits exceeds the sum of the costs by a sufficient margin. Under ideal conditions, the adopted criterion of a cost-benefit analysis – requiring that benefits exceed costs – can be vindicated only by a social judgement, that an economic rearrangement which *could* make everyone better off is 'a good thing'.

There are two points to notice about such a judgement. First, nothing is said about existing institutions, economic, political or legal. But in order to be a valid judgement, the criterion adopted must be *independent* of existing institutions. This is far from being an esoteric refinement, as we shall see later on. Second, and more obvious perhaps, such a judgement does *not* require that everyone shall be made better off, or even that some people shall be made better off while no others are made worse off. The likelihood – a virtual certainty – that some people, possibly most, will be made worse off is tacitly acknowledged. The criterion is met simply if it can be established that, on the adoption of the project, hypothetically costless transfers of money *could* make everyone affected better off than he was before. A project admitted on a cost-benefit analysis is, therefore, quite consistent with an economic arrangement which makes the rich richer and the poor poorer. It is consistent also with transparent inequity: irrespective of the income groups involved, the opportunities for increased profit or pleasure provided by the new project may inflict direct and substantial injury on others.

In order, then, for a project to be socially acceptable, it is not enough to show that the outcome of a cost-benefit calculation is positive – allowing, always, that the evaluation of each of the component items has been thorough and consistent. It must also be established that the resulting distributional effects are not unduly regressive, and that no gross inequities are perpetrated.

In the light of an ideal cost-benefit procedure, what can be said of this Report?

The first thing that ought to be said is that, for Britain at least,[3] the Report has aimed at a level of sophistication that will not be easy to exceed. For the most part it is clearly written and well organized. The theoretical underpinning – much of it summarized in part 1, *Proposed Research Methodology*, and in chapter I of part 2 – is respectable, and the tone is suggestive of a determination not to forsake principle for facility of calculation. The so-called intangibles are believed to be in principle quantifiable, and the research team has not yielded to the temptation to hand back part of its brief to the political process, which had offered it to the economists in the first place.[4] There are occasional manifestations of resourcefulness and ingenuity, as well as determination, in bringing disparate considerations 'into relationship with the measuring rod of money'. Nevertheless, paragraph 1.22 (on page 43) makes it plain that the conditions mentioned above, relating to distribution and equity – though their relevance is acknowledged – are *not* to be taken into consideration in the assessment. For this reason, if for no other, the quantitative findings of the Report cannot be used alone to decide the issue.

3. Cost-benefit studies on the grand scale are more common in the United States, a large proportion being concerned with water resources and construction of dams.

4. Nevertheless, there are one or two blemishes in the proposed methodology which could be damaging in a cost-benefit analysis, though, if they were corrected in this cost-comparison report, they would not be likely to make much difference to the ranking of sites in Table 29.1. (i) On page 38 (para. 1.7), for instance, it is asserted that goods and services are to be valued at their resource costs on grounds that they 'most clearly represent the real cost to the community . . . in terms of resources embodied in their production. Indirect taxes and subsidies . . . are excluded.' This is a valid convention for estimating changes in national income aggregates, but it is an *incorrect* principle for cost-benefit evaluations. The cost to the economy of a resource to be used in the project is determined by the value it creates in the use from which it is to be moved. Consequently, if the resource is moved from the production of some good subject, say, to a 100 per cent tax, its cost to the project must be valued as equal to the price, which is not equal to, but twice, the resource cost. (ii) Again on pp. 42–3 (para. 1.19), in the discussion on the costs of journeys to the airport, mention is made of the preference of some people for using their own cars, and the paragraph ends with the sentence: 'The measure of this benefit is found deductively by

The second thing that ought to be said is that the urgency is apparently not so great as we had been led to believe. If their projections of future air traffic are accepted (and they are large enough in all conscience), the airlines could go on until about 1982 using the existing facilities at Heathrow and Gatwick. Although congestion costs at the existing airports are expected to increase year by year, it will not be until 1982 that they will exceed £22 million, which is the estimated annual worth of postponing construction of the third airport.

The third thing that ought to be said is that the assessment in this volume is *not*, properly speaking, a cost-benefit analysis. It consists only of a comparison of the costs of the four alternative airport sites on the short list: Cublington, Foulness, Nuthampstead and Thurleigh. And in this connection it is important to notice that the full costs of each item are *not* always compared; sometimes only the differences in costs are entered, or a portion of the costs in which the differences are captured. We shall find it revealing to dwell a while on this peculiarity of the Report.

This choice of a relative cost evaluation rather than a cost-benefit evaluation carries with it an implicit presumption that a third airport at any one of the four alternative sites can be justified on economic grounds. There are reasons to doubt this presumption, and we shall turn to them in part 3.

In part 2 we concern ourselves only with the weight to be attached to the comparative figures produced by the Commission in order to rank the four alternative sites on the scale of economic desirability.

2 Costs to passengers and airlines

A comparison of the costs of the four sites discounted to 1975[5] is given by row 22 of Table 29.1 (pp. 490–91). They are ranked

observing what the travelling public is prepared to pay, in time and money, for the convenience, at least in their own eyes . . . of using their own car.' Fair enough, but no allowance is made for the additional congestion costs that are imposed on all *other* vehicles, or for the additional spillover effects on the rest of the population of private transport as compared with public transport.

5. If the costs are discounted to a later date, 1982, the figures above all are roughly doubled, since a discount rate of 10 per cent per annum has been adopted.

below in order of increasing cost:

Cublington	£2265 million	(0)
Thurleigh	£2267 million	(£2 million)
Nuthampstead	£2274 million	(£9 million)
Foulness	£2385 million	(£120 million).

(The figures in the brackets indicate by how much the cost of that particular site exceeds the cost of the lowest site at Cublington.)

It is clear that the differences between the first three sites are too slight in proportion to likely errors to be taken seriously. Foulness – except for bird-lovers, the conservationists' favoured site – stands out clearly as the most costly of the four. One reason is that a loss of potential benefit amounting to about £44 million is chalked up against Foulness in consequence of the smaller air traffic it is expected to generate as compared with the three inland airports, all of which happen to be on the right side of London to attract traffic from the North and the Midlands. In the year 2000, for example, the total number of air passengers in the country is expected to be something between 6 and 10 million less if Foulness is chosen rather than one of the others.

How significant is this difference in cost for the Foulness site? The two largest items in Table 29.1 are those for 'Airspace movement' and 'Passenger user cost'. They account for over 80 per cent of the total costs in the table, and they both depend heavily on the value placed on passengers' time. In particular, it is the additional time and cost of reaching the Foulness Airport site that forces the figure for 'Passenger user cost' there to £1041 million, or £152 million more than the figure for the next most costly site in this respect, Thurleigh.

Value of travel time

It is at such points that one is tempted to challenge the figure of 46s per hour placed on business travel in 1968, rising to 72s per hour (all at 1968 prices) by the year 2000. The figure is derived from an estimate of business firms' average annual expenditure on their airborne representatives of £4626 (in 1968), which sum includes an average business traveller's income of £3200. For 'leisure passengers', in contrast, a mere 4s 7d an hour is deemed appropriate. Both figures are assumed to rise over time at 3 per cent per annum.

Since these estimates, made in consultation with the Ministry of Transport, are likely to be controversial, the Report makes some additional calculations on the side, based on alternative evaluations of the worth of people's time. If, for instance, the value of business time is reduced by 25 per cent of the above figure, and leisure time is not valued at all, the total costs are so revised that the bracketed figures giving the *differences* in cost for the four airports become those shown below:

Thurleigh	(0)
Cublington	(£10 million)
Nuthampstead	(£28 million)
Foulness	(£42 million).

Clearly there is some margin to be got by playing around with such figures, and this makes any choice on economic grounds alone appear somewhat less satisfactory. The figures would appear less reliable still, and the differentials would narrow further,[6] if one could reasonably object to the notion of basing the value of time on a person's earnings. First of all, it is meaningful to say of a person that he values his leisure very little but that he dislikes his work a lot. Travel time for, say, a holiday-maker is simply one way of using his leisure. And it is not to be regarded as equivalent to work unless, at the margin, the person is indifferent as between, say, an hour spent on the train and an hour at work.

Secondly, the assumption of putting a positive value on the extra hour or so of businessmen's time if Foulness is chosen is also open to challenge. Dividing a firm's annual expenditure per travelling representative by the number of hours he is supposed to work produces an average hourly figure which, it can be argued, has no economic significance in this connection. The correct economic concept is the 'opportunity cost' to the firm, or rather to the country, of an hour or so's delay to its representative. Notwithstanding assertions to the contrary, indivisibilities

6. In the limiting case, if no value at all were placed on the time required to reach the airports, the cost ranking of the four airports (with the cost differences given in brackets) would be: Thurleigh (0), Foulness (6), Cublington (7), Nuthampstead (21).

of time are important here. If the delay were of a full day, it could matter to the individual firm – though, again, it might not matter that much for the country. If the difference in delay were of an hour's duration, one might think up circumstances in which it would matter. But such circumstances would not be relevant to the choice under consideration in the Report. If Foulness is chosen, it is not to be supposed that many firms could make profitable use of the extra hour or so of representatives' time saved in travelling to the airport. To most firms, I should imagine, it would make no difference at all. The representative would simply have to get up a little earlier on the appointed day and travel a little longer. And if this is a disutility for him, it has to be taken out of the category of business time and put into the category of passengers' leisure time.

Airline operation costs

Let us suppose, however, that we accept the figures in Table 29.1 as not seriously misleading. We may still wonder what importance we are to attach to them. Large though the absolute figure of £120 million is, it appears as only about 5 per cent of the total discounted costs of any of the sites. Actually, it is a very much smaller proportion of the total future resource costs of any of the airports; for, as mentioned, the table does not reveal all of the costs. The full airport construction costs are given. So also are all the 'passenger user costs' – the resource costs of travelling to each of the four sites, *plus* any difference in the 'disbenefits' of travelling to one airport site rather than another. But the cost of the largest item in the table, 'airspace movement', is only a fraction – presumably unknown – of the total airline operation costs over the future. For, on the assumption that, whichever site is chosen, all the aircraft will fly the same distances to their destinations from some common boundary containing the four sites, the authors of the Report simplified their work by calculating only the costs of reaching this boundary from each of the four sites (allowance being made for the somewhat smaller air traffic expected if Foulness were chosen). If, instead, total airline operation costs were included, the discounted value of *total* resources could be more than double the figures given in row 22 of Table 29.1. Accepting the Report's valuation of time, the excess cost of Foulness would be more like $2\frac{1}{2}$ per cent of the value of the total resources involved. On the Report's optional calculation of business and leisure time, the excess of £42 million for Foulness comes to less than 1 per cent of the value of total resources. On margins thus small, an economic case against the choice of Foulness cannot be seriously maintained.

Supersonic flight

Finally, nothing is said about the particular sorts of damage currently associated with supersonic flight. I have been told that the omission was deliberate, and predicated on the recent White Paper of the previous government, in which it was stated that the Concorde would not fly at supersonic speeds over land. Such a statement of intent may reasonably be regarded with suspicion. If we suppose that there is a chance that, for any of a half-dozen reasons the aircraft industry or the airline companies can think up, supersonic speeds over land may some day become 'essential', the choice of any site other than Foulness would leave us in a sorry and angry state.[7]

3 Is a third airport justified?

Let us now turn to what I regard as the major defect of the Report: that the economic case for the construction of a third London airport was not a part of its terms of reference. In a brief chapter on

7. There are deficiencies also in the measurement of other disbenefits. Their potential impact is probably less significant than that of aircraft noise, but they are worth touching on. For churches located off the airport site, the social losses entered are no more than the costs of strengthening the structures to withstand vibration. On the other hand, the social loss resulting from the demolition of churches and other buildings on the airport site is taken to be equal to the sum of their current market costs, as indicated by their insurance values. For architecturally undistinguished churches there need be no objection on secular grounds. But for irreplaceable churches of unique architectural value, this is obviously unacceptable. If Westminster Abbey is insured for £200,000 against destruction by fire, it does not follow that the nation at large is indifferent as between having Westminster Abbey or the £200,000. But this is the implied logic of accepting the fire insurance figure as the loss equivalence. The loss arising from damage to recreational activities is conventionally treated and arbitrarily quantified. Thus, on page 418 (para. 24.24) we read: 'Most of the recreational activities affected by aircraft noise, of which visiting historic houses, hunting, golf, fresh-water

'The value to the nation of a third London airport', a number of considerations were put forward to convince the public that the benefits were almost self-evident: the popularity of the postwar package tour, it was pointed out, is sure to grow immensely. So also is business travel, conceived as a 'lubricant' of international trade through which the blessings of technology are spread throughout the world. Besides, airports are generators of high income in the surrounding areas, and the growth in traffic should benefit the aircraft construction industry and industry in general; and much more of the same sort of froth. I suspect that this industry sales talk got included in the Report only on the insistence of interested parties. It contrasts with the more professional judgement shown elsewhere and is perhaps not expected to be taken seriously. There is, however, another argument in the earlier part of the chapter which, if it were accepted, would go some way toward establishing a presumption in favour of sufficient benefits to justify the undertaking. This takes the form of a belief that the expected revenues from passengers will be able to cover all the future resource costs involved in airline flights, and that, in addition, the estimated cost of all 'disbenefits' – noise, disamenity, demolition of historic buildings, etc. – could be more than covered by an increase in revenue from raising landing fees.

The intangibles

Before this presumption is accepted, it is necessary to examine the estimates made of the value of the 'intangibles', more particularly to the value of the loss of amenity and recreation to the com-

---

fishing, predominate, are located within moderate noise levels. It was therefore assumed that visits would, on average, be reduced by 10 per cent, and that this would be directly reflected in lower admission revenues. It can be deduced from conventional demand analysis that this reduction in participation could correspond to a reduction of about 20 per cent in the consumer surplus enjoyed by those continuing to visit.' The tone is tentative here: 40 per cent, perhaps 60 per cent, would be no less acceptable. But, frankly, the statement makes no sense as it stands. Admissions could change very little, and yet the loss be far in excess of '20 per cent in the consumer surplus enjoyed by those continuing to visit'. Indeed, the method is in conflict with the guiding principle laid down on page 39 and elsewhere: that the loss of an existing facility is to be measured by the sum necessary to restore the person's original welfare.

munity, or rather to examine the methods used by the authors to estimate these values. For in a comparative costs analysis, whatever the magnitudes of the 'intangibles', one of the alternative projects has to be chosen. Under this constraint, the only relevant question is whether or not introduction of the 'intangibles' will alter the cost ranking of the alternative projects. In a cost-benefit analysis, in contrast, one question to be answered is whether or not any one of the alternative projects is economically feasible. The magnitude of the 'intangibles' can, therefore, be decisive.

By and large, the conceptual underpinning of the Report is, as indicated earlier, sound enough. It is in making the transition from the concepts to the measurement of the relevant effects that one begins to feel critical of the particular devices, ingenious though they sometimes are, which the authors make use of in order to place money values on the damages suffered by others. Thus, in evaluating the potential disbenefits, the authors lay it down on page 39 that 'The analysis has been guided by the principle of accepting the scale of values apparently held by the people concerned, as revealed by their choice and behaviour. For *potential* possessions or activities, they are valued at what people would be prepared to pay to acquire them. For *existing* possessions or activities, things are valued at the minimum which people would be prepared to accept as just compensation for their loss.' As a statement of intent, this reflects the doctrines of modern welfare economics, and is unexceptionable. But, in the event, what do they do?

Households displaced

For those households moving out because of the airport, the loss suffered is reckoned as (a) estimated depreciation of their property, plus (b) removal expenses, plus (c) 'consumer surplus'. Thus, if the market value of a house before the airport is sited in the area is £10,000, but the family enjoys a consumer surplus of £2000 on it (that is, the family would not sell it below £12,000) and would require £500 for removal expenses, a fall in the market price to £7000 would involve the family in a total loss of £5500 – equal to (a) £3000, plus (b) £2000, plus (c) £500. The estimate of (a), depreciation, was derived from consultations with estate agents and by reference to depreciation of properties in those areas around

Gatwick and Heathrow that are subject to various degrees of aircraft disturbance. The estimates for (b) and (c) together, removal expenses plus consumer surplus, resulted from a sample survey in which householders were asked the following question: 'Suppose your house was wanted to form part of a large development scheme and the developer offered to buy it from you, what price would be just high enough to compensate you for leaving this house (flat) and moving to another area?' (p. 381). Subtraction from this subjective price of the existing market price provided an estimate for (b) and (c). A truthful answer to this question would be a satisfactory measure of the subjective value of the house only if the move contemplated by the householder were one that would take him completely out of the noise area (or, more precisely, if there already was some noise in the area, to another area suffering from no greater noise). Yet the question posed does not state how far the householder will have to move. Mention of a developer must surely give the householder the impression that a few acres, within which his house happens to be situated, are required. It would not occur to him that he would have to leave the neighbourhood. And it is, indeed, entirely a different affair if their household is to be displaced either because the site is needed for an airport or because the noise will be all but unbearable. This can be a real wrench for the family. A change of job location, a change of school location, to say nothing of a loss of friends and neighbours, have then to be anticipated. The figures used by the Report in this connection are, therefore, certain to have understated the value of expected losses.

A more obvious reason why the figures derived from the sample answers to the above question understate the amount of compensation is that 8 per cent of those asked said they would not move at any price. The compensatory sum for such a householder was placed, arbitrarily, at £5000. If these people mean what they said, the compensatory sum would be 'infinite' and this would obviously wreck any cost-benefit criterion. Yet, if the answers are believed, consistency of principle requires that an 'infinite sum' be entered. It may be that a good interviewer would have elicited a finite sum, though well in excess of £5000 – perhaps £50,000? or £5 million? And, though unlikely, it is not altogether inconceivable that for some older, or unworldly, people all that money could buy for them would not suffice as compensation for having to live elsewhere. What is certain, however, is that by setting this arbitrary upper limit of £5000 the authors' figure for 'consumer surplus' can be made much smaller than the 'consumer surplus' figure that would have emerged by an uncompromising application of their own adopted principles.

The disbenefits of an increase of the number of flights associated with the establishment of a third London Airport is an under-estimate for another reason, one which the Report itself touches upon – though possibly without recognizing its full significance (inasmuch as it applies to the evaluation of traffic noise in general). On page 368 (para. 20.12) it is observed that 'People buying a house affected by aircraft noise would be very naïve if they did not expect an increase in noise, at least for the next ten years or so.' Precisely! If noise is to increase over the next ten years – and, on present trends, who doubts it? – a family will have to search very much farther afield if they are to discover an equally con-genial neighbourhood with the same degree of quiet. It is scarcely possible for them to discover an area which has reasonable amenities and facilities within commuting distance of work and at the same time is expected over the future to be as quiet as is their present habitation today. Anticipating the spread of noise everywhere, the family, in effect, have only a limited choice: that of staying in the existing area or of moving to a new one, where *both* areas are expected to become much noisier. Indeed, as the level of noise in general increases, the perceived differences are likely to decrease, and so also, therefore, will the sum of money necessary to induce the family to move. But the disbenefit suffered from each contribution to a rising noise level is properly valued only by a sum of money large enough to compensate the family for the loss of the original low-noise situation, this being the sum that will enable them to maintain their original level of welfare.

Households remaining in neighbourhood

The expectation of an increase over the future in the volume and spread of noise is yet more significant in evaluating the loss to the larger population who will continue to live within the noisier zones about the airport – those remaining within the 35 NNI contour line.[8] The statement quoted on page 39 of the Report implies that the measure of the loss experienced by such people would emerge from a truthful answer to the question: 'What is the minimum sum you would accept to reconcile yourself to the increase in aircraft noise to which you are, and in the future will be, subjected?' Yet the loss for this larger group was measured, ultimately, by the expected depreciation of their property alone – that is, no more than the (a)-component of the loss to the household that is moved from the airport site. A good deal of finesse was, of course, employed in working out the exact depreciation to be used for each sort of house in each sort of zone, allowance for sensitivity being made by using the figure for depreciation as the median point of a distribution of noise sensitivity. Again, however, if noise is expected to increase over time, such measures are sure to understate the loss. For as noise grows over time the absolute difference in noise between any two points on a map may be unchanged, and the difference in property values will also remain unchanged – yet people living in areas about these two points will be worse off. Indeed, as noise increases over time, it is far more likely that *differences* in noise will diminish within a given area, and the effect therefore on property values will be smaller – a prospect with which the estate agents consulted can be assumed to be familiar. In such circumstances, the use of differentials in property values does not only understate the loss; as an index of loss it is wholly perverse. In the limiting case in which there is no escape whatever from aircraft noise in all inhabited areas of the country, noise being everywhere uniformly unbearable, noise-induced differences in property values will vanish; the measure of loss for all of us, on this indicator, being zero.

In connection with noise, there is yet another weakness, which at first glance may seem a quibble but in fact is a critical weakness of the cost-benefit technique when extended to non-market disbenefits: its almost unavoidable asymmetry in the weighting of 'imponderables'. To illustrate in the present instance, the authors confine themselves to noise within the 35 NNI contour line, apparently on the grounds that the effects of aircraft disturbance be-

8. NNI is an abbreviation of Noise and Number Index. It was developed as an index of aircraft noise annoyance by the Committee on the Problem of Noise (cmnd 2056).

low 35 NNI are difficult to determine. Now the population within the zones between, say 20 NNI and 35 NNI is several times as large as that within the area enclosed by the 35 NNI contour. Despite the admirable statement of intent on page 39, no loss of welfare is imputed to this larger population. That decision can be justified only if it is known that all families are perfectly indifferent to the increase in noise up to 35 NNI. Yet there will surely be a proportion of such families who, at least, will come to resent the extra noise.

Illusory benefits of air travel

Clearly the reaction of numbers of people in the larger population to noise levels below 35 NNI involves a judgement about significance. It is a purely subjective judgement, however, and it is in just such circumstances that the economist can be misled by a 'misplaced concreteness'. I am not suggesting that the economist is visibly stirred, as we imagine the technocrat to be, by a vision of a vast airport having all the familiar manifestations of highly organized bustle and breathlessness. I am suggesting, however, that market-formed prices and quantities are regarded as somehow more solid than the values attributed to the 'intangibles'. If a person is willing to pay £50 for a flight from London to Palma, there is, indisputably, a figure of £50 of benefit to play with. If the resource cost of the flight were shown to be £40, the economist would have no hesitation in claiming an excess benefit of (at least) £10. Such a flight may well be, for the greater number of future passengers, a whimsical form of indulgence, a fashion good of which the deprivation would be resented in varying degrees – though probably much less as time passed and alternative opportunities were discovered.[9]

   For business travellers, the case is simpler yet. For most of them the company pays air fares from business expenditures, so that, taking income and corporation taxes into account, the true cost to

9. I do not underestimate the extent of the potential protest, initiated by business interests with the support of mass media and inflated by the sheer joy of expressing protest. I speak only of the individual discomfort after the ban against this sort of travel has been generally accepted. Anger at being deprived, or the pleasure of expressing it, is no measure of the loss of utility of a thing.

the firm is less than half the fare. Thus, the marginal value of the air trip to the business firm is, presumably, well below the marginal resource cost.

With the advent of air travel, the number of conferences, business, professional and academic, has been growing at an exponential rate. The same people who now rush about the world reading the same paper at a dozen conferences in as many months are those who, in quieter days, would have found time to read, write, and reflect. At any rate, the value of such trips cannot be measured by the air fare, simply because air travel is not, in such cases, one of the alternative goods a man can buy subject to a budget constraint. The conferees do not pay their own fares. And it is doubtful if the benefit they personally expect to derive from these occasions is such that many would attend the conference without additional inducements. Only the conveners of the conference can be said to benefit. Calling a conference is one among the alternative ways of disposing of funds provided by governments and businesses guided by the principle of self-promotion. Conference-creating activity is one of many growth industries produced by aircraft travel, and one of the many prestige uses of the massive funds accumulated by business foundations. The social benefit of all this hectic to-ing and fro-ing, however, is difficult to evaluate – which is no reason for not assuming that it is probably negative.

There is room for speculation here, but not for doubt, that much of the assumed benefit of air travel is illusory.

Asymmetry in cost-benefit analysis

The purpose of carping at the nature of these assumed benefits is to draw attention to the asymmetry referred to, which arises, in the last resort, from institutional limitations. Whether he is motivated by strong desire, by the spirit of over-indulgence, or by spurious business need, if a man pays £50 twice a year for an air trip a benefit of at least £100 will be entered against the cost of the resources used in the two flights. In contrast, the disbenefit suffered by a person living within the 35 NNI – 20 NNI zone, whether it verges on fury for a hypersensitive minority [10] or whether it is

10. On page 365 the authors refer to the survey conducted by the Committee on the Problem of Noise. In the *quietest* areas covered by the survey,

the bearable annoyance of the majority, does not enter the grand computation at all. Yet it is, at least, a moot point whether the loss of welfare to any person subjected daily (and perhaps nightly also) to this *initially* lower level of noise-annoyance should properly be thought of as meriting no consideration as compared with the gain in welfare of any person who, at some time in the year, does the flight to Palma, or to Hong Kong for that matter.[11] If institutions happened to be the reverse of what they are for this particular case; if, say, the universe were so designed that people could freely sell their quiet in a competitive market at the ruling price while, on the other hand, owing to some institutional factor (say, the cost of fare collecting was fantastically high), a market in airline services were not possible, we should appreciate the asymmetrical treatment better. For then, *all* the disbenefits from noise would be priced on the market, and they would grow with the increasing noise of aircraft. They would be counted as part of the 'solid' price-quantity data, and would be added to the resource costs on the same economic principle – that payment has to be made to induce people to part with things they value, whether it be their property rights, their leisure, or their peace and quiet. And both in virtue of the change to a correct method of evaluating these disbenefits, and in virtue of the extension of the market to the population as a whole, the resulting loss figure would probably be many times that estimated in the Report. On the other hand, in keeping with the current methods used in estimating the values of non-market items, the benefits of the trips would be cal-

---

10 per cent of the population were classified as 'seriously annoyed'. In the noisiest areas, on the other hand, only 10 per cent denied that aircraft noise was a nuisance, and 10 per cent claimed a 'minimal degree of annoyance', leaving 80 per cent claiming more than a minimal degree of annoyance.

11. It might be objected that the person on the ground may, at some other time, be an air passenger on his way to Palma or Hong Kong. But this, as it happens, makes not the slightest difference to the calculation. His losses are no less real for his having benefits also, and vice versa. Nor does the fact that a person who resents aircraft noise also travels by air constitute evidence that, *on balance*, he prefers air travel along with the accompanying disbenefits to no air travel at all. Evidence of the latter proposition must await developments in which he is given the choice of being 'grounded' without any aircraft noise or of putting up with the noise along with the opportunity of flying. This sort of choice is not provided by the market, nor does the Government at present look like presenting it to us.

culated only for a fraction of the potential number of beneficiaries. This would be the fraction having greater claims according to some benefit-scale beyond which the economist would declare it difficult to believe that benefits were at all substantial. Moreover, if the methods used in estimating benefits were deficient in the same respects as those used by the Report in estimating disbenefits, the total value of the benefits calculated even for this fraction of the beneficiaries would be an underestimate.

In sum, under such hypothetical institutions, the outcome of a cost-benefit calculation conducted on the lines of this Report would be vastly different from that reached under the existing institutions, and could fail entirely to justify the building of a third London airport – from which we may conclude, at the very least, that the methods employed in the Report do not meet the conditions of an ideal cost-benefit analysis as laid down at the beginning of this article.

4 Social costs and equity

The conclusion of part 2 was that, on alternative – and, in my opinion, more plausible – estimates of the value of passengers' time over the future, the cost differences between the four sites as a proportion of total resource costs become so small as to be unreliable for the purpose of economic ranking.

In part 3 I gave some reasons for doubting whether, indeed, the construction of a third London airport could be justified by a respectable cost-benefit analysis. The chief reason I gave was that the methods used for the estimate of the benefits and the disbenefits are not independent of existing institutions: because the benefits are registered largely as market phenomena, and disbenefits largely as 'intangibles', the asymmetry of treatment tells heavily in favour of the benefits.

This reason is reinforced when it is discovered that a number of 'intangible' disbenefits have been omitted altogether from the Commission's calculation. There may be some justification for these omissions in a study of cost comparisons; the evidence may suggest that they differ little as between one site and another. But in a cost-benefit study undertaken to establish economic feasibility such disbenefits must be counted. I mention two of these below, neither of which is negligible.

(a) *Loss of life*. Per million passenger miles fatalities may be falling. But what matters in a cost-benefit calculation is the expected rise in absolute numbers attributable to the rise in numbers of passengers brought about by a third London airport. If choice of Foulness implies fewer passenger flights over the future, loss of life will be correspondingly smaller also – something the Commission did not take into account.

(b) Most important of all, however, is the *destruction of natural beauty* at home and abroad. This disbenefit is sometimes rudely referred to as 'tourist blight' – a phenomenon of postwar affluence that has already caused irreparable destruction, all over the Mediterranean area and far beyond, to places of once rare scenic beauty, woodland, coastline, lakes and islands.[12]

The social costs inflicted as a result of air travel facilities may be ignored by governments, but a comprehensive cost-benefit analysis simply cannot ignore them. If they appear intractable to existing methods of computation, the economist must say so, in which case an otherwise favourable cost-benefit calculation must be deemed inconclusive.[13]

Finally, the economist is interested not only in the question whether a given project yields an excess of benefit over cost, but also in the *optimal* operation of an existing or future project.

From Table 4.6, on page 86, one gathers that the number of air passengers taking off in the London area is expected to increase from 18 million per annum in 1969 to 294 million in 37 years' time. Reference to such figures would seem to leave no room for doubt

12. I refer not only to the disfiguration of innumerable coastal resorts, once famed for their beauty, as a result of frantic 'development' in the attempt to accommodate increasing numbers: these are losses to be borne by future generations as well as ourselves. I refer also to the increasing discomforts endured in popular resorts in consequence of the greater numbers of people and the greater traffic. Indeed, in the expectation that in this respect matters can only get worse, there is every incentive to add to the crowds by visiting such places sooner rather than later. The reader will readily appreciate that the economic issue is not *who* should travel, but (thinking in terms of the spillovers borne by the intra-marginal tourists today and other generations to come) *how many*.

13. The *otherwise* excess benefit over cost may be provided by the economist so allowing the public to judge whether such a figure compensates for the damage to be expected over the future.

of the 'need' of a third London airport, and probably of a fourth and fifth also. After all, for every single air passenger today there will be, according to these predictions, as many as seventeen in 37 years' time. And if fares continue to remain much the same relative to the prices of other services, and if there is no restriction on airports or air travel, some of us may live to witness the grand spectacle. But, inasmuch as air travel does impose disbenefits on the public, proper concern with allocation requires that fares be raised to take account of them. If this were done, the numbers would not rise nearly so rapidly. They might hardly rise at all, and the need for a third London airport might not then be in the least apparent. For the disbenefits do not consist only of the noise annoyance, fearful as this is going to be,[14] and increased air pollution – which disbenefits, be it noted, contribute to a spreading background of pollution and perpetual noise, by reference to which further aircraft and automobile projects are the more easily justified by cost-benefit techniques, since the perceptible contribution of each project to noise and air pollution that are already so bad is obviously limited.[15] As already indicated, the chief disbenefit, tourist blight, is the most difficult of all to measure. The popularity of package tourism need not be questioned. Let us accept airline receipts as a measure of benefit. We need attend only to the 'spillover effects' each additional person imposes on all others, present and future, but of which he himself takes no account. Indeed, not being 'very naïve' either, the would-be traveller will expect tourist blight to rise over the future and will hasten to travel the sooner before the destruction is complete.

Measuring these adverse spillover effects would, as suggested, present some difficulties. In view of the commercial interests at stake, and in view of the commitment of governments to compete

14. Unless some effective aircraft-noise preventive device is invented. This does not seem too likely just now, particularly as private and public airlines have no strong incentive to undertake such research – an incentive they would have if they were required to compensate the victims of noise pollution.

15. As has been pointed out frequently during the controversy on noise, the ground traffic is already so heavy in built-up areas that the addition of aircraft noise makes no great difference. So, too, once a third airport is built and the aircraft noise level rises over time and extends over the country, it will be that much easier to justify further noise-creating projects, including a fourth and fifth London airport.

for a share in this growing market (for fear of losing on balance-of-payments account), research into methods for their quantification would also be a thankless task. As things stand, however, the process of destruction through mass tourism, instead of being slowed down by taxes high enough to cover the marginal spill-over effects, is, on the contrary, accelerated by subsidies. In view of the magnitude of these spillovers, it is high time that governments began to think in terms of stiff taxes on air travel. Where the fare may cover only a small part of the social cost, a very roughly calculated tax is almost certainly better than no tax at all – even if it should eventually be found to reduce air travel below the optimum level.

Growth of public protest

Let me conclude with a more general reflection. There are the beginnings in this country and abroad, particularly in the United States, of a strong anti-disamenity movement among the public. At present, political parties are trying to absorb some of its force. My belief is that they underrate the passion behind the protest, and its growing appeal, not least among the young. The movement shows every indication of growing rapidly in the next few years, and also every inclination to achieve its aims by large-scale political changes rather than by 'tinkering with the system'.

Cost-benefit techniques are, indeed, becoming more sophisticated. But they may be too late to exert much influence in the choice of projects which can be related to the 'quality of life' issue. A Report such as the present one, excellent as it is, paying lip service to right principles and secure within its terms of reference, may have the unexpected effect of contributing only to the public's growing impatience with economic expertise, and perhaps with economics in general.

One reason for this impatience is that in such economic calculations *equity* is wholly ignored. If indeed, the business tycoons and the Mallorca holiday-makers are shown to benefit, after paying their fares, to such an extent that they *could* more than compensate the victims of aircraft spillover, the cost-benefit criterion is met. But compensation is *not* paid. The former continue to enjoy the profit and the pleasure; the latter continue to suffer the disamenities. Another reason for growing impatience is even more compelling. In an age of supposedly increasing prosperity, the choice of a more wholesome life than that we seem to be moving into should, it seems, be technically feasible. Yet, despite a succession of governments overtly obsessed with economic growth, we are being offered year by year continuously less choice in the one factor most crucial to our welfare – the physical environment in which we live, and in which we are fast being submerged.

Reference

COMMISSION ON THE THIRD LONDON AIRPORT (1970), *Papers and Proceedings: Stage III Research and Investigation – Assessment of Short-Listed Sites*, vol. 7, parts 1 and 2, HMSO.

Exercises

A channel tunnel

A government is considering building a tunnel across a sea channel which can currently only be crossed by boat or aeroplane.

1. The tunnel will consist of a two-track railway, and cars and passengers will be carried by train. It will cut the crossing time by about two hours for cars and passengers.

2. The relevant categories of traffic are:

(a) cars (and their passengers)
(b) passengers not in cars
(c) freight.

The authorities who would operate the tunnel have decided to charge tolls which would maximize revenue. (Are they right?) By tunnel, the crossing would become cheaper for each category of traffic: for example, for a car the toll would fall from £10 to £8.

3. Because of the quicker and cheaper journeys available, it is forecast that the following traffic per year for the foreseeable future will be diverted from existing methods of travel:

  750,000 cars (with an average of 2 passengers)
3,500,000 passengers not in cars
3,500,000 tons of freight.

In addition, 500,000 extra car journeys will be made. The average wage of all categories of passenger (diverted and additional) is £0.70 per hour and 10 per cent of them are on business.

4. The diverted traffic will reduce direct operating costs of existing ships and aeroplanes by £20m. per year, while at the forecast levels of traffic the maintenance and operating costs of the tunnel will be £4m. Its capital cost is £180m.

5. The government decides to use the Hicks-Kaldor criterion to decide on the tunnel. Assuming the interest rate is 10 per cent and that savings in the economy are optimal, should it be built?

6. If savings were non-optimal what additional information would you need to evaluate the project?

(Adapted and highly simplified from *Proposals for a Fixed Channel Link* (HMSO, 1963, cmnd. 2137), reprinted in Munby (1968).)

A course of education

1. Suppose there is a particular one-year course of full-time education that the State has been providing for some time. It involves a normal working week plus six hours' work in the evening and at weekends. Experience shows that 20 per cent of those who take the course fail the final examination and 10 per cent complete it successfully but immediately emigrate for good.

2. The real recurrent tuition cost per student is £800. The capital cost of a new place is £2000. The students have grants of £200 towards maintenance. Students' average maintenance expenditures are £700. Tuition is free.

3. In the labour force here and abroad people who have successfully taken the course earn on average £2000 a year, irrespective of age; those who have the entrance qualifications to the course but who have not taken it or have failed the final exam earn £1500 irrespective of age. The marginal and average tax rate is 20 per cent.

4. Assuming the interest rate is 10 per cent and that savings in the economy are optimal and capital markets perfect, what is the present value to society of putting one more person through the course? What guidance does this information provide to policy-makers wondering whether to expand their intake to the course?

5. If savings were non-optimal and capital markets imperfect, what more information would you like to have?

6. In considering your answers you will want to give particular consideration to the following issues involved:

Costs
(a) Treatment of maintenance costs.
(b) Treatment of leisure foregone.
(c) Treatment of drop out.
(d) Treatment of capital cost.

Benefits
(a) Possible external effects and psychic benefits.
(b) The effect of ability on income.
(c) Treatment of brain drain.

The appropriate discount rate

The dynamic problem
How far can data, using current prices, guide policy-makers in conditions of changing demand?

The income distribution question
Who benefits from higher education and how far should the method of financing education affect the amount of it considered to be socially optimal?

(For treatment of an analogous problem see W. Lee Hansen in Blaug (1968); or Blaug *et al.* (1967, ch. 7); or Layard *et al.* (1971, ch. 10); or Maglen and Layard (1970)).

Closure of a branch line railway
 (i) The British Rail Board is to meet to consider closing down the branch line passenger service from Little X to Great X. No goods are currently carried by rail.
 (ii) The Board's accountants estimate the annual cost of train movements, track maintenance, signalling and station upkeep at Little X at £76,000, including £6000 depreciation and interest charges. However, in five years' time if the line is to continue in operation, the track will need to be relaid at a cost of £300,000 and the accountants thereafter estimate the annual cost at £102,000 including £32,000 depreciation and interest charges.
(iii) If the line were closed at any time, the diesel train operating on it could be sold to an underdeveloped country for £20,000. Nothing else has any resale value.
(iv) The line is used for 1000 single journeys each day (250 days per year). The single fare is £0.2. So the line is losing money – a deficit met by taxation.
 (v) If the line is closed, it is estimated that of the former daily journeys 800 will be made by bus (at the same fare), and 200

will not be made. The bus fare is the same as the rail fare and the extra bus fares exactly offset the bus operators' extra costs. Bus journeys take an average of twenty minutes longer than the rail journey. The average value of passengers' time is £0.6 per hour.

(vi) Assuming the interest rate is 10 per cent and that savings in the economy are optimal, what should the Board decide to do?

Some questions on valuation

1. Suppose that electricity is sold in Glasgow at more than marginal cost and that potential migrants to Manchester are affected by the relative cost of electricity. If you had to do an investment appraisal for an electricity station in Manchester charging marginal costs, would you consider the benefits to be greater or lower than the area under the demand curve for electricity?

2. In Britain domestic agricultural production is currently subsidized. In evaluating a water control project which would increase production, would you value the increased output at market prices or higher?

3. Suppose a dam raises farmers' output by £100,000 (other inputs constant), but £50,000 is taken from them in water charges. Should the latter be deducted from the social benefits?

4. Suppose a project brings an unemployed worker into work. Do we include the saving on unemployment benefit as a benefit in the project appraisal? Is there any cost to be included as a result of employing him?

5. Suppose a man were living near Cublington. Before the airport was built he was asked 'How much would you need to be paid to compensate you for leaving your house?'. He answered '£4500'. The market price of his house was £4000. The airport was then built. The price of his house fell to £3500. He was then asked a second question 'How much would you need to be paid to compensate you for the noise of the airport?'. He answered '£1500'. Shortly afterwards he sold his house.
(a) What cost did the airport impose on him?
(b) What cost did it impose on the man who bought his house?

Topics for discussion

1. 'If resources can be employed in the private sector on projects with a rate of return of n per cent, it cannot be right to undertake any public sector project with a lower yield'.

2. 'If future benefits are valued less than present ones because people will be richer in future, then contemporaneous benefits to rich and poor should receive different weights in cost-benefit analysis'.

3. 'The only sensible assumption in the cost-benefit analysis of a particular project is that sensible decisions are being made in every other area of government policy (e.g. on tariffs)'.

4. 'Cost-benefit analysis should confine itself to the tangible consequences of decisions'.

5. 'The public sector is so large that the riskiness of its projects can always be safely ignored'.

6. 'The third London airport should have been sited at Cublington, as the Roskill Commission's cost-benefit analysis showed'.

References

BLAUG, M. (ed.) (1968), *Economics of Education, 1*, Penguin.
BLAUG, M., *et al.* (1967), *The Utilisation of Educated Manpower in Industry*, Oliver & Boyd.
LAYARD, P. R. G., *et al.* (1971), *Qualified Manpower and Economic Performance*, Allen Lane, The Penguin Press.
MAGLEN, L., and LAYARD, R. (1970), 'How profitable is engineering education?', *Higher Education Review*, Spring.
MUNBY, D. (ed.) (1968), *Transport*, Penguin.

Further Reading

The reader is referred to the references given at the end of the Introduction.

The best available textbooks on the subject are Mishan (1971) and UNIDO (1972). Good comprehensive survey articles are Prest and Turvey (1965, reading 1), Henderson (1965) reprinted in Turvey (1968), and Eckstein (1961) reprinted in Houghton (1970).

Acknowledgements

Permission to reproduce the following readings in this volume
is acknowledged to the following sources:

1 *Economic Journal*
2 American Economic Association
3 The Brookings Institution
4 *Economic Journal*
5 Organisation for Economic Co-operation & Development, Paris.
6 European Conference of Ministers of Transport, Paris.
7 *Regional Studies*
8 University of Chicago Press
9 *Economic Journal*
10 *Quarterly Journal of Economics*
11 *Quarterly Journal of Economics*
12 Queens University at Kingston, Ontario
13 M. S. Feldstein
14 American Economic Association
15 Macmillan, London & Basingstoke, and Harvard University Press
16 The Brookings Institution
17 A. Flowerdew
18 *Journal of Transport Economics and Policy*

Author Index

Subject Index